NATIONAL COOPERATIVE HIGHWAY RESEARCH PROGRAM

## NCHRP RESEARCH REPORT 1116

# Development of a MASH Barrier to Shield Pedestrians, Bicyclists, and Other Vulnerable Users from Motor Vehicles

Chiara Silvestri Dobrovolny
Sun Hee Park
Shawn Turner
Roger Bligh
James Kovar
TEXAS A&M TRANSPORTATION INSTITUTE
TEXAS A&M UNIVERSITY SYSTEM
College Station, TX

T0295690

*Subscriber Categories*
Pedestrians and Bicyclists • Design • Safety and Human Factors

---

Research sponsored by the American Association of State Highway and Transportation Officials
in cooperation with the Federal Highway Administration

---

NATIONAL ACADEMIES *Sciences Engineering Medicine*

**TRB** TRANSPORTATION RESEARCH BOARD

2024

# NATIONAL COOPERATIVE HIGHWAY RESEARCH PROGRAM

Systematic, well-designed, and implementable research is the most effective way to solve many problems facing state departments of transportation (DOTs) administrators and engineers. Often, highway problems are of local or regional interest and can best be studied by state DOTs individually or in cooperation with their state universities and others. However, the accelerating growth of highway transportation results in increasingly complex problems of wide interest to highway authorities. These problems are best studied through a coordinated program of cooperative research.

Recognizing this need, the leadership of the American Association of State Highway and Transportation Officials (AASHTO) in 1962 initiated an objective national highway research program using modern scientific techniques—the National Cooperative Highway Research Program (NCHRP). NCHRP is supported on a continuing basis by funds from participating member states of AASHTO and receives the full cooperation and support of the Federal Highway Administration (FHWA), United States Department of Transportation, under Agreement No. 693JJ31950003.

The Transportation Research Board (TRB) of the National Academies of Sciences, Engineering, and Medicine was requested by AASHTO to administer the research program because of TRB's recognized objectivity and understanding of modern research practices. TRB is uniquely suited for this purpose for many reasons: TRB maintains an extensive committee structure from which authorities on any highway transportation subject may be drawn; TRB possesses avenues of communications and cooperation with federal, state, and local governmental agencies, universities, and industry; TRB's relationship to the National Academies is an insurance of objectivity; and TRB maintains a full-time staff of specialists in highway transportation matters to bring the findings of research directly to those in a position to use them.

The program is developed on the basis of research needs identified by chief administrators and other staff of the highway and transportation departments, by committees of AASHTO, and by the FHWA. Topics of the highest merit are selected by the AASHTO Special Committee on Research and Innovation (R&I), and each year R&I's recommendations are proposed to the AASHTO Board of Directors and the National Academies. Research projects to address these topics are defined by NCHRP, and qualified research agencies are selected from submitted proposals. Administration and surveillance of research contracts are the responsibilities of the National Academies and TRB.

The needs for highway research are many, and NCHRP can make significant contributions to solving highway transportation problems of mutual concern to many responsible groups. The program, however, is intended to complement, rather than to substitute for or duplicate, other highway research programs.

## NCHRP RESEARCH REPORT 1116

Project 22-37
ISSN 2572-3766 (Print)
ISSN 2572-3774 (Online)
ISBN 978-0-309-71000-8
Library of Congress Control Number 2024942429

## NOTICE

The research report was reviewed by the technical panel and accepted for publication according to procedures established and overseen by the Transportation Research Board and approved by the National Academies of Sciences, Engineering, and Medicine.

The opinions and conclusions expressed or implied in this report are those of the researchers who performed the research and are not necessarily those of the Transportation Research Board; the National Academies of Sciences, Engineering, and Medicine; the FHWA; or the program sponsors.

The Transportation Research Board does not develop, issue, or publish standards or specifications. The Transportation Research Board manages applied research projects which provide the scientific foundation that may be used by Transportation Research Board sponsors, industry associations, or other organizations as the basis for revised practices, procedures, or specifications.

The Transportation Research Board; the National Academies of Sciences, Engineering, and Medicine; and the sponsors of the National Cooperative Highway Research Program do not endorse products or manufacturers. Trade or manufacturers' names or logos appear herein solely because they are considered essential to the object of the report.

*Published research reports of the*

## NATIONAL COOPERATIVE HIGHWAY RESEARCH PROGRAM

*are available from*

National Academies Press
500 Fifth Street, NW, Keck 360
Washington, DC 20001

(800) 624-6242

*and can be ordered through the Internet by going to*

https://nap.nationalacademies.org

Printed in the United States of America

# NATIONAL ACADEMIES

*Sciences*
*Engineering*
*Medicine*

COOPERATIVE RESEARCH PROGRAMS

By Ann M. Hartell
Staff Officer
Transportation Research Board

*NCHRP Research Report 1116: Development of a MASH Barrier to Shield Pedestrians, Bicyclists, and Other Vulnerable Users from Motor Vehicles* provides a detailed design for a crashworthy roadside barrier system for use alongside high-speed roadways that also addresses the needs of nonmotorized users of adjacent multiuse facilities. The report and accompanying resources will be of interest to highway designers seeking a design solution for locations where nonmotorized transportation facilities are adjacent to high-speed roadways.

---

As the number of pedestrians, bicyclists, and users of other active transportation modes continues to grow in the United States, state departments of transportation and other transportation agencies are seeking to improve how these users are accommodated on or adjacent to our nation's roadways. In many locations, limited lateral offsets between the motor vehicle travel lanes and the sidewalks or multiuse paths can reduce actual and perceived safety for these vulnerable users. When the available right-of-way constrains the ability to increase offset distance, an alternative can be to install a positive protection device—a barrier that separates lanes for motorized vehicles and facilities for nonmotorized users.

Traditionally, barriers are designed for a specific need such as shielding motorists from a steep slope or a fixed object, such as a pole or tree. The selection of a barrier is driven by roadway design speed, traffic volume, clear zones, aesthetics, and accommodation of driveways and other access points, snow plowing, and stormwater runoff. However, the use of barriers to separate pedestrians and bicycles from motor vehicles requires the consideration of additional factors. For example, a typical guardrail is designed to redirect motor vehicles but may not be tall enough to protect pedestrians or bicyclists by preventing them from inadvertently encroaching on the roadway. Guardrail designs may have bolts or other features that can snag a wheelchair or bicyclist. A barrier that has gaps between posts may be difficult for people with limited vision to detect with a cane or other mobility device. When struck by a motor vehicle, a barrier may deflect into the path of a nonmotorized user on the adjacent facility.

Under NCHRP Project 22-37, "Development of a MASH Barrier to Shield Pedestrians, Bicyclists, and Other Vulnerable Users from Motor Vehicles," the Texas A&M Transportation Institute was tasked with reviewing existing barrier designs and policies related to safety barriers that separate nonmotorized users from motor vehicles. From this review, design requirements for a new barrier were identified. A preferred design was selected for detailed development and was assessed for impact performance by using finite element computer impact simulations. Finally, a full-scale installation of a refined barrier design was constructed and tested for crashworthiness in accordance with Test Level 3 (TL-3) of the *Manual for Assessing Safety Hardware* (MASH). The barrier was also assessed for comfort and acceptability for people who use wheelchairs, people with limited vision who use canes as a mobility device, pedestrians, and bicyclists. Separate computer simulations and full-scale crash tests were also conducted to assess the crashworthiness of a Thrie beam transition to connect the new barrier to a typical W-beam guardrail.

*NCHRP Research Report 1116* presents a nonproprietary, crashworthy design for use in separating vulnerable users from motor vehicle travel lanes that is

- Tested to the TL-3 criteria (high-speed roadway application) established by AASHTO's *Manual for Assessing Safety Hardware,*
- In compliance with the U.S. Access Board's proposed Public Right-of-Way Accessibility Guidelines (PROWAG),
- Appropriate for a variety of design contexts, and
- Compatible with W-beam guardrail using a Thrie beam transition.

The report includes detailed drawings of the barrier and the transition designs to provide designers with a barrier system that is ready for implementation. Accompanying the report are a set of presentation slides summarizing the project, a memorandum describing activities to promote the adoption and implementation of the new system, a video of all full-scale tests, and 10 appendices provided in two files:

- "Technical Drawings and Information for FHWA Eligibility Filing: Appendices B, E, F, and J" (Appendices B, E, and F are also included in this report) and
- "Survey, Crash Test Data, and Supporting Certification Documents: Appendices A, C, D, G, H, and I."

All of these materials can be found on the National Academies Press website (nap.national academies.org) by searching for *NCHRP Research Report 1116: Development of a MASH Barrier to Shield Pedestrians, Bicyclists, and Other Vulnerable Users from Motor Vehicles* and looking under "Resources."

# CONTENTS

# Development of a MASH Barrier to Shield Pedestrians, Bicyclists, and Other Vulnerable Users from Motor Vehicles

The number of vulnerable road users continues to grow within the United States, as do crashes between motorists and vulnerable road users. Vulnerable users such as pedestrians and bicyclists are expected to jointly use facilities that have constrained lateral offsets between the travel lanes and vulnerable user transportation facilities such as sidewalks and multiuse paths. On many of these facilities, right of way (ROW), fiscal, or geographical constraints prohibit transportation agencies from increasing the offset distance.

At present, no positive barrier systems have been designed specifically for the purpose of providing positive protection between vulnerable user transportation facilities and motorized facilities. A critical need exists to develop new multifunctional barrier systems that comply with the specific accommodation requirements of pedestrians, bicyclists, and motor vehicles. Such a system should ideally be affordable from a constructability and installation standpoint, be appealing from an aesthetic perspective, take into consideration adequate and proper sight distance, and be designed to safely contain direct hits from motorized users.

The objective of this research was to develop a barrier that accommodates the safety needs of pedestrian, bicyclist, and motor vehicle traffic. In developing a new barrier design, consideration was given to commonly encountered design contexts such as the test standards of the *Manual for Assessing Safety Hardware* (MASH) and the criteria of the Public Right-of-Way Accessibility Guidelines. This research consisted of eight tasks to meet the objectives of NCHRP Project 22-37, "Development of a MASH Barrier to Shield Pedestrians, Bicyclists, and Other Vulnerable Users from Motor Vehicles."

The research team identified and reviewed relevant national and international literature and standards that included methodology and related research about the physical separation of pedestrians or bicyclists and motor vehicles. The researchers identified several sources of information regarding the needs of both crashworthy roadside barriers and vulnerable users. The research team also solicited information from transportation agencies; design consultants; vulnerable user groups; and, as appropriate, transportation agencies outside the United States on typical project types and design contexts where a tested barrier to separate motor vehicles from vulnerable users is needed.

The research team then developed a nonproprietary barrier for use in separating pedestrians, bicyclists, and other vulnerable users—including people who use a wheelchair and people with visual impairments who use canes—from motor vehicles. Six barrier design options were proposed, with ratings based on their anticipated advantages and disadvantages for further investigation through computer simulation. On the basis of discussions with the research panel, finite element simulations and full-scale crash tests were conducted on a selected barrier design, and the barrier met the requirements of MASH Test Level 3 (TL-3) (high speed). The barrier is considered appropriate for a variety of contexts, such as where ROW constraints reduce lateral offset between a roadway and a shared-use path.

It was noted that implementation of the barrier by state departments of transportation (DOTs) required a transition system to standard guardrail. Thus, as part of the project, the research team developed a design that transitioned the new multifunction barrier system to conventional strong-post W-beam guardrail. Different transition designs were proposed and investigated through computer simulations. A Thrie beam transition system was selected and incorporated design details on the upstream end that have been previously evaluated and are considered MASH compliant. The downstream end of the Thrie beam transition design was further investigated through full-scale crash testing according to MASH TL-3 criteria, which included MASH Test 3-20 and MASH Test 3-21. Full detailed drawings of the successfully tested multifunctional barrier and associated transition design are included in this report.

# Introduction

The number of vulnerable road users continues to grow within the United States, as do crashes between motorists and vulnerable users. A large percentage of the nation's roadways have limited space to safely accommodate vulnerable users. Thus, vulnerable users such as pedestrians and bicyclists are expected to jointly use facilities that have constrained lateral offsets between the travel lanes and vulnerable user facilities such as sidewalks and multiuse paths. On many of these facilities, right of way (ROW), fiscal, or geographical constraints prohibit transportation agencies from increasing the offset distance.

Prior to the research conducted for this report, no positive barrier systems had been designed specifically for the purpose of providing positive protection between vulnerable user facilities and motorized facilities. To provide safe travel for vulnerable road users, state departments of transportation (DOTs) are implementing accommodations on the roadside. When enough ROW exists, DOTs increase the separation between pedestrians/bicyclists and the motor vehicle traffic. However, increasing this separation is not always an option. Therefore, DOTs are searching for effective means to provide positive protection and separation between pedestrian/bicycle and motor vehicle traffic.

A new, properly designed barrier could provide not only protection against errant motorists, but also a safer travel space for pedestrian and bicycle traffic. Typical roadside barriers incorporate concrete systems and post-and-beam guardrail barriers. Concrete barriers undergo no deflections upon motorized vehicle impact, representing the safest option to serve as a multifunctional barrier; however, their construction is cost prohibitive in many cases. Guardrail systems, though not as expensive as concrete barriers, might provide unacceptable lateral deflection, which would be hazardous for pedestrians and bicyclists. A commonly used post-and-beam system might also create tripping and snagging hazards for pedestrians and bicyclists.

Thus, a critical need exists to develop a new multifunctional barrier system that complies with the specific accommodation requirements of vehicles, pedestrians, and cyclists. This system should be affordable from the standpoint of constructability and installation, be appealing from an aesthetic perspective, consider adequate and proper sight distance, and be designed to safely contain direct hits from motorized users.

Under NCHRP Project 22-37, "Development of a MASH Barrier to Shield Pedestrians, Bicyclists, and Other Vulnerable Users from Motor Vehicles," the research team developed a nonproprietary barrier for use in separating pedestrians, bicyclists, and other vulnerable users—including people who use a wheelchair and people who are blind or have low vision—from motor vehicles. Simulation models and full-scale crash tests were conducted, and the barrier met the requirements of the AASHTO *Manual for Assessing Safety Hardware* (MASH) (*1*) for Test Level 3 (TL-3) (high speed).

The barrier is appropriate for a variety of contexts, such as where ROW constraints reduce lateral offset between a roadway and a shared-use path. However, state DOTs might be unable to implement the new system until a transition system that connects the new barrier to a typical guardrail installation is designed and evaluated. Therefore, as part of the project, the research team also proposed a design of a transition system. The crashworthiness of the proposed design was preliminarily evaluated through finite element (FE) computer simulations to determine needed design modifications and to identify critical impact locations for vehicular testing. On the basis of the simulation results, MASH Tests 3-20 and 3-21 were conducted on the final transition design by impacting at each critical impact point.

This report presents details on the tasks completed to meet the objectives of this project. Chapter 2 provides a review of U.S. and international literature on roadside safety devices and corresponding design for vulnerable road users to highlight the current state of roadside safety.

In addition to the literature review, the research team conducted an agency survey to collect information on (a) projects/design contexts in which a barrier to separate vulnerable users from motor vehicles is needed; (b) existing standard drawings of a barrier to separate vulnerable users from motor vehicles; (c) implemented retrofit options of an existing barrier to separate vulnerable users from motor vehicles; and (d) preferences in terms of barrier design options. Chapter 3 describes the survey designed to solicit information from transportation agencies and design consultants and presents the findings.

On the basis of the results of the literature review and survey, the research team developed six preliminary barrier designs to address and balance system needs from the perspective of both vehicular impact performance and pedestrian/bicyclist accessibility; this information is presented in Chapter 4. The anticipated advantages and disadvantages of each design alternative, along with the perceived performance benefits and application limitations, are included.

Chapter 5 summarizes modeling done with LS-PrePost, including calibration of the newly developed model, to verify whether the system would behave realistically. The results obtained from the calibration models are compared with actual crash tests from the past.

Chapter 6 then provides details about the modifications made to the FE model described in Chapter 5 to optimize the model and make it more realistic. Using LS-DYNA, the researchers investigated the crashworthiness and critical impact point for the proposed multifunctional barrier design according to MASH TL-3 criteria.

Chapters 7 through 9 present details on the MASH testing and evaluation plan for the proposed multifunctional barrier system. The construction materials, test requirements, and test conditions are included.

Chapters 10 and 11 then summarize the full-scale crash tests conducted in accordance with MASH Tests 3-10 [passenger car, 62 miles per hour (mi/h), 25-degree (deg) orientation angle] and 3-11 (pickup truck, 62 mi/h, 25-deg orientation angle), respectively.

Next, Chapters 12 and 13 describe the transition system that was developed to connect the proposed multifunctional barrier system to a typical guardrail system. The two transition designs were (a) utilizing a W-beam transition system with additional rub rail and (b) a Thrie beam transition system. Using LS-PrePost, the researchers developed an FE transition model and investigated its crashworthiness according to MASH TL-3 criteria.

Chapters 14 and 15 then describe full-scale test plans for the proposed Thrie beam transition system, and Chapters 16 and 17 summarize the crash tests conducted according to MASH Tests 3-20 (passenger car, 62 mi/h, 25-deg orientation angle) and 3-21 (pickup truck, 62 mi/h, 25-deg orientation angle), respectively, including the test results. Finally, Chapter 18 presents the conclusions on the recommended multifunctional barrier and transition system and offers suggestions for future research.

# CHAPTER 2

# Literature Review

This chapter provides a review of U.S. and international literature on roadside safety devices and corresponding designs for vulnerable road users. The chapter consists of four key sections:

- Design characteristics of roadside safety devices for accommodating vulnerable users.
- Safety and planning implications of the relevant types of vulnerable road user facilities. This section also reviews relevant sections of the AASHTO *Guide for the Development of Bicycle Facilities*, 4th ed. (*2*) and the U.S. Access Board's Public Right-of-Way Accessibility Guidelines (*3*) for public ROW and shared-use paths.
- Vegetation control methods for guardrail installations based on application conditions, and
- MASH testing standards.

## Review of Crashworthy Roadside Barriers and Railings

While roadside safety barriers are not new, no current barrier has been both tested for redirective crashworthiness in relation to vulnerable road users and designed to specifically accommodate the needs of these vulnerable users. Such a barrier would need to safely redirect a vehicle away from a vulnerable user on the backside of the device during an impact and also provide necessary protections for that vulnerable user, such as handrails. The first portion of this literature review summarizes various barrier systems and guidelines for systems that involve vulnerable user protection.

While this project focused on developing a crashworthy pedestrian/bicyclist barrier, many agencies incorporate systems that focus solely on protecting pedestrian/bicyclist traffic from hazards. The Vermont Agency of Transportation has various types of barriers focused on protecting vulnerable road user traffic (*4*). Table 1 and Figure 1 show some general examples of the types of barriers that can be implemented to protect pedestrians and bicyclists.

The Texas Department of Transportation (TxDOT) maintains standards on handrail designs (*5*). One such design is the PR11 pedestrian railing, which is a steel pipe rail system designed for pedestrian loads. This system has not been crash tested and is not intended for exposure to traffic. Table 2 shows the specifications for this railing, and Figure 2 shows the railing.

In addition to geometric requirements, the handrail must also be designed for strength considerations (*6*). AASHTO specifies loading requirements for both the rail elements and the posts. Figure 3 shows the minimum requirements for combination railing.

AASHTO also recognizes the need for accommodating the requirements of the Americans with Disabilities Act (ADA) (*6*). For example, AASHTO discusses the addition of certain elements to the rail system to aid in cane navigation. A rail or plate element along the base of the rail system will allow cane users to properly navigate along the length of the rail.

**Table 1. General types of barriers (4).**

| Type | Examples |
|------|----------|
| Hard | Fences (e.g., metal, wood, picket, pipe railing, wrought iron, chain-link), railings |
| Live | Vegetation, trees, bushes, plants |
| Terrain | Naturally occurring boundaries (e.g., rock walls) |

(a) Chain-link fence          (b) Metal fence

(c) Wood railing

**Figure 1. Examples of pedestrian or bicyclist barriers (4).**

**Table 2. TxDOT PR11 specifications (5).**

**Classification:** Pedestrian.

**Description:** Six pipe rails, with 3.5-inch (in.) hollow structural section (HSS) steel pipe for the top rail and 2.375-in. HSS steel pipe for the lower rails. Its 5-in.-wide steel plate posts are spaced a maximum of 10 feet (ft) apart.

**Approved test criteria and level:** The PR11 railing is designed for pedestrian loads only. It has not been crash-tested and it is not intended for exposure to traffic. If this railing is used on a bridge or culvert, it must be protected from vehicular impact by an approved bridge rail type.

**Nominal height:** 42 in.

**Minimum height after maintenance overlays:** 42 in.

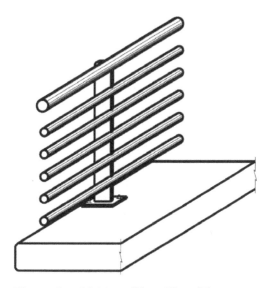

*Figure 2. PR11 traffic railing (5).*

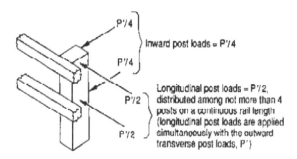

P' = the outward transverse post load applied to the post
at each rail location (P, P/2, or P/3 from Figure 10-4)

**(a) Inward and longitudinal post loads followed by AASHTO requirements**

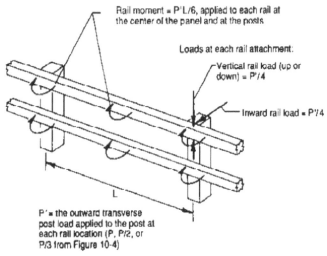

**(b) Moments and loads locations on the railing according to AASHTO requirements**

*Figure 3. AASHTO loading requirements for handrails (6).*

The Midwest Roadside Safety Facility (MwRSF) has investigated pedestrian rails that will be implemented near the roadside (7). The outside diameter of the gripping surface of a circular cross section of the handrail must be 2 in. Noncircular cross sections must be between 4 and 6.25 in. in perimeter measurement. Figure 4 explains the ADA dimensions for the noncircular cross section. According to the AASHTO *LRFD Bridge Design Specifications* (also known as the Bridge Design Guide), the design height of the railing for pedestrians must be at a minimum of 42 in. above the walking surface (8). In addition, the railing must be able to support a live load of at least 50 pounds (lb)/ft, with a concentrated live load of 200 lb. Figure 4 also shows how the loading is applied to the railing.

According to the International Building Code, handrails must be between 34 and 38 in. above the surface (7). Handrails must have minimum clearance space of 1.5 in. between a wall and any other surfaces. Additionally, the Occupational Safety and Health Administration (OSHA) provides guidelines for railings. The standard railing must have a height of 42 in. The nominal diameter of posts, pipe railings, and intermediate railings should be a minimum of 1.5 in. OSHA provides a maximum of 8 ft of space between posts. With regard to loading requirements, OSHA requires the top railing to be able to support a 200-lb load at any point in any direction.

Barriers can incorporate nontraditional structural materials, including timber, high-density polyethylene (HDPE), fiber-reinforced polymer (FRP), and polyvinyl chloride (PVC) (7). These materials are typically used for handrails because of their durability and resistance to corrosion. Figure 5 shows examples of these barriers as well as others that are typically found. Table 3 and Table 4 show a comparative view of these types of materials versus traditional structural materials such as steel and aluminum.

In the review of barriers currently used to protect pedestrians and bicyclists from motor vehicles, the research team identified several designs that could provide inspiration for this project. Practical uses of these barriers are shown in Figure 6.

## Review of Pedestrian and Bicyclist Facility Guidelines

AASHTO publishes two guides that are intended to be the national standard for pedestrian and bicyclist facility design:

- *Guide for the Planning, Design, and Operation of Pedestrian Facilities* (9, 10), also known as the Pedestrian Guide, and
- *Guide for the Development of Bicycle Facilities*, 4th ed. (2), also known as the Bike Guide.

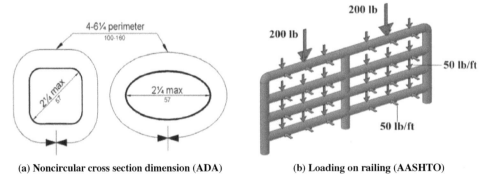

(a) Noncircular cross section dimension (ADA)          (b) Loading on railing (AASHTO)

***Figure 4.   Handrail requirements (7).***

(a) Wooden fence

(b) HDPE fence

(c) FRP fence

(d) PVC fence

*Figure 5. Various types of pedestrian rails (7).*

Table 3. Comparison of materials used for barrier designs (7).

| Consideration/ Condition | Material | | | | | |
|---|---|---|---|---|---|---|
| | **Steel** | **Aluminum** | **PVC** | **FRP** | **HDPE** | **Wood** |
| Bending strength ($f_b$) | Very high | High | Low | Medium | Very low | Very low |
| Modulus of elasticity ($E$) | Very high | High | Low | Medium | Very low | Medium |
| Brittleness | Low | Medium | High | High | Medium | High |
| Formability | Very high | Low | N/A | N/A | N/A | N/A |
| Cost | Medium | High | Medium | Very high | Medium | Low |
| Component weight | Medium | Very low | High | Low | High | Very high |
| Prefabricated connections | Yes | Yes | Yes | Yes | No | No |
| Corrosion resistance | Medium | Very high | Very high | Very high | Very high | Low |
| Temperature degradation | Very low | Very low | High | Low | Very high | Very low |
| Degradation from UV light exposure | Very low | Very low | High | High | High | Very low |

Note: UV = ultraviolet.

**Table 4.  Relevant material properties (7).**

| Material | Bending Strength ($f_b$) | | Modulus of Elasticity ($E$) | | Density | |
|---|---|---|---|---|---|---|
| | psi | kPa | ksi | MPa | lb/ft³ | kg/m³ |
| Steel | 50,000 | 345,000 | 29,000 | 199,950 | 503 | 8,060 |
| Aluminum | 40,000 | 276,000 | 10,000 | 68,950 | 169 | 2,710 |
| FRP | 24,000 | 165,000 | 2,320 | 16,000 | 108 | 1,730 |
| PVC | 14,450 | 100,000 | 400 | 2,760 | 90 | 1,440 |
| HDPE | 4,800 | 33,000 | 200 | 1,380 | 59 | 950 |
| Wood | 1,550 | 11,000 | 1,700 | 11,720 | 31 | 500 |

Note: psi = pounds per square inch; kPa = kilopascals; ksi = kips per square inch; MPa = megapascals; lb/ft³ = pounds per cubic foot; kg/m³ = kilograms per cubic meter.

Many state DOTs either adopt the AASHTO guides as their prevailing design guidance or adapt the AASHTO guidelines with minor modifications. Therefore, this section reviews the AASHTO guidelines as the prevailing national design guidance for which there is consensus among all state DOTs.

The 2012 AASHTO Bike Guide contains several design parameters that are relevant for barrier design: (*a*) bicyclist design dimensions, (*b*) bridge railing or barrier height, (*c*) side clearance on shared-use paths, and (*d*) bicycle handlebar rub railing (*2*). Figure 7 and Table 5 show the bicyclist dimensions from which several facility design dimensions are derived.

In Section 4.12.3 ("Bridges, Viaducts, Tunnels"), the Bike Guide says the following about barrier height (underline emphasis added, italics in original):

> In locations where bicyclists will operate in close proximity to bridge railings or barriers, the railing or <u>barrier should be a</u> *minimum* <u>of 42 in. (1.05 m) high</u>. On bridges where bicycle speeds are likely to be high (such as on a downgrade), and where a bicyclist could impact a barrier at a 25 degree angle or greater (such as on a curve), a higher 48-in. (1.2-m) railing may be considered. Where a barrier is less than 42 in. (1.2 m) high, an aluminum rail with posts is usually mounted on top of the barrier. If the shoulder is sufficiently wide so that a bicyclist does not operate in close proximity to the rail, lower rail heights are acceptable. (*2*)

In the past, there has been considerable debate over a 42-in. versus a 54-in. railing height for bicyclists, and there was even inconsistency between previous editions of the Bike Guide and the Bridge Design Guide. However, the current editions of the Bike Guide and the Bridge Design Guide both specify a minimum railing/barrier height of 42 in. for bicyclists.

In Section 5.2.1 ("Shared-Use Path Width and Clearance"), the Bike Guide indicates that a minimum of 2 ft of clearance is needed for signs, poles, and other lateral obstructions (Figure 8). The accompanying text indicates that a minimum of 1 ft of clearance is needed for smooth features, such as a railing or fence (*2*).

The Bike Guide says the following about shared-use path clearance (underline emphasis added, italics in original):

> <u>At a minimum, a 2 ft (0.6 m) graded area with a maximum 1V [vertical]:6H [horizontal] slope should be provided for clearance from lateral obstructions</u> such as bushes, large rocks, bridge piers, abutments, and *poles*. The MUTCD requires a minimum 2 ft (0.6 m) clearance to post-mounted signs or other traffic control devices (*7*). <u>Where "smooth" features such as bicycle railings or fences are introduced</u> with appropriate flaring end treatments (as described below), <u>a lesser clearance (not less than 1 ft [0.3 m]) is acceptable</u>. If adequate clearance cannot be provided between the path and lateral obstructions, then warning signs, object markers, or enhanced conspicuity and reflectorization of the obstruction should be used. (*2*)

(a) Wave delineator, Los Angeles

(b) Copenhagen bridge barrier

(c) Tokyo Bay

(d) Asakusa Dori bicycle rail

(e) Sands Street, Brooklyn, NY

*Figure 6.  Examples of pedestrian and bicycle barriers.*

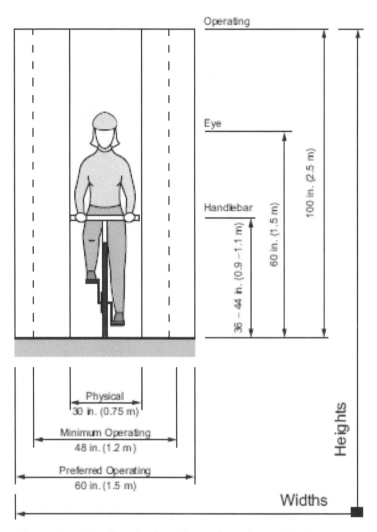

*Figure 7.   Bicyclist design dimensions from 2012 AASHTO Bike Guide (2).*

Table 5.   Bicyclist design dimensions from 2012 AASHTO Bike Guide (2).

| User Type | Feature | Dimension | |
|---|---|---|---|
| | | U.S. Customary (in.) | Metric (m) |
| Typical upright adult bicyclist | Physical width (95th percentile) | 30 | 0.75 |
| | Physical length | 70 | 1.8 |
| | Physical height of handlebars (typical dimension) | 44 | 1.1 |
| | Eye height | 60 | 1.5 |
| | Center of gravity (approximate) | 33–44 | 0.8–10 |
| | Operating width (minimum) | 48 | 1.2 |
| | Operating width (preferred) | 60 | 1.5 |
| | Operating height (minimum) | 100 | 2.5 |
| | Operating height (preferred) | 120 | 3.0 |

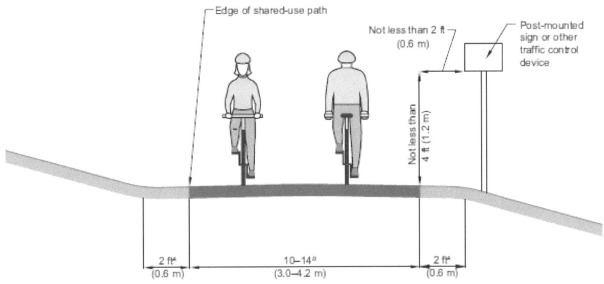

Notes:
[A] (1V:6H) Maximum slope (typ.)
[B] More if necessary to meet anticipated volumes and mix of users, per the *Shared Use Path Level of Service Calculator* (https://www.fhwa.dot.gov/publications/research/safety/pedbike/05138/)

***Figure 8.  Shared-use path width and clearance from 2012 AASHTO Bike Guide (2).***

In Section 5.2.2 ("Shared-Use Paths Adjacent to Roadways"), the Bike Guide says the following about separating shared-use paths and roadways (italics for emphasis added):

> A wide separation should be provided between a two-way side path and the adjacent roadway to demonstrate to both the bicyclist and the motorist that the path functions as an independent facility for bicyclists and other users. The minimum recommended distance between a path and the roadway curb (i.e., face of curb) or edge of traveled way (where there is no curb) is 5 ft (1.5 m). Where a paved shoulder is present, the separation distance begins at the outside edge of the shoulder. Thus, a paved shoulder is not included as part of the separation distance. Similarly, a bike lane is not considered part of the separation; however, an unpaved shoulder (e.g., a gravel shoulder) can be considered part of the separation. *Where the separation is less than 5 ft (1.5 m), a physical barrier or railing should be provided between the path and the roadway.* Such barriers or railings serve both to prevent path users from making undesirable or unintended movements from the path to the roadway and to reinforce the concept that the path is an independent facility. A barrier or railing between a shared-use path and adjacent highway should not impair sight distance at intersections, and should be designed to limit the potential for injury to errant motorists and bicyclists. The barrier or railing need not be of size and strength to redirect errant motorists toward the roadway, unless other conditions indicate the need for a crashworthy barrier. *Barriers or railings at the outside of a structure or a steep fill embankment that not only define the edge of a side path but also prevent bicyclists from falling over the rail to a substantially lower elevation should be a minimum of 42 in. (1.05 m) high. Barriers at other locations that serve only to separate the area for motor vehicles from the side path should generally have a minimum height equivalent to the height of a standard guardrail.*
>
> When a side path is placed along a high-speed highway, a separation greater than 5 ft (1.5 m) is desirable for path user comfort. If greater separation cannot be provided, use of a crashworthy barrier should be considered. Other treatments such as rumble strips can be considered as alternatives to physical barriers or railings, where the separation is less than 5 ft (1.5 m). However, as in the case of rumble strips, an alternative treatment should not negatively impact bicyclists who choose to ride on the roadway rather than the side path. (2)

In Section 5.2.10 ("Bridges and Underpasses"), the Bike Guide says the following about separating shared-use paths and roadways (italics for emphasis added):

> A bridge or underpass may be needed to provide continuity to a shared-use path. The "receiving" clear width on the end of a bridge (from inside of rail or barrier to inside of opposite rail or barrier) *should allow 2 ft (0.6 m) of clearance on each side of the pathway,* as recommended in Section 5.2.1, but under constrained conditions may taper to the pathway width.

*Protective railings, fences, or barriers on either side of a shared-use path on a stand-alone structure should be a minimum of 42 in. (1.05 m) high.* There are some locations where a 48-in. (1.2 m) high railing should be considered in order to prevent bicyclists from falling over the railing during a crash. This includes bridges or bridge approaches where high-speed, steep-angle (25 deg or greater) impacts between a bicyclist and the railing may occur, such as at a curve at the foot of a long, descending grade where the curve radius is less than that appropriate for the design speed or anticipated speed.

Openings between horizontal or vertical members on railings should be small enough that a 6 in. (150 mm) sphere cannot pass through them in the lower 27 in. (0.7 m). For the portion of railing that is higher than 27 in. (0.7 m), openings may be spaced such that an 8 in. (200 mm) sphere cannot pass through them. This is done to prevent children from falling through the openings. Where a bicyclist's handlebar may come into contact with a railing or barrier, a smooth, wide rub rail may be installed at a height of about 36 in. (0.9 m) to 44 in. (1.1 m), to reduce the likelihood that a bicyclist's handlebar will be caught by the railing (see Figure 5-11). (*2*)

Figure 9 shows Figure 5-11 from the Bike Guide.

The edition of the AASHTO Pedestrian Guide referenced under this project was published in 2004 (*9*), 8 years prior to the publication of the 2012 AASHTO Bike Guide. The discussion of shared-use paths in Chapter 3, "Pedestrian Facility Design" of the 2004 AASHTO Pedestrian Guide refers extensively to the most recent (at that time) AASHTO Bike Guide (the 1999 edition). The design dimensions are substantially unchanged in the 2012 AASHTO Bike Guide (*2*):

- Clearance zone of 2 ft on side of shared-use path and
- Minimum of 5 ft of separation between roadways and shared-use path.

The 2004 AASHTO Pedestrian Guide (*9*) also refers extensively to U.S. Access Board guidelines when discussing the accessibility of shared-use paths to persons with disabilities. The most recent accessibility guidelines at that time were published in 1999.

Because the 2004 edition of the AASHTO Pedestrian Guide is 20 years old and has extensive references to other design guidelines that have since been updated, the research team used the most recent versions of incorporated references to determine design parameters. An updated version of the AASHTO Pedestrian Guide was published in 2021, after completion of this phase of NCHRP Project 22-37 (*10*). The guidance in this new version is in line with the decisions made on this project.

The ADA was enacted as national law in 1990 and prohibited discrimination against individuals with disabilities. The U.S. Access Board is the federal agency that was charged with developing national standards to ensure compliance with the ADA (*3*).

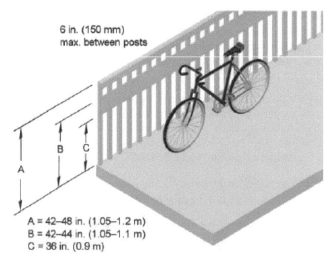

6 in. (150 mm)
max. between posts

A = 42–48 in. (1.05–1.2 m)
B = 42–44 in. (1.05–1.1 m)
C = 36 in. (0.9 m)

***Figure 9.   Bridge railing schematic from the 2012
AASHTO Bike Guide (2).***

The U.S. Access Board has worked with numerous stakeholders over the past two decades to develop specific guidance for how best to accommodate persons with disabilities in transportation and public ROW settings. In late 2019, the prevailing guidance (not yet law) was the Public Right-of-Way Accessibility Guidelines (PROWAG). The U.S. Access Board published the initial PROWAG in the *Federal Register* on July 26, 2011, with the intended application being on "sidewalks, pedestrian street crossings, pedestrian signals, and other facilities for pedestrian circulation and use." The U.S. Access Board issued a supplemental notice of proposed rulemaking on February 13, 2013 (78 FR 10110). The accessibility guidance in this supplemental notice was essentially the same as that issued in July 2011, but it was issued to clarify that shared-use paths should meet the same accessibility standards as sidewalks and pedestrian street crossings. The final rule, "Accessibility Guidelines for Pedestrian Facilities in the Public Right-of-Way" (36 CFR Part 1190) was issued August 8, 2023, after the work for NCHRP Project 22-37 had been completed. Although the 2011 and 2013 PROWAG guidance had not been enacted as law at the time this research was conducted, many states and cities had adopted (or adapted with minor changes) PROWAG as part of their roadway design standards. Therefore, the research team included a review of PROWAG, since it was the prevailing national consensus on accommodating persons with disabilities in transportation facilities. The following discussion of PROWAG refers to the February 13, 2013, supplemental notice of proposed rulemaking (78 FR 10110).

PROWAG contains several design parameters that are relevant for barrier design:

- No protruding objects,
- Bottom edge treatment (cane detection), and
- Handrail.

These parameters are summarized in the following sections.

Section R402 of PROWAG deals with protruding objects in the pedestrian circulation path. Section R402.2 indicates the following (also see Figure 10):

> Objects with leading edges more than 685 mm (2.25 ft) and not more than 2 m [meters] (6.7 ft) above the finish surface shall protrude 100 mm (4 in) maximum horizontally into pedestrian circulation paths.

Section R402.3 indicates the following for post-mounted objects (see Figure 11):

> Where objects are mounted on free-standing posts or pylons and the objects are 685 mm (2.25 ft) minimum and 2030 mm (6.7 ft) maximum above the finish surface, the objects shall overhang pedestrian circulation paths 100 mm (4 in) maximum measured horizontally from the post or pylon base. The base

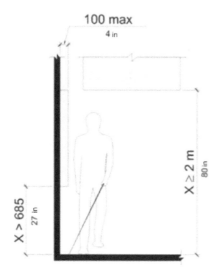

***Figure 10.   Protrusion limits from PROWAG.***

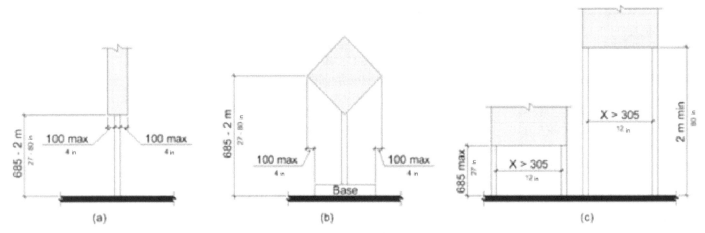

*Figure 11.*    ***Post-mounted objects from PROWAG.***

dimension shall be 64 mm (2.5 in) thick minimum. Where objects are mounted between posts or pylons and the clear distance between the posts or pylons is greater than 305 mm (1.0 ft), the lowest edge of the object shall be 685 mm (2.25 ft) maximum or 2 m (6.7 ft) minimum above the finish surface. (*2*)

Section R409 of PROWAG deals with handrails and indicates their need on ramps but not necessarily on level pedestrian circulation paths. Section R409.1 says,

> Handrails are required on ramp runs with a rise greater than 150 mm (6 in) (see R407.8) and stairways (see R408.6). Handrails are not required on pedestrian circulation paths. However, if handrails are provided on pedestrian circulation paths, the handrails must comply with R409 (see R217). The requirements in R409.2, R409.3, and R409.10 apply only to handrails at ramps and stairways, and do not apply to handrails provided on pedestrian circulation paths.

Section R409.4 of PROWAG deals with handrail height:

> Top of gripping surfaces of handrails shall be 865 mm (2.8 ft) minimum and 965 mm (3.2 ft) maximum vertically above walking surfaces, ramp surfaces, and stair nosings. Handrails shall be at a consistent height above walking surfaces, ramp surfaces, and stair nosings.

A review of literature by Sarkar attempted to subdivide different types of separations based on their unique physical and regulatory attributes and compared their performance in safety, equity, comfort, and convenience to the different road users (especially pedestrians and bicyclists) (*11*). The review found that there are four types of separations: (*a*) horizontal separation, (*b*) time separation, (*c*) vertical separation, and (*d*) soft separation.

Each of these types of separation requires different design and planning requirements that use physical, psychological, visual, and legal tools to eliminate conflicts. Sarkar's work also discusses the performance of each type of separation in eliminating or promoting the following:

1. Elimination of conflicts;
2. Safety of vulnerable groups such as the elderly, children, and the physically/mentally impaired;
3. Elimination of barriers for non-motorists;
4. Optimal use of public space for outdoor pedestrian activities;
5. Equitable use of the public space;
6. Comfort and convenience; and
7. Ensuring conformance. (*11*)

Separating vulnerable users from traffic can also help improve both safety and comfort of all roadway users. A study by Sanders examined the design preferences regarding multimodal roadways in a policy era focused on complete streets (*12*). The study found that alignment between drivers and cyclists for roadway designs can meet the needs of both user groups while sharing the road, with both groups preferring greater separation on multilane roadways. The findings also support past research on bicyclists' preferences and U.S. federal policy encouraging more substantial accommodation for cyclists on roadways. In addition, with the movement toward complete streets, practitioners need an understanding of roadway designs that maximize comfort and safety for all roadway users. More specifically, Sanders presented findings from research exploring perceptions of adult bicycling risks, experiences bicycling, and roadway design preferences among bicycling drivers, nonbicycling drivers, and nondriving bicyclists in the San Francisco Bay Area. The results showed that bicyclists of all types—and particularly potential cyclists—prefer greater separation from motorists. Also, the results provided new information about motorists' preferences for sharing the road with bicyclists, indicating that motorists also prefer greater separation. These findings suggest an alignment between roadway user groups' design preferences for multilane commercial streets and provide additional evidence of the benefits of complete streets for all roadway users. Methodologically, these findings also suggest advantages from studying the preferences of multiple user groups regarding shared facilities.

In another study by Sanders, the author examined roadway design preferences when bicycling alone, bicycling with children, and driving on multilane commercial streets (*13*). The findings were based on results from a survey exploring attitudes toward driving and bicycling, bicycling habits, barriers to bicycling, and roadway design preferences among Michigan residents. Regarding roadway design preferences, respondents were asked a series of questions about their level of comfort and experience riding and driving on seven different roadway designs. The findings overwhelmingly suggested a preference for more bicycle accommodations and more separated facilities. Seventy-five percent of respondents indicated that separated bicycle facilities would encourage them to bicycle more, with almost twice as many rare cyclists choosing separated bike facilities over more facilities in general. The findings also suggested that the presence of bicycle facilities increased respondents' comfort and willingness to try bicycling on a roadway. Most respondents felt more comfortable bicycling on a roadway with any type of bike facility, and this preference was even stronger when the facility was separated from drivers by any physical barrier. Separation was even more important when considering bicycling with children. Respondents also indicated that their comfort level increased while driving with greater separation from bicyclists.

A study by Li et al. found that physical environments can influence bicyclists' perceptions of comfort on separated and on-street bicycle facilities (*14*). Their investigation, conducted in Nanjing, China, found that physical environmental factors significantly influenced bicyclists' perception of comfort on the two types of facilities. Comfort was mainly influenced by the road geometry and surrounding conditions, such as the width of a path, presence of a slope, presence of a bus stop, physical separation from pedestrians, surrounding land use, and bicycle flow rate. For on-street bicycle facilities, comfort was influenced by factors including the width of the bicycle lane, the width of the curb lane, the presence of a slope, the presence of a bus stop, the amount of occupied car parking spaces, the bicycle flow rate, the motor vehicle flow rate, and the rate of use of electric bicycles. The researchers also found that physically separated paths provided greater comfort when there was light bicycle traffic and when there was traffic congestion on the street, while on-street bicycle lanes were preferred when bicycle volume was heavy.

A study by DuBose also found that separated bikeways encouraged more people to bicycle (*15*). Many people do not bicycle because they have safety concerns. Therefore, installing separated bikeways can improve bicyclist comfort while also helping reduce collision rates as drivers come to expect encounters with bicyclists more regularly.

A study by Huybers et al. (*16*) found that pavement markings and signs can reduce pedestrian casualties and injuries. They performed two experiments. In Experiment 1, use of a "yield here to pedestrians" sign alone reduced pedestrian/motor vehicle conflicts and increased motorists' yielding distance. The results of Experiment 1 indicated that the addition of advance yield pavement markings was associated with a further decrease in conflicts and a further increase in motorist yielding distance. These results rule out the possibility that the lack of effectiveness of the yellow-green sign was due to a floor effect for conflicts or a possible ceiling effect for yielding farther behind the crosswalks. The results also suggest that signs made with yellow-green sheeting may be more easily recognizable and that it is possible that the motorists were attending more to the fluorescent yellow-green sheeting than to the message of the sign that was printed on it. Use of fluorescent yellow-green sheeting as the background of the sign did not help increase the effectiveness of the sign. In Experiment 2, the researchers used advance yield pavement markings alone and found that doing so was as effective at reducing pedestrian/motor vehicle conflicts and increasing yielding distance as the combination of a sign and pavement markings. The researchers suggested that the pavement markings were the essential component for reducing conflicts and increasing yielding distance.

A study by McNeil et al. (*17*) suggested that buffered and protected bike lanes can increase people's sense of safety and comfort when bicycling. The project used data collected from surveys for a multicity study of newly constructed protected bike lanes. Participants were current bicyclists and residents who were potential bicyclists. The bicyclists agreed that buffers made them feel safer, and residents strongly believed that buffers effectively separated and protected bikes from vehicles, thereby increasing safety when bicycling. These findings suggest that bike lanes with an extra buffered space can increase the safety and comfort of bicycling for both current and potential bicyclists, which would make people more likely to ride a bicycle for transportation. The findings also suggest that both current bicyclists and potential bicyclists would feel comfortable riding on a busy commercial street if there were a bike lane with a physical barrier.

## Review of Use of Vegetation Control

Various concepts for the multifunctional barrier system developed under this project incorporated different elements on the field side of the barrier to accommodate pedestrians (including those with disabilities) and bicyclists. These added elements can make cutting or trimming vegetation around the barrier more time consuming, which can increase both the cost and the safety risk associated with vegetation maintenance. Use of vegetation control was, therefore, a design element considered during the development of the new barrier system. Vegetation control can reduce maintenance costs and risk to workers associated with hand mowing or trimming around a barrier. Literature pertaining to the use of vegetation control for barrier systems is presented in the sections below.

### Caltrans Roadside Management Toolbox

The Caltrans [California Department of Transportation] Roadside Management Toolbox is a web-based decision-making tool designed to improve the safety and maintainability of transportation projects (*18*). The management, maintenance, and control of vegetation on roadsides has become increasingly difficult as the miles of roadway and acres of roadside have increased while maintenance resources decreased. Historical methods of vegetation control (manual, mechanical, and chemical) have been sharply curtailed due to local development, increased traffic volumes, public concerns, and other economic and environmental issues.

The toolbox includes treatments composed of both materials familiar to traditional highway construction contractors (such as asphalt concrete, portland cement concrete, and road base), as well as less conventional materials or products (such as polyurea coatings, rubber mats, and fiber weed control mats). Figure 12 shows examples of vegetation control recommended by Caltrans.

(a) Minor concrete vegetation control

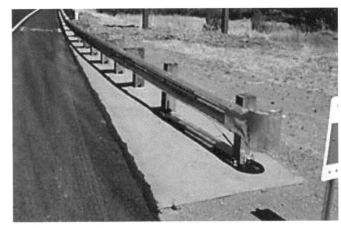

(b) Example of weed control mat (fiber)

(c) Examples of asphalt composite control

(d) Weed control mat (rubber)

(e) Native vegetation

*Figure 12. Examples of vegetation control recommended by Caltrans (18).*

### Evaluation of DuroTrim Vegetation Control Mats

Dunn investigated the performance of DuroTrim Vegetation Control Mats for eliminating trimming around roadside delineator and guardrail posts and weighed the cost of purchasing and placing the mats versus hand trimming (*19*). Dunn found that the DuroTrim Vegetation Control Mats would be required to perform well for 9 to 21 years, on average, in order to recoup the cost of installation. This calculation includes the durability of the product, but not the cost of repair due to traffic damage, snowplow and wing damage, or damage caused by mowing operations.

DuroTrim Vegetation Control Mats are 2- × 2-ft tiles composed of shredded used tires bound together with a urethane resin binder. The manufacturer recommends use of two tiles per delineator post for a 4- × 2-ft mat. The mats weigh approximately 4.25 lb/ft² and are connected and sealed at the joints with a one-part urethane adhesive. Figure 13 shows DuroTrim Vegetation Control Mats before and after a vehicle collision.

The use of the weed control mats could be justified in areas that are dangerous to maintenance workers, such as guardrail installations in high traffic areas. Because the delineator posts are farther from the edge of the traveled roadway, the risk to the maintenance workforce while hand trimming is reduced.

Because the DuroTrim Vegetation Control Mats appear to have performed adequately in the field trial, they could be considered for use where safety conditions warrant. That use should be limited, however, given the considerable initial cost. Applications should be limited to instances where the use of the mats would have a significant impact on the safety of roadside maintenance workers. The cost savings from elimination of trimming and mowing alone are not enough to justify the use of these mats in most situations.

### Vegetation Management Under Guardrail for North Carolina Roads

Yelverton and Gannon (*20*) designed and then determined the influence of herbicides and plant growth regulators on the establishment of centipede grass, evaluated treatments for vegetation management under guardrails, and determined whether nitrogen fertility levels affected the establishment of centipede grass sod. They conducted experiments to attempt to correlate centipede grass and zoysia grass problem areas with geographical areas or soil parameters as well as to compare the establishment of common centipede grass and El Toro zoysia grass from sod simulating vegetation under a guardrail.

*Figure 13. DuroTrim Vegetation Control Mats before* (left) *and after* (right) *vehicle collision (19).*

The researchers also determined management plans for these areas where centipede grass or zoysia grass was sodded into existing vegetation. Management plans included tolerance of herbicides and plant growth regulators as well as practices to transition the roadside to centipede grass or zoysia grass in an effort to achieve a monoculture turfgrass stand. The experiments included the tolerance of centipede grass to herbicides and plant growth regulators applied at seeding and soon thereafter, the survival of centipede grass when subjected to various fertility regimes, and the establishment of zoysia grass versus centipede grass from sod under roadside conditions.

## Dynamic Response of Guardrail Systems Encased in Mow Strips

Bligh et al. examined the effect of pavement post encasement on the crashworthiness of strong post guardrail systems (21). The performance of these systems used experimental testing and numerical simulation. Seventeen configurations of wood and steel guardrail posts embedded in various mow strip systems and confinement conditions were subjected to dynamic impact testing with a bogie vehicle. Along with enhanced impact performance, it was suggested that mow strip configurations featuring leave-outs were also more practical, on the basis of ease of repair after an impact. Crash tests of a steel post guardrail system and wood post guardrail system encased in a selected concrete mow strip with low-strength grout-filled leave-outs were successful. While the number of full-scale tests conducted was limited, the structure of subcomponent analysis and testing provided additional insight into the performance of guardrail posts encased in a mow strip.

Recommendations regarding the acceptable ranges for some key mow strip parameters, such as mow strip material and dimensions, leave-out dimensions, leave-out backfill material, and guardrail post location were provided as part of this study.

## Evaluation of Tire-Rubber Antivegetation Tiles

Raine conducted a project to allow TxDOT to evaluate the ease of installation, cost, and effectiveness of antivegetation tiles made from recycled tires (22). The purpose of the project was to evaluate the ease and cost of installing antivegetation tiles made from recycled tires to control vegetation around guardrails and signposts. The project also compared the tiles' effectiveness and life-cycle costs with those of other TxDOT-approved designs, such as using grout or concrete installed around guardrail posts or signposts. If tire-rubber tiles for guardrail and signposts are eventually accepted for use in new construction, retrofits, and maintenance to control vegetation, more than 500,000 tires worth of scrap tire rubber that is generated in Texas each year could be consumed.

## Alternatives to Labor-Intensive Tasks in Roadside Vegetation Maintenance

Arsenault et al. addressed herbicide use and the feasibility of replacing herbicides with alternative mechanical vegetation control technologies (23). The use of hot foam application, radiant heating, and high-pressure water application was compared with the use of mowing and herbicide application in the maintenance of areas around posts and guardrails, mow strips, and paved surfaces. The reduction of herbicides was important because Caltrans had mandated that herbicide use be reduced to 80% of 1994 levels by 2012.

According to the report, the current major vegetation control methods included (a) herbicide application, (b) mechanical mowing, and (c) no vegetation maintenance. The alternative vegetation control technologies included the following:

- Hot water, hot foam, steam application: The hot water melts the waxy coating of the vegetation, leading to severe dehydration (Figure 14).

*Figure 14.   Hot foam treatment unit (23).*

- Hydromechanical obliteration: High-pressure application of water is used to cut/mow vegetation. When held at a distance of 1 m (3 ft), the nozzle clears most brush without disturbing the soil.
- Thermal weed treatments: Open flames or radiant heat or ultraviolet heat are used to control weeds (Figure 15).

The benefits and drawbacks of each method are discussed in the report in detail, along with the cost calculations for roadside application.

The report also includes recommendations on the combination of alternative and current technologies. A combination of two or more methods may lead to the development of more-effective and efficient control methods. In this way, some of the vegetation control technologies, when combined, will perform better than each respective technology alone. The combination options are (*a*) hot foam and radiant heat, (*b*) hot foam and mowing, and (*c*) hot foam and other attachments for the Advanced Roadway Debris Vacuum (ARDVAC).

## Alternative Design of Guardrail Posts in Asphalt or Concrete

Arrington et al. focused on testing alternative materials for the leave-out sections around guardrail posts encased in a pavement mow strip (*24*). Figure 16 shows the tested guardrail posts

*Figure 15.   Thermal weed control unit in operation (23).*

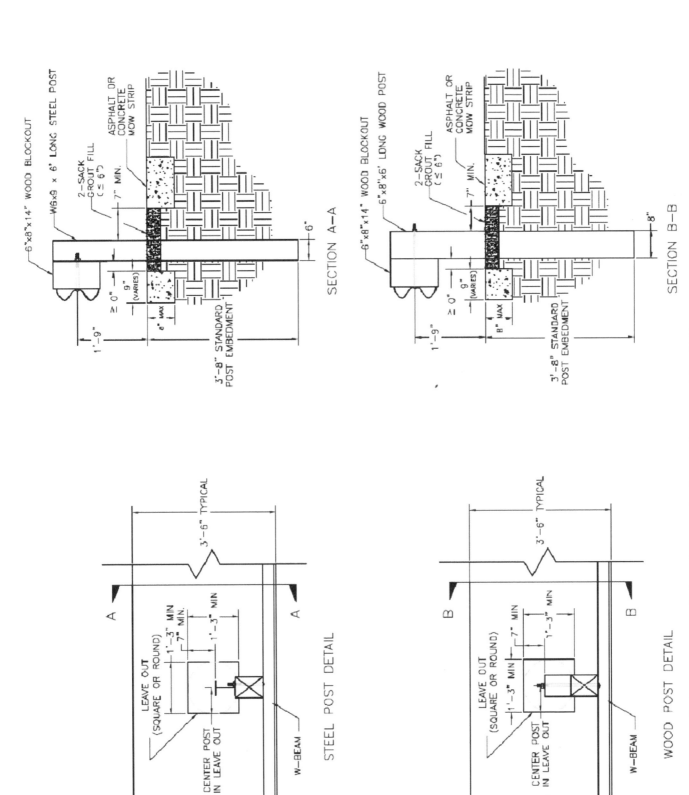

*Figure 16. Installation recommendations for guardrail posts in mow strips (24).*

in mow strips. A two-sack grout mixture that had been successfully crash tested previously was used as a baseline reference for acceptable impact performance. Static laboratory and dynamic bogie impact testing was conducted to evaluate the various products. The long-term durability of these products was not evaluated.

The products that were investigated included a two-part urethane foam, a molded rubber product that had an insert fabricated to match the size of the leave-out, a flat recycled rubber mat that rested on top of a leave-out backfilled with soil, and a new pop-out concrete wedge.

All of the products except the flat rubber mat were considered to have acceptable impact performance. The acceleration levels associated with the flat rubber mat significantly exceeded the baseline threshold established from the test results of the two-sack grout mixture. The soil confined within the leave-out was responsible for the high acceleration. Since the soil was compressed between the post and the back face of the leave-out, without any void space, the added height and confinement of the soil led to the high acceleration levels.

The other tested products were considered to be acceptable alternatives to the two-sack grout mix from the standpoint of impact performance and vegetation control. However, the advantages and disadvantages regarding cost, availability, and ease of installation and inspection should be considered before selecting the product.

## Assessment of Alternatives in Vegetation Management at Pavement Edge

Willard et al. documented findings from case studies at 43 locations throughout the state of Washington that compared and contrasted vegetation management alternatives at the pavement edge (*25*). The traditional Washington State DOT practice of maintaining a bare ground strip at the pavement edge was being reevaluated as a result of concerns about potential effects to the environment from these types of herbicide applications and because satisfactory results could be achieved without the use of herbicides at many locations. This study implemented strategies to either establish and maintain vegetation up to the pavement edge or maintain a bare strip of ground through nonchemical methods.

Alternative approaches were grouped into five categories: managed vegetation up to the edge of the pavement, pavement edge design, cultivation, weed barriers, and nonselective herbicides. The set of alternatives studied in the category of managed vegetation up to the edge of pavement was the most extensive group of experiments. This alternative focused on establishing desirable vegetation (grasses) on the nonpaved shoulder and maintenance with selective chemical and/or mechanical means (mowing and grading) in a variety of situations.

The category of pavement edge design included two locations where some form of paved break/edge drop was already present or constructed at the edge of the paved shoulder. The category of cultivation included situations in which a band 2 to 3 ft wide was annually turned and repacked with a tractor-mounted disking tool followed by a grader. The category of weed barriers tested a series of products/materials designed as soil cover/matting material for use under a guardrail. The category of nonselective herbicides evaluated annual treatment of a 2- to 4-ft band with various mixtures of nonselective, pre- and postemergent herbicides each spring.

The first two categories focused on a vegetative treatment at the pavement edge, while the last three described various methods of providing a nonvegetative pavement edge. Both of these conditions are now referred to as a "Zone 1" treatment.

Evaluation of alternatives was based on a comparison of costs and results. Maintenance costs were averaged per mile and per year, since some activities might occur more or less than once per year. Results included impacts on maintenance objectives such as traffic safety, worker safety, environmental factors, and preservation of pavement and roadside hardware.

The results varied significantly between eastern and western Washington, in part due to precipitation and vegetative growth. In eastern Washington, particularly in the more arid areas, it was found that desirable grasses could be established up to the edge of the pavement. This was accomplished either through soil preparation and planting with new construction or through efforts by maintenance to manage the transition from bare ground shoulders to naturally occurring grasses over a series of years. In cases where desirable grasses were successfully established, there were no adverse impacts on maintenance objectives, and the level of effort and cost to maintenance was shown to decrease over time.

In western Washington, where the climate promotes more vegetative growth, there was a corresponding increase in required maintenance resulting from impacts on traffic safety and stormwater management. Where tall grasses blocked sight distance at intersections and curves in the spring and early summer, increased mowing was required at a greater cost than if these areas had been maintained with a vegetation-free pavement edge. In locations where stormwater flowed to the edge of the pavement, it was found that the presence of grass at the pavement edge resulted in a buildup of soil and debris and subsequent problems related to standing water on the roadway shoulder. Over the course of the study period, a number of maintenance innovations were proven effective in removing edge buildup and improving the efficiency of mowing operations. However, in the majority of cases in western Washington where vegetation was allowed to grow at the edge of the pavement, there was an increased cost and level of effort compared with the use of herbicides to maintain a vegetation-free pavement edge.

Information supports the continued or renewed application of residual herbicides at the pavement edge in certain locations, such as under guardrails and on western Washington highways with narrow paved shoulders and abundant vegetative growth. In some areas where shoulders were allowed to grow vegetation, bare-ground treatments were to be reestablished with a narrow (2- to 3-ft) strip at the edge of the pavement. In areas with unique environmental constraints, or where it had proven effective to manage the pavement edge with mowing, grading, sweeping, or other routine maintenance practices, those practices were to be continued. In eastern Washington, areas would continue to minimize and phase out bare-ground pavement edge strips as appropriate.

## Guardrail Vegetation Management in Delaware

To explore alternatives to traditional herbicide treatments under guardrails, Barton and Budischak evaluated the following (26):

- Three herbicide formulations:
  - Formulation 1: Standard Delaware DOT New Castle County Formulation composed of DuPont™ Karmex® DF Herbicide (diuron), BASF Plateau (imazapic ammonium salt), Dow AgroSciences Accord® XRT (glyphosate), and BASF Pendulum (pendimethalin).
  - Formulation 2: Sensitive areas formulation composed of BASF Plateau (imazapic ammonium salt), Dow AgroSciences Accord® XRT (glyphosate), and BASF Pendulum (pendimethalin).
  - Formulation 3: Dow AgroSciences Accord® XRT (glyphosate).
  Formulations 1 and 2 provided adequate control of vegetation under guardrails when applied once per year. Formulation 3 did not provide adequate control. Herbicide treatments resulted in a bare ground condition for much of the year and resulted in an unsightly edge between dead and live vegetation on the median.

- Four weed control barriers:
  - U-Teck™ WeedEnder standard installation (a permeable recycled fiber material).
  - U-Teck™ WeedEnder custom installation (a product designed to reach the road edge and accommodate variances in post width).
  - Universal Weed Cover (a semirigid panel made of 100% recycled plastic.
  - TrafFix (a rubber mat with three punched guardrail cutouts for flexible installation).

  Weed control barriers performed differently, depending on the barrier. The Universal Weed Cover provided inadequate control, and the U-Teck™ WeedEnder (standard or custom cut installation) and TrafFix barriers provided adequate control. Weed barriers that were not installed adjacent to the road surface allowed a strip of vegetation to grow between the barrier and the roadway, resulting in an unacceptable condition. Examples of weed barrier products are shown in Figure 17.
- Competitive vegetation:
  - Low fescue: difficult to establish reliably under guardrail but, when established, provided a desirable uniform cover with minimal maintenance.
  - Zoysia seed: not established from seed during the first growing season.
  - Zoysia sod: established successfully and almost entirely eliminated weeds under the guardrail and required no trimming during the first year.
  - FlightTurf: only established at the end of the 2012 growing season.
- Hand trimming: Hand trimming was required once or twice per year depending on the site, weather, and timing.
- Pavement under guardrail: When conducted once per year, hand trimming was the most cost-effective treatment and provided a green mat of vegetation below the guardrail.

## Crash Tests on Guardrail System Embedded in Asphalt Vegetation Barriers

The Georgia Department of Transportation (GDOT) authorized tests to be performed on guardrails installed in accordance with GDOT Standard Detail S-4-2002, which was used in Georgia prior to 2017 and includes an asphalt mow strip with nearby curb (27). The University of Nebraska's MwRSF was selected to perform the tests in accordance with AASHTO's MASH. Test Vehicle 1100C, a small passenger car, was used to perform a single crash test. The crash test results exceeded multiple MASH safety evaluation criteria, including occupant compartment deformation, windshield crushing, and maximum allowable occupant ridedown acceleration. Thus, the Midwest Guardrail System (MGS) installed in an asphalt mow strip with a curb placed behind the barrier was deemed to be unacceptable, according to the TL-3 safety performance criteria for Test 3-10 provided in MASH.

GDOT no longer uses the S-4-2002 mow strip configuration. Beginning March 15, 2017, GDOT directed that all new guardrail construction projects on Georgia roadways use asphalt layers that are paved up to the face of the post, leaving the post itself and the area behind unrestrained. Figure 18 shows the actual test bed site behind posts.

## MASH Evaluation of 31-in. W-Beam Guardrail with Wood and Steel Posts in Concrete Mow Strip

The performance of a 31-in.-tall W-beam guardrail system installed in a concrete mow strip with wood and steel posts, respectively, was evaluated (28). Figure 19 shows the system details. The presence of a mow strip prevents growth of vegetation around the posts, and thus helps

*Figure 17.    Weed barrier products tested at time of installation (26).*

*Figure 18.   View of GDOT test bed site showing area directly behind post (27).*

reduce maintenance for the guardrail system. MASH Tests 3-10 and 3-11 were performed for both wood and steel guardrail systems.

## Review of MASH Testing Standards

### MASH Testing Standards

AASHTO's MASH (*1*) is the latest in a series of documents that provide guidance on testing and evaluation of roadside safety features. This document was initially published in 2009 and represents a comprehensive update to crash test and evaluation procedures to reflect changes in the vehicle fleet, operating conditions, and roadside safety knowledge and technology. It superseded *NCHRP Report 350: Recommended Procedures for the Safety Performance Evaluation of Highway Features* (*29*).

MASH was developed to incorporate significant changes and additions to the procedures for the safety performance of roadside safety hardware, including new design vehicles that better reflected the changing character of vehicles using the highway network. Like *NCHRP Report 350*, MASH defines six test levels for longitudinal barriers (the type of barrier designed/investigated through this project). Each test level places an increasing level of demand on the structural capacity of a barrier system.

MASH Test Level 2 (TL-2) is recommended for investigating the behavior of roadside safety hardware (including longitudinal barriers) when impacted by passenger vehicles to evaluate the placement of such roadside safety hardware on low-speed roadways. MASH recommends two tests for evaluating longitudinal barriers according to TL-2:

- MASH Test 2-10: 2,240-lb vehicle impacting the length of need (LON) section at a speed of 44 mi/h and an angle of 25 deg.
- MASH Test 2-11: 5,000-lb pickup truck impacting the LON section at a speed of 44 mi/h and an angle of 25 deg.

MASH TL-3 is recommended for investigating the behavior of roadside safety hardware (including longitudinal barriers) when impacted by passenger vehicles to evaluate the placement of such roadside safety hardware on high-speed roadways. MASH recommends two tests for evaluating longitudinal barriers according to TL-3:

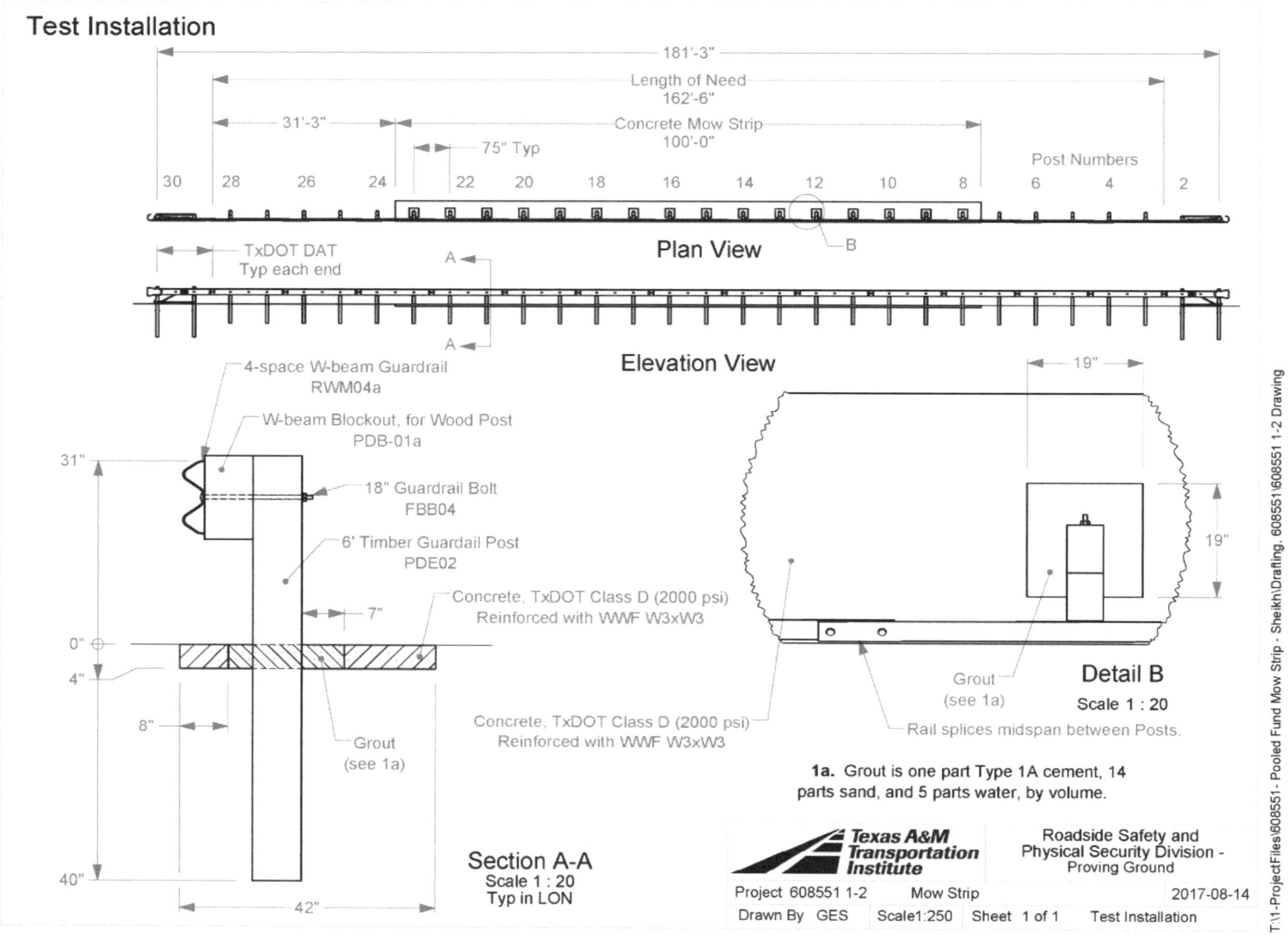

Test Installation

Figure 19. *Overall details for 31-in. W-beam guardrail on wood posts in a concrete mow strip (28).*

- MASH Test 3-10: 2,240-lb vehicle impacting the LON section at a speed of 62 mi/h and an angle of 25 deg.
- MASH Test 3-11: 5,000-lb pickup truck impacting the LON section at a speed of 62 mi/h and an angle of 25 deg.

Due to higher impact energy, Test 3-11 results in greater lateral deflection and helps evaluate connection strength and the tendency of the barriers to rotate. Test 3-10 is needed to evaluate occupant risk and potential for vehicle snagging and occupant compartment intrusion.

The target critical impact point (CIP) for each test is determined according to information provided in MASH and is revised through computer simulations and engineering analysis to help support the decision on the proposed CIPs.

According to the MASH standards, the impact performance of tested roadside safety systems is judged on the basis of the following factors:

- Structural adequacy, which is judged on the ability of the system to contain and redirect the vehicle.
- Risk of occupant compartment deformation or intrusion by detached elements, fragments, or other debris from the test article, which evaluates the potential risk of hazard to occupants and, to some extent, other traffic, pedestrians, or workers in construction zones, if applicable.
- Occupant risk values, for which longitudinal and lateral occupant impact velocity and ridedown accelerations for the 1100C and 2270P test vehicles must be within the limits specified in MASH and which determine the risk of injury to the occupants.

**Table 6. Safety evaluation criteria for full-scale crash testing (1).**

**MASH Test 10**

Structural Adequacy
A. Test article should contain and redirect the vehicle or bring the vehicle to a controlled stop; the vehicle should not penetrate, underride, or override the installation although controlled lateral deflection of the test article is acceptable.

Occupant Risk
D. Detached elements, fragments, or other debris from the test article should not penetrate or show potential for penetrating the occupant compartment, or present an undue hazard to other traffic, pedestrians, or personnel in a work zone.
Deformations of, or intrusions into, the occupant compartment should not exceed limits set forth in Section 5.3 and Appendix E of MASH.
F. The vehicle should remain upright during and after collision. The maximum roll and pitch angles are not to exceed 75 degrees.
H. Longitudinal and lateral occupant impact velocities should fall below the preferred value of 30 ft/s, or at least below the maximum allowable value of 40 ft/s.
I. Longitudinal and lateral occupant ridedown accelerations should fall below the preferred value of 15.0 Gs, or at least below the maximum allowable value of 20.49 Gs.

**MASH Test 11**

Structural Adequacy
A. Test article should contain and redirect the vehicle or bring the vehicle to a controlled stop; the vehicle should not penetrate, underride, or override the installation although controlled lateral deflection of the test article is acceptable.

Occupant Risk
D. Detached elements, fragments, or other debris from the test article should not penetrate or show potential for penetrating the occupant compartment, or present an undue hazard to other traffic, pedestrians, or personnel in a work zone.
Deformations of, or intrusions into, the occupant compartment should not exceed limits set forth in Section 5.3 and Appendix E of MASH.
F. The vehicle should remain upright during and after collision. The maximum roll and pitch angles are not to exceed 75 degrees.
H. Longitudinal and lateral occupant impact velocities should fall below the preferred value of 30 ft/s, or at least below the maximum allowable value of 40 ft/s.
I. Longitudinal and lateral occupant ridedown accelerations should fall below the preferred value of 15.0 Gs, or at least below the maximum allowable value of 20.49 Gs.

- Postimpact vehicle trajectory, which considers the potential for secondary impact with other vehicles or fixed objects creating further risk of injury to occupants of the impacting vehicle and/or the risk of injury to occupants in other vehicles.

Table 6 shows the safety evaluation criteria from Table 5-1 of MASH, which are used to evaluate the full-scale crash tests (*1*).

## MASH Implementation Plan

The AASHTO Technical Committee on Roadside Safety and FHWA adopted a new MASH implementation plan that has compliance dates for installing MASH hardware that differ by hardware category. After December 31, 2019, all new installations of roadside safety devices on the National Highway System must have been successfully evaluated according to the 2016 edition of MASH. FHWA no longer issues eligibility letters for highway safety hardware that has not been successfully evaluated to MASH performance criteria.

CHAPTER 3

# Agency Survey

This chapter describes the survey designed to solicit information from transportation agencies and design consultants on

- Projects/design contexts in which a barrier to separate vulnerable users from motor vehicles is needed,
- Existing standard drawings of a barrier to separate vulnerable users from motor vehicles,
- Implemented retrofit options of an existing barrier to separate vulnerable users from motor vehicles, and
- Preferences in terms of barrier design options.

The information collected served to determine the initial parameters and improved characteristics to be considered while developing preliminary design options for the proposed system. A copy of the survey instrument is provided in Appendix A. The survey was designed to incorporate a logic to redirect the respondents to different survey portions on the basis of the offered responses.

The survey was administered online with Qualtrics and was sent to all state DOTs and Ontario, Canada. The survey was distributed via email. A total of 25 state DOTs responded to the submitted survey.

Since the survey employed logic that redirected respondents to specific questions on the basis of certain responses, the total number of responses to specific questions may not equal the number of participants in the survey. Conversely, some questions allowed for multiple selections to be made, which resulted in a total number of responses greater than the number of participants in the survey. Although the survey was submitted to both state DOTs and design consultants, the project team received responses primarily from state DOTs. Followings are the 25 state and local agencies that participated in the survey: Alaska, Arkansas, Baltimore City, Colorado, Delaware, Florida, Iowa, Louisiana, Massachusetts, Michigan, Minnesota, Missouri, New Jersey, New Mexico, New York State, North Carolina, Oregon, Pennsylvania, Texas, Utah, Virginia, Washington State, West Virginia, Wisconsin, and Wyoming.

## Survey Responses

### Needs and Solutions at Locations with Barrier Separation Needs

Almost all the respondent agencies (the exception being the Arkansas DOT) indicated that they have locations where barrier separation of vulnerable users from motor vehicles is a consideration. Table 7 shows the solutions some respondent agencies described for separating vulnerable users from motor vehicles.

**Table 7.    State agency comments on consideration for barrier separation of vulnerable users from motor vehicles.**

| Agency (DOT) | Comment |
|---|---|
| Colorado | We will have a barrier between pedestrians and roadway for any situations with a speed limit of >45 mi/h. |
| Florida | We address it where we can with the use of concrete barriers, especially for high-speed conditions and on bridges. |
| Louisiana | Typically, we do not install a barrier, since doing so would reduce the already limited space available for pedestrians. Also, the additional weight of the barrier could cause structural issues when installed on a bridge. Typically, the only thing separating pedestrians from traffic is an 8- to 10-in. curb. |
| Minnesota | Typically move bus stations out of the clear zone rather than install a barrier. |
| Missouri | Depending on traffic volumes, speed, and other factors, we will install pedestrian barriers. |
| New York | We often install a barrier, but traffic speeds, offsets, and vehicular and pedestrian volumes are also taken into consideration. |
| Oregon | ODOT [Oregon Department of Transportation] has guidance to consider installing a barrier—usually concrete barrier—for high-speed locations. |
| Texas | In some instances, an MBGF [metal beam guard fence] application or CTB [concrete traffic barrier] application will be used to provide protection. |
| Utah | We often have barrier located between pedestrians and vehicles on bridges or through interchanges, but we are developing a standard for temporary traffic control that does not include barrier separation—at least not anything capable of protecting a pedestrian from a TL-3 hit. We install cast-in-place barrier on a case-by-case basis. Could use guidance on standard practice and design. |

## Agency Standard Barriers

The agencies were asked whether they had approved standard drawings in their roadside safety hardware standard that they could use to separate vulnerable users from motor vehicles (see Figure 20). Eight state agencies indicated that they had an approved standard and provided related information (Tables 8 through 11).

On the basis of the feedback, it appears that the majority of the respondent DOTs utilize either a concrete barrier or a combination concrete-metal (on top) barrier as their standard for those locations where a barrier separation of vulnerable users from motor vehicles is needed. There are a few exceptions, such as the Delaware DOT, which indicated use of a standard 31-in. guardrail in roadway areas, with the understanding that this is not a statewide practice but used only in certain areas. The New York State DOT also specified use of a heavy-post blocked-out (HPBO) beam median barrier, indicating that "the face towards the path users shields them from its posts." The New York State DOT also identified use of a box-beam median barrier with rounded corners, indicating the post corners are not directly accessible to path users since the posts are underneath the rail and have paddles that extend up into transverse slots in the bottom of the rail.

## Agency Nonstandard Barriers

The agencies were asked whether they had nonstandard barriers they could utilize to separate vulnerable users from motor vehicles (Figure 21). Six agencies indicated that they had a nonstandard barrier for such use; however, only New York State provided details regarding the nonstandard system currently used:

If the path is to be closer than 3 ft to the barrier, then a barrier must be used that does not have any post corners exposed to the path users. We have one special option for barriers that satisfy this condition: roadside box or roadside HPBO with timber rail bolted to the back (path side) of the posts. This typically consists of a pressure-treated 2 × 12 or 2 × 10 bolted to the flange of the steel post so that the top of the plank is an inch or two above the top of post.

| Agency (DOT) | Approved standard for barrier design to separate vulnerable users from motor vehicles? |
|---|---|
| Alaska | No |
| Arkansas | N/A |
| Baltimore City | No |
| Colorado | N/A |
| Delaware | Yes |
| Florida | N/A |
| Iowa | Yes |
| Louisiana | N/A |
| Massachusetts | No |
| Michigan | Yes |
| Minnesota | No |
| Missouri | N/A |
| New Jersey | N/A |
| New Mexico | Yes |
| New York State | Yes |
| North Carolina | N/A |
| Oregon | No |
| Pennsylvania | Yes |
| Texas | N/A |
| Utah | N/A |
| Virginia | Yes |
| Washington State | No |
| West Virginia | No |
| Wisconsin | Yes |
| Wyoming | No |

**(a) Recipient response**

Note: N/A = not applicable.

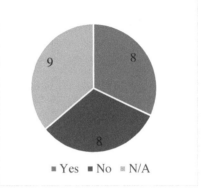

**(b) Distribution of recipient response**

| Answer | Count | DOT |
|---|---|---|
| Yes | 8 | Delaware, Iowa, Michigan, New Mexico, New York State, Pennsylvania, Virginia, Wisconsin |
| No | 8 | Alaska, Baltimore City, Massachusetts, Minnesota, Oregon, Washington State, West Virginia, Wyoming |
| N/A | 9 | Arkansas, Colorado, Florida, Louisiana, Missouri, New Jersey, North Carolina, Texas, Utah |

**(c) Categorization of recipient response**

*Figure 20. State agency responses regarding approved standard barrier designs.*

**Table 8.   State agency standards for barrier separation of vulnerable users from motor vehicles: Delaware, Iowa, and Michigan.**

| Agency (DOT) | Comment |
| --- | --- |
| Delaware | Some of our newer bridges are designed with a parapet separating pedestrians. Some roadway areas have guardrail installed. This is not a statewide practice, just certain areas.<br>We used standard F-shaped barrier on bridges and standard 31-in. guardrail in roadway areas. |
| Iowa | Iowa state provided a rendering of their standard barrier used for shared-use path.<br>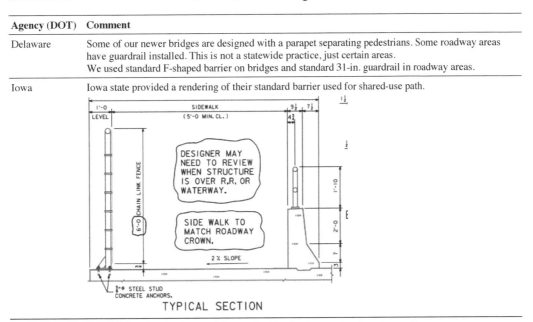<br>TYPICAL SECTION |
| Michigan | Michigan provided a picture of the standard barrier they use for shared-use path.<br>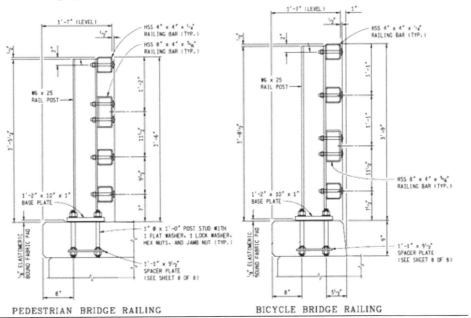<br>PEDESTRIAN BRIDGE RAILING          BICYCLE BRIDGE RAILING |

**Table 9. State agency standards for barrier separation of vulnerable users from motor vehicles: New Mexico and Pennsylvania.**

| Agency (DOT) | Comment |
|---|---|
| New Mexico | https://dot.state.nm.us/content/dam/nmdot/Plans_Specs_Estimates/2019_Standard_Drawings.pdf (543-05) |

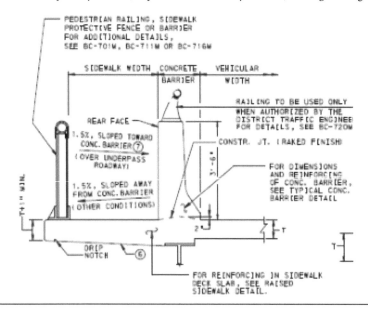

| | |
|---|---|
| Pennsylvania | PennDOT has standards for barriers on bridges for highspeed environments, see attached. However, for along highways, if a buffer cannot be provided, standard F-shape concrete barriers are typically used.<br><br>For bicycle requirements, they follow AASHTO requirements, meaning that height is 42 in. |

Note: PennDOT = Pennsylvania Department of Transportation.

**Table 10. State agency standards for barrier separation of vulnerable users from motor vehicles: Virginia and Wisconsin.**

| Agency (DOT) | Comment |
|---|---|
| Virginia | At this time, we use W-beam to shield the parapet on bridges. The shared-use path transitions away from the roadway beyond the bridge.<br>Standard 27¾-in. W-beam or MGS is used to shield the parapet, which is then terminated with a W-beam energy-absorbing terminal. |
| Wisconsin | https://wisconsindot.gov/dtsdManuals/strct/manuals/bridge/ch30.pdf<br>https://wisconsindot.gov/rdwy/fdm/fd-11-35.pdf#fd11-35-1.6<br>From the manuals provided, the minimum height of a barrier for shared-use path is 42 in. |

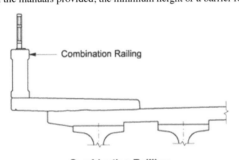

**Combination Railling**
Design Speeds of 45 mph or Less

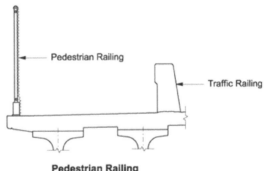

**Pedestrian Railing**
All Design Speeds

"Combination Railings can be used concurrently with a raised sidewalk on roadways with a design speed of 45 mph or less. Combination Railings can be composed of, but are not limited to: single slope **concrete parapets** with chain link fence, vertical face **concrete parapets with tubular steel railings** such as type 3T, and aesthetic concrete parapets with combination type C1-C6 railings."

**Table 11. State agency standards for barrier separation of vulnerable users from motor vehicles: New York State.**

| Agency (DOT) | Comment |
|---|---|
| New York State | If the path is to be closer than 3 ft to the barrier, then a barrier must be used that does not have any post corners exposed to the path users. We have three standard barrier options (…). |

1. **Heavy-Post Blocked-Out (HPBO) Corrugated Beam Median Barrier.** While it has a somewhat sharp top edge, the face towards the path users shields them from its posts.
2. **Box Beam Median Barrier.** This railing has a 6-in.-tall × 8-in.-wide steel box beam with rounded corners. The posts that support it are underneath the rail and have "paddles" that extend up into transverse slots in the bottom of the rail. The post corners are therefore not directly accessible to path users.
3. **Single-Slope Concrete Median Barrier.** To my knowledge, we have not yet resorted to the use of this option due to its cost. The advantages of the option are that it has almost no deflection and therefore provides maximum protection for path users. Additionally, its 42-in. height reduces the chances for a bicyclist to fall over it.

**Box Beam Median Barrier**

https://www.dot.ny.gov/main/business-center/engineering/cadd-info/drawings/standard-sheets-us-repository/606-05.pdf

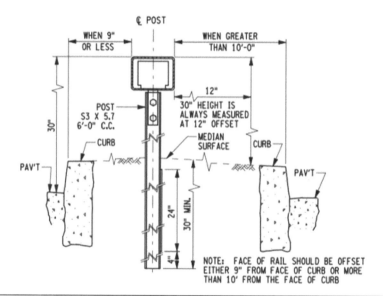

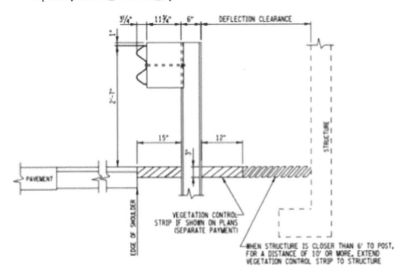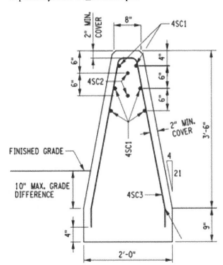

## Table 11. (Continued).

| Agency (DOT) | Comment |
|---|---|

**HPBO (Heavy-Post Blocked-Out) Median Barrier**
https://www.dot.ny.gov/main/business-center/engineering/cadd-info/drawings/standard-sheets-us-repository/606-09_050814e2_0.pdf

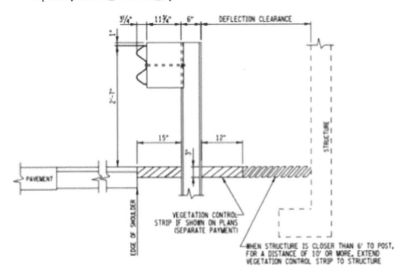

**Single-Slope Concrete Median Barrier**
https://www.dot.ny.gov/main/business-center/engineering/cadd-info/drawings/standard-sheets-us-repository/606-14_090612.pdf

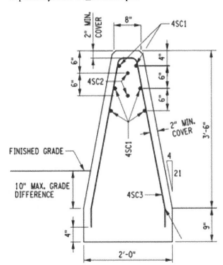

| Agency (DOT) | Approved standard for barrier design to separate vulnerable users from motor vehicles? |
|---|---|
| Alaska | No |
| Arkansas | N/A |
| Baltimore City | Yes |
| Colorado | N/A |
| Delaware | No |
| Florida | N/A |
| Iowa | Yes |
| Louisiana | N/A |
| Massachusetts | Yes |
| Michigan | No |
| Minnesota | No |
| Missouri | N/A |
| New Jersey | N/A |
| New Mexico | No |
| New York State | N/A |
| North Carolina | N/A |
| Oregon | Yes |
| Pennsylvania | Yes |
| Texas | N/A |
| Utah | N/A |
| Virginia | No |
| Washington State | No |
| West Virginia | No |
| Wisconsin | Yes |
| Wyoming | No |

(a) Recipient response

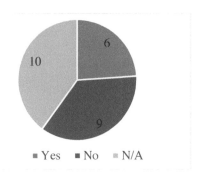

(b) Distribution of recipient response

| Answer | Count | DOT |
|---|---|---|
| Yes | 6 | Baltimore City, Iowa, Massachusetts, Oregon, Pennsylvania, Wisconsin |
| No | 9 | Alaska, Delaware, Michigan, Minnesota, New Mexico, Virginia, Washington State, West Virginia, Wyoming |
| N/A | 10 | Arkansas, Colorado, Florida, Louisiana, Missouri, New Jersey, New York State, North Carolina, Texas, Utah |

(c) Categorization of recipient response

**Figure 21. State and local agency responses regarding nonstandard barrier designs.**

Table 12 and Table 13 provide additional information on testing and evaluation of existing barriers used by the DOTs for separation of vulnerable users from motor vehicles.

## Agency Needs

The agencies were asked whether the barrier options they were using satisfied all their needs, given considerations in regard not only to errant motorists, but also to protecting vulnerable users. Figure 22 illustrates the feedback obtained from the respondent agencies.

Tables 14 through 18 record feedback from the respondent agencies regarding a general description of the roadway types (e.g., functional class or design/posted speed or both) and pedestrian/bicyclist facilities (e.g., bike lanes, shared-use paths, separated bikeways) where a barrier to separate vulnerable users from motor vehicles could be helpful.

Tables 19 through 22 present feedback from the respondent agencies regarding required/ desirable characteristics for the development of a new barrier for separation of vulnerable users from motor vehicles.

Tables 23 through 25 summarize the roadside barriers currently available/in use by the agencies for separation of vulnerable users from motor vehicles.

## Table 12.  Testing/evaluation information from state agencies on reported barriers used for separation of vulnerable users from motor vehicles: Massachusetts, New Mexico, Oregon, Virginia, and Wyoming.

| Agency (DOT) | Comment |
|---|---|
| Massachusetts | Barrier was used to separate a multiuse path from an Interstate on a bridge. Barrier was just a standard bridge rail that had previously been crash tested to *NCHRP Report 350* [29]. |
| New Mexico | Since we do not have testing facilities, we use other approved devices from other states. |
| Oregon | We have been using Tuff Curb with vertical delineators for our first physically separated bike lanes on state facilities. We selected this product because it is included on ODOT's Qualified Products List (QPL), which means it has been crash tested and approved for use on state highways. Tuff Curb is currently only approved in the QPL as a temporary traffic control device, so we will need to do before/after studies on our pilot bikeway installations to get it approved for permanent use. |
| Virginia | Standard 27¾-in, W-beam or MGS is used to shield the parapet, which is then terminated with a W-beam energy-absorbing terminal. |
| Wyoming | We used our standard box beam guardrail that is used to mitigate against roadside hazards. |

## Table 13.  Testing/evaluation information from state agencies on reported barriers used for separation of vulnerable users from motor vehicles: Iowa.

| Agency (DOT) | Comment |
|---|---|
| Iowa | The concrete safety shape barrier we use as the basis of our standard separator has been crash tested, though the steel railing attachment has not. Our TL-2 nonstandard separator is based on a crash tested 32-in. vertical parapet, but the back-mounted steel railing attachment has not been crash tested. |

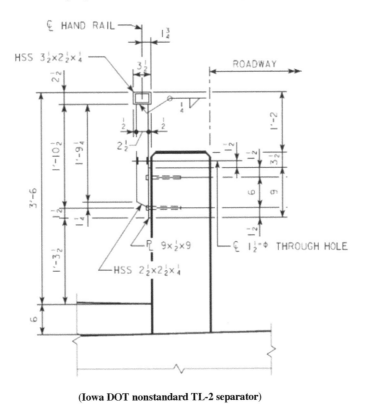

(Iowa DOT nonstandard TL-2 separator)

*(continued on next page)*

**Table 13. (Continued).**

| Agency (DOT) | Comment |
| --- | --- |
| | Our TL-4 nonstandard separator is a Michigan BR 27C barrier modified by the Vermont Agency of Transportation to include a bicycle railing. Both nonstandard design evaluations can be found here: https://static.tti.tamu.edu/tti.tamu.edu/documents/FHWA-RD-93-058.pdf |

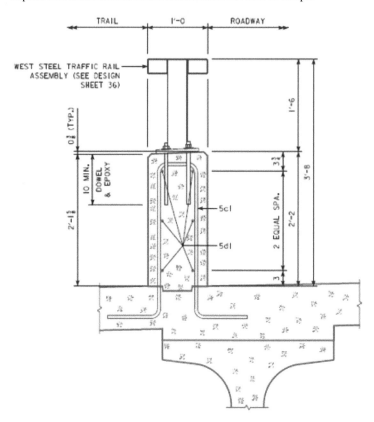

(Iowa DOT nonstandard TL-4 separator)

While many would characterize our separators as *NCHRP Report 350*–compliant [*29*], their actual crash testing was performed under *NCHRP Report 230* (*30*) with the possible exception of the concrete safety shape. The barriers in *NCHRP Report 230* were carried forward under *NCHRP Report 350*.

| Agency (DOT) | Approved standard for barrier design to separate vulnerable users from motor vehicles? |
|---|---|
| Alaska | No |
| Arkansas | N/A |
| Baltimore City | No |
| Colorado | N/A |
| Delaware | Yes |
| Florida | N/A |
| Iowa | Yes |
| Louisiana | N/A |
| Massachusetts | Yes |
| Michigan | Yes |
| Minnesota | Yes |
| Missouri | N/A |
| New Jersey | N/A |
| New Mexico | Yes |
| New York State | N/A |
| North Carolina | N/A |
| Oregon | No |
| Pennsylvania | Yes |
| Texas | N/A |
| Utah | N/A |
| Virginia | No |
| Washington State | Yes |
| West Virginia | N/A |
| Wisconsin | No |
| Wyoming | Yes |

(a) Recipient response

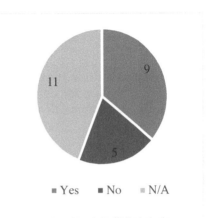

■ Yes    ■ No    ■ N/A

(b) Distribution of recipient response

| Answer | Count | DOT |
|---|---|---|
| Yes | 9 | Delaware, Iowa, Massachusetts, Michigan, Minnesota, New Mexico, Pennsylvania, Washington State, Wyoming |
| No | 5 | Alaska, Baltimore City, Oregon, Virginia, Wisconsin |
| N/A | 11 | Arkansas, Colorado, Florida, Louisiana, Missouri, New Jersey, New York State, North Carolina, Texas, Utah, West Virginia |

(c) Categorization of recipient response

**Figure 22.  State agency responses regarding satisfaction of needs by barrier options used.**

**Table 14. Additional information from state and local agencies on facilities needing barrier separation for vulnerable users: Alaska, Baltimore City, Colorado, Delaware, Florida, Louisiana, Michigan, Minnesota, and New Mexico.**

| Agency (DOT) | Comment |
|---|---|
| Alaska | Major arterial or above, speed limits ≥5 mi/h, and crash data to suggest the barrier is needed. In most cases, that would lead to separating the path/trail behind a ditch and/or outside of the clear zone. Where that is not practicable and crash data warrant further protection, then MASH-tested guardrail or concrete barrier have been our current solutions of choice. |
| Baltimore City | Arterial roadways with a low posted/target speed of 25 mi/h to 30 mi/h, but with a high 85th percentile speed, that include a mix of bicycle and pedestrian traffic based on adjacent land uses (e.g., parks, dense residential). |
| Colorado | We provide barrier between roadway and pedestrian when speed is >45 mi/h. |
| Delaware | 45- to 50-mi/h roadways that run adjacent to shared-use paths. It is mostly when the shared-use path and roadway merge together at a pinch point (e.g., bridge, ROW issue). |
| Florida | We use concrete barriers on bridges and where there are higher-speed conditions. Florida does not have the solution you are seeking. |
| Louisiana | This is typically a concern in urban areas where the sidewalk is carried across the bridge. These routes are typically high ADT but low speed (45 mi/h or less), and the only thing separating pedestrians from the vehicles is an 8- to 10-in. curb. |
| Michigan | Bridges with posted speeds of 45 mi/h or greater and a pedestrian and/or bicyclist facility. Barrier separation is required on bridges with pedestrian/shared-use facilities and a posted speed limit greater than 40 mi/h. |
| Minnesota | Considering a BRT system in a 50-mi/h road using 14-in. platforms located in the clear zone. Arterials, low and high speed, shared-use trails. |
| New Mexico | Several busy arterials; barrier has been used for pedestrian and bicycle facilities on bridges. The facilities have been separated from vehicles with a barrier and railing has been installed for the pedestrian protection from drop-offs. |

Note: ADT = average daily traffic; BRT = bus rapid transit.

**Table 15.   Additional information from state and local agencies on facilities needing barrier separation for vulnerable users: Iowa, Missouri, New York State, Pennsylvania, Texas, Virginia, and West Virginia.**

| Agency (DOT) | Comment |
|---|---|
| Iowa | Our highest need for separators is on bridges that carry both vehicles and shared-use paths (pedestrians/bicyclists). Approach roadways leading to these structures also require these separators. The new MASH-tested separator we have under development at MwRSF is a potential solution to most of these installations, since the majority occur in TL-2 conditions. However, our new MASH policy states that we cannot be the only state to employ any individual piece of barrier hardware. We need additional states to adopt our proposed separator in order for the Iowa DOT to use it. This project may provide a venue for other states to see this proposed bridge separator and consider its use. The Iowa DOT's occasional needs for TL-4 separators can be handled by the use of TL-4 traffic barriers that meet the 42-in. minimum height specifications for this hardware (e.g. BR 27C, Texas T80HT), if those barriers are carried forward under MASH. We have not had other instances arise where similar positive separation of vulnerable users from traffic is necessary, but that does not mean we will never have this need. It would be beneficial to have ready options available for future applications of this type. |
| Missouri | Barrier construction is based on traffic volumes, speed, and other factors. This is done on a project-by-project need. We also work with our planning partners on their community needs for vulnerable road users. |
| New York State | Numerous such possibilities exist. The final decision generally comes down to a question of the likelihood that a path user might be struck by an errant vehicle. One common scenario involves a narrow corridor where a popular recreation path will need to be close to a high-volume, high-speed highway. Another scenario involves park areas where children could be path users adjacent to medium-speed park roads. A double standard exists, as urban sidewalks are not separated from high-volume urban traffic. "Paths" are more likely to receive special treatment. |
| Pennsylvania | When sidewalks are provided on bridges with a posted vehicular speed greater than 45 mph or structures longer than 200 ft (regardless of the speed), the sidewalk shall be protected by a barrier, unless waived by the Department. An example where the Department may waive the sidewalk barrier requirement is a structure longer than 200 ft. in an urban environment where a curbed approach walkway exists and the posted vehicular speed is less than or equal to 45 mph. When a barrier is required on a bridge to protect the sidewalk, the barrier shall be transitioned to the appropriate roadway protection device (e.g., guide rail, barrier, curb) beyond the end of the structure and maintain pedestrian access. |
| Texas | Higher-level functional classifications and those with higher design speeds would be likely candidates for a barrier to protect pedestrians on sidewalk. A barrier application for shared-use paths that are not significantly separated from the traveled way would also be helpful. |
| Virginia | We would like to have a positive barrier that can be used for the entire length of the shared-use path (or other path types) other than the W-beam. The W-beam must have a rail on the back to shield the posts if it remains adjacent to the path. |
| West Virginia | Most locations are multilane with TWLTLs and sidewalks on either side. Speed limits vary from 35 to 55 and are in urban locations. |

Note: TWLTL = two-way left-turn lane.

**Table 16.   Additional information from state agency on facilities needing barrier separation for vulnerable users: Oregon.**

| Agency (DOT) | Comment |
|---|---|
| Oregon | ODOT will be adopting a separation chart similar to the draft AASHTO bike facility selection chart where speeds and volume are the primary factors.<br><br>At slower speeds (say, 35 and below), the separation treatment does not need to redirect a motor vehicle; it only needs to be very visible, which means it probably needs a vertical component. The treatment needs to be sufficiently crashworthy that it does not cause an errant vehicle to lose control or become a hazard to the occupants or any nearby vulnerable road users. The treatment needs to be [able] to withstand a vehicle hit and not require extensive maintenance.<br><br>At higher speeds (say 40 and above), the separation treatment does need to be capable of redirecting an errant vehicle. ODOT's Pedestrian and Bicycle Design guide includes a separation matrix that advises on where to physically separate bikeways from traffic based on speed and volume of the roadway. ODOT is currently finalizing the Blueprint for Urban Design, which includes an updated bikeway selection process, which is essentially the new FHWA Bikeway Selection model with minor modifications.<br><br>ODOT has guidance in the Traffic Control Plans design manual for when to consider positive protection for pedestrians. See pages 85 & 86, table 3.3.<br>https://www.oregon.gov/ODOT/Engineering/Docs_TrafficEng/TCP-Design-Manual.pdf |

*Table 3.3 – TPAR Traffic Control Measure Selection Guide*

| | Pre-Construction Posted Speed (mph) | USING SHOULDER, or MAKING NO/MINIMAL CHANGES to PEDESTRIAN PATHWAY ALIGNMENT * | | USING CLOSED/PARTIAL LANE, or MAKING MAJOR CHANGES to PEDESTRIAN PATHWAY ALIGNMENT ** | |
|---|---|---|---|---|---|
| | | Between Traffic & TPAR | Between TPAR & Work Area | Between Traffic & TPAR | Between TPAR & Work Area |
| URBAN | ≤ 40 | If Off Sidewalk: Surface-mounted tubular markers @ 5-10 ft spacing; PCD or similar | PCD, or other barrier system. Consider adding Contractor escort for long, elaborate TPARs. | Surface-mounted tubular markers @ 5-10 ft spacing; PCD or similar | PCD, or other barrier system. Consider adding Contractor escort for long, elaborate TPARs. |
| | ≥ 45 | If Off Sidewalk: Rigid barrier system (e.g. steel, concrete), with protected ends | PCD, or other barrier system. Also consider Contractor escort for long, elaborate TPARs. | Rigid barrier system (e.g. steel or concrete), with protected ends | PCD, or other barrier system. Consider adding Contractor escort for long, elaborate TPARs. |
| RURAL | ≤ 40 | Existing/temporary pavement markings; tubular markers @ 10-20 ft spacing | PCD, or tubular markers @ 5-10 ft spacing. Consider substituting Contractor escort for very long TPARs. | Surface-Mounted Tubular Markers @ 5-10 ft spacing; PCD or similar | PCD, or other barrier system. Consider substituting Contractor escort for very long TPARs. |
| | ≥ 45 | Existing/temporary pavement markings; tubular markers @ 10-20 ft spacing | PCD, or tubular markers @ 5-10 ft spacing. Consider substituting Contractor escort for very long TPARs. | Rigid barrier system (e.g. steel or concrete), with protected ends | PCD, or other barrier system. Consider substituting Contractor escort for very long TPARs. |

NOTES:

* **Minimal Change:** Shifting alignment by one or two feet, without encroaching onto a separate portion of the roadway (e.g. traffic lane).

** **Major Change:** Examples might include shifting from a sidewalk to a full/partial traffic lane; or, multi-use path onto a shoulder. Provide traffic lane closures, lane shifts, and shoulder closures according to ODOT Standard Drawings. Use a Buffer Space "B" between the end of the lane closure taper and start of the TPAR shift where it moves pedestrians into the roadway shoulder or traffic lane.

◑ "Other Barrier System": Refers to temporary concrete or steel barrier; or, other continuous system that includes a handrail and detectable edge; and, will restrict pedestrian access from the work area. All barrier systems must include crashworthy end treatments for ends exposed to vehicular traffic.

◑ **Urban:** Higher traffic volumes; multiple pedestrian facilities/crossings; high anticipated pedestrian presence/usage; large pedestrian traffic generators.

◑ **Rural:** Low traffic volumes; few to no specific pedestrian facilities; low to very-low anticipated pedestrian presence/usage.

Note: TPAR = temporary pedestrian-accessible route.

**Table 17.  Additional information from state agency on facilities needing barrier separation for vulnerable users: Wisconsin.**

| Agency (DOT) | Comment |
|---|---|
| Wisconsin | The majority of bicycle accommodations in rural areas will be provided through paved shoulders and in urban areas through bike lanes. If a bridge or approaching highway has either pavement-marked bike lanes or is signed as a bicycle route and the bicycle accommodation is immediately adjacent to the bridge railing, the railing height should be a lower minimum of 42-in. If the bridge/highway is not marked or signed as a bicycle facility, then use the typical 32-in. barrier height on the bridge (i.e., even if the bridge/highway has a paved shoulder wider than typical paved width shoulder and is not marked or signed as a bicycle facility, use the typical barrier height). Refer to FDM 11-46-15 for additional information on bicycle accommodations.<br><br>Two-way shared-use paths are required to be separated from the traveled way for all posted speeds with a 42-in. barrier wall, except that a 32-in. barrier wall may be considered if<br><br>• There is 5 ft or more separation (i.e., shoulder or bike accommodation) between the outside edge of the traveled lane and the face of barrier, or<br>• There is a shared-use path on a short bridge (less than 75 ft).<br><br>There is another unique option for a shared-use path that allows the elimination of the barrier wall if the posted speed is 40 mph or less. That option is to provide a 16-ft-wide raised curb shared-use path across the structure. This option provides the 5-ft space separation and the shared-use path as a combined raised curb section.<br><br>Facilities Development Manual 11-35 <<https://wisconsindot.gov/rdwy/fdm/fd-11-35.pdf#fd11-35>> There is criteria when inadequate separation cannot be provided from motor vehicles or along bridge structures, etc. https://wisconsindot.gov/rdwy/fdm/fd-11-35.pdf#fd11-35-1.6 |

A structure shall include a parapet or barrier wall to separate the roadway from a sidewalk based on Table 1.2 for the proposed posted speed. Barrier requirements for shared use paths are discussed below in the Shared Use Paths section.

*Table 1.2 Barrier Wall Separation Required Between Roadway and Sidewalk [5]*

| For new, reconstructed, or rehabilitated structures with a posted speed >= 45 mph | For other existing structures with a posted speed >= 45 mph | For any structure with a posted speed <= 40 mph |
|---|---|---|
| Yes | No, unless requested by community and agreed to by the Department.¹ | No, unless requested by community and agreed to by the Department¹ |

*¹ The designer and community may decide that a parapet/barrier wall separation is a desirable safety solution, especially for posted speeds of 35 mph and greater. Bear in mind that installing a parapet or barrier on a structure is considered structure rehabilitation. Consider the adjacent roadway character, shy distance between traveled way and raised curb sidewalk, pedestrian volume, length of structure*

*1. Part of reasonable justification to provide separation is if the adjacent roadway character is rural.*

*2. Another reasonable justification to provide separation is if there is a narrow shoulder or gutter (< 1.8-ft) located between the travel lane and the sidewalk.*

*3. High, seasonal or year around, pedestrian volume may suggest that separation is desirable.*

*4. A long structure may be more likely to include separation than a short structure.*

*Justification to include parapet/barrier wall separation in the Design Study Report is not required, but is encouraged.*

The lower minimum height for a barrier wall/parapet separating the sidewalk from the roadway is 32-inches for posted speeds of 40 mph or greater (see Attachment 1.1, Section C-C). A lower barrier meeting NCHRP 350 TL2 may be considered for posted speeds of 35 mph or less.

The lower minimum height for a barrier wall/parapet on the outside of the sidewalk is 42-inches (see Attachment 1.1, Section B-B to visualize the raised curb sidewalk option). Keep in mind that certain areas require Protective Screening, to discourage people from dropping or throwing objects onto vehicles passing under the structure. See FDM 11-35-1.8 for guidance on Protective Screening.

Also, see Table 1.2, "Roadside Barrier and End Treatment for Parapets, Barrier Walls and Sidewalk/Paths" in FDM 11-45-1.4.3, "Transitions to Bridges or Concrete Barrier Wall".

**Table 18.   Additional information from state agency on facilities needing barrier separation for vulnerable users: Utah.**

| Agency (DOT) | Comment |
| --- | --- |
| Utah | We typically use barriers in and around freeways—for instance, at diverging diamond interchanges, we will use barrier on both sides of the median walkway. We will also in some cases place the walkway to the outside of the TL-3 parapet and use chain link for the outside railing. Arterials on structures, arterials at grade interchanges, diverging diamond interchanges, high-speed road with narrow ROW, separate light and heavy rail, routing pedestrians in the road during temporary traffic control. |

Use of barrier for center walkway in a diverging diamond interchange

**Table 19.   State and local agency feedback on the development of a new barrier for separation of vulnerable users: Alaska, Baltimore City, Colorado, Delaware, Florida, Louisiana, and Massachusetts.**

| Agency (DOT) | Comment |
|---|---|
| Alaska | Barrier should protect the vulnerable user but also at minimal increased risk to the motor vehicle user. |
| Baltimore City | 1. Durability/maintenance requirements/ease of replacement when damaged<br>2. Aesthetics<br>3. Visibility<br>4. Ease of deployment<br>5. Cost<br>6. Anchoring requirements<br>7. Ease of storing when not deployed |
| Colorado | Preferably, the barrier would include standard crash-tested barrier with additional height or rail to provide appropriate requirements for pedestrians. Challenge has been that pedestrians/bikes are generally on an elevated sidewalk, so 42-in. barrier at roadway level is still too short for 42-in. rub rail at sidewalk height. Should have a concrete barrier and metal barrier options. Add-ons for pedestrian requirements should not affect the crashworthiness of the roadway barrier, i.e., create additional snagging points, etc. |
| Delaware | Meet TL-3 requirements. |
| Florida | We would like you to develop a steel railing with horizontal steel members for use in lower-speed conditions. We feel that a TL-2 test level is appropriate for this barrier. There would likely be horizontal members on the bicycle face as well to prevent snagging of the bicyclist on the steel posts. The challenge will be the termination of these barriers. There will be a lot of breaks in the barrier for driveways and side streets. We would want to see a TL-2 crashworthy end treatment. |
| Louisiana | It would be helpful if this was a retrofit type of detail that could be applied to bridges already in service, not just new construction. Also, I think deflection should be kept as low as possible, since the barrier should not excessively deform or break apart into the sidewalk area. It would be helpful if this was a retrofit type of detail that could be applied to roadways and sidewalks already in service, not just new construction. Also, I think deflection should be kept as low as possible, since the barrier should not excessively deform or break apart into the sidewalk area. For installations on bridges with sidewalks, a low-weight barrier would be preferred. |
| Massachusetts | In general, MassDOT will only consider barrier-separating motor vehicles from vulnerable road users in cases where a bridge is shared by both users. In those cases, we would be looking for a bridge-rail style design that meets MASH TL-4. |

Note: MassDOT = Massachusetts Department of Transportation.

**Table 20. State agency feedback on the development of a new barrier for separation of vulnerable users: Iowa.**

| Agency (DOT) | Comment |
|---|---|
| Iowa | For the Iowa DOT to be able to employ barriers that meet our own MASH policy on file with FHWA, they must have the full suite of crash tests for the test level, and all components of the complete system (transitions, end sections, joints, etc.) must be tested. This level of completeness currently results in an FHWA eligibility letter, which is what our policy prioritizes. It would be ideal if any new nonproprietary separator hardware had an FHWA eligibility letter and is adopted by multiple states, so that Iowa can use it and meet the 1st priority of our policy. And, again, we hope that this project can bring attention to our proposed MASH TL-2 bridge separation barrier with bicycle railing under development at MwRSF, in the hopes that other states will adopt it. |

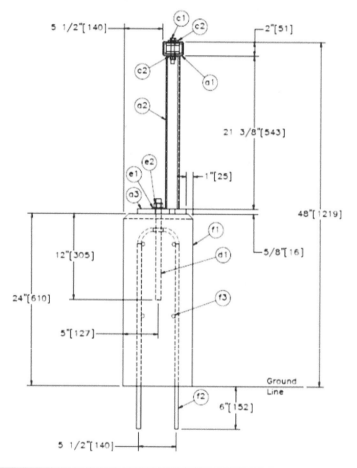

**Table 21.  State agency feedback on the development of a new barrier for separation of vulnerable users: Michigan, Minnesota, Missouri, New Mexico, New York State, and Oregon.**

| Agency (DOT) | Comment |
|---|---|
| Michigan | Speed, facility (bridge versus roadway).<br>Even though a 42-in. tall barrier is acceptable, the Michigan DOT prefers to use a 54-in.-tall barrier when it is necessary to shield a shared-use facility on a bridge. |
| Minnesota | Would need to have openings for transit users to access three BRT bus doors in a seamless fashion. Verify that the barrier selected is appropriate for the current and future roadway characteristics. |
| Missouri | We have currently not established that criteria. |
| New Mexico | Barrier need is assessed based on the test level requirement in the mainline, so it varies. |
| New York State | Barrier system needs to be free from sharp corners or edges that could injure a pedestrian or bicyclist who runs into them. The typical steel guide rail posts have quite hazardous corners.<br><br>Rail systems for bicyclists need to be tall enough so that a bicyclist will not fall over them and into traffic.<br><br>The barrier system exposed to vehicles needs to minimize the number and strength of any vertical elements that an impacting vehicle will be able to snag on.<br><br>The system needs to be modular, with bolted connections, so that a damaged section may be readily replaced. |
| Oregon | At slow speeds, visibility is the most important factor. Crashworthiness and low maintenance needs are other criteria. The barrier should ideally have some ability to redirect slightly errant vehicles, but that is not the most important criteria.<br><br>At high speeds, the treatment's ability to redirect vehicles becomes more of a factor. A treatment's inability to fully redirect vehicles should not automatically disqualify it from further consideration by this research project or by an agency that is considering its use.<br><br>Barriers need to be crashworthy and recoverable if a vehicle hits them (e.g., tested and on ODOT's Qualified Products List), or outside of the clear zone. Maintenance is also a major consideration.<br><br>Width is important; the narrower the barrier is the better to facilitate limited spaces. Deflection is important; if have to design for deflection and provide clear space for the deflection, [it] just uses the already limited space available for both vehicles and pedestrians. |

**Table 22. State agency feedback on the development of a new barrier for separation of vulnerable users: Pennsylvania, Texas, Utah, Virginia, West Virginia, Wisconsin, and Wyoming.**

| Agency (DOT) | Comment |
| --- | --- |
| Pennsylvania | Meet MASH, ADA, and AASHTO bicycle requirements. |
| Texas | MASH-compliant for impacting vehicle.<br>Minimal deflection into the area of the sidewalk or shared-use path.<br>Easily installed for varying site conditions. |
| Utah | End treatments are an important element; in the photo of the DDI, we are using a sloped end section, which is probably OK in a DDI, where the geometry of the interchange limits speed. When we do pedestrian protection on a bridge, the question is always how to protect the blunt end. The other issue we deal with is in temporary applications, where we place precast barrier—how do we control deflection of the barrier into the pedestrian walkway? This is particularly important when we are placing barrier on a surface that we do not want to drive pins into. On top of structure, when you reach the end of structure, how to protect barrier blunt ends with limited ROW or space in general. In work zones, how to limit deflection with minimal damage to road surface. |
| Virginia | We would like to see a barrier that has a height range (42 in. plus additional height if zone of intrusion is considered) and, possibly, a handrail, if needed on the back side. Another consideration would be drainage along the wall and whether the barrier will have adjacent curb and gutter. |
| West Virginia | Concerns have been sight distance at intersections and width of barrier since sidewalk width is less than 5 ft. |
| Wisconsin | Barrier causing a pinch point on ADA sidewalk. Barrier working width and risk of having sidewalk close to a barrier. Bikes or pedestrians interacting with post or other edges.<br>It seems that most information is provided from the motor vehicle's needs. It is unclear if you wanted to have barriers to separate between bike/pedestrian or other types of vehicles (e.g., snowmobiles, ATVs). |
| Wyoming | The Wyoming DOT generally does not use barriers to separate pathway users from motor vehicles. We have installed box beam barrier in one location within the state that I am aware of, where pathway was within the clear zone of the highway. |

Note: DDI = diverging diamond interchange; ATV = all-terrain vehicle.

**Table 23. Barriers state agencies reported using for separation of vulnerable users from motor vehicles: Wisconsin and Michigan.**

| Agency (DOT) | Drawing | Test Level | Testing Standards |
|---|---|---|---|
| Wisconsin | | TL-2 and TL-3 | *NCHRP Report 350* (*29*), MASH (*1*) |
| Michigan | | TL-4 | *NCHRP Report 350* (*29*) |

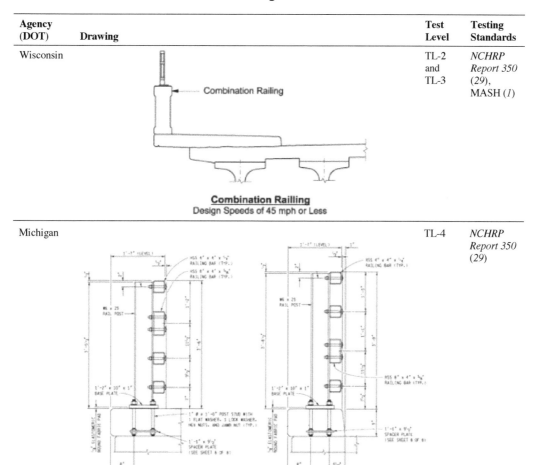

**Table 24.  Barriers state agencies reported using for separation of vulnerable users from motor vehicles: New Mexico and Pennsylvania.**

| Agency (DOT) | Drawing | Test Level | Testing Standards |
|---|---|---|---|
| New Mexico | | TL-2 and TL-5 | MASH (*1*) |
| | 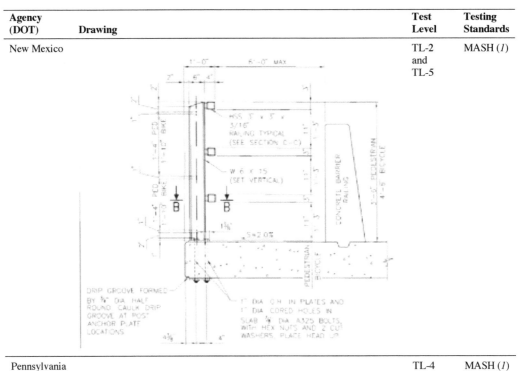 | | |
| Pennsylvania | | TL-4 | MASH (*1*) |

**Table 25.  Barriers state agencies reported using for separation of vulnerable users from motor vehicles: Iowa and New York.**

| Agency (DOT) | Drawing | Test Level | Testing Standards |
|---|---|---|---|
| Iowa | 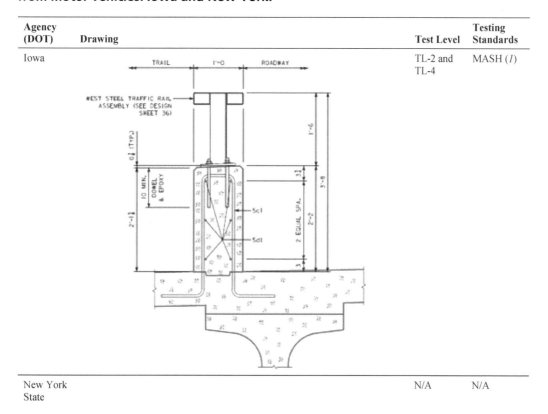 | TL-2 and TL-4 | MASH (*1*) |
| New York State | 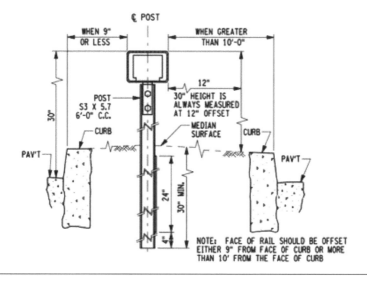 | N/A | N/A |

## Conclusions

Most existing barrier systems that are currently utilized to shield vulnerable users from the roadway are rigid concrete or concrete and metal combination rails (a concrete parapet or concrete curb with metal railing on top). Some DOTs also utilize metal-only barrier options; however, those are generally considered for bridge applications. Currently, few existing systems of this type have passed MASH requirements for high-speed applications and can be directly implemented where needed. However, the cost for these combination concrete barriers is a factor that represents a limitation for some agencies, which would prefer having a more economical metal-only system option.

Table 26 and Table 27 summarize the design preferences suggested by the survey respondents for consideration during the development of the new barrier to shield vulnerable users from errant vehicles. The tables are organized to identify specific design preferences, barrier material type and minimum height, and system crashworthiness level (Table 26), and consider other barrier characteristics, such as working width, damage, and maintenance requirements (Table 27).

When the development of a metal-only barrier system is being considered, special attention needs to be given to dynamic deflection of the barrier when it is impacted by errant vehicles as well as working width and vehicle zone of intrusion. This is especially true for barriers that could potentially be implemented to shield vulnerable users from the roadway. In addition, maintenance is also an important factor for metal-only barriers. However, metal-only barriers can offer acceptable sight distance or drainage capability as compared with a concrete-only barrier option.

Specific design considerations also must be given to potential protruding railing elements or sharp post or rail edges. The barrier would need to be designed to account for potential interaction between vulnerable users and the barrier system; therefore, protruding and sharp elements would need to be avoided or shielded through a proper barrier design. In addition, consideration needs to be given to specific elements that might need to be added to comply with PROWAG/ADA requirements, with the understanding that add-ons for pedestrian requirements should not create additional snagging points for errant vehicles.

Some DOTs offered feedback with respect to the roadway-posted speed conditions where this new barrier should be deployed. While some DOTs specified that the majority of installations for these types of barriers would be for MASH TL-2 conditions—meaning low speeds (≤45 mi/h posted speed limit) and urban areas—a similar number of respondent DOTs indicated a need for a barrier meeting MASH TL-3 requirements (high posted speed of ≥45 mi/h).

**Table 26. Design preferences for development of a new barrier to shield vulnerable users from errant vehicles.**

| Design Consideration for Vulnerable Users | Material | Height | Road Speed |
|---|---|---|---|
| • W-beam must have a rail on the back to shield posts if adjacent to path (Virginia)<br>• Horizontal members on the bicycle face as well to prevent snagging of the bicyclist on the steel posts (Florida)<br>• Bikes and pedestrians interacting with post or other edges (Wisconsin)<br>• Possibly handrail on the back side (Virginia)<br>• Preferably include standard crash test barrier with additional height or rail to provide appropriate requirements for pedestrians (Colorado)<br>• Add-ons for pedestrian requirements should not create additional snagging points for errant vehicles (Colorado)<br>• Bridge-rail style design that meets MASH TL-4 (Massachusetts) | • Rigid barrier system (steel or concrete) (Oregon)<br>• Should have a concrete barrier and metal barrier options (Colorado)<br>• Steel railing (Florida) | • 42 in. [Colorado (with consideration of sidewalk height), Iowa, Michigan (acceptable), Virginia (≥42 in.), Wisconsin]<br>• 32 in. for 40 mph or greater (Wisconsin)<br>• 54 in. preferred (Michigan) | • Low-speed conditions (TL-2) (Iowa, Louisiana, Florida, West Virginia)<br>• High-speed conditions (TL-3) (Delaware, New York, Oregon, Pennsylvania, Wisconsin)<br>• Occasionally, TL-4 separators handled by use of TL-4 traffic barriers (Iowa) |

**Table 27. Other considerations for development of a new barrier to shield vulnerable users from errant vehicles.**

| Suggesting Agency | Considerations |
|---|---|
| Baltimore City | • Durability/maintenance requirements/ease of replacement when damaged.<br>• Aesthetics<br>• Visibility<br>• Ease of deployment<br>• Cost<br>• Anchoring requirements<br>• Ease of storing when not deployed |
| Florida | • Challenge is termination of the barrier—would like to see a TL-2 crashworthy end treatment |
| Iowa | • Need full suite of crash tests |
| Louisiana | • Low weight barrier (especially if for bridges)<br>• Helpful if it was a retrofit type of detail to apply to roadways already in service<br>• Minimize deflection |
| Utah | • Minimal damage to road surface for work zone applications<br>• End treatment |
| Virginia | • Drainage considerations |
| Wisconsin | • Minimize deflection—working width |
| West Virginia | • Sight distance<br>• Width of barrier |

## Recommendations

On the basis of the literature review and the survey responses, the research team compiled recommendations for barrier development (Table 28). Feedback was requested from the project panel to guarantee that the panel's directions and guidance were followed through the preliminary options design phase.

**Table 28. Research team recommendations for development of a new barrier to shield vulnerable users from errant vehicles.**

| Required | Minimum barrier rail height: 42 in.<br>[AASHTO Bike Guide (2) and AASHTO Bridge Design Specifications (8)]. |
|---|---|
| Required | No protruding objects (PROWAG)—objects with leading edges between 27 and 80 in. shall not protrude more than 4 in. |
| Preferred | Open metal-only rail. |
| Preferred | Handrail not required on pedestrian circulation paths (PROWAG); however, the Texas Department of Licensing and Registration requires handrails at 34 to 38 in. when running slope is 1:20.<br>The TTI research team still suggests including this feature in the proposed barrier design. |
| Preferred | Safety toe rail or curb—serves as cane detection—maximum of 15 in. above sidewalk.<br>It is preferred (and not required) as long as the bottom edge of metal barrier is lower than 27 in.<br>If bottom edge is higher than 27 in., then this is required. |
| Preferred | MASH TL-3 (high-speed) conditions. |

Note: TTI = Texas A&M Transportation Institute.

# CHAPTER 4

# Preliminary Design Options

The research team reviewed the information presented in the previous chapters and developed several design options addressing the needs of this research study to present to the NCHRP project panel for consideration. The proposed options were designed to address and balance system needs from the perspectives of both vehicular impact performance and pedestrian/bicyclist accessibility while minimizing material cost and installation complexity. The research team developed the proposed design options with the objective of meeting the relevant standards and guidelines, such as AASHTO's MASH (1) and *Roadside Design Guide* (31) and PROWAG (3). Design elements identified in the previous tasks, such as barrier height and implementation of PROWAG criteria, were highlighted for each proposed barrier option.

The research team also addressed basic requirements for the barrier systems, including accommodation of service loads to meet impact performance requirements, while providing other desirable functional characteristics. As an example, the research team took into consideration placement and attachment of barrier design elements to increase the safety of vulnerable users while still optimizing vehicular driver safety during an impact.

The design concepts were not presented as yet fully engineered and detailed at this stage but were sufficient for initial assessment of the feasibility of rail behavior and capability. The research team documented the anticipated advantages and disadvantages of each design alternative, including any perceived performance benefits and application limitations.

The proposed options were as follows:

- Option A: Steel-only open rail system with longitudinal hollow structural section (HSS).
- Option B: Steel-only open rail system with longitudinal HSS and metal mesh.
- Option C: W-beam guardrail system with rails.
- Option D: W-beam guardrail system with metal mesh.
- Option E: Steel-only open rail system with covering HSS top rail.
- Option F: Steel-only open rail system with covering HSS top rail and metal mesh.

## Design of Multifunctional Barrier Components

TTI researchers developed a preliminary design of the components of the guardrail system meant to address vulnerable user concerns. This included a pedestrian handrail, a bicycle handrail, and a cane detection rail. The preliminary design of these components was then incorporated into a further analysis and computer simulation efforts.

To design the multifunctional rail, the TTI researchers followed the design guidelines described by ADA standards and AASHTO specifications (2). Because of the lack of guidance with regard to the structural design of bicycle handrails, the research team employed the same design loads and methodology used for the pedestrian rail. The preliminary design of the pedestrian handrail consisted of two components: the geometric concerns and the structural concerns. The geometric concerns consisted of items such as the diameter of the handrails and the spacing of the vertical supports. The structural concerns involved the flexural capacity of the rails and the combination loads resisted in the vertical supports. Some overlap did exist between these two concerns, for example, the diameter of the round steel tubes affecting the flexural capacity of the handrail.

The selection of the outer diameter of the handrails was based on the requirements set forth by ADA standards (Figure 23*a*). The design loads on the handrails were according to AASHTO specifications (Figure 23*b*). The wall thickness of the handrails was chosen on the basis of the flexural capacity of the HSS member. The section of this handrail size was also based on material availability. The vertical support was designed for both axial load and combined axial-flexural loading arising from the horizontal offset between the handrails and the vertical supports. The vertical supports were spaced to match the spacing of a standard quarter-post spacing guardrail system. This quarter-post spacing was desired because of its reduced dynamic deflection compared with standard guardrail spacing.

The size of the cane detection rail was based on material availability, cost effectiveness, and crashworthiness. This design was further evaluated during the computer simulation effort.

## Option A: Steel-Only Open Rail System with Longitudinal HSS

Option A was a steel-only open rail system bolted to a concrete slab. The total height of the railing system was 42 in., which included a post height of 32 in. and an additional bicycle railing to reach the required 42 in. The bolted connection between the post and the concrete slab could be located on the side of the post aligned with the longitudinal deployment of the system to prevent interference with the shared-use path.

The proposed option utilized 30-in.-long steel posts, which could be either a wide flange or an HSS section. The anticipated post spacing was approximately 10 ft; however, detailed engineering analysis would be required to define post spacing on the basis of the system characteristics. Depending on the post option (i.e., wide flange or HSS), different types of connections could be used. Steel angles were suggested for attachment of the horizontal HSS railing to the post. A steel plate could be included in the design to cover the steel post top, providing an element of protection in case of direct contact between the vulnerable user and the sharper edges along the

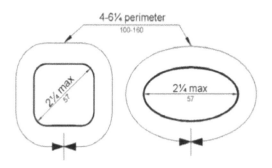
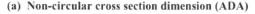

**(a)  Non-circular cross section dimension (ADA)**

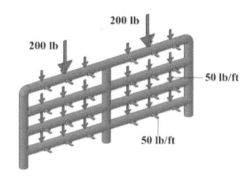

**(b)  Loading on railing (AASHTO)**

*Figure 23.   Handrail constraints.*

top of the post. The Option A design did not include continuous protection along the back side of the railing. Consequently, Option A still resulted in considerable post exposure to vulnerable users. If the post were designed to be an HSS member, however, the post would not present significant exposed edges.

The barrier included a total of three horizontal steel HSS railings. The horizontal railings would be adequately spaced to limit snagging potential during vehicular impact. Furthermore, the lower railing would be required to prevent any vehicle underriding.

Option A included two additional preferred design elements: a handrail for pedestrians and a lower rail for cane detection. Both the bicycle and the pedestrian rails had a 2-in. diameter to comply with AASHTO requirements and were adequately spaced away from the posts to allow for hand gripping. Both rails were connected to a plate that could be bolted to the back side of the post. The lower small rail (for cane detectors) was connected to the back of the posts and positioned a few inches above the ground surface to allow for water drainage.

Option A could be designed to significantly limit deflections of the system during vehicular impact events. However, these details would significantly increase the cost for construction of the system. All of the material proposed for the construction of Option A was expected to be readily available.

Table 29 summarizes anticipated advantages and disadvantages of the Option A barrier system. Figure 24 illustrates a perpendicular view of Option A, and Figure 25 shows a three-dimensional rendering of Option A from the traffic and pedestrian sides.

## Option B: Steel-Only Open Rail System with Longitudinal HSS and Metal Mesh

Option B was a steel-only open rail system bolted to a concrete slab. The main difference between Option A and Option B was that Option B included a metal mesh at the back of the rail system on the vulnerable users' side. The metal mesh was connected to the bicycle railing plate and extended to the lower cane detector rail. The metal sheet would need to be constructed with a mesh size to prevent any snagging of vulnerable users with the system in the event of accidental fall or impact. Option B is depicted in Figure 26 as a system without a pedestrian handrail. However, a pedestrian handrail could be incorporated in the proposed system design if desired.

The total height of the railing system was 42 in., which included a post height of 32 in. and an additional bicycle railing to reach the required 42 in. The bolted connection between the post and the concrete slab could be located on the side of the post along the longitudinal deployment of the system to prevent interference with the shared-use path.

**Table 29. Option A barrier system: Perceived advantages and disadvantages.**

| Advantages | Disadvantages |
|---|---|
| • Material availability | • Installed cost |
| • Visibility | • Post exposure on wide flange option |
| • Aesthetics | • Lack of continuous protection |
| • Limited exposed edges on HSS option | |
| • Includes both handrail and top rail (as preferred) | |
| • Minimal deflection | |
| • Drainage | |
| • Snow clearing | |

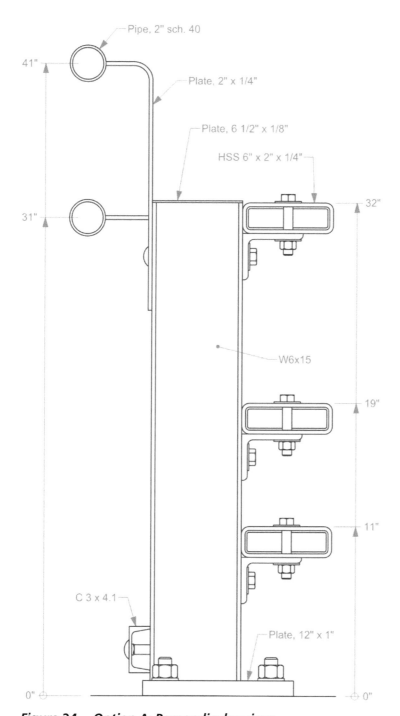

**Figure 24.  Option A: Perpendicular view.**

The proposed option utilized 30-in.-long steel posts, which could be either a wide flange or an HSS section. Because this design included continuous protection along the back side of the railing (proposed metal sheet), Option B does not result in post exposure to vulnerable users. Utilization of wide flange steel posts, therefore, would not present an exposed edge problem, given that the vulnerable users would be shielded from the entire post by the metal sheet protection system. Therefore, an HSS section would not be required to prevent interaction of vulnerable users with exposed edges. The anticipated post spacing was approximately 10 ft; however, detailed engineering analysis would be required to define post spacing on the basis of the system characteristics.

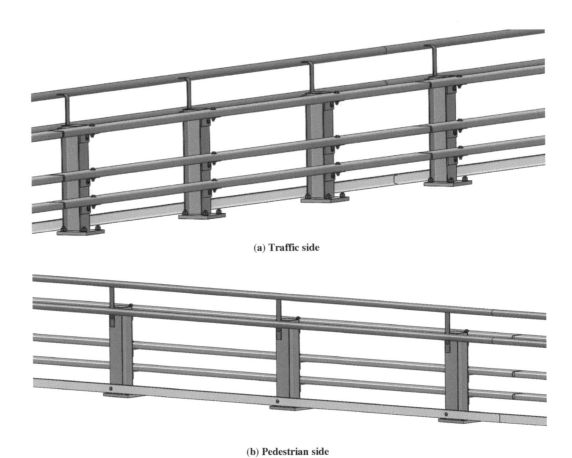

(a) Traffic side

(b) Pedestrian side

*Figure 25.   Option A: Perspective view.*

Steel angles were suggested for attachment of the horizontal HSS railing to the post. A steel plate could be included in the design to cover the steel post top, providing an element of protection in case of direct contact between the vulnerable user and the sharper edges along the top of the post.

The barrier included a total of three horizontal steel HSS railings. The horizontal railings would be adequately spaced to limit snagging potential in case of vehicular impact. Furthermore, the lower railing would be required to prevent any vehicle underriding.

Option B included a lower rail for cane detection, which was connected to the back of the posts and positioned a few inches from the ground surface. This setup would allow water drainage through the barrier system.

Option B could be designed to significantly limit deflections of the system during vehicular impact events. However, these details would significantly increase the cost for the system construction. All of the material proposed for construction of Option B was expected to be readily available.

With inclusion of the metal sheet, Option B represented a more challenging system with regard to snow clearing. In addition, aesthetic considerations and visibility through the barrier option would be compromised because of the presence of the metal mesh.

Table 30 summarizes the anticipated advantages and disadvantages of the Option B barrier system. Figure 27 illustrates a perpendicular view of Option B, and Figure 28 shows a rendering of Option B from the traffic and pedestrian sides. Figure 29 shows an elevation view from the pedestrian side.

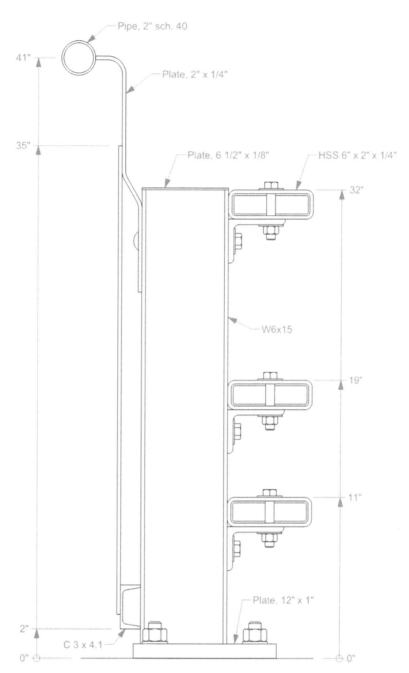

*Figure 26.    Option B: Perpendicular view.*

**Table 30.    Option B barrier system: Perceived advantages and disadvantages.**

| Advantages | Disadvantages |
|---|---|
| • Material availability | • Installed cost |
| • Continuous protection | • Snow clearing |
| • Limited post exposure | • Aesthetics |
| • Limited exposed edges (due to inclusion of metal mesh) | • Low visibility |
| • Minimal deflection | |
| • Drainage | |

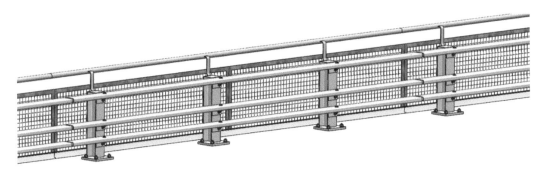

*Figure 27.  Option B: Perspective view, traffic side.*

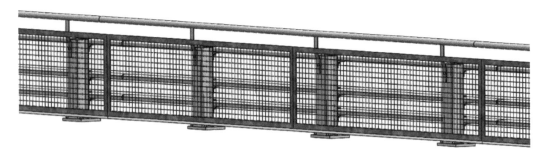

*Figure 28.  Option B: Perspective view, pedestrian side.*

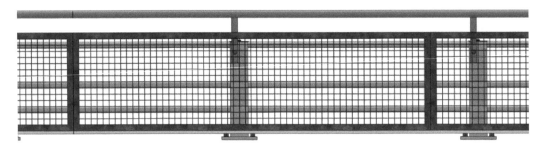

*Figure 29.  Option B: Elevation view.*

## Option C: W-Beam Guardrail System with Rails

Option C was a steel post, wood blockout W-beam rail system embedded in soil and surrounded by a low-strength grout to minimize vegetation maintenance. The total height of the railing system was 42 in., which included a post height of 32 in. and an additional bicycle railing to reach the required 42 in.

The proposed option utilized a commonly available wide flange 72-in.-long steel post. The anticipated post spacing, based on previous research completed by the research team, was 18¾ in. Previous testing on a steel post W-beam guardrail system with 18¾-in. post spacing showed the lateral deflection during vehicular impact (i.e., deflection into the shared-use path) to be approximately 20 in. The Option C design did not include a continuous protection system along the back side of the railing. Consequently, Option C still resulted in considerable post exposure as well as edges exposed to vulnerable users.

Option C included two additional preferred design elements: a handrail for pedestrians and a lower rail for cane detection. Both bicycle and pedestrian rails had a 2-in. diameter to comply with AASHTO requirements and were adequately spaced away from the posts to allow for hand gripping. Both rails were connected to a plate that could be bolted to the back side of the post. The lower small rail (for cane detectors) was connected to the back of the posts and positioned a few inches above the ground surface to allow for water drainage.

All material proposed for construction of Option C was expected to be readily available, and the construction cost was estimated to be comparable to that of a commonly deployed 31-in. W-beam guardrail embedded in soil and surrounded by a low-strength grout.

Table 31 summarizes the anticipated advantages and disadvantages of the Option C barrier system. Figure 30 illustrates a perpendicular view of Option C, and Figure 31 and Figure 32 show a rendering of Option C from the traffic and pedestrian sides, respectively. Figure 33 and Figure 34 show an elevation view from the pedestrian and traffic sides, respectively.

## Option D: W-Beam Guardrail System with Metal Mesh

Option D was a steel post, wood blockout W-beam rail system embedded in soil and surrounded by a low-strength grout to minimize vegetation maintenance. The total height of the railing system was 42 in., which includes a post height of 32 in. and an additional bicycle railing to reach the required 42 in.

The proposed option utilized a commonly available wide flange 72-in.-long steel post. The anticipated post spacing, based on previous research and testing studies, was 18¾ in. Previous testing on a steel post W-beam guardrail system with 18¾-in. post spacing showed the lateral deflection during vehicular impact (i.e., deflection into the shared-use path) to be approximately 20 in.

**Table 31. Option C barrier system: Perceived advantages and disadvantages.**

| Advantages | Disadvantages |
|---|---|
| • Material availability | • Drainage |
| • Installed cost | • Aesthetics |
| | • Post exposure |
| | • Exposed edges |
| | • Snow clearing |
| | • Low visibility |
| | • Larger deflection |

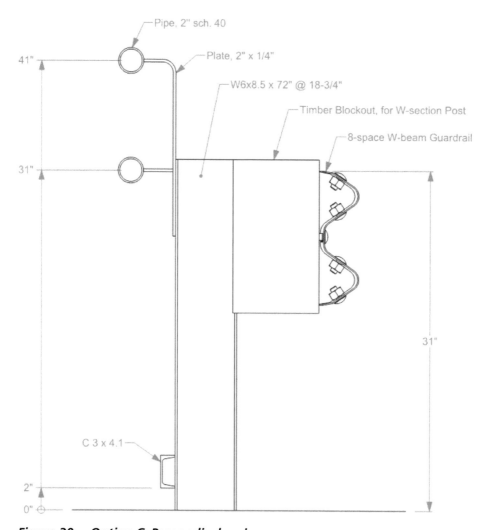

*Figure 30.  Option C: Perpendicular view.*

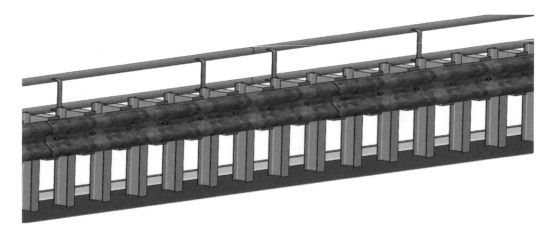

*Figure 31.  Option C: Perspective view, traffic side.*

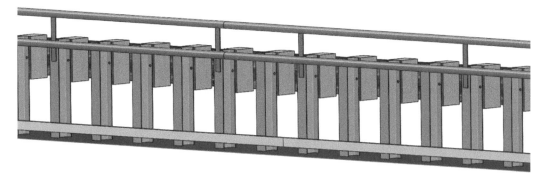

*Figure 32.   Option C: Perspective view, pedestrian side.*

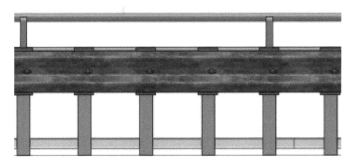

*Figure 33.   Option C: Elevation view, pedestrian side.*

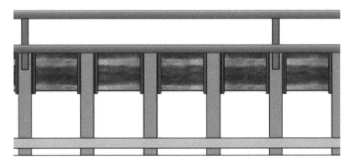

*Figure 34.   Option C: Elevation view, traffic side.*

The Option D design included a continuous protection system along the length of the back side of the railing. The metal mesh was connected to the bicycle railing plate and extended to the lower cane detector rail. The metal sheet would need to be constructed with a mesh size that would prevent any snagging of vulnerable users with the system in the event of accidental fall or impact. Option D was a system without a pedestrian handrail. However, a pedestrian handrail could be incorporated in the proposed system design if desired.

Option D included a lower rail for cane detection. The lower small rail (for cane detectors) was connected to the back of the posts and positioned a few inches from the ground surface to still allow for proper drainage.

The material proposed for the construction of Option D was expected to be readily available.

**Table 32. Option D barrier system: Perceived advantages and disadvantages.**

| Advantages | Disadvantages |
|---|---|
| • Material availability | • Drainage |
| • Continuous protection | • Aesthetics |
| • Post exposure | • Visibility |
| • Exposed edges | • Larger deflection |
| • Installed cost | • Snow clearing |

Table 32 summarizes the anticipated advantages and disadvantages of the Option D barrier system. Figure 35 illustrates a perpendicular view of Option D, and Figure 36 and Figure 37 show a rendering of Option D from the traffic and pedestrian sides, respectively. Figure 38 shows an elevation view from the pedestrian side.

With inclusion of the metal mesh, Option D represented a more challenging system with regard to snow clearing. In addition, aesthetic considerations and visibility through the barrier option would be compromised, because of the presence of the metal mesh covering most of the railing portion.

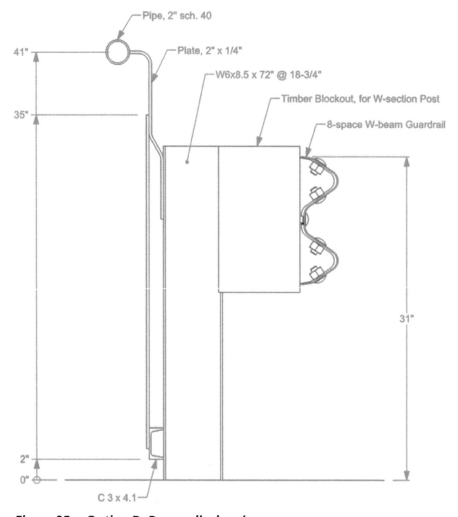

*Figure 35. Option D: Perpendicular view.*

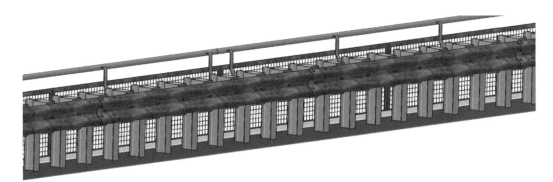

*Figure 36.   Option D: Perspective view, traffic side.*

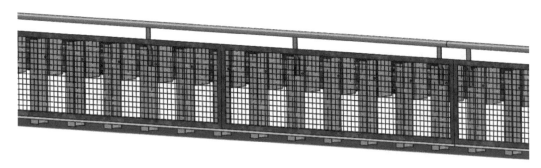

*Figure 37.   Option D: Perspective view, pedestrian side.*

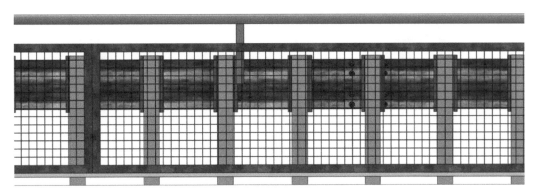

*Figure 38.   Option D: Elevation view.*

## Option E: Steel-Only Open Rail System with Covering HSS Top Rail

Option E was a steel-only open rail system bolted to a concrete slab. The total height of the railing system was 42 in., which included a post height of 32 in. and an additional bicycle railing to reach the required 42 in. The bolted connection between the post and the concrete slab could be located on the side of the post aligned with the longitudinal deployment of the system to prevent interference with the shared-use path.

The proposed option utilized steel posts approximately 24 in. long, which could be either a wide flange or an HSS section. The anticipated post spacing was approximately 10 ft; however, detailed engineering analysis would be required to define post spacing on the basis of the system characteristics. A 6-in.-tall longitudinal HSS railing element was placed on top of the steel posts and connected to them with steel angles. The 6-in.-tall longitudinal railing provided adequate barrier strength to vehicular impacts while providing continuous top post protection in case of direct contact with the sharper edges on the top of the post by the vulnerable user.

The Option E design did not include a continuous protection system along the length of the back side of the railing. Consequently, Option E still resulted in considerable post exposure as well as edges exposed to vulnerable users. However, were the post designed to be an HSS section, it would not present significant exposed edges.

Option E was proposed with inclusion of an additional horizontal steel HSS railing. The horizontal railing would be needed, properly located along the height of the system, to limit snagging potential in case of vehicular impact.

Option E included two additional preferred design elements: a lower rail for cane detection and a handrail for pedestrians, as depicted in Figure 39. Both bicycle and pedestrian rails had a 2-in. diameter to comply with AASHTO requirements and were adequately spaced from the posts' back side to allow for easy hand gripping. Both rails were connected to a plate that could be bolted to the posts' back side. The lower small rail (for cane detectors) was connected to the back of the posts and positioned a few inches above the ground surface to allow for proper drainage.

Option E could be designed to significantly limit deflections of the system during vehicular impact events; these details, however, might increase the cost for the system construction significantly. The material proposed for construction of Option E was anticipated to be readily available.

Table 33 summarizes the anticipated advantages and disadvantages of the Option E barrier system. Figure 39 illustrates a perpendicular view of Option E, and Figure 40 and Figure 41 show a rendering of Option E from the traffic and pedestrian sides, respectively.

## Option F: Steel-Only Open Rail System with Covering HSS Top Rail and Metal Mesh

Option F was a steel-only open rail system bolted to a concrete slab. The total height of the railing system was 42 in., which included a post height of 32 in. and an additional bicycle railing to reach the required 42 in. The bolted connection between the post and the concrete slab could be located on the side of the post along the deployment of the system to prevent interference with the shared-use path.

The proposed option utilized steel posts approximately 24 in. long, which could be either a wide flange or an HSS type. The anticipated post spacing was approximately 10 ft; however, detailed engineering analysis would be required to define post spacing on the basis of the system

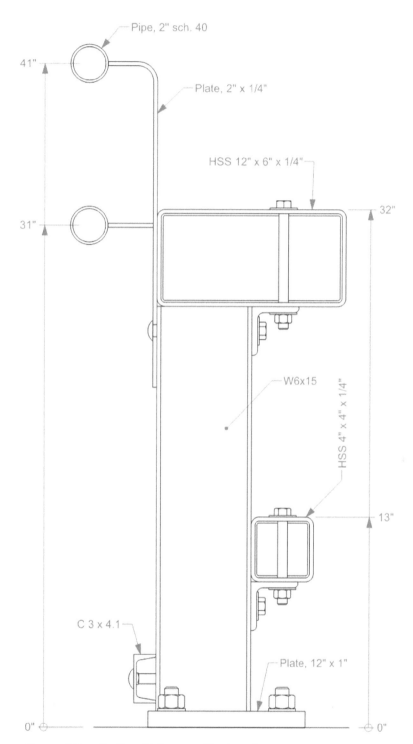

*Figure 39.* *Option E: Perpendicular view.*

**Table 33. Option E barrier system: Perceived advantages and disadvantages.**

| Advantages | Disadvantages |
|---|---|
| • Visibility | • No continuous protection on back side of post |
| • Minimal deflection | • Post exposure |
| • Drainage | • Exposed edges on wide flange option |
| • Material availability | • Installed cost |
| • Aesthetics | |
| • No exposed edges on HSS option | |
| • Snow clearing | |
| • Continuous protection along the top of post | |

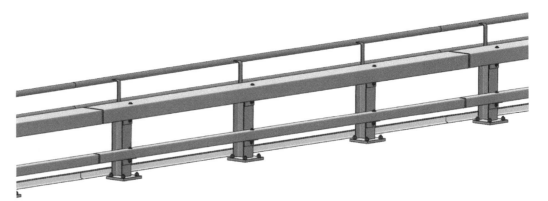

*Figure 40. Option E: Perspective view, traffic side.*

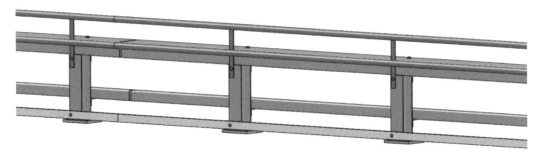

*Figure 41. Option E: Perspective view, pedestrian side.*

characteristics. A 6-in.-tall longitudinal HSS railing element was placed on top of the steel posts and connected to them through steel angle. The 6-in.-tall longitudinal railing served as a steel beam element, offering adequate barrier strength to vehicular impacts and, at the same time, providing continuous top post protection against direct contact by the vulnerable user with the sharp edges on the top of the post.

The Option F design included a continuous protection system along the length of the back side of the railing. The metal mesh was connected to the bicycle railing plate and extended to the lower cane detector rail. The metal sheet would need to be constructed with a mesh size that would prevent any snagging of vulnerable users with the system in the event of accidental fall or impact. Option F is depicted in Figure 42 as a system without a pedestrian handrail. However, a pedestrian handrail could be incorporated in the proposed system design if desired.

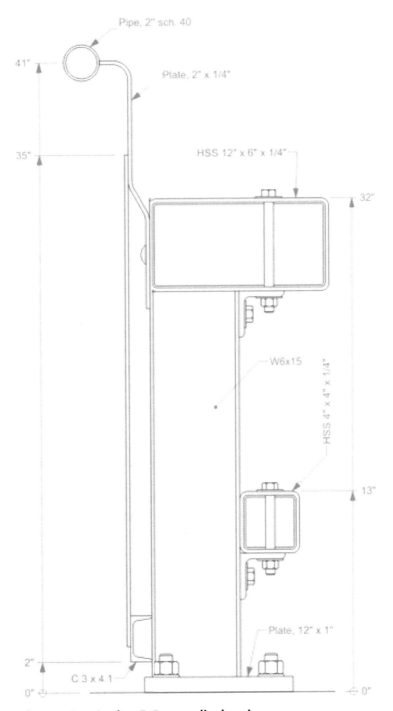

Pipe, 2" sch. 40

Plate, 2" x 1/4"

HSS 12" x 6" x 1/4"

41"

35"

32"

W6x15

HSS 4" x 4" x 1/4"

13"

Plate, 12" x 1"

2"

C 3 x 4.1

0"

0"

*Figure 42.    Option F: Perpendicular view.*

**Table 34.   Option F barrier system: Perceived advantages and disadvantages.**

| Advantages | Disadvantages |
|---|---|
| • Minimal deflection | • Installed cost |
| • Material availability | • Visibility |
| • Exposed edges | • Drainage |
| • Post exposure | • Aesthetics |
| • Continuous protection | • Snow clearing |

Option F was proposed with inclusion of an additional horizontal steel HSS railing. The horizontal railing would be needed, properly located along the height of the system, to limit snagging potential in case of vehicular impact.

Option F included two preferred additional design elements: a lower rail for cane detection and a handrail for pedestrians, as shown in Figure 42. The lower small rail (for cane detectors) was connected to the back of the posts and positioned a few inches from the ground surface to allow for proper drainage.

Option F could be designed to significantly limit deflections of the system during vehicular impact events; these details, however, might increase the cost for the system construction significantly. The material proposed for construction of Option F was expected to be readily available.

Table 34 summarizes the anticipated advantages and disadvantages of the Option F barrier system, and Figure 42 illustrates a perpendicular view of the system. With inclusion of the metal mesh, Option F represented a more challenging system with regard to snow clearing. In addition, aesthetic considerations and visibility through the barrier option would be compromised because of the presence of the metal mesh covering most of the railing portion.

## Design Comparison

Table 35 summarizes the six different options reported in this chapter. The research team compared the perceived advantages and disadvantages for each proposed option. To help compare the proposed system designs in an objective manner, the research team suggested a rating for each of the proposed systems based on the anticipated advantages and disadvantages. A rating of one, two, or three stars for each element considered during the barrier design process was suggested. Three stars indicates a barrier concept better addresses that design aspect than a barrier concept that has one star for that design aspect. For example, installed cost of Option C is significantly lower in comparison to some of the other design options. Thus, Option C was assigned three stars for installation cost and other design concepts (e.g., Option A) received only one star for installation cost.

## Design Recommendation and Modification

The preliminary designs for the pedestrian and bicycle handrails and the cane detection rail are shown in Figure 43. This is a variation of Option E derived from discussion with the project panel. Although some of the original concepts included a base-plated post bolted to a concrete slab or pavement, the project panel selected a direct embedded post option. Direct post embedment reduces cost by eliminating the need for a structural slab for mounting of the barrier. It was further decided that vegetation control should be incorporated around the barrier system. This consisted of a concrete mow strip on both the traffic and field sides of the barrier and an interior soil strip into which the barrier posts are embedded. The top 4 in. of this soil strip,

**Table 35.    System option comparison.**

| Rating | Option A | Option B | Option C | Option D | Option E | Option F |
|---|---|---|---|---|---|---|
| ★ ★ ★ | Visibility, aesthetics, deflection, drainage, material availability, exposed edges (HSS), snow clearing | Deflection, drainage, material availability, continuous protection, post exposure, exposed edges | Material availability, installed cost | Material availability, continuous protection, post exposure, exposed edges | Visibility, deflection, drainage, material availability, exposed edges (HSS), aesthetics, snow clearing, continuous protection (post top only) | Deflection, material availability, exposed edges, post exposure, continuous protection |
| ★ ★ | Post exposure | Visibility, aesthetics | Drainage, aesthetics, post exposure, snow clearing, visibility | Drainage, installed cost | Continuous protection (post body only), post exposure | Visibility, aesthetics, drainage |
| ★ | Installed cost, continuous protection, exposed edges (wide flange) | Installed cost, snow clearing | Deflection, exposed edges | Aesthetics, visibility, deflection, snow clearing | Installed cost | Installed cost, snow clearing |

corresponding to the thickness of the mow strip, were filled with a low-strength grout to provide vegetation control around the posts. The cane detection rail on the bottom field side of the barrier was changed from a structural channel to a steel plate, which reduced its projection from the post and its cost. This preliminary design was subject to change pending further analysis and computer simulation.

This section provides information about preliminary drawings with proposed changes to the design after several simulation iterations were performed. After considering several design options, the research team decided to provide post spacing of 22 in., 44 in., and 66 in. for performance of further simulations to choose a final option for testing. The models were checked for deformation and economic feasibility.

Some modifications in design to optimize the overall system were as follows:

1. Post spacing was increased to 22 in., 44 in., and 66 in. to obtain economic options from the viewpoint of construction, production, and cost effectiveness.
2. For the 22-in. post spacing options, the angle brackets used to connect the rails to the posts were at each post for the lower rub rail.
3. The spliced box sections for both the rails were replaced with simple plate splices.
4. The rub rail thickness was increased from ⅛ in. to ¼ in. after preliminary simulations indicated vehicle instability issues due to the light rub rail section.
5. The handrail design was modified to further optimize it from the perspective of cost, fabrication, installation, and transportation.

The 44-in. post spacing design was similar to the 22-in.-tall design, except that the traffic side of the rub rail was extended to match the plane of the top traffic rail, as mentioned before.

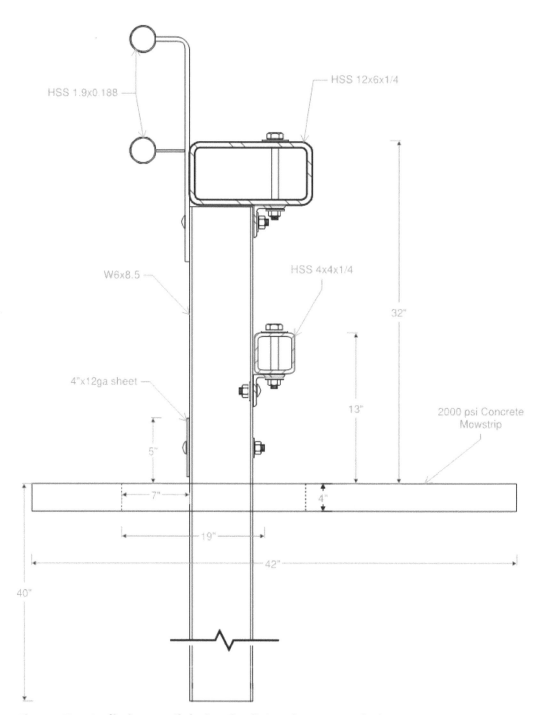

***Figure 43. Preliminary rail design for finite element analysis.***

When considering the simulation results obtained from the 22-in. and 44-in. post spacing, the researchers saw the opportunity to increase the post spacing and further optimize the design. The post spacing was increased to 66 in., and simulations were conducted to check the MASH limits along with the maximum deflection requirements. The research team terminated further investigation after the results for the 66-in. post spacing option were analyzed, since the deflection results were very close to the desired deflection limit of 24 in. proposed by the project panel in the kickoff meeting. The simulation results for this option are provided in the next chapter.

# CHAPTER 5

# Finite Element Computer Modeling and Calibration

This chapter discusses the finite element (FE) modeling aspect of this project. As discussed earlier, calibration of the new developed model was required to verify whether the system would behave realistically. Before using LS-PrePost to develop the FE model, the researchers needed to calibrate the model and confirm that the modeling techniques, contacts, material cards, and other information to be used in the final model would give realistic results and replicate the interaction between the systems and vehicles. To do this, they compared the results obtained from the calibration models with actual crash tests done in the past. This chapter discusses the calibration simulations and results obtained. Calibration tests were performed to determine the behavior of the steel HSS, steel connections, and concrete mow strip to be used in the new developed model. This chapter is broadly divided into three parts: (*a*) calibration of the HSS model, (*b*) mow strip calibration, and (*c*) the multifunctional barrier model and validation.

## Calibration of the HSS Model

The LS-DYNA FE software package was used to simulate the behavior of vehicular impacts with a steel median barrier system. LS-DYNA is an all-purpose, explicit FE analysis code. It is extensively used to simulate the nonlinear, dynamic response of three-dimensional problems and to capture the intricate interactions of a vehicle with a Triborough Bridge and Tunnel Authority (TBTA) steel bridge rail system. LS-DYNA is also capable of producing dynamic load time history responses for any impact. Before modeling the actual system, the researchers used an earlier study by TTI to calibrate the LS-DYNA FE analysis model (N. M. Sheikh, W. L. Menges, and D. L. Kuhn, "MASH TL-5 Testing and Evaluation of the TBTA Bridge Rail, No. 603911-1," unpublished report, TTI, 2017; see also *32*). LS-DYNA was used to perform critical impact simulations that used the developed sign support system and available vehicle models.

### Finite Element Computer Models for HSS Calibration

Figure 44 illustrates the available FE vehicle models. These models include (*a*) the Toyota Yaris model, representing a 2,420-lb (1100C) MASH small car test vehicle and (*b*) the Chevrolet Silverado model, representing a 5,000-lb (2270P) MASH pickup truck test vehicle.

The researchers used a TBTA steel bridge rail tested for HNTB New York Engineering and Architecture, P.C., under the aforementioned TTI project for calibration of the LS-DYNA FE model (N. M. Sheikh, W. L. Menges, and D. L. Kuhn, "MASH TL-5 Testing and Evaluation of the TBTA Bridge Rail, No. 603911-1," unpublished report, TTI, 2017; see also *32*). Figure 45 illustrates the actual constructed TBTA bridge rail. In the TBTA project, MASH Tests 5-10 and 5-11 were conducted on the TBTA steel bridge rail system because of the high volume of freight traffic on the bridge where it would be located. The tests were only used to calibrate the FE models. To calibrate

(a) Toyota Yaris FE model

(b) Chevrolet Silverado FE model

*Figure 44. Available FE models of vehicles.*

the results of the developed model in LS-DYNA, vehicle impact behavior and stability as well as occupant risk factors upon vehicle impact were compared.

The Test Risk Assessment Program (TRAP) was used to evaluate vehicle stability, occupant risk, and structural adequacy. Vehicle angular velocities, also known as roll, pitch, and yaw angles, were used to evaluate vehicle stability. MASH specifies that the maximum roll and pitch angles should not exceed 75 deg. Occupant risk describes the risk of hazard to occupants. It was evaluated on the basis of the data collected by the accelerometer located at the center of gravity (CG) in the vehicle. Two factors were mainly analyzed in preliminary simulations on the basis of the acceleration data: occupant impact velocity (OIV) and occupant ridedown acceleration (ORA). OIV and ORA are, respectively, the changes in velocity that the hypothetical occupant feels at impact and the acceleration from the collision just after impact. MASH requires the OIV to be lower than 40 ft/s and the ORA to be less than 20.49 $g$ (acceleration due to gravity) in the longitudinal and lateral directions.

A 2010 Kia Rio passenger car and 2010 Dodge Ram 1500 pickup truck were used in the full-scale crash tests. The actual impact speed and angle for both the tests were 62 mi/h and 25 deg, respectively.

LS-PrePost was used to develop a TBTA steel bridge rail. A steel bridge rail was developed with multiple different material and section properties. W-sections were modeled with MAT024 (Piecewise Linear Plasticity) to define the material properties of the steel posts. MAT024 was also used to define the material properties of the base plates and both HSS sections. Constrained

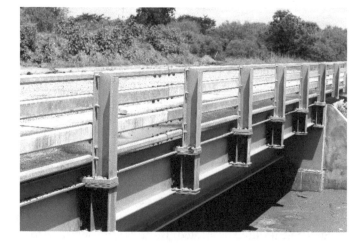

*Figure 45. TBTA bridge rail.*

Nodal Rigid Body (CNRB) connections were used to connect the base plates to the W-section and the HSS sections to the W-sections. Figure 46 shows the LS-DYNA model of the TBTA steel bridge rail system used for calibration.

## MASH Test 5-10 Calibration (Test 603911-1)

The researchers used a validated Toyota Yaris FE model to represent the test vehicle. The weight of the Toyota Yaris model was similar to that of the Kia Rio used in the actual crash test. The test vehicle's actual impact speed and angle orientation were implemented in the computer simulation. Figure 47 shows sequential photos of the simulated impact event and compares frames from the actual full-scale crash test with the calibrated computer model's simulation of the impact. Table 36 summarizes occupant risk, vehicle stability information, and system deflection values from the comparison between the actual crash test and the simulated impact event.

## MASH Test 5-11 Calibration (Test 603911-2): Passenger-Side Impact

The researchers used a validated Chevrolet Silverado FE model to represent the test vehicle. The weight of the Silverado model was similar to that of the Dodge Ram used in the actual crash test. The test vehicle's actual impact speed and angle orientation were implemented in the computer

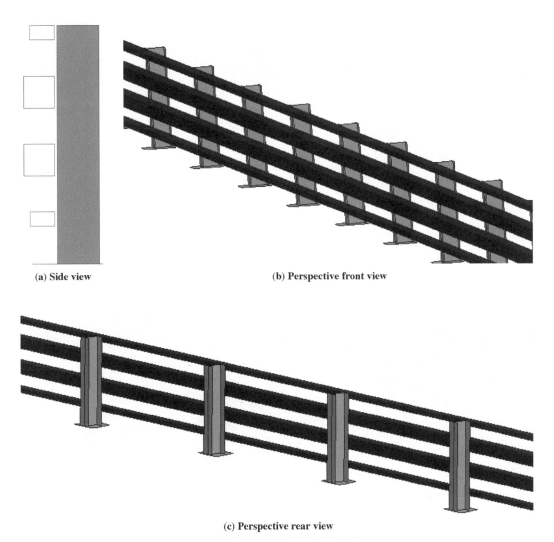

(a) Side view          (b) Perspective front view

(c) Perspective rear view

*Figure 46.   LS-DYNA model for calibration of the barrier system.*

0.0 s

0.1 s

 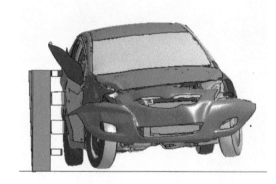

0.2 s

 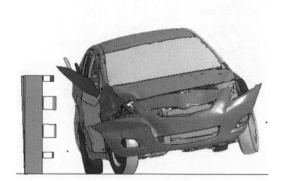

0.3 s

*Figure 47. Comparison of actual crash test (Test 5-10) (left) and LS-DYNA simulation (right).*

**Table 36. Comparison of test results (occupant risk factors) from full-scale crash test (Test 5-10) and FE impact simulation.**

| Occupant Risk Factor | Actual Crash Test | FE Simulation |
|---|---|---|
| Impact velocity (ft/s) | | |
| X | 22.0 | 20.59 |
| Y | 34.8 | −30.43 |
| Ridedown acceleration (g) | | |
| X | 4.1 | −4.3 |
| Y | 10.9 | 21.9 |
| THIV (km/h) | 44.8 | 42.7 |
| PHD (g) | 10.9 | 21.9 |
| ASI | 2.82 | 2.6 |
| Maximum 0.050-s average (g) | | |
| X | −13.1 | −13.3 |
| Y | 21.2 | 20.2 |
| Vertical | 3.2 | 4.8 |
| Maximum angle (deg) | | |
| Roll | 9 | 11.5 |
| Pitch | 8 | 2.2 |
| Yaw | 74 | 35.7 |

Note: THIV = theoretical head impact velocity; PHD = peak head deceleration; ASI = acceleration severity index.

simulation. Figure 48 compares frames from the actual full-scale crash test and the calibrated computer model's simulation of the impact. Table 37 summarizes occupant risk, vehicle stability information, and system deflection values from the comparison between the actual crash test and the simulated impact event.

## Conclusion

A comparison of LS-DYNA simulation results and actual crash test values revealed that the computer models (system and vehicle) could be considered calibrated. The results from the simulated impact events closely matched those from the actual crash test events. The ridedown acceleration value was slightly over predicted in the computer model as compared with the result obtained through the full-scale crash test. Generally, however, the FE model closely replicated the testing outcomes in terms of vehicle stability and general behavior during the impact event.

## Validation of the Mow Strip Model

The LS-DYNA FE software package was used to simulate the behavior of vehicular impacts with a steel barrier system embedded in a mow strip and soil. As noted previously, LS-DYNA is an all-purpose, explicit FE analysis code. It is extensively used to simulate the nonlinear, dynamic response of three-dimensional problems and to capture the intricate interactions of a vehicle with a steel guardrail system. LS-DYNA is also capable of producing dynamic load-time history responses for any impact. Before modeling the actual system, the researchers used the earlier study by TTI to calibrate the LS-DYNA FE analysis model (N. M. Sheikh, W. L. Menges, and D. L. Kuhn,

0.0 s

0.1 s

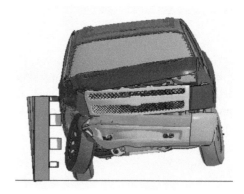

0.2 s

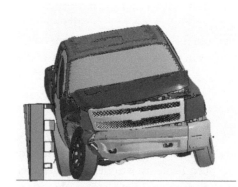

0.3 s

Figure 48. Comparison of actual crash test (Test 5-11) (left) and LS-DYNA simulation (right, passenger side).

**Table 37. Comparison of test results (occupant risk factors) from full-scale crash test (Test 5-11) and FE impact simulation on the passenger side.**

| Occupant Risk Factor | Actual Crash Test | FE Simulation |
|---|---|---|
| Impact velocity (ft/s) | | |
| $X$ | 17.4 | 28.2 |
| $Y$ | 28.5 | −28.2 |
| Ridedown acceleration ($g$) | | |
| $X$ | 6.0 | −15.9 |
| $Y$ | 10.7 | 14.7 |
| THIV (km/h) | 44.8 | 37.1 |
| PHD ($g$) | 10.9 | 10.8 |
| ASI | 2.82 | 1.92 |
| Max 0.050-s average ($g$) | | |
| $X$ | −8.5 | −13.3 |
| $Y$ | −15.2 | 14.2 |
| Vertical | 2.8 | 3.8 |
| Maximum angle (deg) | | |
| Roll | 10 | 11.3 |
| Pitch | 4 | 16.9 |
| Yaw | 43 | 30.3 |

"MASH TL-5 Testing and Evaluation of the TBTA Bridge Rail, No. 603911-1," unpublished report, TTI, 2017; see also *32*). LS-DYNA was used to perform critical impact simulations that used the developed system and available vehicle models.

## MASH Test 5-11 Calibration (Test 603911-2): Driver Side Impact

For more accurate calibration, the researchers also validated the driver side of the pickup truck for MASH Test 5-11. The test vehicle's actual impact speed and angle orientation were implemented in the computer simulation. Figure 49 compares frames from the actual full-scale crash test and the calibrated computer model's simulation of the impact. Table 38 summarizes occupant risk, vehicle stability information, and system deflection values from the comparison between the actual crash test and the simulated impact event.

## Finite Element Mow Strip Model

Figure 50 illustrates the available FE vehicle model, a 2018 Dodge Ram model representing a 5,000-lb (2270P) MASH pickup truck test vehicle.

The researchers used a 31-in. W-beam guardrail system with steel posts in a concrete mow strip, as tested by TTI (*28*) to calibrate the LS-DYNA FE analysis model. The researchers at TTI conducted MASH Tests 5-10 and 5-11 on this guardrail system, which was used to calibrate the results of the developed system in LS-DYNA by comparing vehicle impact behavior and stability as well as occupant risks and performance upon vehicle impact.

TRAP was used to evaluate vehicle stability, occupant risk, and structural adequacy. Vehicle angular velocities, also known as roll, pitch, and yaw angles, were used to evaluate vehicle stability. MASH specifies that the maximum roll and pitch angles should not exceed 75 deg. Occupant risk describes the risk of hazard to occupants. It was evaluated on the basis of the data collected by the

0.0 s

0.1 s

 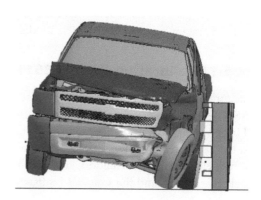

0.2 s

 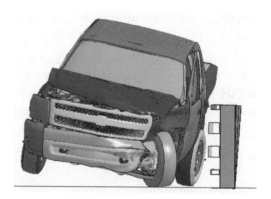

0.3 s

**Figure 49. Comparison of actual crash test (Test 5-11) (left) and LS-DYNA simulation (right, *driver side*).**

**Table 38. Comparison of test results (occupant risk factors) from full-scale crash test (Test 5-11) and FE impact simulation on the driver side.**

| Occupant Risk Factor | Actual Crash Test | FE Simulation |
|---|---|---|
| Impact velocity (ft/s) | | |
| X | 17.4 | 21.648 |
| Y | 28.5 | 29.192 |
| Ridedown acceleration (g) | | |
| X | 6.0 | −5.7 |
| Y | 10.7 | −16.9 |
| THIV (km/h) | 44.8 | 37.1 |
| PHD (g) | 10.9 | 10.8 |
| ASI | 2.82 | 1.92 |
| Max 0.050-s average (g) | | |
| X | −8.5 | −11.6 |
| Y | −15.2 | −15 |
| Vertical | 2.8 | 2.9 |
| Maximum angle (deg) | | |
| Roll | 10 | −12.8 |
| Pitch | 4 | 9 |
| Yaw | 43 | 31.5 |

accelerometer located at the CG in the vehicle. Two factors were mainly analyzed in preliminary simulations through the acceleration data: OIV and ORA. OIV and ORA are, respectively, the change in velocity that the hypothetical occupant feels at impact and the acceleration from the collision just after impact. MASH requires the OIV to be lower than 40 ft/s and ORA to be less than 20.49 g in the longitudinal and lateral directions.

The test article developed by Sheikh et al. (*28*) consisted of a 31-in. W-beam guardrail with steel posts. The guardrail system was installed with 26 posts, with 16 posts in the concrete mow strip. Figure 51 is a drawing of the actual installation.

A standard 12-gauge W-beam rail was provided. The top of the W-beam was 31 in. above the ground, and the posts were spaced at 6 ft 3 in. A 10-in. bolt was used to attach 8-in. wood (timber) blockouts to the posts to keep the rail and blockout attached to the posts. Guardrail posts with section W6 × 8.5 ASTM A36 structural steel were used. The embedment of the posts was 40 in. deep in the soil.

*Figure 50. 2018 Dodge Ram FE model.*

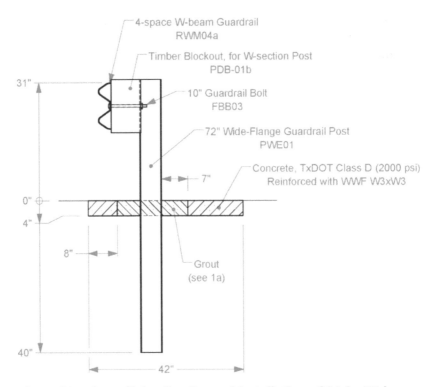

*Figure 51. Overall details of actual installation of 31-in. W-beam guardrail with steel posts in concrete mow strip (28).*

The concrete mow strip was 100 ft long, 42 in. wide, and 4 in. thick. Each post had a 19-in. square leave-out. Leave-outs were allocated 8 in. from the traffic-side edge of the strip. Posts were installed with a back face edge distance of 7 in. from the leave-outs. After installation of the posts and strip, the 4-in. deep leave-outs were filled with low-strength grout.

The material properties of the concrete and grout were assessed before the test. The specified concrete strength of the mow strip was 3 ksi. The grout strength was 150 psi on the date of the first test. Figure 52 provides the installation pictures before the test was performed.

The FE model was developed by replicating the test installation used in the study by Sheikh et al. (*28*). The spacing and dimensions of the posts were kept the same as those in the actual installation. The section property assigned in the software keywords was used to replicate the dimensions

(a) Perspective rear view of the installation

(b) Perspective front view of the installation

*Figure 52. Perspective view of actual test installation (28).*

of the actual test article. Thus, FE steel posts with section properties of W6 × 8.5 steel were used with 40 in. of embedment in soil. Further, the dimensions of the grout around the post were kept approximately the same as those of the actual installation. The depth of the concrete mow strip was kept at 4 in. The 8-in. wood blockout was also used with the same section properties. A W-beam rail was used with a 12-gauge steel section property with splices in the middle of the two posts.

The steel posts, W-beam rail, and bolt exteriors were provided with shell elements. The blockout, soil, grout, and mow strip concrete layer were provided with solid elements. CNRB elements were used for the bolts keeping the rail and blockout attached to posts. Discrete mass elements were used at the ends of the longitudinal rail to provide a simulated end terminal effect in an effort to restrain the free movement of the ends. The bolt center was provided with beam element with nodes to tie the constrained nodes to the center of the bolt axis.

Material properties of the model were provided on the basis of the anticipated behavior of the model compared with the actual testing. A material property representing linear plasticity was used for steel bolts, W-beam, and steel posts. For the concrete mow strip, rigid body elements were used. Springs or discrete mass elements were used instead of an anchorage system at the ends of the rail. Soil, wood block out, and concrete for the grout leave-outs near the posts were used with their corresponding material properties. Figure 53 shows the perspective views of the developed model in LS-PrePost.

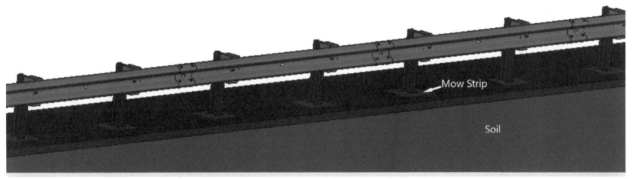

(a) **Front perspective view of the developed FE model**

(b) **Rear perspective view of the developed FE model**

*Figure 53.* **LS-PrePost FE model for 31-in. W-beam guardrail with steel posts in concrete mow strip.**

## MASH Test 3-11 Calibration

The researchers used a validated 2018 Dodge Ram FE model to represent the test vehicle. The weight of the Dodge Ram model was similar to that of the crash-tested Dodge Ram. The test vehicle's actual impact speed and angle orientation were implemented in the computer simulation. Figure 54 provides some frames from the results of the predictive impact simulation. Materials such as MAT_072, MAT_084, MAT_159, MAT_272, and MAT_273 were considered to determine the material properties of the grout and mow strip concrete.

After performing several simulations with the material combinations mentioned above, the researchers changed the material properties of the grout and mow strip on the basis of the results obtained. Several errors were obtained due to the constraints of the material card used in the model, so the material properties had to be altered to eliminate the errors. After eliminating the errors, the researchers verified whether the behavior of the soil, mow strip, and grout was realistic and if it could be compared with the actual crash test.

The latest results were obtained by using the MAT_025 Geologic Cap Model for the grout and MAT_159 Continuous Surface Cap Model (CSCM) Concrete for the mow strip. The impact location, speed, and angle were kept the same as for the actual test. Figure 55 and Figure 56 show sequential images comparing the actual crash test and simulation results for the grout/mow strip calibration model. These figures show that the behavior of the FE model was similar to the actual

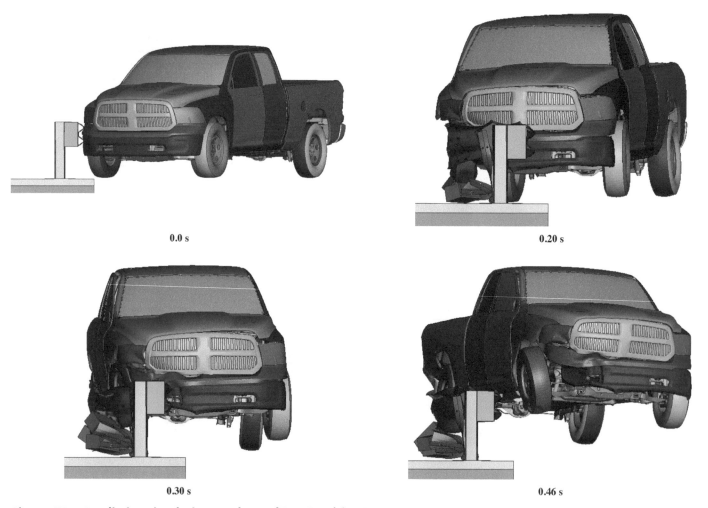

0.0 s                                    0.20 s

0.30 s                                    0.46 s

*Figure 54.  Predictive simulation crash test (Test 3-11) in LS-DYNA.*

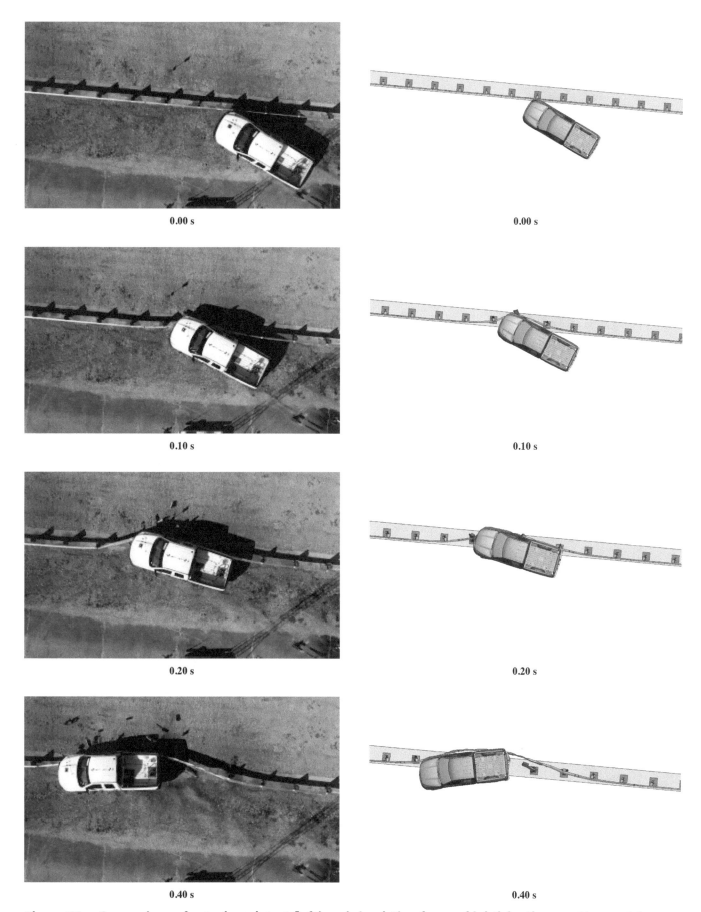

*Figure 55. Comparison of actual crash test (left) and simulation frames (right) for the grout/mow strip calibration model (top view).*

0.00 s                    0.00 s

0.10 s                    0.10 s

0.20 s                    0.20 s

0.40 s                    0.40 s

*Figure 56. Comparison of actual crash test (left) and simulation frames (right) for the grout/ mow strip calibration model (side view).*

**Table 39. Comparison of TRAP values for actual crash test and FE simulation results.**

| Occupant Risk Factor | Actual Crash Test | FE Simulation |
|---|---|---|
| Impact velocity (ft/s) | | |
| *X* | 15.4 | 17.71 |
| *Y* | 14.4 | 14.4 |
| Ridedown acceleration (*g*) | | |
| *X* | 7.0 | 11.2 |
| *Y* | 7.3 | 10.6 |
| Maximum angle (deg) | | |
| Roll | 16 | 4.1 |
| Pitch | 4 | 2.6 |
| Yaw | 40 | 41.1 |

crash test results for most of the crash time period. Table 39 presents the comparison of the TRAP values obtained for the purpose of determining the occupant risk factors after the impact. As shown in the comparison, the values are close, with no significant difference in the TRAP values.

After calibration of the mow strip model, TTI researchers tried to validate the model with the Roadside Safety Verification and Validation Program (RSVVP) MATLAB compiler. For this, the acceleration and angular displacement values were obtained from the simulation through postprocessing and compared with the data available from the actual crash test. All such data were imported into the compiler, and the metrics evaluation was obtained after the curves were filtered. This evaluation tried to determine several parameters that could judge the similarity between the true crash and the simulation tests. An image from the RSVVP test results is shown in Figure 57. In the figure, all the evaluation parameters indicate a pass for the comparison; therefore, the model was considered near to being validated. Furthermore, the maximum dynamic deflection values for true test and simulation were also similar, at 50.6 in. and 47 in., respectively. Thus, the soil model used for the calibration was used in developing the multifunctional barrier model after the proposed design was incorporated. The barrier design is discussed in the next section and includes drawings, modifications in the design, and FE simulation results.

## Validation of the Multifunctional Barrier Model

The TTI researchers used LS-PrePost software to develop the FE model for the proposed MASH multifunctional barrier. The purpose of developing this model was to obtain a preliminary simulation result without calibration. Figure 58 shows the proposed model drawing used for preliminary purposes. Figure 59 provides a detailed drawing of different components of the proposed system. The drawings were only used for the FE model and were modified for the actual test installation later.

## Finite Element Multifunctional Barrier Model

This section discusses the calibration of the multifunctional barrier model. Although researchers calibrated each component of the system model, as explained in previous sections, the entire barrier model needed to be calibrated after all components of the system were combined. As shown in Figures 58 and 59, the proposed barrier consists of a mow strip with grout along with steel posts.

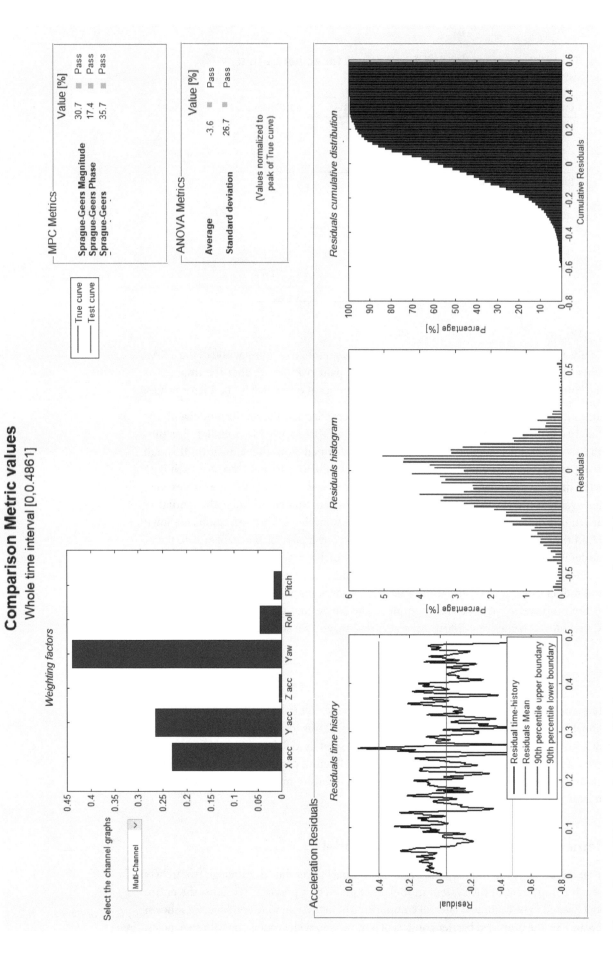

*Figure 57. RSVVP results for validating concrete mow strip model.*

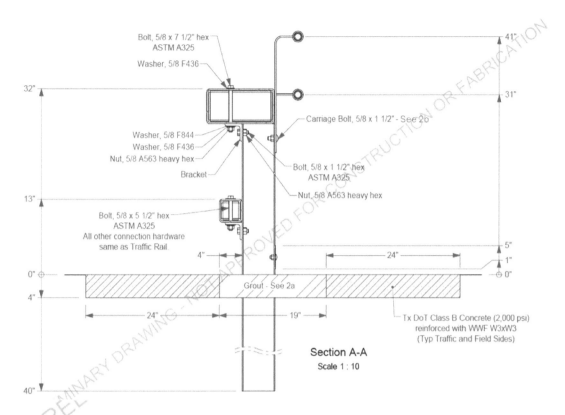

**2a.** Grout is 2719 pounds sand, 188 pounds Type I or II cement, and 550 pounds of water per cubic yard.

**2b.** Carriage Bolts are Grade 5, with Grade 5 nuts.

*Figure 58.   Preliminary drawing for MASH multifunctional barrier to shield pedestrians, bicyclists, and other vulnerable users from motor vehicles.*

The HSS rails connected to the posts are attached with brackets. The two handrails attached to the post have bolted connections. A cane detection rail is attached to the bottom of the post near the mow strip level.

To prepare the FE model of the system in LS-PrePost, researchers obtained different components from the respective calibration models and combined the files to prepare the final model. The HSS rails were obtained from the HSS calibration model, and the mow strip with soil was obtained from the mow strip calibration model. Additional parts of the barrier system, such as handrails and cane detection, were modeled separately.

Section properties of the model were based on the thickness and length of different components of the system shown in the drawing. The material properties of A36 steel were used with all the components of the system except the soil and mow strip. Instead of modeling a terminal, the researchers used springs and discrete mass elements at the ends of the rail. Soil and grout were modeled with Material ID 025—MAT_GEOLOGIC_CAP_MODEL, while mow strip concrete was modeled with the material properties of a concrete.

The connections of the different components of the system were based on calibration experience with HSS rails and mow strips. CNRB was used for the connection between the HSS traffic rail and rub rail with posts. Spot-welds were used for the connection of the internal joints between all rail sections. Similarly, spot-welds were used for the connections between the handrails and

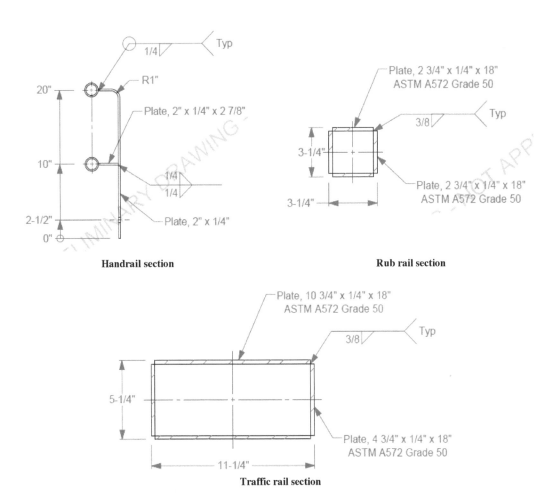

*Figure 59. Preliminary drawing for different components of proposed MASH multifunctional barrier.*

the posts and between the cane detection system and the posts. No brackets were used in the FE model, since the connections were made with CNRB and spot-welds.

The mow strip had the dimensions of depth and leave-outs, as per the calibration model. This included the depth of concrete and grout in the strip at 4 in. thick. The properties of the soil and mow strip with grout were kept the same as those of the calibration model. Figure 60 and Figure 61 show the FE model prepared in LS-PrePost.

## MASH Test 3-11 Calibration

The researchers calibrated the FE model of the multifunctional rail length of need (LON) system against full-scale crash testing to validate the chosen properties and modeling techniques. Specifically, the calibration was conducted to achieve similar lateral deformation of the LON system during the impact by the pickup truck, which reflects system stiffness. Calibration of system stiffness was needed to anticipate potential vehicle pocketing/snagging behavior during the impact event against the transition system.

Figure 62 and Figure 63 compare actual MASH Test 3-11 test frames and results with the FE simulation outcome (top view and front view, respectively). This comparison indicates that the FE model acceptably predicts the general system behavior and vehicle interaction during the impact event.

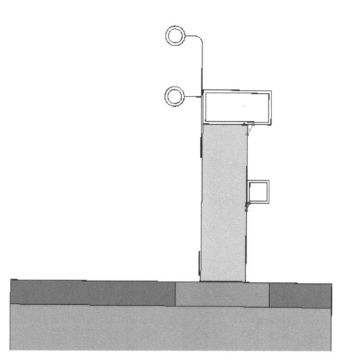

*Figure 60. Preliminary FE model of proposed MASH multifunctional barrier.*

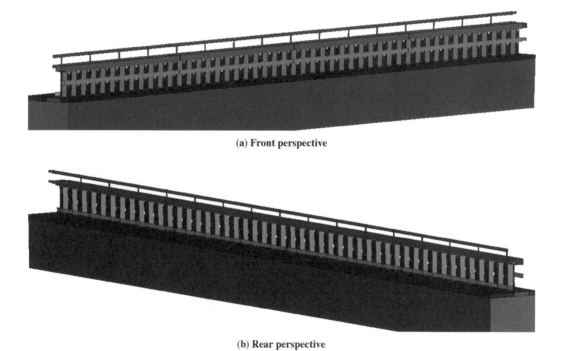

(a) Front perspective

(b) Rear perspective

*Figure 61. Different views of FE model proposed for MASH multifunctional barrier.*

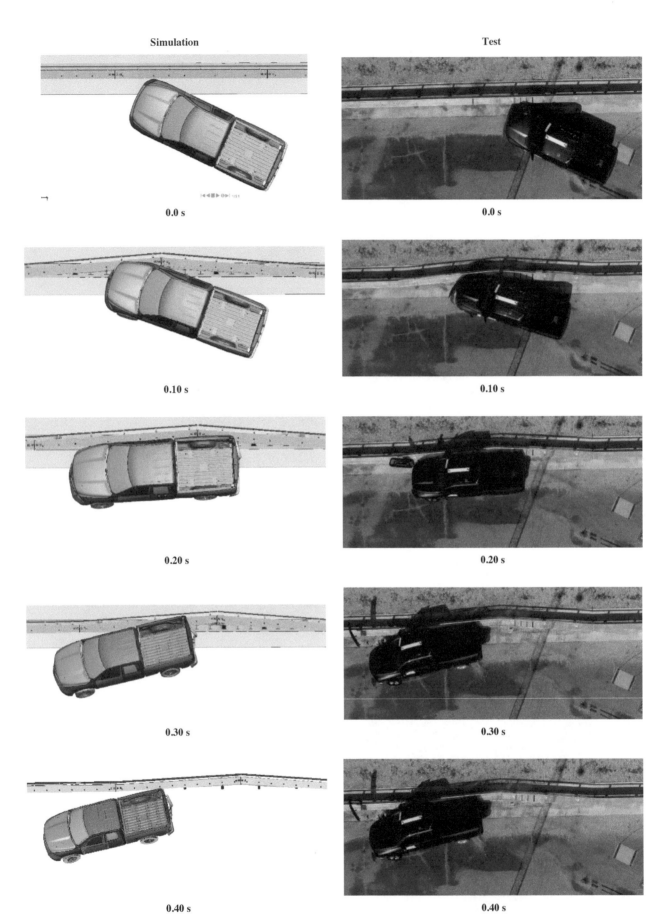

**Figure 62.** *Comparison of FE simulation and crash test results under MASH Test 3-11 (top view).*

Simulation                                    Test

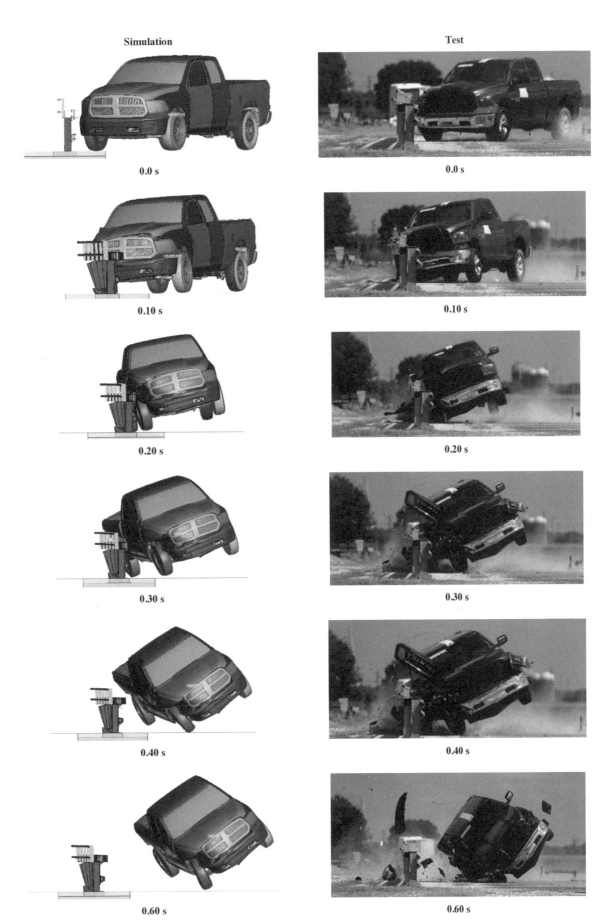

Figure 63.    Comparison of FE simulation and crash test results under MASH Test 3-11 (front view).

Table 40 shows the comparison of occupant risk factors associated with the crash test and the FE simulation. The FE model appeared to underpredict the maximum vehicle roll angle during the impact event, which was a finding that needed consideration when the simulations for the transition impact behavior were being revised. At the same time, the computer model seemed to overpredict the dynamic lateral deflection of a few inches.

On the basis of the results, the FE model of the LON multifunctional barrier was considered calibrated for the purpose of the transition investigation. This model was utilized in conjunction with the newly developed transition model design to conduct predictive simulations for system crashworthiness. The calibration of the LON model aided in the investigation of vehicles' snagging or pocketing potential due to differences in stiffness between the LON and the transition component.

**Table 40. Occupant risk factors comparison of crash test and FE simulation results under MASH Test 3-11.**

| Occupant Risk Factor | Actual Crash Test | FE Simulation |
|---|---|---|
| Impact point (ft) | | |
| Upstream of Post 17 | 1.6 | 1.6 |
| Upstream of splice | 4.4 | 4.4 |
| OIV (ft/s) | | |
| X | 14.0 | 14.3 |
| Y | 22.9 | 22.8 |
| Ridedown acceleration (g) | | |
| X | 5.6 | 4.6 |
| Y | 9.6 | 13.5 |
| Maximum angle (deg) | | |
| Roll | 46.3 | 27.4 |
| Pitch | 7.0 | 4.0 |
| Yaw | 38.7 | 41.9 |
| Maximum deflection (in.) | | |
| Dynamic | 16.0 | 21.3 |
| Permanent | 9.6 | 14.6 |

# CHAPTER 6

# Finite Element Analysis for Barrier System Design Option

This chapter provides details about the FE model developed to address the modifications discussed in the previous chapter. The overall modeling technique was the same as discussed in Chapter 5. Some changes were incorporated to optimize the model and make it more realistic. The CNRB connections between the posts and the rails were replaced with a bolted connection along with brackets. The details for the bolts and brackets were obtained from the drawings. The handrail was connected with the traffic rail via spot-weld connection. The cane rail with splice was attached to the posts with CNRBs.

Other modifications in the FE model design were as follows:

1. Post spacing was increased to 22 in., 44 in., and 66 in.
2. For the 22-in. post spacing options, the angle brackets used to connect the rails to the posts were at each post for the lower rub rail.
3. The spliced box sections for both the rails were replaced with simple plate splices with a thickness of 0.5 in.
4. The rub rail thickness was increased from ⅛ in. to ¼ in. after several preliminary simulations indicated vehicle instability issues due to a light rub rail section.

Figure 64 shows the updated FE model with the latest modifications for 22-in. post spacing. The model has a different handrail design than shown in the figure, however, as the handrail design was modified after preliminary simulations to further optimize it from the perspective of cost, fabrication, installation, and transportation. The researchers anticipated that such minor changes in the design would not interfere with the crashworthiness of the system. The remaining parts of the modeled design stayed the same as the final proposed options. Thus, the researchers anticipated that MASH test results would not be affected by the minor changes to the handrail design. Also, the new handrail design protrudes less outside the plane of vertical posts, which makes it more conservative with regard to deflection as compared with the simulation model. This chapter discusses the predictive simulations for MASH Tests 3-10 and 3-11 and presents the results.

## Predictive Simulations with LS-DYNA for MASH Test 3-11 on Developed Barrier Models

Simulations with the available pickup truck model were performed on the developed barrier with the different post spacing under consideration (22 in. and 44 in.).

### Simulations with 22-in. Post Spacing

To parametrically evaluate the barrier system, simulations with different impact points were performed. As discussed, MASH requires that full-scale crash tests be conducted at the critical

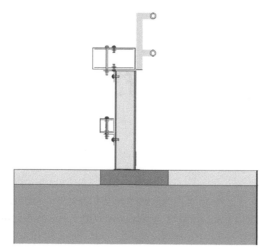

(a) Preliminary FE model of proposed MASH barrier

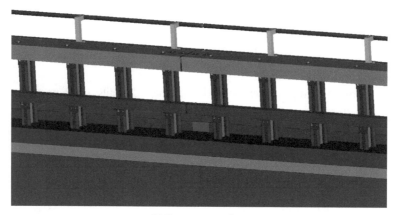

(b) Front perspective

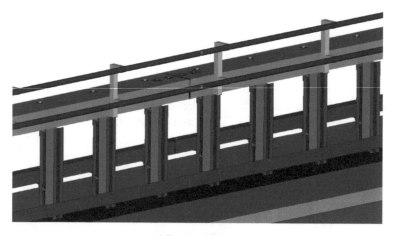

(c) Rear perspective

*Figure 64. Different views of the 22-in. post spacing for the MASH barrier.*

impact point (CIP) to maximize the potential that the crashworthiness of the system will fail. To determine the CIP for the system, different impact points are considered to evaluate the system within the range of tolerances. Simulations with a truck impacting at 2.3 ft, 4.3 ft, and 6.3 ft upstream of the splice were performed to parametrically evaluate the system. The distance of 4.3 ft corresponds to the CIP distance in MASH for Test 3-11 with the pickup truck for rigid barriers. Since the multifunction barrier is not rigid, the impact location was varied ±2 ft from this point to determine the appropriate CIP for the barrier. The results are shown in Figure 65. The postprocessing results for each simulation conducted are summarized in Table 41.

The results showed that all simulations satisfied the MASH limits for crashworthiness. Note that the MASH limit for stability (75 deg) is only applicable to roll and pitch. The TTI researchers

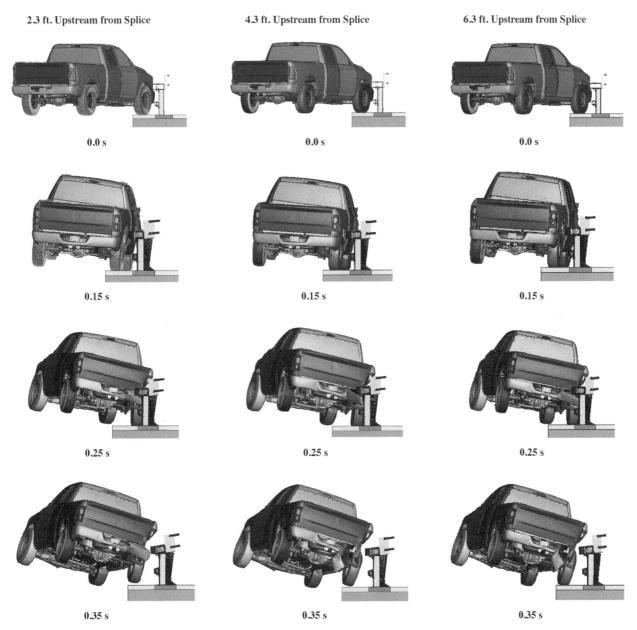

**2.3 ft. Upstream from Splice**  **4.3 ft. Upstream from Splice**  **6.3 ft. Upstream from Splice**

0.0 s   0.0 s   0.0 s

0.15 s   0.15 s   0.15 s

0.25 s   0.25 s   0.25 s

0.35 s   0.35 s   0.35 s

*Figure 65.   Sequential images of pickup truck impacting at 2.3 ft, 4.3 ft, and 6.3 ft upstream from the splice.*

**Table 41.  Summary table of MASH Test 3-11 CIP analysis (22 in.).**

| Variable | Measurement | MASH Limits |
|---|---|---|
| **2.3 ft Upstream from Splice** | | |
| Deflection (in.) | | |
| Handrail | 11.11 | N/A |
| Traffic rail | 10.71 | N/A |
| Rub rail | 7.44 | N/A |
| OIV (ft/s) | | |
| $X$ | 7.22 | 40 |
| $Y$ | 32.5 | 40 |
| Stability (deg) | | |
| Roll | 14.7 | 75 |
| Pitch | 11.3 | 75 |
| Yaw | 46.5 | — |
| Ridedown acceleration ($g$) | | |
| $X$ | 5.0 | 20.49 |
| $Y$ | 15.5 | 20.49 |
| **4.3 ft Upstream from Splice** | | |
| Deflection (in.) | | |
| Handrail | 10.67 | N/A |
| Traffic rail | 10.32 | N/A |
| Rub rail | 7.6 | N/A |
| OIV (ft/s) | | |
| $X$ | 5.91 | 40 |
| $Y$ | 30.51 | 40 |
| Stability (deg) | | |
| Roll | 14 | 75 |
| Pitch | 11.4 | 75 |
| Yaw | 57.5 | — |
| Ridedown acceleration ($g$) | | |
| $X$ | 5.4 | 20.49 |
| $Y$ | 15.5 | 20.49 |
| **6.3 ft Upstream from Splice** | | |
| Deflection (in.) | | |
| Handrail | 9.65 | N/A |
| Traffic rail | 9.33 | N/A |
| Rub rail | 6.5 | N/A |
| OIV (ft/s) | | |
| $X$ | 4.6 | 40 |
| $Y$ | 30.18 | 40 |
| Stability (deg) | | |
| Roll | 13.8 | 75 |
| Pitch | 16.2 | 75 |
| Yaw | 110.8 | — |
| Ridedown acceleration ($g$) | | |
| $X$ | 7.4 | 20.49 |
| $Y$ | 15 | 20.49 |

suggested the CIP for the pickup truck impacting the system be at 6.3 ft upstream of the splice of the rails for Test 3-11 (22 in.) after the deflection results, occupant risk results, and overall stability of the pickup truck in the predictive crash test simulations were compared.

## Simulations with 44-in. Post Spacing (with Smaller Rub Rail)

To parametrically evaluate the barrier system, simulations with different impact points were performed. Simulations with the truck impacting at 2.3 ft, 4.3 ft, and 6.3 ft upstream from the splice were performed.

The 44-in. option was simulated with the same size rub rail as the 22-in. option. However, preliminary simulations suggested the pickup truck rolling over in one of the CIP evaluation crash tests. Thus, researchers modified the bottom rub rail with a larger size to reduce tire interaction and prevent a higher roll angle of the truck. Simulation with the truck rollover is shown in Figure 66. The postprocessing results for each simulation conducted are summarized in Table 42.

Since preliminary simulations suggested the pickup truck rolling over in one of the CIP evaluation crash tests, researchers modified the bottom rub rail with a larger size to reduce tire interaction and prevent a higher roll angle of the truck. Even though the simulation results satisfied the MASH criteria for two of the impact points, one point failed the evaluation tests and, thus, per the MASH CIP recommendation, that would be the critical location for testing. The maximum dynamic deflection of 17 in. was obtained at the impact location of 2.3 ft upstream from the splice. This was higher than the preferred limit of 12 in. (1 ft). The permanent deflection in the same case was 12.3 in., which was close to the preferred limit of 12 in. (1 ft).

## Simulations with 44-in. Post Spacing with Modification (Larger Rub Rail)

As discussed in the previous section, the preliminary simulations suggested the pickup truck rolling over in one of the CIP evaluation crash tests. Thus, the researchers had to modify the bottom rub rail with a larger size to reduce tire interaction and prevent a higher roll angle of the truck. The results for the larger rub rail model with the truck impacting at 2.3 ft, 4.3 ft, and 6.3 ft upstream from the splice are shown in Figure 67. The postprocessing results for each simulation conducted are shown in Table 43.

Results show that all simulations satisfied the MASH limits for crashworthiness. Note that the MASH limit for stability (75 deg) is only applicable to roll and pitch. The maximum dynamic deflection of 16.6 in. was obtained at the impact location of 2.3 ft upstream from the splice. This was smaller than the desired deflection limit of 24 in. (2 ft) proposed by project panel members in the kickoff meeting, and it was higher than the preferred limit of 12 in. (1 ft). The permanent deflection in the same case was 12.1 in., which was very close to the preferred limit of 12 in. (1 ft). On the basis of the simulation results, the TTI researchers suggested the CIP for the pickup impacting the system at 4.3 ft upstream of the splice of the rails for Test 3-11 (44 in.) after the occupant risk results, deflection values, and overall stability of the truck in the crash test simulations were compared.

## Predictive Simulations with LS-DYNA for MASH Test 3-10 on Developed Barrier Models

Simulations with the available passenger car model were performed on the developed barrier with different post spacings under consideration (22 in. and 44 in.).

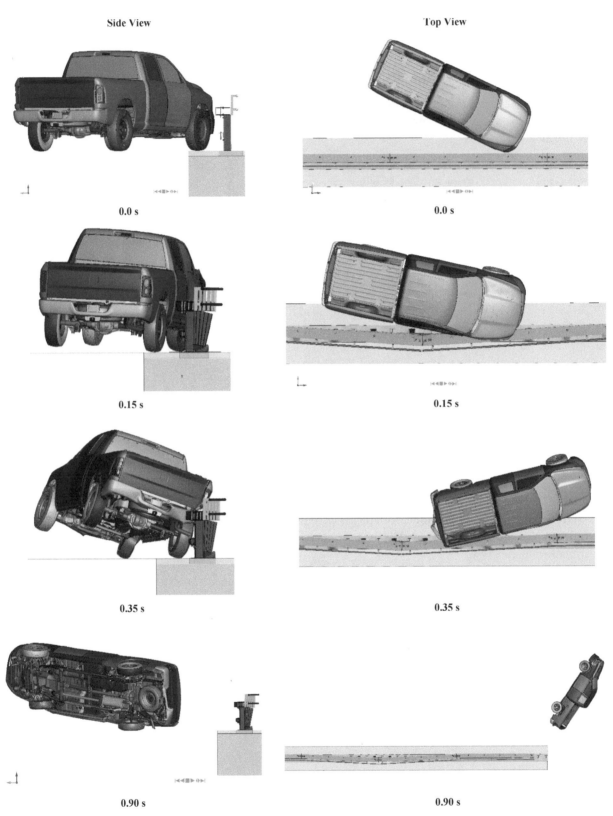

Side View          Top View

0.0 s          0.0 s

0.15 s          0.15 s

0.35 s          0.35 s

0.90 s          0.90 s

*Figure 66.   Sequential images of pickup truck impacting at 4.3 ft. upstream from splice (rollover case with smaller rub rail).*

**Table 42.   Summary table of MASH Test 3-11 CIP analysis (44 in. with smaller rub rail).**

| Variable | Measurement | MASH Limits |
|---|---|---|
| **2.3 ft Upstream from Splice** | | |
| Maximum deflection[a] (in.) | | |
|   Handrail | 17.0 (12.3) | N/A |
|   Traffic rail | 16.2 (11.9) | N/A |
|   Rub rail | 9.9 (7.7) | N/A |
| OIV (ft/s) | | |
|   X | 20.0 | 40 |
|   Y | 24.9 | 40 |
| Stability (deg) | | |
|   Roll | 14.4 | 75 |
|   Pitch | 3.2 | 75 |
|   Yaw | 47.8 | — |
| Ridedown acceleration (g) | | |
|   X | 6.8 | 20.49 |
|   Y | 12.0 | 20.49 |
| **4.3 ft Upstream from Splice** | | |
| Maximum deflection[a] (in.) | | |
|   Handrail | 15.9 (11.5) | N/A |
|   Traffic rail | 15.2 (11.2) | N/A |
|   Rub rail | 11.2 (7.9) | N/A |
| OIV (ft/s) | | |
|   X | 21.6 | 40 |
|   Y | 24.6 | 40 |
| Stability (deg) | | |
|   Roll | 80.4 (over limit) | 75 |
|   Pitch | 8.2 | 75 |
|   Yaw | 79.8 | — |
| Ridedown acceleration (g) | | |
|   X | 17.6 | 20.49 |
|   Y | 10.7 | 20.49 |
| **6.3 ft Upstream from Splice** | | |
| Maximum deflection[a] (in.) | | |
|   Handrail | 15.2 (11.1) | N/A |
|   Traffic rail | 14.4 (10.9) | N/A |
|   Rub rail | 9.6 (7.0) | N/A |

*(continued on next page)*

**Table 42.   (Continued).**

| Variable | Measurement | MASH Limits |
|---|---|---|
| OIV (ft/s) | | |
| X | 16.7 | 40 |
| Y | 21.7 | 40 |
| Stability (deg) | | |
| Roll | 26.4 | 75 |
| Pitch | 6.4 | 75 |
| Yaw | 98.9 | — |
| Ridedown acceleration ($g$) | | |
| X | 7.4 | 20.49 |
| Y | 12.6 | 20.49 |

[a]Permanent deflection is given in parentheses.

### Simulations with 22-in. Post Spacing

To parametrically evaluate the barrier system, simulations with different impact points were performed. Simulations with the car impacting at 1.6 ft, 3.6 ft, and 5.6 ft upstream from the splice were performed. The distance of 3.6 ft corresponds to the CIP distance in MASH for Test 3-10 with the passenger car for rigid barriers. Since the multifunction barrier is not rigid, the impact location was varied ±2 ft from this point to determine the appropriate CIP for the barrier. The results are shown in Figure 68. The postprocessing results for each simulation are summarized in Table 44.

The results show that all simulations satisfied the MASH limits for crashworthiness. On the basis of the simulation results, the TTI researchers suggested the CIP for the car impacting the system at 3.6 ft upstream of the splice of the rails for Test 3-10 (22 in.) after the occupant risk results and overall stability of the car in the crash test simulations were compared.

### Simulations with 44-in. Post Spacing

To parametrically evaluate the barrier system, simulations with different impact points were performed. Simulations with the car impacting at 1.6 ft, 3.6 ft, and 5.6 ft upstream from the splice were performed. The results are shown in Figure 69. The postprocessing results for each simulation conducted are summarized in Table 45.

The results show that all simulations satisfied the MASH limits for system crashworthiness. On the basis of the simulation results, the researchers suggested the CIP for the car impacting the system at 3.6 ft upstream of the splice of the rails for Test 3-10 (44 in.). The test article included a larger rub rail in the design for the 44-in. post spacing because the 44-in. post spacing with a small rub rail failed Test 3-11.

### Predictive Simulations for MASH Tests 3-10 and 3-11 on Barrier Models with 66-in. Post Spacing

Considering the results obtained from the tests of 22-in. and 44-in. post spacing, the researchers saw the opportunity to increase the post spacing and further optimize the design. For this purpose, the post spacing was increased to 66 in., and simulations were conducted to check the MASH limits along with maximum deflection requirements. This option would reduce the number of posts and connections, making the system much more cost effective as compared with previous options.

| 2.3 ft Upstream from Splice | 4.3 ft Upstream from Splice | 6.3 ft Upstream from Splice |
|:---:|:---:|:---:|

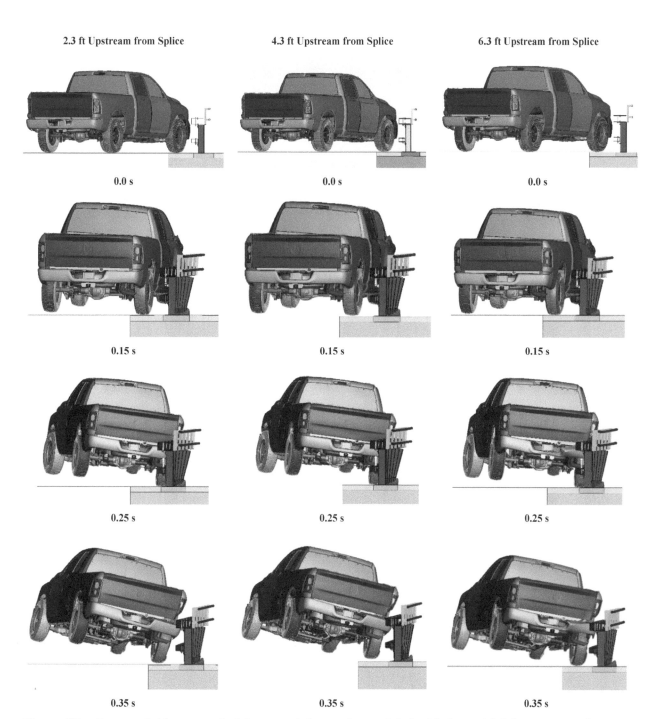

| 0.0 s | 0.0 s | 0.0 s |
|:---:|:---:|:---:|
| 0.15 s | 0.15 s | 0.15 s |
| 0.25 s | 0.25 s | 0.25 s |
| 0.35 s | 0.35 s | 0.35 s |

*Figure 67. Sequential images of pickup truck impacting at 2.3 ft, 4.3 ft, and 6.3 ft upstream from the splice.*

Table 43. Summary table of MASH Test 3-11 CIP analysis
(44 in. with larger rub rail).

| Variable | Measurement | MASH Limits |
|---|---|---|
| **2.3 ft Upstream from Splice** | | |
| Maximum deflection[a] (in.) | | |
| Handrail | 16.6 (12.1) | N/A |
| Traffic rail | 15.4 (11.7) | N/A |
| Rub rail | 10.4 (7.9) | N/A |

*(continued on next page)*

**Table 43. (Continued).**

| Variable | Measurement | MASH Limits |
|---|---|---|
| OIV (ft/s) | | |
| X | 20.0 | 40 |
| Y | 24.9 | 40 |
| Stability (deg) | | |
| Roll | 27.6 | 75 |
| Pitch | 4.6 | 75 |
| Yaw | 81.1 | — |
| Ridedown acceleration (g) | | |
| X | 7.0 | 20.49 |
| Y | 11.4 | 20.49 |
| **4.3 ft Upstream from Splice** | | |
| Maximum deflection[a] (in.) | | |
| Handrail | 16.1 (11.4) | N/A |
| Traffic rail | 15.3 (11.1) | N/A |
| Rub rail | 10.1 (7.5) | N/A |
| OIV (ft/s) | | |
| X | 19.4 | 40 |
| Y | 23.3 | 40 |
| Stability (deg) | | |
| Roll | 30.6 | 75 |
| Pitch | 4.5 | 75 |
| Yaw | 93.7 | — |
| Ridedown acceleration (g) | | |
| X | 5.0 | 20.49 |
| Y | 15.5 | 20.49 |
| **6.3 ft Upstream from Splice** | | |
| Maximum deflection[a] (in.) | | |
| Handrail | 15.0 (10.5) | N/A |
| Traffic rail | 14.4 (10.4) | N/A |
| Rub rail | 9.4 (6.9) | N/A |
| OIV (ft/s) | | |
| X | 17.7 | 40 |
| Y | 21.7 | 40 |
| Stability (deg) | | |
| Roll | 27.4 | 75 |
| Pitch | 5.4 | 75 |
| Yaw | 104.9 | — |
| Ridedown acceleration (g) | | |
| X | 6.6 | 20.49 |
| Y | 13.6 | 20.49 |

[a]Permanent deflection is given in parentheses.

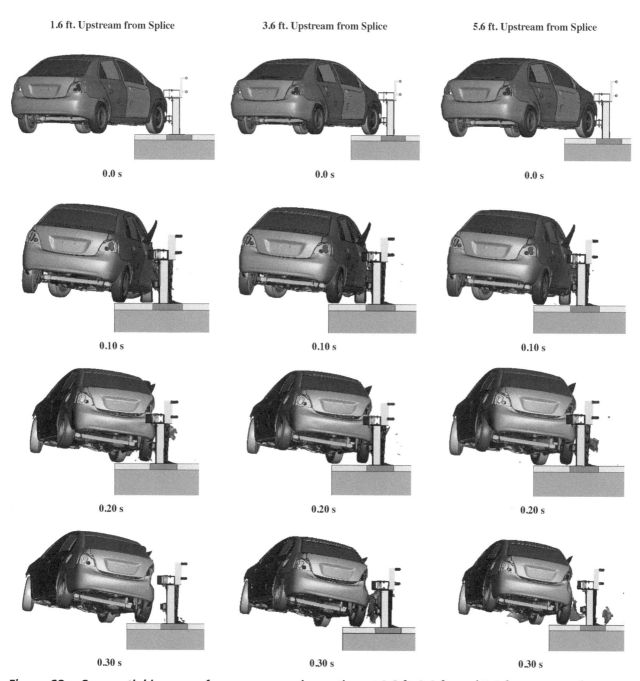

*Figure 68.    Sequential images of passenger car impacting at 1.6 ft, 3.6 ft, and 5.6 ft upstream from the splice.*

**Table 44.  Summary Table of MASH Test 3-10 CIP Analysis (22 in.).**

| Variable | Measurement | MASH Limits |
|---|---|---|
| **1.6 ft Upstream from Splice** | | |
| Deflection (in.) | | |
|   Handrail | 5.32 | N/A |
|   Traffic rail | 5.08 | N/A |
|   Rub rail | 3.98 | N/A |
| OIV (ft/s) | | |
|   $X$ | 23.62 | 40 |
|   $Y$ | 32.15 | 40 |
| Stability (deg) | | |
|   Roll | 9.9 | 75 |
|   Pitch | 2.2 | 75 |
|   Yaw | 39.4 | — |
| Ridedown acceleration ($g$) | | |
|   $X$ | 10.6 | 20.49 |
|   $Y$ | 9.6 | 20.49 |
| **3.6 ft Upstream from Splice** | | |
| Deflection (in.) | | |
|   Handrail | 4.84 | N/A |
|   Traffic rail | 4.69 | N/A |
|   Rub rail | 3.67 | N/A |
| OIV (ft/s) | | |
|   $X$ | 23.29 | 40 |
|   $Y$ | 32.15 | 40 |
| Stability (deg) | | |
|   Roll | 10.7 | 75 |
|   Pitch | 1.8 | 75 |
|   Yaw | 38.8 | — |
| Ridedown acceleration ($g$) | | |
|   $X$ | 10.2 | 20.49 |
|   $Y$ | 9.5 | 20.49 |
| **5.6 ft Upstream from Splice** | | |
| Deflection (in.) | | |
|   Handrail | 4.53 | N/A |
|   Traffic rail | 4.25 | N/A |
|   Rub rail | 2.96 | N/A |
| OIV (ft/s) | | |
|   $X$ | 22.96 | 40 |
|   $Y$ | 32.15 | 40 |
| Stability (deg) | | |
|   Roll | 9.3 | 75 |
|   Pitch | 1.8 | 75 |
|   Yaw | 36 | — |
| Ridedown acceleration ($g$) | | |
|   $X$ | 7.4 | 20.49 |
|   $Y$ | 9.9 | 20.49 |

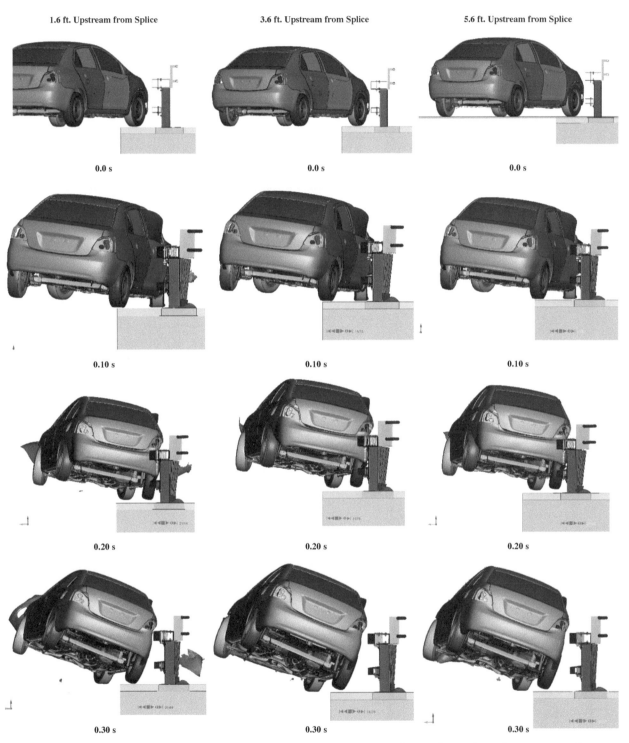

*Figure 69.    Sequential images of passenger car impacting at 1.6 ft, 3.6 ft, and 5.6 ft upstream from the splice.*

**Table 45.    Summary table of MASH Test 3-10 CIP analysis (44 in.).**

| Variable | Measurement | MASH Limits |
|---|---|---|
| **1.6 ft Upstream from Splice** | | |
| Maximum deflection[a] (in.) | | |
| Handrail | 7.6 (4.5) | N/A |
| Traffic rail | 7.2 (4.3) | N/A |
| Rub rail | 5.2 (3.0) | N/A |
| OIV (ft/s) | | |
| $X$ | 19.0 | 40 |
| $Y$ | 27.2 | 40 |
| Stability (deg) | | |
| Roll | 24.9 | 75 |
| Pitch | 2.4 | 75 |
| Yaw | 34 | — |
| Ridedown acceleration ($g$) | | |
| $X$ | 6.6 | 20.49 |
| $Y$ | 12.3 | 20.49 |
| **3.6 ft Upstream from Splice** | | |
| Maximum deflection[a] (in.) | | |
| Handrail | 7.0 (3.9) | N/A |
| Traffic rail | 6.7 (3.7) | N/A |
| Rub rail | 4.4 (2.5) | N/A |
| OIV (ft/s) | | |
| $X$ | 19.0 | 40 |
| $Y$ | 26.2 | 40 |
| Stability (deg) | | |
| Roll | 21.1 | 75 |
| Pitch | 2.4 | 75 |
| Yaw | 32.9 | — |
| Ridedown acceleration ($g$) | | |
| $X$ | 5.5 | 20.49 |
| $Y$ | 13.7 | 20.49 |
| **5.6 ft Upstream from Splice** | | |
| Maximum deflection[a] (in.) | | |
| Handrail | 7.8 (4.8) | N/A |
| Traffic rail | 7.6 (4.5) | N/A |
| Rub rail | 5.6 (3.4) | N/A |

**Table 45.  (Continued).**

| Variable | Measurement | MASH Limits |
|---|---|---|
| OIV (ft/s) | | |
| X | 20.7 | 40 |
| Y | 27.9 | 40 |
| Stability (deg) | | |
| Roll | 23.4 | 75 |
| Pitch | 1.8 | 75 |
| Yaw | 35.6 | — |
| Ridedown acceleration (g) | | |
| X | 6.2 | 20.49 |
| Y | 11.3 | 20.49 |

[a]Permanent deflection is given in parentheses.

## MASH Test 3-11 Simulations with 66-in. Post Spacing

To parametrically evaluate the barrier system, simulations with different impact points were performed. Simulations with the truck impacting at 2.3 ft, 4.3 ft, and 6.3 ft upstream from the splice were performed. These impact distances were selected for the pickup in consideration of the CIP distance for rigid barriers in MASH, as previously discussed. The results are shown in Figure 70.

The postprocessing values for all three simulations indicated stable behavior of the truck, with values well within the MASH limits. The maximum dynamic deflection of 23.54 in. was obtained at the impact location of 4.3 ft upstream from the splice. This was very close to the desired deflection limit of 24 in. (2 ft) and much higher than the preferred limit of 12 in. (1 ft). The permanent deflection in the same case was 16.38 in., which again was more than the preferred limit of 12 in. (1 ft).

## MASH Test 3-10 Simulations with 66-in. Post Spacing

To parametrically evaluate the barrier system, simulations with different impact points were performed, as recommended by MASH (starting with recommendations from Table 2-6 in MASH). Simulations with the Toyota Yaris impacting at 1.6 ft, 3.6 ft, and 5.6 ft upstream from the splice were performed. These impact distances were selected for the passenger car in consideration of the CIP distance for rigid barriers in MASH, as previously discussed. The results are shown in Figure 71.

The postprocessing values for all three simulations indicated stable behavior of the Yaris, with values well within the MASH limits. The maximum dynamic deflection of 11.0 in. was obtained at the impact location of 5.6 ft upstream from the splice. This was less than the preferred limit of 12 in. (1 ft). The permanent deflection in the same case was 4.2 in., which was less than half of the preferred limit of 12 in. (1 ft).

## Conclusions

The researchers evaluated three similar barrier design options that varied predominantly with regard to post spacing (i.e., 22 in., 44 in., and 66 in.). These three variations were proposed to obtain recommendations, if any, from the project panel regarding the system that best addressed its needs. The post spacing was increased to allow the design to be more economical from the perspective of installation, fabrication, transportation, and feasibility while still maintaining the structural ability

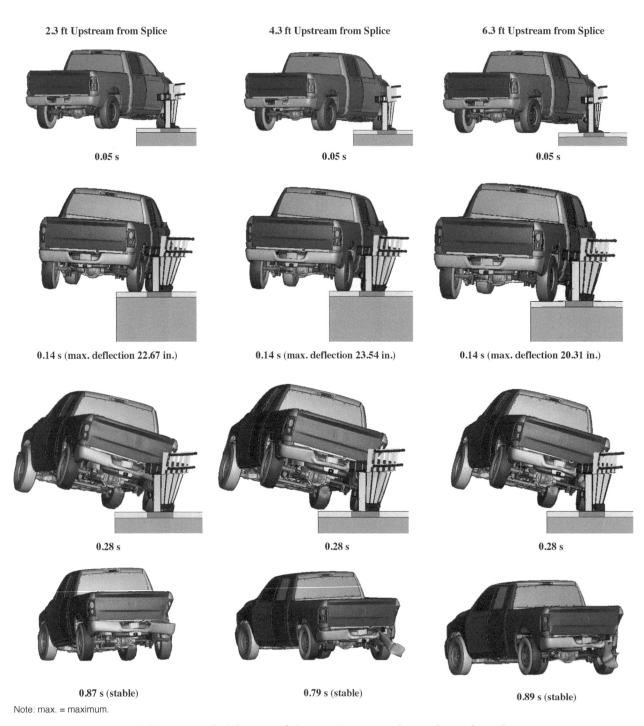

**2.3 ft Upstream from Splice**     **4.3 ft Upstream from Splice**     **6.3 ft Upstream from Splice**

0.05 s     0.05 s     0.05 s

0.14 s (max. deflection 22.67 in.)     0.14 s (max. deflection 23.54 in.)     0.14 s (max. deflection 20.31 in.)

0.28 s     0.28 s     0.28 s

0.87 s (stable)     0.79 s (stable)     0.89 s (stable)

Note: max. = maximum.

*Figure 70.   Sequential images of pickup truck impacting at 2.3 ft, 4.3 ft, and 6.3 ft upstream from splice.*

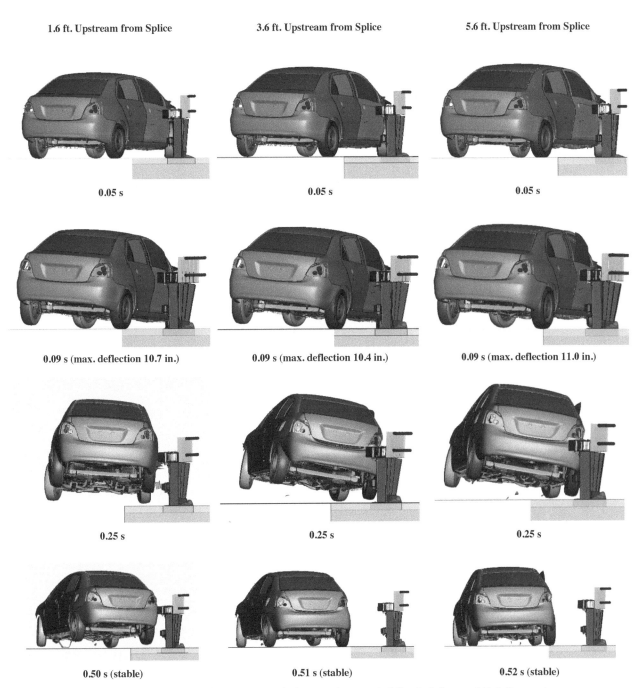

**Figure 71.  Sequential images of Toyota Yaris impacting at 1.6 ft., 3.6 ft., and 5.6 ft. upstream from splice.**

to contain and redirect an errant vehicle and meet the crashworthiness requirements. Closer post spacing would yield lower maximum deflection values, resulting in a more conservative design for pedestrian and bicyclist safety. The handrail design was optimized to address construction, installation, repair, and aesthetic criteria. When revising the FE predictive simulations, the researchers also gave special consideration to the maximum system deflection (including handrails) during impact, the preferred value of which was set by the project panel to be less than 24 in.

On the basis of the simulation results, the TTI researchers suggested the CIP for the car and pickup truck impacting the system for each of the proposed design options. The CIPs were suggested after the occupant risk results, deflection values, and overall stability of the vehicle in the crash test simulations were compared. Table 46 summarizes the simulation results for all the design options.

**Table 46.  Summary table for MASH testing of the three investigated designs.**

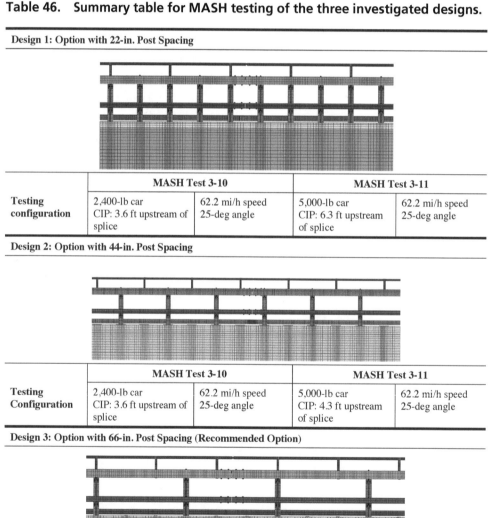

**Design 1: Option with 22-in. Post Spacing**

| Testing configuration | MASH Test 3-10 | | MASH Test 3-11 | |
|---|---|---|---|---|
| | 2,400-lb car CIP: 3.6 ft upstream of splice | 62.2 mi/h speed 25-deg angle | 5,000-lb car CIP: 6.3 ft upstream of splice | 62.2 mi/h speed 25-deg angle |

**Design 2: Option with 44-in. Post Spacing**

| Testing Configuration | MASH Test 3-10 | | MASH Test 3-11 | |
|---|---|---|---|---|
| | 2,400-lb car CIP: 3.6 ft upstream of splice | 62.2 mi/h speed 25-deg angle | 5,000-lb car CIP: 4.3 ft upstream of splice | 62.2 mi/h speed 25-deg angle |

**Design 3: Option with 66-in. Post Spacing (Recommended Option)**

| Testing Configuration | MASH Test 3-10 | | MASH Test 3-11 | |
|---|---|---|---|---|
| | 2,400-lb car CIP: 5.6 ft upstream of splice | 62.2 mi/h speed 25-deg angle | 5,000-lb car CIP: 4.3 ft upstream of splice | 62.2 mi/h speed 25-deg angle |

The researchers recommended the 66-in. post spacing option for construction and full-scale crash testing according to MASH TL-3 high-speed conditions. This proposed option maximizes the cost efficiency for system construction while maintaining all performance requirements and preferences specified by the project panel, such as lateral deflection. A three-dimensional rendering of the recommended system is provided in Figure 72.

(a) **Traffic side view**                    (b) **Field side view**

*Figure 72.    Visualization of three-dimensional perspective views of the system with 66-in. post spacing.*

# System Details for MASH 3-10 and 3-11 Tests

## Test Article and Installation Details

The length of the test installation was 185 ft 7½ in. and consisted of a traffic rail and rub rail on the traffic side and pedestrian rails on the field side. Each end of the installation was anchored with a steel post W-beam cable anchorage system that was approximately 9 ft 4 in. long. The traffic rail was constructed of an HSS with dimensions of $12 \times 6 \times ¼$ in. with its top located 32 in. above grade. The rub rail was an HSS with dimensions of $4 \times 4 \times ¼$ in. with its top located 13 in. above grade. The rails were supported by W6 × 8.5 posts spaced at 66 in. on center.

Two field side handrails were fabricated of HSS tubing 1.90 in. in diameter by 0.145 in. thick. Their centers were located 35 in. and 41 in. above grade. A cane rail, also on the field side, was fabricated of 11 gauge 4-in.-wide plate with its bottom edge 1 in. above grade.

The posts were set in a 19-in.-wide, 4-in.-thick continuous area of low-strength grout with 24-in.-wide, 4-in.-thick concrete slabs on both sides. The traffic side faces of the posts were 4 in. from the joint between the concrete and grout.

Figure 73 presents overall information on the multifunctional barrier, and Figure 74 provides photographs of the installation. Appendix B provides further details on the multifunctional rail. Drawings were provided by the TTI Proving Ground, and construction was performed by MBC Management and supervised by TTI Proving Ground personnel.

## Design Modifications During Tests

No modifications were made to the installation during the testing phase.

## Material Specifications

Appendix I provides material certification documents for the materials used to install and construct the multifunctional barrier. Table 47 shows the average compressive strength of the concrete.

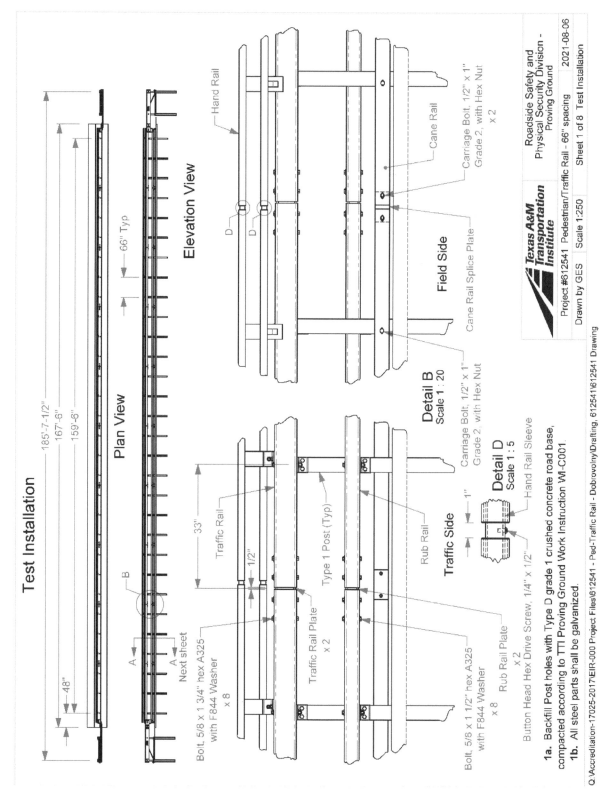

**Figure 73. Details of the multifunctional barrier.**

*Figure 74.    Multifunctional barrier prior to testing.*

**Table 47.  Concrete strength.**

| Location | Design Strength (psi) | Average Strength (psi) | Age (days) | Detailed Location |
|---|---|---|---|---|
| Concrete | 2,000 | 5,030 | 77 | Traffic and field side concrete |
| Grout | 100–220 | 170 | 21 | All grout for first test |
| Grout | 100–220 | 160 | 17 | Grout for Posts 15 through 20 for second test |

## Soil Conditions

The test installation was installed in standard soil meeting Type 1 Grade D of AASHTO standard specification M147-17 "Materials for Aggregate and Soil Aggregate Subbase, Base, and Surface Courses." In accordance with Appendix B of MASH, the soil strength was measured the day of the crash test. During installation of the multifunctional barrier for full-scale crash testing, two 6-ft-long W6 × 16 posts were installed in the immediate vicinity of the multifunctional barrier with the same fill materials and installation procedures used in the test installation and the standard dynamic test. Table I.1 in Appendix I presents minimum soil strength properties established through the dynamic testing performed in accordance with MASH Appendix B.

The minimum post loads are shown in Table 48 and Table 49. Table 48 shows the loads on the posts at the specified deflections on the day of Test 3-10, September 14, 2021. The backfill material in which the multifunctional barrier was installed met the minimum MASH requirements for soil strength. Table 49 shows the loads on the posts at the specified deflections on the day of Test 3-11, August 24, 2021. The backfill material in which the multifunctional barrier was installed met the minimum MASH requirements for soil strength.

**Table 48.  Soil strength for Test 3-10 (Test 612541-01-2).**

| Displacement (in.) | Post Load (lb) | |
|---|---|---|
| | Minimum | Actual |
| 5 | 4,420 | 10,575 |
| 10 | 4,981 | 11,090 |
| 15 | 5,282 | 10,454 |

**Table 49.  Soil strength for Test 3-11 (Test 612541-01-1).**

| Displacement (in.) | Post Load (lb) | |
|---|---|---|
| | Minimum | Actual |
| 5 | 4,420 | 7,484 |
| 10 | 4,981 | 8,212 |
| 15 | 5,282 | 8,424 |

# Test Requirements and Evaluation Criteria for MASH 3-10 and 3-11 Tests

## Performed Crash Test Matrix

Table 50 shows the test conditions and evaluation criteria for MASH TL-3 for longitudinal barriers. The target CIPs for each test were determined on the basis of the FE simulations described in Chapter 6 and the information provided in MASH Section 2.2.1 and Section 2.3.2. Figure 75 shows the target CIP for MASH Tests 3-10 and 3-11 on the multifunctional barrier. The crash tests and data analysis procedures were in accordance with guidelines presented in MASH. Chapter 9 of this report presents brief descriptions of these procedures.

**Table 50. Test conditions and evaluation criteria specified for MASH TL-3 longitudinal barriers.**

| Test Designation | Test Vehicle | Impact Conditions | | Evaluation Criteria[a] |
| --- | --- | --- | --- | --- |
| | | Speed (mi/h) | Angle (deg) | |
| 3-10 | 1100C | 62 | 25 | A, D, F, H, I |
| 3-11 | 2270P | 62 | 25 | A, D, F, H, I |

[a]Details on the evaluation criteria are given in Table 51.

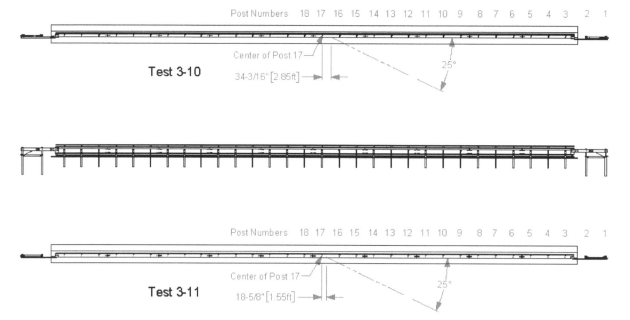

*Figure 75. Target CIP for MASH TL-3 tests on multifunctional barrier.*

# Evaluation Criteria

The appropriate safety evaluation criteria from Tables 2.2 and 5.1 of MASH were used to evaluate the crash tests reported herein. Table 50 lists the test conditions and evaluation criteria required for MASH TL-3, and Table 51 provides detailed information on the evaluation criteria.

**Table 51.  Evaluation criteria required for MASH testing.**

| Evaluation Factor | Evaluation Criteria |
|---|---|
| Structural adequacy | A.  Test article should contain and redirect the vehicle or bring the vehicle to a controlled stop; the vehicle should not penetrate, underride, or override the installation, although controlled lateral deflection of the test article is acceptable. |
| Occupant risk | D.  Detached elements, fragments, or other debris from the test article should not penetrate or show potential for penetrating the occupant compartment or present undue hazard to other traffic, pedestrians, or personnel in a work zone.<br><br>Deformations of, or intrusions into, the occupant compartment should not exceed limits set forth in Section 5.2.2 and Appendix E of MASH. |
|  | F.  The vehicle should remain upright during and after collision. The maximum roll and pitch angles are not to exceed 75 deg. |
|  | H.  Occupant impact velocities (OIVs) should satisfy the following limits: preferred value of 30 ft/s or maximum allowable value of 40 ft/s. |
|  | I.  The occupant ridedown accelerations should satisfy the following limits: preferred value of 15.0 $g$, or maximum allowable value of 20.49 $g$. |

CHAPTER 9

# Test Conditions

## Test Facility

The full-scale crash tests reported herein were performed at the TTI Proving Ground, an International Organization for Standardization (ISO)/International Electrotechnical Commission (IEC) 17025–accredited laboratory with American Association for Laboratory Accreditation (A2LA) Mechanical Testing Certificate 2821.01. The full-scale crash tests were performed according to TTI Proving Ground quality procedures as well as MASH guidelines and standards.

The test facilities of the TTI Proving Ground are located on the RELLIS Campus of the Texas A&M University System, which consists of a 2,000-acre complex of research and training facilities situated 10 mi northwest of the flagship campus of Texas A&M University. The site, formerly a U.S. Army Air Corps base, has large expanses of concrete runways and parking aprons well suited to experimental research and testing in the areas of vehicle performance and handling, vehicle–roadway interaction, highway pavement durability and efficacy, and roadside safety hardware and perimeter protective device evaluation. The site selected for construction and testing is along the edge of an out-of-service apron/runway. The apron/runway consists of an unreinforced jointed-concrete pavement in 12.5- × 15-ft blocks nominally 6 in. deep. The aprons were built in 1942, and the joints have some displacement but are otherwise flat and level.

## Vehicle Tow and Guidance System

For the testing utilizing the 1100C and 2270P vehicles, each vehicle was towed into the test installation with a steel cable guidance and reverse tow system. A steel cable for guiding the test vehicle was tensioned along the path, anchored at each end, and threaded through an attachment to the front wheel of the test vehicle. An additional steel cable was connected to the test vehicle, passed around a pulley near the impact point and through a pulley on the tow vehicle, and then anchored to the ground, such that the tow vehicle moved away from the test site. A 2:1 speed ratio between the test and tow vehicle existed with this system. Just prior to impact with the installation, the test vehicle was released and ran unrestrained. The vehicle remained freewheeling (i.e., no steering or braking inputs) until it cleared the immediate area of the test site.

## Data Acquisition Systems

### Vehicle Instrumentation and Data Processing

Each test vehicle was instrumented with a self-contained onboard data acquisition system (DAS). The signal conditioning and acquisition system was a multichannel DAS produced by Diversified Technical Systems Inc. The accelerometers, which measure the $x$, $y$, and $z$ axes of vehicle acceleration, were strain gauge type with linear millivolt output proportional to acceleration. The angular rate sensors measuring vehicle roll, pitch, and yaw rates were ultra-small, solid-state units designed for crash test service. The data acquisition hardware and software conformed to the latest SAE J211, Instrumentation for Impact Test. Each of the channels was capable of providing precision amplification, scaling, and filtering based on transducer specifications and calibrations. During the test, data were recorded from each channel at a rate of 10,000 samples per second with a resolution of one part in 65,536. Once data were recorded, internal batteries backed these up inside the unit in case the primary battery cable were to be severed. Initial contact of the pressure switch on the vehicle bumper provided a time zero mark and initiated the recording process. After each test, the data were downloaded from the DAS unit into a laptop computer at the test site. The TRAP software then processed the raw data to produce detailed reports of the test results.

Each DAS is returned to the factory annually for complete recalibration and to ensure that all instrumentation used in the vehicle conforms to the specifications outlined by SAE J211. All accelerometers are calibrated annually by means of an Endevco® 2901 precision primary vibration standard. This standard and its support instruments are checked annually and receive a National Institute of Standards Technology (NIST) traceable calibration. The rate transducers used in the data acquisition system receive calibration via a Genisco Rate-of-Turn Table. The subsystems of each data channel are also evaluated annually with instruments with current NIST traceability, and the results are factored into the accuracy of the total data channel per SAE J211. Calibrations and evaluations are also made any time data are suspect. Acceleration data are measured with an expanded uncertainty of ±1.7% at a confidence factor of 95% ($k = 2$).

TRAP uses the DAS-captured data to compute the occupant/compartment impact velocities, time of occupant/compartment impact after vehicle impact, and highest 10-millisecond (ms) average ridedown acceleration. TRAP calculates change in vehicle velocity at the end of a given impulse period. In addition, maximum average accelerations over 50-ms intervals in each of the three directions are computed. For reporting purposes, the data from the vehicle-mounted accelerometers are filtered with an SAE Class 180-Hz low-pass digital filter, and acceleration versus time curves for the longitudinal, lateral, and vertical directions are plotted with TRAP.

TRAP uses the data from the yaw, pitch, and roll rate transducers to compute angular displacement in degrees at 0.0001-s intervals and then plots yaw, pitch, and roll versus time. These displacements are in reference to the vehicle-fixed coordinate system with the initial position and orientation being initial impact. The rate of rotation data is measured with an expanded uncertainty of ±0.7% at a confidence factor of 95 percent ($k = 2$).

## Anthropomorphic Dummy Instrumentation

An Alderson Research Laboratories Hybrid II, 50th-percentile male anthropomorphic dummy restrained with lap and shoulder belts was placed in the front seat on the impact side of the 1100C vehicle. The dummy was not instrumented.

According to MASH, use of a dummy in the 2270P vehicle is optional. However, MASH recommends that a dummy be used when testing "any Longitudinal Barrier with a height greater than or equal to 33 in." More specifically, use of the dummy in the 2270P vehicle is recommended for tall rails to evaluate the "potential for an occupant to extend out of the vehicle and come into direct contact with the test article." Although this information is reported, it is not part of the performance evaluation of the impact. Since the rail height of the multifunctional barrier was 41 in., a dummy was placed in the front seat of the 2270P vehicle on the impact side and restrained with lap and shoulder belts.

## Photographic Instrumentation Data Processing

Photographic coverage of each test included three digital high-speed cameras:

- One located overhead with a field of view perpendicular to the ground and directly over the impact point,
- One placed upstream from the installation at an angle to have a field of view of the interaction of the rear of the vehicle with the installation, and
- A third placed with a field of view parallel to and aligned with the installation at the down-stream end.

A flashbulb on the impacting vehicle was activated by a pressure-sensitive tape switch to indicate the instant of contact with the installation. The flashbulb was visible from each camera. The video files from these digital high-speed cameras were analyzed to observe phenomena occurring during the collision and to obtain time event, displacement, and angular data. A digital camera recorded and documented the conditions of each test vehicle and the installation before and after the test.

# CHAPTER 10

# MASH Test 3-10 (Crash Test 612541-01-2)

## Test Designation and Actual Impact Conditions

The impact conditions and exit parameters for MASH Test 3-10 (Crash Test 612541-01-2) are reported in Table 52 and Table 53, respectively. Figure 76 and Figure 77 depict the target impact setup.

## Weather Conditions

Table 54 provides the weather conditions for Crash Test 612541-01-2.

**Table 52. Impact conditions for MASH Test 3-10 (Crash Test 612541-01-2).**

| Test Parameter | Specification | Tolerance | Measured |
|---|---|---|---|
| Impact speed (mi/h) | 62 | ±2.5 | 63.7 |
| Impact angle (deg) | 25 | ±1.5 | 25.5 |
| Impact severity (kip-ft) | 51 | ≥51 | 61.4 |
| Impact location [distance (ft) upstream of centerline of Post 17] | 2.85 | ±1 | 3.1 |

**Table 53. Exit parameters for MASH Test 3-10 (Crash Test 612541-01-2).**

| Exit Parameter | Measured |
|---|---|
| Speed (mi/h) | 53.3 |
| Trajectory (deg) | 11 |
| Heading (deg) | 11 |
| Brakes applied post impact (s) | 2.1 |
| Vehicle at rest position | 311 ft downstream of impact point<br>34 ft to the traffic side<br>2 deg left |
| Comments | Vehicle remained upright and stable.<br>Vehicle crossed the exit box[a] at 75 ft downstream from loss of contact and satisfied the exit box criteria described in MASH. |

[a]Not less than 32.8 ft downstream from loss of contact for cars and pickups is optimal.

*Figure 76. Pedestrian traffic rail/test vehicle geometrics for Crash Test 612541-01-2.*

*Figure 77. Pedestrian traffic rail/test vehicle impact location for Crash Test 612541-01-2.*

**Table 54. Weather conditions for Crash Test 612541-01-2 (2021-09-14, AM).**

| Condition | Measurement |
|---|---|
| Wind speed (mi/h) | 12 |
| Wind direction (deg) | 47 |
| Temperature (°F) | 75 |
| Relative humidity (%) | 88 |
| Vehicle traveling (deg) | 195 |

## Test Vehicle

Figure 78 and Figure 79 show the 2015 Nissan Versa used for the crash test. Table 55 shows the vehicle measurements. Table C.1 in Appendix C, Section C.1, gives additional dimensions and information about the vehicle.

## Test Description

Table 56 lists events that occurred during Crash Test 612541-01-2. Figures C.1 and C.2 in Appendix C, Section C.2, present sequential photographs during the test.

## Damage to Test Installation

The rails were scuffed at the location of the impact and downstream of the impact. Maximum permanent deflection was 2.3 in. at the joint between Posts 17 and 18. The soil was disturbed at Post 1, there was significant grout damage between Posts 17 and 18, and there was slight separation between the grout and concrete on the traffic and field sides from Posts 14 to 21.

*Figure 78. Impact side of test vehicle before Crash Test 612541-01-2.*

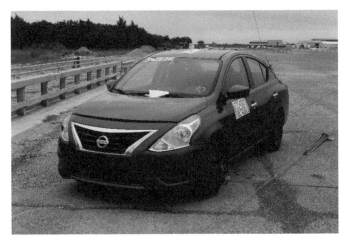

*Figure 79. Opposite of the impact side of the test vehicle before Crash Test 612541-01-2.*

**Table 55.  Vehicle measurements for Crash Test 612541-01-2.**

| Test Parameter | MASH | Allowed Tolerance | Measured |
|---|---|---|---|
| Dummy (if applicable)[a] (lb) | 165 | N/A | 165 |
| Inertial weight (lb) | 2,420 | ±55 | 2,443 |
| Gross static[a] (lb) | 2,585 | ±55 | 2,608 |
| Wheelbase (in.) | 98 | ±5 | 102.4 |
| Front overhang (in.) | 35 | ±4 | 32.5 |
| Overall length (in.) | 169 | ±8 | 175.4 |
| Overall width (in.) | 65 | ±3 | 66.7 |
| Hood height (in.) | 28 | ±4 | 30.5 |
| Track width[b] (in.) | 59 | ±2 | 58.4 |
| CG aft of front axle[c] (in.) | 39 | ±4 | 41.1 |
| CG above ground[c,d] (in.) | N/A | N/A | N/A |

[a]If a dummy is used, the gross static vehicle mass includes the mass of the dummy.
[b]Average of front and rear axles.
[c]For test inertial mass.
[d]2270P vehicle must meet minimum CG height requirement.

**Table 56.  Events during Crash Test 612541-01-2.**

| Time (s) | Event |
|---|---|
| 0.0000 | Vehicle impacted the installation. |
| 0.0130 | Vehicle began to redirect. |
| 0.0263 | Post 17 began to move toward field side due to contact with front bumper. |
| 0.1530 | Vehicle was parallel with installation. |
| 0.1650 | Rail began to move back toward field side due to rear bumper contact. |
| 0.2920 | Vehicle exited the installation at 53.3 mi/h with a heading of 11 deg and trajectory of 11 deg. |

Table 57 presents the data on the post displacement and lean. Table 58 describes the deflection and working width of the multifunctional barrier. Figure 80 and Figure 81 show the damage to the multifunctional barrier.

## Damage to Test Vehicle

Figure 82 and Figure 83 show the damage sustained by the vehicle. Figure 84 and Figure 85 show the interior of the vehicle after the test. Table 59 and Table 60 provide details on the occupant compartment deformation and exterior vehicle damage, respectively. Tables C.2 and C.3 in Appendix C, Section C.1, provide exterior crush and occupant compartment measurements, respectively.

**Table 57.  Post displacement details for multifunctional barrier for Crash Test 612541-01-2.**

| Post | Soil Gap (in.) | | Lean from Vertical Toward Field Side (deg) |
|---|---|---|---|
| | Traffic Side | Field Side | |
| 16 | ¼ | ½ | 2 |
| 17 | ¼ | 1¼ | 9 |
| 18 | ½ | 1¼ | 8 |
| 19 | ¼ | ⅜ | 7 |

**Table 58. Deflection and working width of the multifunctional barrier for Crash Test 612541-01-2.**

| Test Parameter | Measured |
|---|---|
| Permanent deflection/location (in.) | 2.3 toward field side, at the joint between Posts 17 and 18 |
| Dynamic deflection (in.) | 8.4 toward field side |
| Working width[a] and height (in.) | 24.1 at a height of 35 in. |

[a]Per MASH, "The working width is the maximum dynamic lateral position of any major part of the system or vehicle. These measurements are all relative to the preimpact traffic face of the test article." In other words, the working width is the total barrier width plus the maximum dynamic intrusion of any portion of the barrier or test vehicle past the field side edge of the barrier.

*Figure 80. Multifunctional barrier at impact location after Crash Test 612541-01-2.*

*Figure 81. In-line view of the multifunctional barrier after Crash Test 612541-01-2.*

*Figure 82. Impact side of test vehicle after Crash Test 612541-01-2.*

*Figure 83. Rear impact side of test vehicle after Crash Test 612541-01-2.*

*Figure 84. Overall interior of test vehicle after Crash Test 612541-01-2.*

*Figure 85. Interior of test vehicle on impact side after Crash Test 612541-01-2.*

**Table 59. Occupant compartment deformation in Crash Test 612541-01-2.**

| Test Parameter | Specification (in.) | Measured (in.) |
|---|---|---|
| Roof | ≤4.0 | 0 |
| Windshield | ≤3.0 | 0 |
| A and B pillars | ≤5.0 overall, ≤3.0 lateral | 0 |
| Foot well/toe pan | ≤9.0 | 0 |
| Floor pan/transmission tunnel | ≤12.0 | 0 |
| Side front panel | ≤12.0 | 0.5 |
| Front door (above seat) | ≤9.0 | 0 |
| Front door (below seat) | ≤12.0 | 0.5 |

**Table 60. Exterior vehicle damage in Crash Test 612541-01-2.**

| Part of Vehicle | Damage |
|---|---|
| Side windows | Right front side window shattered. The cause was torsion of the vehicle body due to impact with rail. |
| Maximum exterior deformation | 8 in. in the front plane at bumper height |
| VDS | 01RFQ5 |
| CDC | 01FREW3 |
| Fuel tank damage | None |
| Description of damage to vehicle | The front bumper hood and grill, right headlight and quarter fender, right front tire and rim, right front strut, windshield (crack caused by torsion of vehicle body due to impact with rail), right front door and glass, right front floor pan, right rear door, right rear quarter fender, right taillight, and rear bumper were damaged. |

Note: VDS = vehicle damage scale; CDC = collision deformation classification.

## Occupant Risk Factors

Data from the accelerometers were digitized for evaluation of occupant risk; the results are shown in Table 61. Figure C.3 in Appendix C, Section C.3, shows the vehicle angular displacements, and Figures C.4 through C.6 in Appendix C, Section C.4, show acceleration versus time traces.

## Test Summary

Figure 86 summarizes the results of MASH Crash Test 612541-01-2.

**Table 61.  Occupant risk factors for Crash Test 612541-01-2.**

| Test Parameter | MASH[a] | Measured | Time (s) |
|---|---|---|---|
| OIV (ft/s) | | | |
| X | ≤40.0 *30.0* | 14.9 | 0.0794 on right side of interior |
| Y | ≤40.0 *30.0* | 28.9 | 0.0794 on right side of interior |
| Ridedown (g) | | | |
| X | ≤20.49 *15.0* | 4.1 | 0.0960–0.1060 |
| Y | ≤20.49 *15.0* | 9.6 | 0.0980–0.1080 |
| THIV (m/s) | N/A | 9.9 | 0.0779 on right side of interior |
| ASI | N/A | 2.2 | 0.0460–0.0960 |
| Max. 0.050-s average (g) | | | |
| X | N/A | –8.4 | 0.0134–0.0634 |
| Y | N/A | –16.5 | 0.0268–0.0768 |
| Vertical | N/A | –2.3 | 0.0331–0.0831 |
| Roll (deg) | ≤75 | 17 | 2.0000 |
| Pitch (deg) | ≤75 | 4 | 0.3106 |
| Yaw (deg) | N/A | 38 | 0.4486 |

[a]Values in italics are the preferred MASH values.

| Sequential Photographs | Test Agency | Texas A&M Transportation Institute (TTI) |
|---|---|---|
| **0.000 s** | Test Standard/Test No. | MASH 2016, Test 3-10 |
| | TTI Project No. | 612541-01-2 |
| | Test Date | 2021-09-14 |
| | **TEST ARTICLE** | |
| | Type | Longitudinal barrier |
| | Name | Multifunctional barrier |
| | Length | 185 ft 7½ in. |
| | Key Materials | Traffic side: HSS 12- × 6- × ¼-in. rail, and HSS 4- × 4- × ¼-in. rub rail on W6 × 8.5 posts spaced on 66-in. centers<br>Field side: Two HSS 1.90-in.-diameter × 0.145-in.-thick (Sch 40) tubes, and one 12-gauge, 4-in-wide plate cane rail |
| **0.200 s** | Soil Type and Condition | AASHTO M147-17, Type 1, Grade D crushed concrete |
| | **TEST VEHICLE** | |
| | Type/Designation | 1100C |
| | Year, Make and Model | 2015 Nissan Versa |
| | Inertial Weight (lb) | 2,443 |
| | Dummy (lb) | 165 |
| | Gross Static (lb) | 2,608 |
| | **IMPACT CONDITIONS** | |
| | Impact Speed (mi/h) | 63.7 |
| | Impact Angle (deg) | 25.5 |
| **0.400 s** | Impact Location | 3.1 ft upstream from the centerline of Post 17 |
| | Impact Severity (kip-ft) | 61.4 |
| | **EXIT CONDITIONS** | |
| | Exit Speed (mi/h) | 53.3 |
| | Trajectory/Heading Angle (deg) | 11/11 |
| | Exit Box Criteria | Vehicle crossed the exit box 75 ft downstream from loss of contact. |
| | Stopping Distance | 311 ft downstream<br>34 ft to the traffic side |
| | **TEST ARTICLE DEFLECTIONS** | |
| | Dynamic (in.) | 8.4 |
| | Permanent (in.) | 2.3 |
| **0.600 s** | Working Width/Height (in.) | 24.1/35 |
| | **VEHICLE DAMAGE** | |
| | VDS | 01RFQ5 |
| | CDC | 01FREW3 |
| | Max. Ext. Deformation (in.) | 8 |
| | Max. Occupant Compartment Deformation | 0.5 in. in the front door below the seat and the side panel |

**OCCUPANT RISK VALUES**

| | | | | | | | |
|---|---|---|---|---|---|---|---|
| Long. OIV (ft/s) | 14.9 | Long. Ridedown (g) | 4.1 | Max. 50-ms Long. (g) | -8.4 | Max. Roll (deg) | 17 |
| Lat. OIV (ft/s) | 28.9 | Lat. Ridedown (g) | 9.6 | Max. 50-ms Lat. (g) | -16.5 | Max. Pitch (deg) | 4 |
| THIV (m/s) | 9.9 | ASI | 2.2 | Max. 50-ms Vert. (g) | -2.3 | Max. Yaw (deg) | 38 |

Note: Sch = schedule; ext. = exterior; long. = longitude; lat. = latitude; vert. = vertical.

**Figure 86. Summary of results for MASH Test 3-10 (Crash Test 612541-01-2) on multifunctional barrier.**

CHAPTER 11

# MASH Test 3-11
# (Crash Test 612541-01-1)

## Test Designation and Actual Impact Conditions

The MASH impact conditions and exit parameters for Crash Test 612541-01-1 are given in Table 62 and Table 63, respectively. Figure 87 and Figure 88 depict the setup of the target impact.

## Weather Conditions

Table 64 provides the weather conditions for Crash Test 612541-01-1.

**Table 62.  Impact conditions for MASH Test 3-11 (Crash Test 612541-01-1).**

| Test Parameter | Specification | Tolerance | Measured |
|---|---|---|---|
| Impact speed (mi/h) | 62 | ±2.5 | 60.3 |
| Impact angle (deg) | 25 | ±1.5 | 25.1 |
| Impact severity (kip-ft) | 106 | ≥106 | 110 |
| Impact location [distance (ft) upstream of center of Post 17] | 1.55 | ±1 | 1.1 |

**Table 63.  Exit parameters for MASH Test 3-11 (Crash Test 612541-01-1).**

| Exit Parameter | Measured |
|---|---|
| Speed (mi/h) | 51 |
| Trajectory (deg) | 6 |
| Heading (deg) | 14 |
| Brakes applied post impact (s) | 3.2 |
| Vehicle at rest position | 235 ft downstream of impact point 26 ft to the field side 25 deg right |
| Comments | Vehicle remained upright and stable. Vehicle did not cross the exit box[a] and therefore failed to meet the exit box criteria described in MASH. |

[a]Not less than 32.8 ft downstream from loss of contact for cars and pickups is optimal.

*Figure 87. Multifunctional barrier/test vehicle geometrics for Crash Test 612541-01-1.*

*Figure 88. Multifunctional barrier/test vehicle impact location for Crash Test 612541-01-1.*

**Table 64. Weather conditions for Crash Test 612541-01-1 (2021-08-24, AM).**

| Condition | Measurement |
|---|---|
| Wind speed (mi/h) | 5 |
| Wind direction (deg) | 181 |
| Temperature (°F) | 87 |
| Relative humidity (%) | 76 |
| Vehicle traveling (deg) | 195 |

## Test Vehicle

Figure 89 and Figure 90 show the 2015 Ram 1500 used for the crash test. Table 65 shows the vehicle measurements. Table D.1 in Appendix D, Section D.1, gives additional dimensions and information about the vehicle.

**Figure 89.    Impact side of test vehicle before Crash Test 612541-01-1.**

**Figure 90.    Opposite of the impact side of the test vehicle before Crash Test 612541-01-1.**

**Table 65.    Vehicle measurements for Crash Test 612541-01-1.**

| Test Parameter | MASH | Allowed Tolerance | Measured |
|---|---|---|---|
| Dummy (if applicable)[a] (lb) | 165 | N/A | 165 |
| Inertial weight (lb) | 5,000 | ±110 | 5,027 |
| Gross static[a] (lb) | 5,165 | ±110 | 5,192 |
| Wheelbase (in.) | 148 | ±12 | 140.5 |
| Front overhang (in.) | 39 | ±3 | 40 |
| Overall length (in.) | 237 | ±13 | 227.5 |
| Overall width (in.) | 78 | ±2 | 78.5 |
| Hood height (in.) | 43 | ±4 | 46 |
| Track width[b] (in.) | 67 | ±1.5 | 68.3 |
| CG aft of front axle[c] (in.) | 63 | ±4 | 61.1 |
| CG above ground[c,d] (in.) | 28 | ≥28 | 28.6 |

[a]If a dummy is used, the gross static vehicle mass includes the mass of the dummy.
[b]Average of front and rear axles.
[c]For test inertial mass.
[d]2270P vehicle must meet minimum CG height requirement.

## Test Description

Table 66 lists events that occurred during Crash Test 612541-01-1. Figures D.1 and D.2 in Appendix D, Section D.2, present sequential photographs from the test.

## Damage to Test Installation

The rails were scuffed at the location of the impact and downstream of the impact. The soil was disturbed at Post 1, and there was slight separation between the grout and concrete on the traffic and field sides from Posts 14 to 21. The grout was also cracked and broken up around Posts 15 to 20.

Table 67 presents the data on the post displacement and lean. Table 68 reports the deflection and working width of the multifunctional barrier. Figure 91 and Figure 92 show the damage to the multifunctional barrier.

**Table 66.   Events during Crash Test 612541-01-1.**

| Time (s) | Event |
|---|---|
| 0.0000 | Vehicle impacted the installation. |
| 0.0175 | Post 17 began to deflect toward the field side. |
| 0.0250 | Post 18 began to deflect toward the field side. |
| 0.0338 | Post 19 began to deflect toward the field side. |
| 0.0430 | Vehicle began to redirect. |
| 0.1040 | Front driver's side tire lifted off the pavement. |
| 0.1310 | Back driver's side tire lifted off the pavement. |
| 0.1820 | Vehicle was parallel with installation. |
| 0.3460 | Front passenger's side tire lifted off the pavement. |
| 0.3690 | Vehicle exited the installation at 51.1 mi/h with a heading of 14 deg and a trajectory of 6 deg. |
| 0.3730 | Front passenger's side tire contacted the pavement. |

**Table 67.   Post displacement details for multifunctional barrier for Crash Test 612541-01-1.**

| Post | Soil Gap (in.) | | Lean from Vertical Toward Field Side (deg) |
|---|---|---|---|
| | **Traffic Side** | **Field Side** | |
| 14 | Grout disturbed | | 1 |
| 15 | ¼ | ⅛ | 1 |
| 16 | 1⅜ | ½ | 5 |
| 17 | 3 | 2 | 7 |
| 18 | 3¼ | 2 | 9 |
| 19 | 1¾ | 1 | 6 |
| 20 | ½ | ½ | 2 |
| 21 | Grout disturbed | | — |

**Table 68.  Deflection and working width of the multifunctional barrier for Crash Test 612541-01-1.**

| Test Parameter | Measured |
|---|---|
| Permanent deflection/location (in.) | 9.6 toward field side, at the joint between Posts 17 and 18 |
| Dynamic deflection (in.) | 16 toward field side |
| Working width[a] and height (in.) | 33.1, at a height of 32.2 |

[a]Per MASH, "The working width is the maximum dynamic lateral position of any major part of the system or vehicle. These measurements are all relative to the pre-impact traffic face of the test article." In other words, the working width is the total barrier width plus the maximum dynamic intrusion of any portion of the barrier or test vehicle past the field side edge of the barrier.

*Figure 91.  Multifunctional barrier at impact location after Crash Test 612541-01-1.*

*Figure 92.  Multifunctional barrier at Post 17 after Crash Test 612541-01-1.*

## Damage to Test Vehicle

Figure 93 and Figure 94 show the damage sustained by the vehicle. Figure 95 and Figure 96 show the interior of the test vehicle. Table 69 and Table 70 provide details on the occupant compartment deformation and exterior vehicle damage. Tables D.2 and D.3 in Appendix D, Section D.1, provide exterior crush and occupant compartment measurements, respectively.

## Occupant Risk Factors

Data from the accelerometers were digitized for evaluation of occupant risk; the results are shown in Table 71. Figure D.3 in Appendix D, Section D.3, shows the vehicle angular displacements, and Figures D.4 through D.6 in Appendix D, Section D.4, show acceleration versus time traces.

*Figure 93.   Impact side of test vehicle after Crash Test 612541-01-1.*

*Figure 94.   Rear impact side of test vehicle after Crash Test 612541-01-1.*

*Figure 95. Overall interior of test vehicle after Crash Test 612541-01-1.*

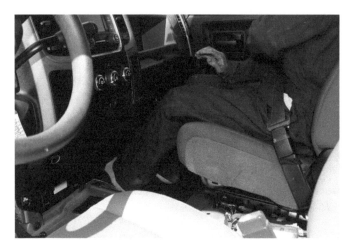

*Figure 96. Interior of test vehicle on impact side after Crash Test 612541-01-1.*

**Table 69. Occupant compartment deformation in Crash Test 612541-01-1.**

| Test Parameter | Specification (in.) | Measured (in.) |
|---|---|---|
| Roof | ≤4.0 | 0 |
| Windshield | ≤3.0 | 0 |
| A and B pillars | ≤5.0 overall, ≤3.0 lateral | 0 |
| Foot well/toe pan | ≤9.0 | 0 |
| Floor pan/transmission tunnel | ≤12.0 | 0 |
| Side front panel | ≤12.0 | 0 |
| Front door (above seat) | ≤9.0 | 0 |
| Front door (below seat) | ≤12.0 | 0 |

**Table 70.   Exterior vehicle damage in Crash Test 612541-01-1.**

| Part of Vehicle | Damage |
|---|---|
| Side windows | No damage |
| Maximum exterior deformation | 10 in. in the front and side planes at the right front corner at and above bumper height |
| VDS | 01RFQ5 |
| CDC | 01FREW3 |
| Fuel tank damage | None |
| Description of damage to vehicle | The front bumper, grill, right headlight, right front tire and rim, right front door, right rear door, right rear quarter fender, and right taillight were all damaged. The right front door had a 3-in. gap at the top. |

**Table 71.   Occupant risk factors for Crash Test 612541-01-1.**

| Test Parameter | MASH[a] | Measured | Time (s) |
|---|---|---|---|
| OIV (ft/s) | | | |
| X | ≤40.0 <br> *30.0* | 14 | 0.1098 on right side of interior |
| Y | ≤40.0 <br> *30.0* | 22.9 | 0.1098 on right side of interior |
| Ridedown (*g*) | | | |
| X | ≤20.49 <br> *15.0* | 5.6 | 0.1184–0.1284 |
| Y | ≤20.49 <br> *15.0* | 9.6 | 0.1098–0.1198 |
| THIV (m/s) | N/A | 8 | 0.1073 on right side of interior |
| ASI | N/A | 1.2 | 0.0566–0.1066 |
| Max. 0.050-s average (*g*) | | | |
| X | N/A | –5.6 | 0.0408–0.0908 |
| Y | N/A | –9.3 | 0.0322–0.0822 |
| Vertical | N/A | –4 | 1.1427–1.1927 |
| Roll (deg) | ≤75 | 46 | 0.6108 |
| Pitch (deg) | ≤75 | –7 | 1.0474 |
| Yaw (deg) | N/A | –39 | 0.6938 |

[a]Values in italics are the preferred MASH values.

## Test Summary

Figure 97 summarizes the results of MASH Crash Test 612541-01-1. The dynamic deflection of the barrier was only 16 in. There was no debris from the barrier. There was debris from the impacting vehicle that traveled beyond the field edge of the barrier. This flying debris, which comprised the plastic grill guard and smaller plastic pieces from the vehicle, could potentially interact with vulnerable users behind the rail. The debris would require removal to maintain full function of any nonmotorized facility behind the barrier for bicyclists and other users.

| Sequential Photographs | | Test Agency | Texas A&M Transportation Institute (TTI) |
|---|---|---|---|
| **0.000 s** | | Test Standard/Test No. | MASH 2016, Test 3-11 |
| | | TTI Project No. | 612541-01-1 |
| | | Test Date | 2021-08-24 |
| | | **TEST ARTICLE** | |
| | | Type | Longitudinal barrier |
| | | Name | Multifunctional barrier |
| | | Length | 185 ft 7½ in. |
| | | Key Materials | Traffic side: HSS 12- × 6- × ¼-in. rail, and HSS 4- × 4- × ¼-in. rub rail on W6 × 8.5 posts spaced on 66-in. centers<br>Field side: Two HSS 1.90-in.-diameter by 0.145-in.-thick (Sch 40) tubes and one 12-gauge, 4-in.-wide plate cane rail |
| **0.200 s** | | Soil Type and Condition | AASHTO M147-17, Type 1, Grade D crushed concrete |
| | | **TEST VEHICLE** | |
| | | Type/Designation | 2270P |
| | | Year, Make and Model | 2015 Ram 1500 |
| | | Inertial Weight (lb) | 5,027 |
| | | Dummy (lb) | 165 |
| | | Gross Static (lb) | 5,192 |
| | | **IMPACT CONDITIONS** | |
| **0.400 s** | | Impact Speed (mi/h) | 60.3 |
| | | Impact Angle (deg) | 25.1 |
| | | Impact Location | 1.1 ft upstream of the center of Post 17 |
| | | Impact Severity (kip-ft) | 110 |
| | | **EXIT CONDITIONS** | |
| | | Exit Speed (mi/h) | 51 |
| | | Trajectory/Heading Angle (deg) | 6/14 |
| | | Exit Box Criteria | Vehicle did not cross the exit box. |
| | | Stopping Distance | 235 ft downstream<br>26 ft to the field side |
| | | **TEST ARTICLE DEFLECTIONS** | |
| **0.600 s** | | Dynamic (in.) | 16 |
| | | Permanent (in.) | 9.6 |
| | | Working Width/Height (in.) | 33.1/32.2 |
| | | **VEHICLE DAMAGE** | |
| | | VDS | 01RFQ5 |
| | | CDC | 01FREW3 |
| | | Max. Ext. Deformation (in.) | 10 |
| | | Max. Occupant Compartment Deformation | No occupant compartment damage |

| OCCUPANT RISK VALUES | | | | | | | |
|---|---|---|---|---|---|---|---|
| Long. OIV (ft/s) | 14 | Long. Ridedown (g) | 5.6 | Max. 50-ms Long. (g) | −5.6 | Max. Roll (deg) | 46 |
| Lat. OIV (ft/s) | 22.9 | Lat. Ridedown (g) | 9.6 | Max. 50-ms Lat. (g) | −9.3 | Max. Pitch (deg) | −7 |
| THIV (m/s) | 8 | ASI | 1.2 | Max. 50-ms Vert. (g) | −4 | Max. Yaw (deg) | −39 |

**Figure 97. Summary of results for MASH Test 3-11 (Crash Test 612541-01-1) on the multifunctional barrier.**

# CHAPTER 12

# Finite Element Analysis for Preliminary Transition Designs Utilizing W-Beam and Rub Rail

In the previous chapters, a multifunctional barrier system was designed and verified to use in a variety of contexts, such as where ROW constraints reduce lateral offset between a roadway and a shared-use path. To limit separation of the multiuse path and roadway traffic, it is also likely that the barrier needs to be terminated in the clear zone, particularly at crossroads and intersections. Therefore, it is necessary to connect the barrier to a crashworthy terminal.

This chapter presents the preliminary transition design options, which used W-beam. Computer simulations helped determine the crashworthiness of the proposed design and served as a design aid, as needed.

## Predictive Finite Element Analysis of Crashworthiness of the Preliminary W-Beam Transition System

MASH recommends two tests to evaluate transitions to TL-3:

- **MASH Test Designation 3-20:** A 2,425-lb vehicle impacting the CIP of the LON of the barrier at a nominal impact speed and angle of 62 mi/h and 25 deg, respectively. This test investigates a barrier's ability to successfully contain and redirect a small passenger vehicle.
- **MASH Test Designation 3-21:** A 5,000-lb pickup truck impacting the CIP of the LON of the barrier at a nominal impact speed and angle of 62 mi/h and 25 deg, respectively. This test investigates a barrier's ability to successfully contain and redirect light trucks and sport utility vehicles.

The multifunctional barrier would be connected to the 50-ft-long W-beam guardrail and nonproprietary terminal via a W-beam transition component. The proposed preliminary design of the transition system included a W-beam segment directly attached to a properly positioned spacer through a W-beam terminal connector. The proposed transition length was 6.25 ft and was supported by a standard W6 × 8.5 × 72-in. steel post with half post spacing (37.5 in.).

The cane rail terminated behind the last post of the multifunctional barrier LON, while the traffic rail, handrail, and rub rail of the multifunctional barrier LON extend past the LON's last post. The rub rail (HSS 4 × 4 × ¼ × 30 in.) was flared behind the second post of the proposed transition to limit potential for snagging of the impacting vehicle. A terminal handrail component is suggested to connect the two hand railings of the system's LON.

The W-beam transition was connected to the traffic rail and a spacer (HSS 12 × 8 × ¼ × 30 in.) through a terminal connector. The spacer was connected to the traffic rail through three ¾- × 16-in. hex A449 bolts.

Figure 98 and Figure 99 provide a general overview, as well as specific details of the FE model of the proposed transition. The overall modeling technique and material/contact properties were similar to those utilized and described in the discussion of the multifunctional barrier LON in Chapter 6.

### MASH Test 3-21: Predictive Investigation of Crashworthiness of Transition

The research team conducted simulations to replicate the impact of the pickup truck vehicle (2270P) at various locations of the proposed transition design. MASH recommends performing a parametric investigation of the critical location of impact to identify the system CIP, which is the impact point that maximizes the risk of failure of the system's crashworthiness. The following impact points were considered in the investigation of the system's crashworthiness during the 2270P impact (Figure 100):

- Case 1: Impact location = 2 ft upstream of the fourth transition post.
- Case 2: Impact location = at the fourth transition post.
- Case 3: Impact location = 2 ft downstream of the fourth transition post.
- Case 4: Impact location = 2 ft upstream of the second transition post.

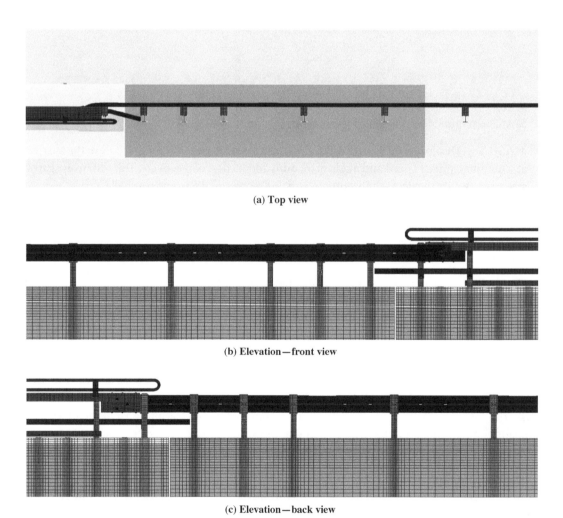

(a) Top view

(b) Elevation—front view

(c) Elevation—back view

*Figure 98.   Proposed FE transition model (various views).*

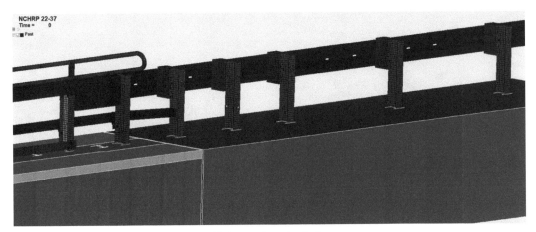

(a) **Perspective—back view**

(b) **Front view—connections details**

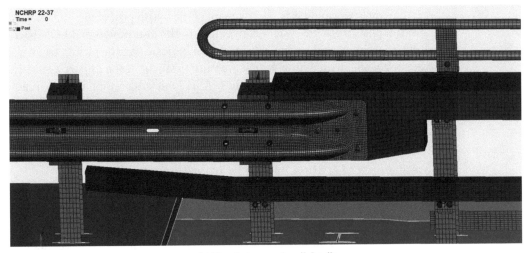

(c) **Front view—rub rail details**

*Figure 99.   Details of proposed FE transition model (various views).*

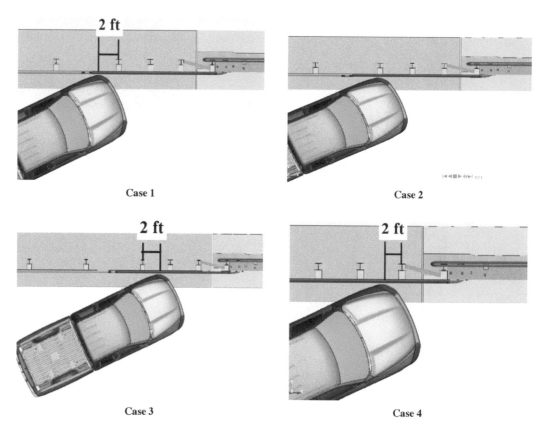

**Figure 100.** *Test 3-21: Investigation of critical impact location.*

The selection of impact points was based on previous experience with transition design and testing, with the objective of maximizing the potential for vehicle instability and pocketing on the multifunctional barrier end (near the transition connection).

### Case 1: Impact Location 2 ft Upstream of Fourth Transition Post

Table 72 summarizes the results from the predictive impact simulation of MASH Test 3-21 when the impact location was 2 ft upstream of the fourth post of the transition rail (counting the transition posts from the system connection to the multifunctional LON barrier system). The results from this predictive impact simulation indicate that the pickup truck was contained and redirected while maintaining vehicle stability throughout the impact event. The occupant risk factors (OIV and ORA) were all within MASH limits. According to these predicted results, the conducted simulation indicated that the transition design system was likely to perform acceptably per MASH Test 3-21 and evaluation criteria when the system was impacted 2 ft upstream of the fourth transition post.

### Case 2: Impact Location at Fourth Transition Post

Table 73 summarizes the results from the predictive impact simulation of MASH Test 3-21 when the impact location was at the fourth post of the transition rail (counting the transition posts from the system connection to the multifunctional LON barrier system). The results from this predictive impact simulation indicated that the pickup truck was contained and redirected while maintaining vehicle stability throughout the impact event. The occupant risk factors (OIV and ORA) were all within MASH limits. According to these predicted results, the conducted simulation indicated that the transition design system was likely to perform acceptably per MASH Test 3-21 and evaluation criteria when impacted at the fourth transition post.

**Table 72.   Predictive impact simulation of MASH Test 3-21: Case 1—impact location 2 ft upstream of fourth transition post.**

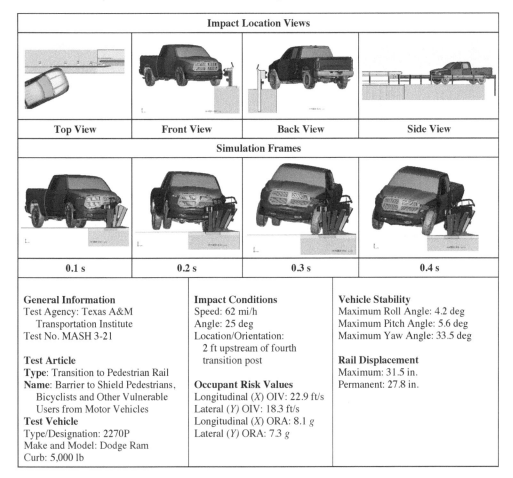

| General Information | Impact Conditions | Vehicle Stability |
|---|---|---|
| Test Agency: Texas A&M Transportation Institute | Speed: 62 mi/h | Maximum Roll Angle: 4.2 deg |
| | Angle: 25 deg | Maximum Pitch Angle: 5.6 deg |
| Test No. MASH 3-21 | Location/Orientation: 2 ft upstream of fourth transition post | Maximum Yaw Angle: 33.5 deg |
| **Test Article** | | **Rail Displacement** |
| **Type**: Transition to Pedestrian Rail | | Maximum: 31.5 in. |
| **Name**: Barrier to Shield Pedestrians, Bicyclists and Other Vulnerable Users from Motor Vehicles | **Occupant Risk Values** | Permanent: 27.8 in. |
| **Test Vehicle** | Longitudinal ($X$) OIV: 22.9 ft/s | |
| Type/Designation: 2270P | Lateral ($Y$) OIV: 18.3 ft/s | |
| Make and Model: Dodge Ram | Longitudinal ($X$) ORA: 8.1 $g$ | |
| Curb: 5,000 lb | Lateral ($Y$) ORA: 7.3 $g$ | |

## Case 3: Impact Location 2 ft Downstream of Fourth Transition Post

Table 74 summarizes the results from the predictive impact simulation of MASH Test 3-21 when the impact location was 2 ft downstream of the fourth post of the transition rail (counting the transition posts from the system connection to the multifunctional LON barrier system). The results from this predictive impact simulation indicated that the pickup truck was contained and redirected while maintaining vehicle stability throughout the impact event. The occupant risk factors (OIV and ORA) were all within MASH limits. According to these predicted results, the conducted simulation indicated that the transition design system was likely to perform acceptably per MASH Test 3-21 and evaluation criteria when impacted 2 ft downstream of the fourth transition post.

## Case 4: Impact Location 2 ft Upstream of Second Transition Post

Table 75 summarizes the results from the predictive impact simulation of MASH Test 3-21 when the impact location was 2 ft upstream of the second post of the transition rail (counting the transition posts from the system connection to the multifunctional LON barrier system). The results from this predictive impact simulation indicated that the pickup truck was contained and redirected while maintaining vehicle stability throughout the impact event. The occupant risk factors (OIV and ORA) were all within MASH limits. According to these predicted results, the conducted simulation indicated that the transition design system was likely to perform

**Table 73. Predictive impact simulation of MASH Test 3-21: Case 2—impact location at the fourth transition post.**

| Impact Location Views | | | |
|---|---|---|---|
| | | | |
| Top View | Front View | Back View | Side View |
| Simulation Frames | | | |
| | | | |
| 0.1 s | 0.2 s | 0.3 s | 0.4 s |

**General Information**
Test Agency: Texas A&M Transportation Institute
Test No. MASH 3-21

**Test Article**
**Type**: Transition to Pedestrian Rail
**Name**: Barrier to Shield Pedestrians, Bicyclists and Other Vulnerable Users from Motor Vehicles
**Test Vehicle**
Type/Designation: 2270P
Make and Model: Dodge Ram
Curb: 5,000 lb

**Impact Conditions**
Speed: 62 mi/h
Angle: 25 deg
Location/Orientation: At fourth transition post

**Occupant Risk Values**
Longitudinal (X) OIV: 19.4 ft/s
Lateral (Y) OIV: 18.1 ft/s
Longitudinal (X) ORA: 7.7 g
Lateral (Y) ORA: 9.9 g

**Vehicle Stability**
Maximum Roll Angle: 10.2 deg
Maximum Pitch Angle: 5.6 deg
Maximum Yaw Angle: 40.9 deg

**Rail Displacement**
Maximum: 30.6 in.
Permanent: 25.7 in.

acceptably per MASH Test 3-21 and evaluation criteria when impacted 2 ft upstream of the second transition post.

*Conclusion*

Table 76 provides a comprehensive summary of the results of the 2270P predictive simulation. The conducted simulations seem to indicate that the design of the transition system is likely to perform acceptably per MASH Test 3-21 and evaluation criteria. Case 1 recorded the largest dynamic lateral deflection of the transition system upon impact, which could be an indication of a greater potential for pocketing and snagging on the end of the multifunctional barrier.

## MASH Test 3-20: Predictive Investigation of Crashworthiness of Transition

The research team conducted a parametric investigation of the potential CIP for the passenger car vehicle (1100C), similar to the investigation conducted for the pickup truck. Only one of the conducted cases is reported here, however, since the simulation results predicted the potential for the transition system to perform unacceptably per MASH Test 3-20 and evaluation criteria.

Figure 101 presents sequential screenshots from the results of the predictive impact simulation of MASH Test 3-20 when the impact location was 1.5 ft upstream of the fourth post of the

**Table 74.   Predictive impact simulation of MASH Test 3-21: Case 3—impact location 2 ft downstream of fourth transition post.**

| Impact Location Views | | | |
|---|---|---|---|
| Top View | Front View | Back View | Side View |
| **Simulation Frames** | | | |
| 0.1 s | 0.2 s | 0.3 s | 0.4 s |

| General Information | Impact Conditions | Vehicle Stability |
|---|---|---|
| Test Agency: Texas A&M Transportation Institute<br>Test No. MASH 3-21<br><br>**Test Article**<br>Type: Transition to Pedestrian Rail<br>Name: Barrier to Shield Pedestrians, Bicyclists and Other Vulnerable Users from Motor Vehicles<br>**Test Vehicle**<br>Type/Designation: 2270P<br>Make and Model: Dodge Ram<br>Curb: 5,000 lb | Speed: 62 mi/h<br>Angle: 25 deg<br>Location/Orientation:<br>2 ft downstream of the fourth transition post<br><br>**Occupant Risk Values**<br>Longitudinal (X) OIV: 19.3 ft/s<br>Lateral (Y) OIV: 18.2 ft/s<br>Longitudinal (X) ORA: 6.9 g<br>Lateral (Y) ORA: 10.0 g | Maximum Roll Angle: 18.2 deg<br>Maximum Pitch Angle: 4.9 deg<br>Maximum Yaw Angle: 40.5 deg<br><br>**Rail Displacement**<br>Maximum: 29.1 in.<br>Permanent: 23.5 in. |

transition rail (counting the transition posts from the system connection to the multifunctional LON barrier system).

Table 77 summarizes the results of the predictive impact simulation of MASH Test 3-20 when the impact location was 1.5 ft upstream of the fourth post of the transition rail. The results from this predictive impact simulation indicate high values for occupant risk factors. Specifically, the predicted OIV in the longitudinal direction was 42.4 ft/s, which is higher than the maximum value allowed by MASH of 40 ft/sec.

The high (and unacceptable) occupant risk value seems to originate from snagging of the passenger car and the post/rub rail system. The simulation frames indicate that the vehicle tire underrides the W-beam system and fully engages the impacted transition posts. The transition post immediately adjacent to the end of the rub rail seems to be constrained from deflecting longitudinally by the presence of the rub rail itself. The limitation of the post movement results in high-impact velocity for the impacting passenger car. The passenger car, in fact, is not efficiently redirected upon impact, as desired.

These predicted results from the conducted simulation indicate that the transition design system would likely not perform per MASH Test 3-20 and evaluation criteria when impacted at 1.5 ft upstream of the fourth transition post. Design modifications are required to address the potential for snagging and pocketing of the passenger car vehicle during the impact event.

**Table 75. Predictive impact simulation of MASH Test 3-21: Case 4—impact location 2 ft upstream of second transition post.**

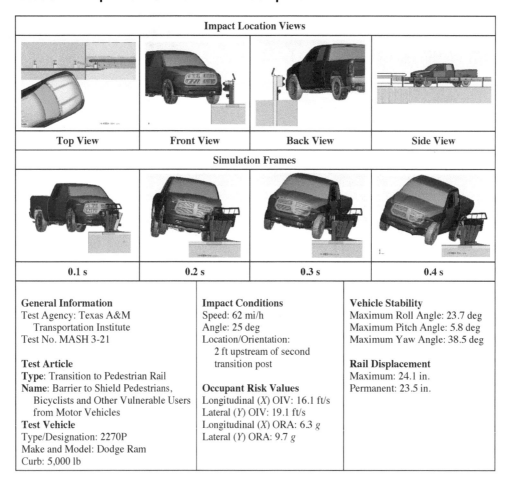

| Impact Location Views | | | |
|---|---|---|---|
| Top View | Front View | Back View | Side View |
| Simulation Frames | | | |
| 0.1 s | 0.2 s | 0.3 s | 0.4 s |

| General Information | Impact Conditions | Vehicle Stability |
|---|---|---|
| Test Agency: Texas A&M Transportation Institute<br>Test No. MASH 3-21<br><br>**Test Article**<br>**Type**: Transition to Pedestrian Rail<br>**Name**: Barrier to Shield Pedestrians, Bicyclists and Other Vulnerable Users from Motor Vehicles<br>**Test Vehicle**<br>Type/Designation: 2270P<br>Make and Model: Dodge Ram<br>Curb: 5,000 lb | Speed: 62 mi/h<br>Angle: 25 deg<br>Location/Orientation:<br>  2 ft upstream of second<br>  transition post<br><br>**Occupant Risk Values**<br>Longitudinal (X) OIV: 16.1 ft/s<br>Lateral (Y) OIV: 19.1 ft/s<br>Longitudinal (X) ORA: 6.3 g<br>Lateral (Y) ORA: 9.7 g | Maximum Roll Angle: 23.7 deg<br>Maximum Pitch Angle: 5.8 deg<br>Maximum Yaw Angle: 38.5 deg<br><br>**Rail Displacement**<br>Maximum: 24.1 in.<br>Permanent: 23.5 in. |

**Table 76.   Summary table of MASH Test 3-21 CIP analysis.**

| Variable | Measurement | Variable | Measurement |
|---|---|---|---|
| **Case 1: 2270P—2 ft upstream of fourth transition post** | | **Case 3: 2270P—2 ft downstream of fourth transition post** | |
| Deflection (in.) | | Deflection (in.) | |
| Dynamic | 32.5 | Dynamic | 29.1 |
| Permanent | 28.0 | Permanent | 23.5 |
| OIV (ft/s) | | OIV (ft/s) | |
| $X$ | 22.9 | $X$ | 19.3 |
| $Y$ | 18.3 | $Y$ | 18.2 |
| Stability (deg) | | Stability (deg) | |
| Roll | 4.2 | Roll | 18.2 |
| Pitch | 5.6 | Pitch | 4.9 |
| Yaw | 33.5 | Yaw | 40.5 |
| Ridedown acceleration ($g$) | | Ridedown acceleration ($g$) | |
| $X$ | 8.1 | $X$ | 6.9 |
| $Y$ | 7.3 | $Y$ | 10 |
| **Case 2: 2270P—at fourth transition post** | | **Case 4: 2270P—2 ft upstream of second transition post** | |
| Deflection (in.) | | Deflection (in.) | |
| Dynamic | 30.6 | Dynamic | 24.5 |
| Permanent | 25.7 | Permanent | 19.7 |
| OIV (ft/s) | | OIV (ft/s) | |
| $X$ | 19.4 | $X$ | 16.1 |
| $Y$ | 18.1 | $Y$ | 19.1 |
| Stability (deg) | | Stability (deg) | |
| Roll | 10.2 | Roll | 23.7 |
| Pitch | 5.6 | Pitch | 5.8 |
| Yaw | 40.9 | Yaw | 38.5 |
| Ridedown acceleration ($g$) | | Ridedown acceleration ($g$) | |
| $X$ | 7.7 | $X$ | 6.3 |
| $Y$ | 9.9 | $Y$ | 9.7 |

Side View · Top View

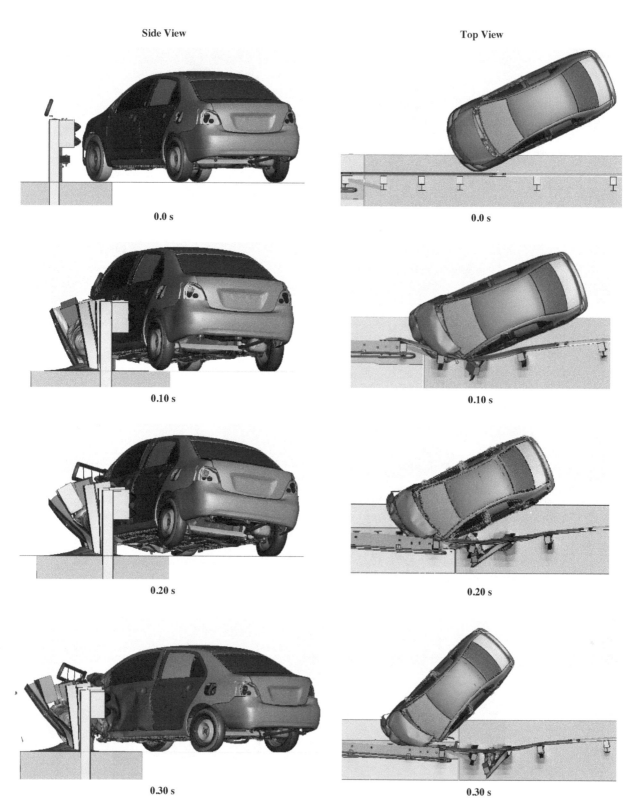

*Figure 101. Sequential images of MASH Test 3-20 (impact location 1.5 ft upstream of fourth transition post).*

**Table 77. Predictive impact simulation of MASH Test 3-20: Impact location 1.5 ft upstream of fourth transition post.**

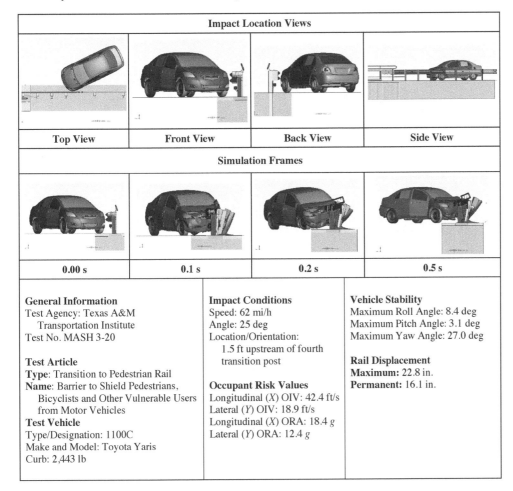

| Impact Location Views | | | |
|---|---|---|---|
| Top View | Front View | Back View | Side View |

| Simulation Frames | | | |
|---|---|---|---|
| 0.00 s | 0.1 s | 0.2 s | 0.5 s |

| General Information | Impact Conditions | Vehicle Stability |
|---|---|---|
| Test Agency: Texas A&M Transportation Institute<br>Test No. MASH 3-20<br><br>**Test Article**<br>**Type**: Transition to Pedestrian Rail<br>**Name**: Barrier to Shield Pedestrians, Bicyclists and Other Vulnerable Users from Motor Vehicles<br>**Test Vehicle**<br>Type/Designation: 1100C<br>Make and Model: Toyota Yaris<br>Curb: 2,443 lb | Speed: 62 mi/h<br>Angle: 25 deg<br>Location/Orientation:<br>  1.5 ft upstream of fourth transition post<br><br>**Occupant Risk Values**<br>Longitudinal ($X$) OIV: 42.4 ft/s<br>Lateral ($Y$) OIV: 18.9 ft/s<br>Longitudinal ($X$) ORA: 18.4 $g$<br>Lateral ($Y$) ORA: 12.4 $g$ | Maximum Roll Angle: 8.4 deg<br>Maximum Pitch Angle: 3.1 deg<br>Maximum Yaw Angle: 27.0 deg<br><br>**Rail Displacement**<br>**Maximum:** 22.8 in.<br>**Permanent:** 16.1 in. |

## Predictive Finite Element Analysis of Crashworthiness of the Modified W-Beam Transition Design with Extended Rub Rail

Following an initial discussion with the project panel members, the project team members prioritized the continued investigation of a W-beam transition with added rub rail. This section provides the details for the transition system with extended rub rail and computer simulation results. The computer simulations helped determine the crashworthiness of the proposed design.

Figure 102 shows the general overview of the FE model of the proposed extended rub rail design. The multifunctional barrier would be connected to the 50-ft-long W-beam guardrail and nonproprietary terminal via a W-beam transition component. Figure 103 provides specific details of the FE model of the proposed transition. The proposed design of the transition system included a W-beam segment directly attached to the traffic rail and a spacer (HSS $12 \times 8 \times \frac{1}{4} \times 30$ in.) through a W-beam terminal connector. The spacer was connected to the traffic rail through three $\frac{3}{4}$- $\times$ 16-in. hex A449 bolts (see Figure 103a).

The cane rail was terminated behind the last post of the multifunctional LON barrier, while the traffic rail, handrail, and rub rail of the multifunctional LON barrier were extended past the LON's last post (see Figure 102b and Figure 103a). A terminal handrail component is suggested to connect the two handrails of the system's LON.

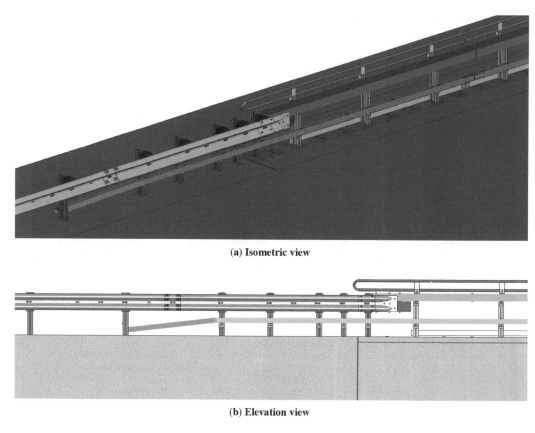

(a) Isometric view

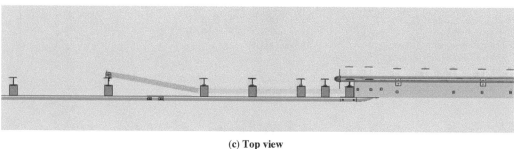

(b) Elevation view

(c) Top view

*Figure 102.  FE model of transition system with extended rub rail.*

As shown in Figure 102c, the rub rail (HSS 4 × 4 × ¼ × 30 in.) was flared behind the first post of the second W-beam of the proposed transition to limit the potential for snagging of the impacting vehicle. The end of the rub rail was connected to the post to eliminate the potential issues caused by the relatively long hanging rub rail (Figure 103b).

The proposed transition length was 6.25 ft and was supported by five standard W6 × 8.5 × 72-in. steel posts with two 9.375-in. spacings and two quarter (18.75 in.) spacings. The overall modeling technique and material/contact properties were similar to those utilized and described in the discussion of the multifunctional barrier LON in Chapter 6.

The full MASH TL-3 matrix includes two tests: MASH Test 3-20 (passenger car, 62-mi/h nominal speed and 25-deg nominal orientation angle) and MASH Test 3-21 (pickup truck, 62-mi/h nominal speed and 25-deg nominal orientation angle). The research team conducted simulations to replicate the impact of the passenger car vehicle (1100C) at various locations of the proposed transition design, since the passenger car showed more critical behavior than the pickup truck (2270P), as addressed in the previous section.

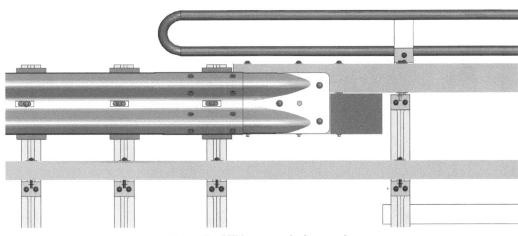

**(a) Details of W-beam terminal connection**

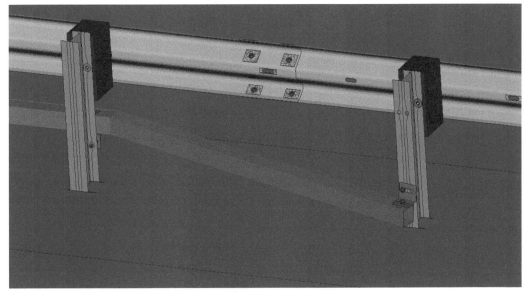

**(b) Details of rub rail connection**

*Figure 103.   Details of the FE model of the proposed transition.*

MASH recommends performing a parametric investigation of the critical location of impact to identify the system CIP, which is the impact point that maximizes the risk of failure of the system's crashworthiness. The following impact points were considered in the investigation of the system's crashworthiness during the 1100C impact (Figure 104):

- Case 1: Impact location = 1 ft upstream of fifth transition post.
- Case 2: Impact location = 1 ft downstream of fifth transition post.
- Case 3: Impact location = 3 ft upstream of fifth transition post.
- Case 4: Impact location = 7 ft upstream of sixth transition post (end of rub rail).
- Case 5: Impact location = 4 ft upstream of sixth transition post (end of rub rail).

The selection of impact points was based on previous transition design and testing experience. Cases 1 through 3 were selected to maximize the potential for vehicle instability and pocketing on the end of the multifunctional barrier (at the downstream transition location, i.e., near the transition connection with the multifunctional LON barrier system). Cases 4 and 5 were selected

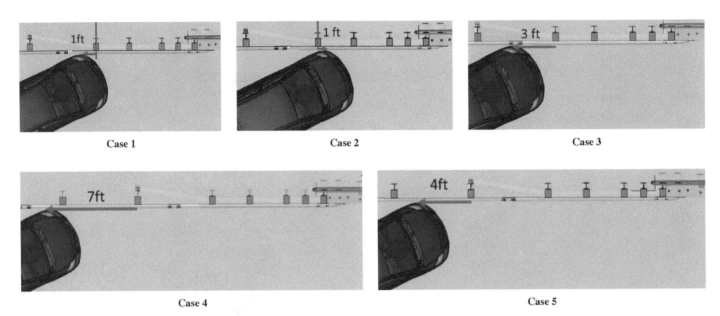

**Figure 104.  MASH Test 3-20: Critical impact locations investigated.**

to maximize the interaction between the end of the rub rail and the vehicle at the upstream location (i.e., near the transition connection with the W-beam guardrail LON).

According to the computational investigation of downstream impact points (Cases 1, 2, and 3), the passenger car was successfully contained and redirected. Moreover, the occupant risk factors met the MASH TL-3 evaluation criteria.

Simulations for Cases 4 and 5 were conducted to investigate the interaction between the end of the rub rail and the vehicle. While the results of Case 4 met the MASH TL-3 evaluation criteria, the OIV in Case 5 was 45.9 ft/s, which exceeded the maximum MASH TL-3 limit of 40 ft/s. Figure 105 shows sequential images of the impact simulation in Case 5. Table 78 shows the occupant risk factors that were determined with TRAP.

Closer analysis of the Case 5 simulation results found little interaction between the impacting passenger car and the end of the rub rail, and vehicle deceleration that led to the high OIV were attributed to wheel-post snagging. Absent additional constraints on the post, a guardrail post would not typically be expected to generate wheel snagging forces that result in unacceptable OIV. It was, therefore, theorized that these unacceptably high post snagging forces could be attributable to limitations in the vehicle suspension model and absence of applicable suspension failure modes. Another computer simulation (Case 6) was conducted to further investigate the behavior of the FE vehicle model. In this simulation, the rub rail was removed from the transition system to create a configuration that should behave similarly to a conventional MGS with 8-in. offset blocks. The same impact point used in Case 5 (i.e., 4 ft upstream of sixth transition post) was used in this new simulation. Table 79 lists the occupant risk factors computed from the simulation results, and Figure 106 shows the sequential images from this Case 6 simulation.

Since the system for Case 6 did not have a rub rail at the impact point and was essentially a W-beam guardrail section with standard 6-ft 3-in. post spacing, the results of the simulation were expected to be similar to those of a previous MASH Test 3-10 conducted on an MGS with 8-in. offset blocks (33). However, as shown in Figure 106, the vehicular behavior and occupant risk indices were more similar to those of Case 5 on the upstream end of the transition and rub rail rather than to the MASH TL-3 compliant guardrail system. The degree of snagging on the posts was excessive. In fact, the OIV was slightly higher in Case 6 without the rub rail (48.2 ft/s)

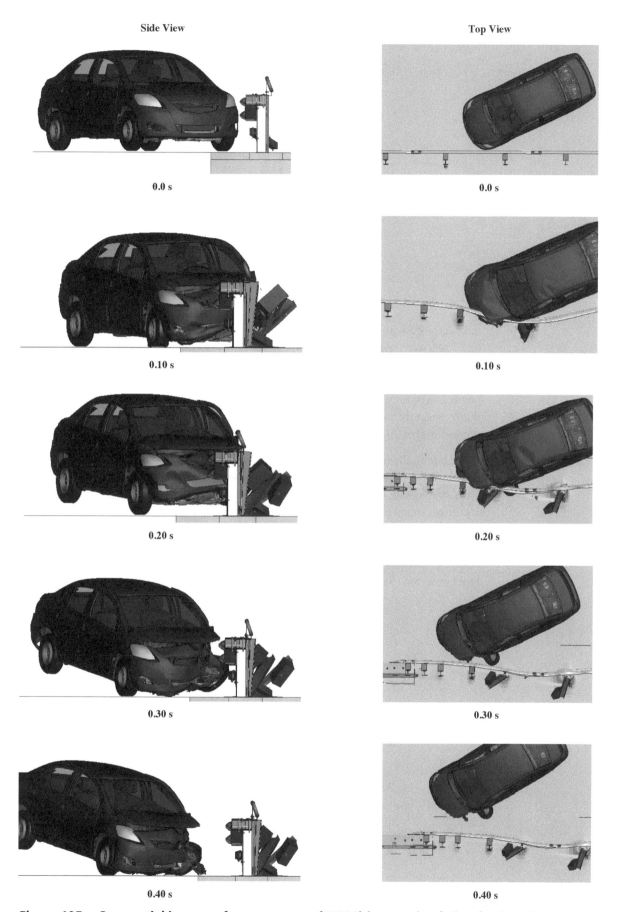

***Figure 105.    Sequential images of passenger car (1100C) impact simulation for Case 5.***

**Table 78. Occupant risk factors for Case 5 (TRAP results).**

| Variable | Value |
|---|---|
| Impact velocity (ft/s) | |
| $X$ | 45.9 |
| $Y$ | −20.3 |
| Ridedown acceleration ($g$) | |
| $X$ | −15.6 |
| $Y$ | 11.1 |
| Maximum angle (deg) | |
| Roll | 12.5 |
| Pitch | 10.3 |
| Yaw | −15.6 |

than in Case 5 with the rub rail (45.9 ft/s). It became apparent that the high OIV values computed for Case 5 were related to limitations in the vehicle model suspension that created wheel contact forces that were likely not realistic or reflective of the behavior of the transition system. However, the available project resources were insufficient to conduct the further investigations that would be necessary to validate changes to the vehicle model and further evaluate the performance of the W-beam transition with rub rail. Without this further evaluation, it is difficult to provide any professional opinion on the upstream transition.

Therefore, the research team decided to further evaluate the Thrie beam transition system as an alternative option because the project budget included only two transition crash tests for the downstream end. Whereas the W-beam transition with rub rail would require additional testing on the upstream end for a total of four crash tests (two on the downstream end and two on the upstream end), the Thrie beam transition could be evaluated with two tests on the downstream end, since the MASH compliance of the upstream end of the Thrie beam transition had already been established through a professional opinion developed under the Roadside Safety Pooled Fund program (*34*).

**Table 79. Occupant risk factors for Case 6 (TRAP results).**

| Variable | Value |
|---|---|
| Impact velocity (ft/s) | |
| $X$ | 48.2 |
| $Y$ | −16.4 |
| Ridedown acceleration ($g$) | |
| $X$ | −16.5 |
| $Y$ | 6.6 |
| Maximum angle (deg) | |
| Roll | 12.0 |
| Pitch | 10.2 |
| Yaw | −34.6 |

Side View    Top View

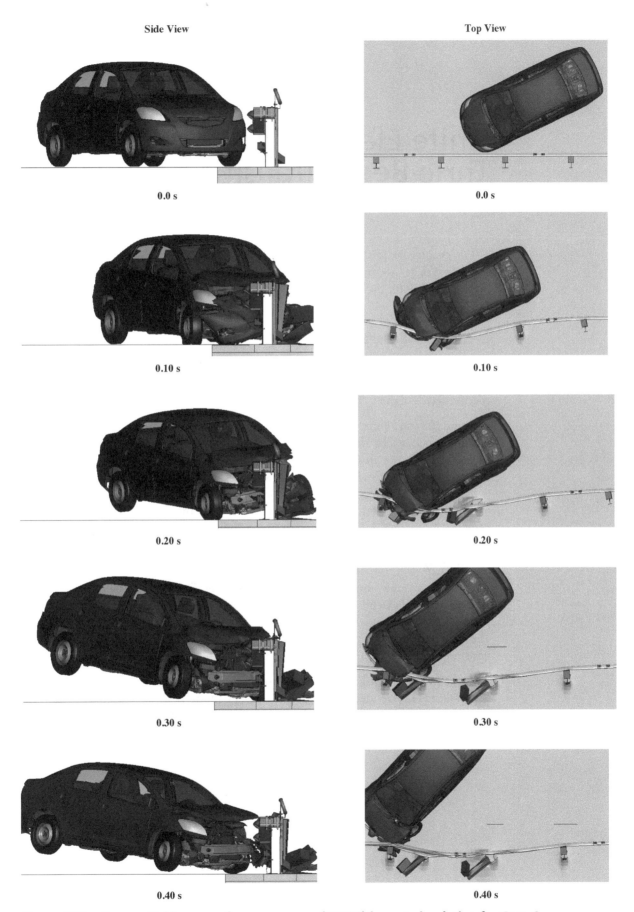

0.0 s    0.0 s

0.10 s    0.10 s

0.20 s    0.20 s

0.30 s    0.30 s

0.40 s    0.40 s

*Figure 106.    Sequential images of passenger car (1100C) impact simulation for Case 6.*

CHAPTER 13

# Finite Element Analysis for Final Thrie Beam Transition System

This chapter describes the design of the transition system and the results of the computer simulation that was conducted to determine the crashworthiness of the proposed design and to identify the CIP for the full-scale crash test.

## Transition Design with Thrie Beam

The proposed Thrie beam transition system was designed by adapting and modifying the standard TxDOT Thrie beam transition design (see Figure 107). Figures 108 through 112 present specific details of the transition design.

Figure 108 and Figure 109 show specific details of the connection between the Thrie beam and the multifunctional barrier. Two Thrie beam sections are nested and connected to the multifunctional barrier by the proposed transition connector, as shown in Figure 110. The rub rail of the multifunctional barrier (HSS $4 \times 4 \times \frac{1}{4} \times 30$ in.) is terminated at the connector. The rub rail's end is connected to the back of the connector, and the flared portion of the connector is designed to minimize interaction with an impacting vehicle. As the TxDOT Thrie beam transition suggested, 7-ft-long W6 $\times$ 8.5 steel posts and 6-ft-long W6 $\times$ 8.5 steel posts were used at the Thrie beam and at the asymmetric beam locations, respectively, with half-post spacing (3 ft 1.5 in.), as shown in Figure 112.

The cane rail ended behind the last post of the multifunctional LON barrier, while the traffic rail and handrail extended past the LON's last post (see Figure 109). A terminal handrail component is suggested to connect the two handrails of the system's LON, as shown in Figure 111. The upstream (W-beam portion) of the proposed design is the same as the TxDOT Thrie beam transition (Figure 112).

Figure 113 shows the general overview of the FE model of the proposed Thrie beam transition, while Figure 114 provides specific details of the FE model of the proposed transition. The overall modeling technique and material/contact properties were similar to those utilized and described in the discussion of the multifunctional LON barrier in Chapter 6.

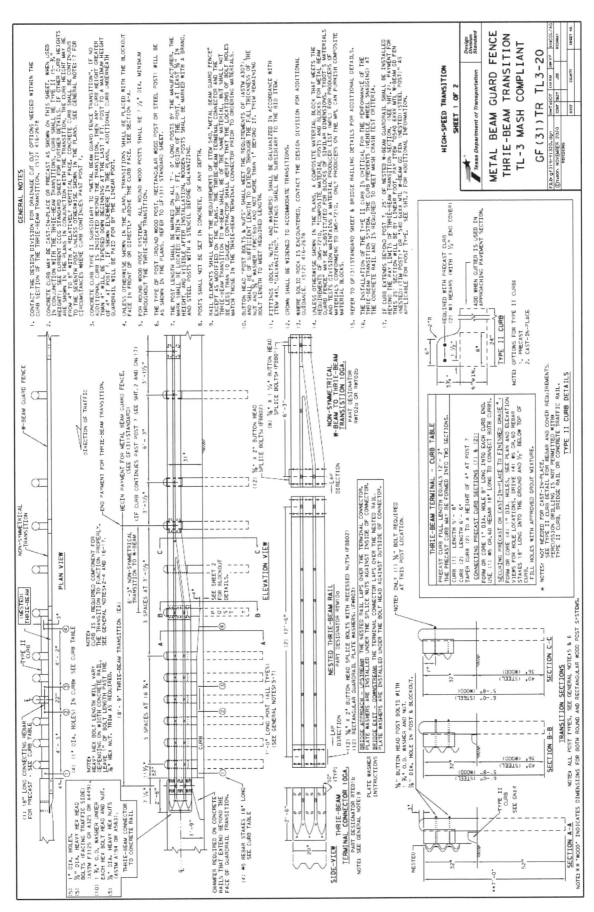

Figure 107. *Standard TxDOT MASH TL-3-compliant Thrie beam transition.*

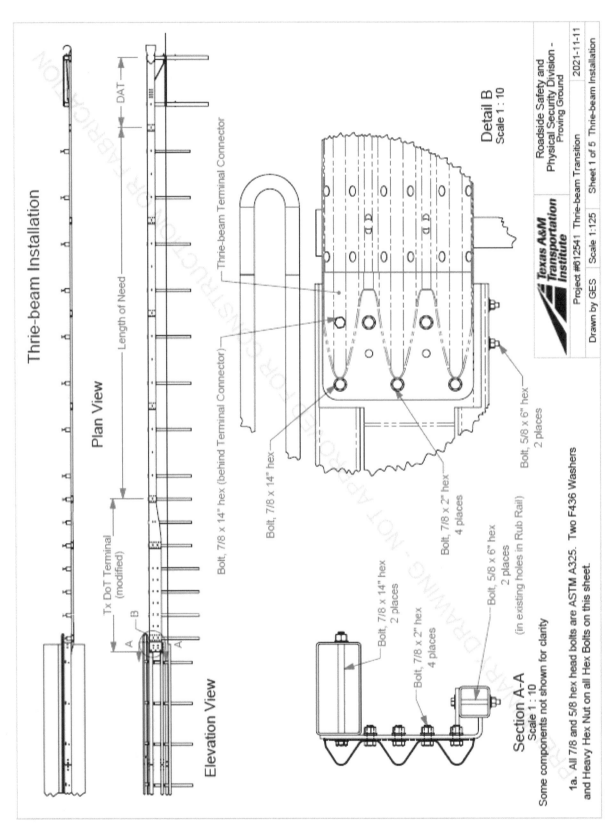

Figure 108. *Thrie beam transition overview and connection details.*

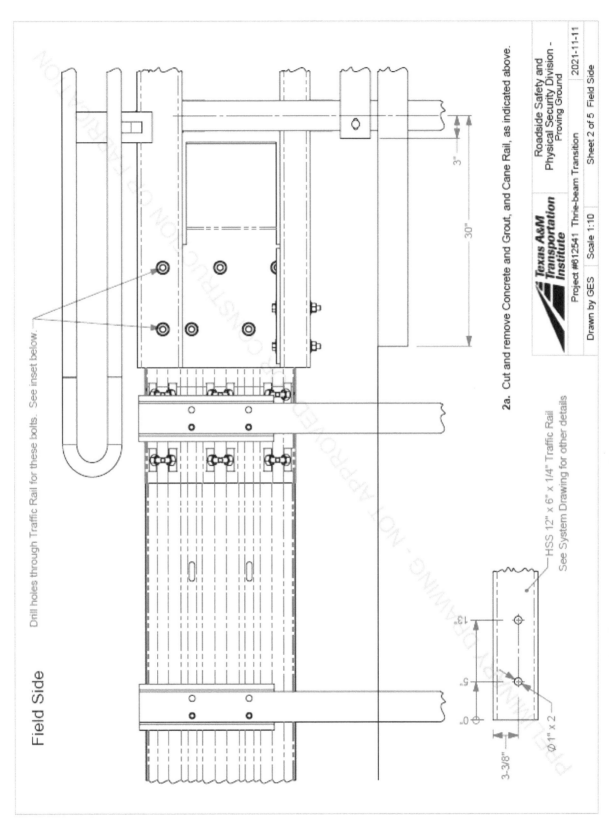

Figure 109.    *Details of Thrie beam connection to rub rail end and multifunctional rail (field side view).*

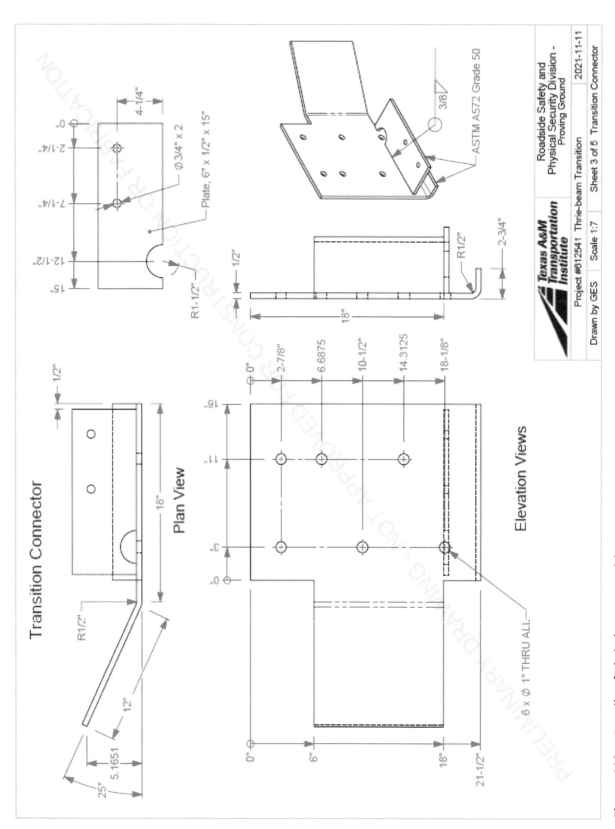

**Figure 110. Details of Thrie beam transition connector.**

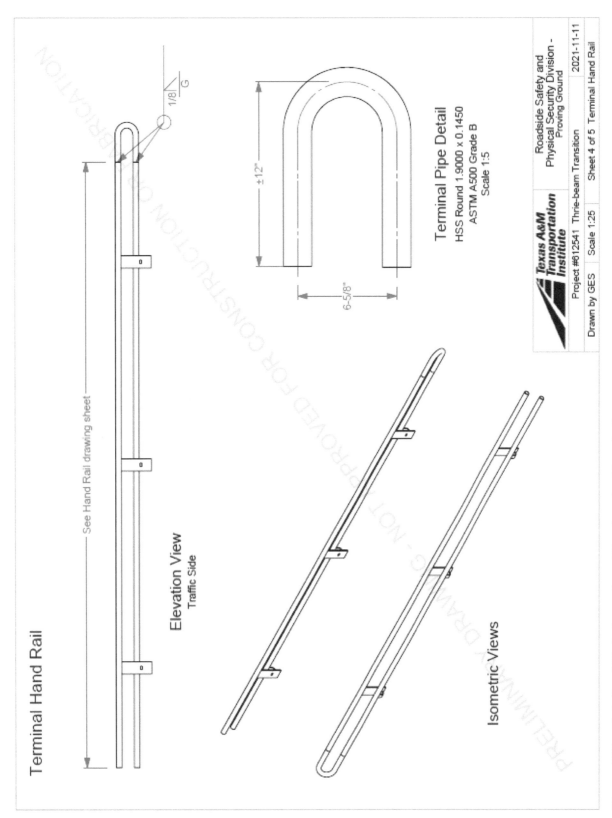

**Figure 111.** *Details of Thrie beam transition terminal handrail.*

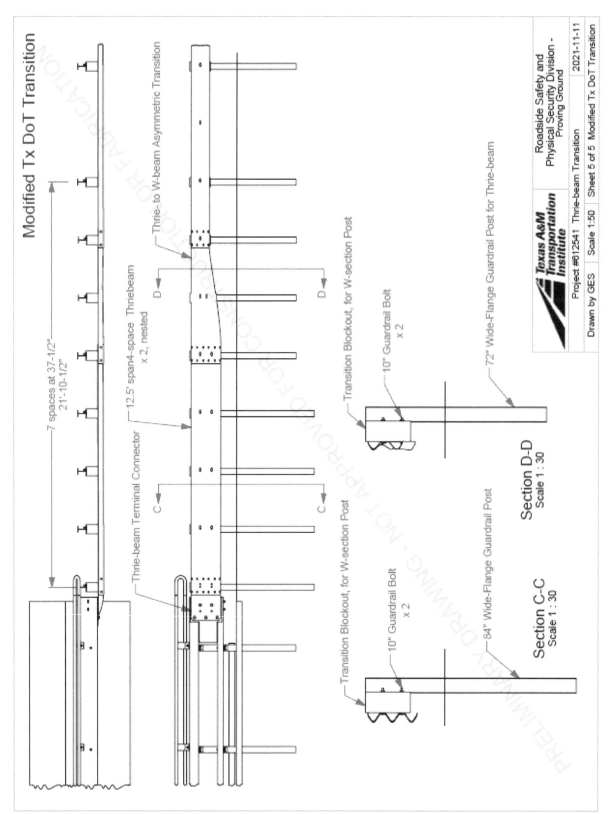

*Figure 112. Details on posts and wood blockout for Thrie beam transition.*

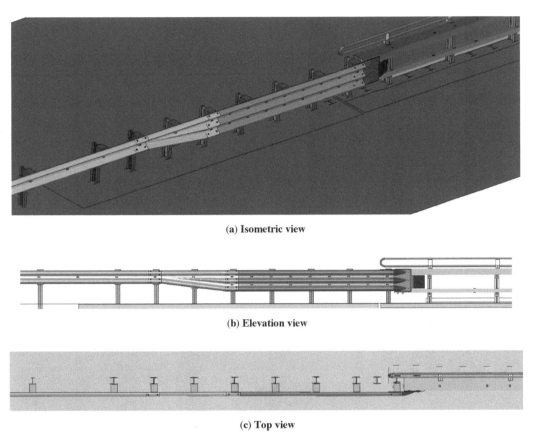

(a) Isometric view

(b) Elevation view

(c) Top view

*Figure 113. FE model of transition system with Thrie beam.*

## Predictive Investigation of Crashworthiness of Transition

The research team conducted simulations to replicate the impact vehicles at various locations of the proposed Thrie beam transition. Since the passenger car (1100C) showed more critical behavior than the pickup truck (2270P), the passenger car simulations in accordance with MASH Test 3-20 were conducted prior to the pickup truck simulations. MASH recommends performing a parametric investigation of the critical location of impact, to identify the system CIP, which is the impact point that maximizes the risk of failure of the system's crashworthiness.

### MASH Test 3-20 Simulations (1100C)

Since the upstream configuration of the proposed Thrie beam transition was the same as the TxDOT Thrie beam transition, the research team agreed to focus on investigating the system's crashworthiness at its downstream location, that is, at the attachment between the transition and the multifunctional rail. A professional opinion is available for the upstream location (i.e., the connection between the transition and the W-beam guardrail LON) (*34*). Therefore, the downstream impact locations were selected for the preliminary CIP investigation. The following impact locations were considered in the investigation of the system's crashworthiness during the 1100C impact (Figure 115):

- Case 1: Impact location = 1 ft upstream of fourth transition post.
- Case 2: Impact location = at fifth transition post.
- Case 3: Impact location = 1 ft downstream of fourth transition post.

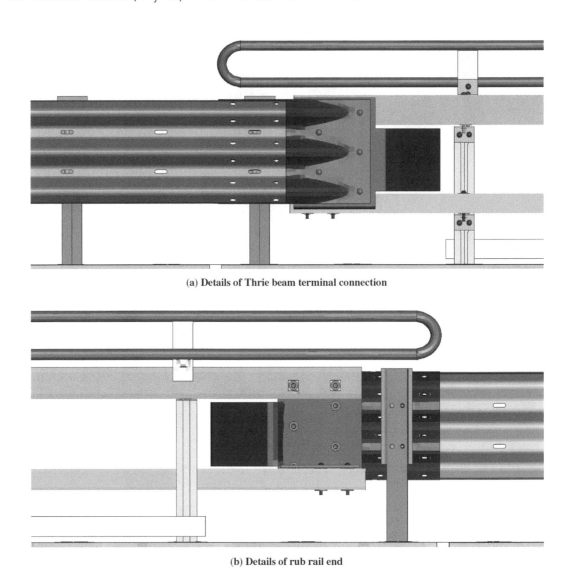

(a) Details of Thrie beam terminal connection

(b) Details of rub rail end

***Figure 114. Details of the proposed Thrie beam transition FE model.***

The selection of the impact locations was based on previous transition design and testing experience. Cases were selected with the objective of maximizing the potential for vehicle instability and pocketing on the end of the multifunctional barrier (near the transition connection).

According to the computational investigation of downstream impact points (Cases 1, 2, and 3), the passenger car was successfully contained and redirected and maintained its stability throughout the impact event. Figures 116 through 118 show sequential frames of the impact simulations for Cases 1 through 3. Table 80 shows the summary of numerical and TRAP analysis results. The occupant risk factors for all cases met the MASH TL-3 evaluation criteria.

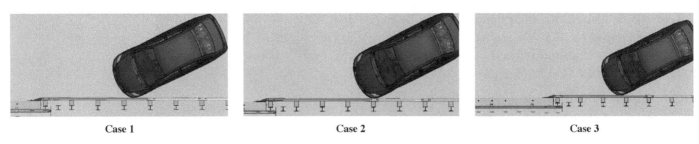

Case 1            Case 2            Case 3

***Figure 115. MASH Test 3-20: Downstream critical impact locations investigated for the Thrie transition.***

Side View                                                                  Top View

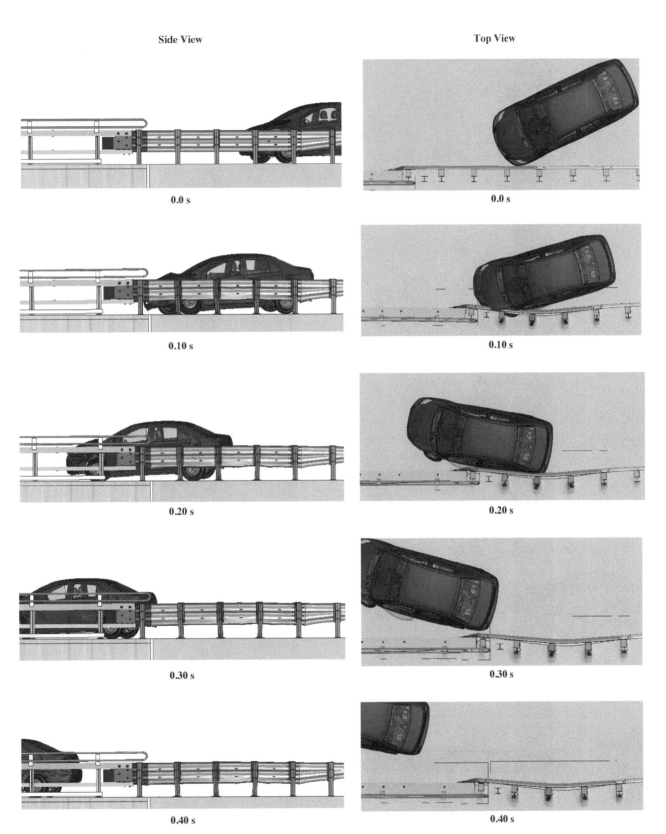

*Figure 116.   Sequential images of passenger car (1100C) impact simulation for Thrie beam transition, Case 1.*

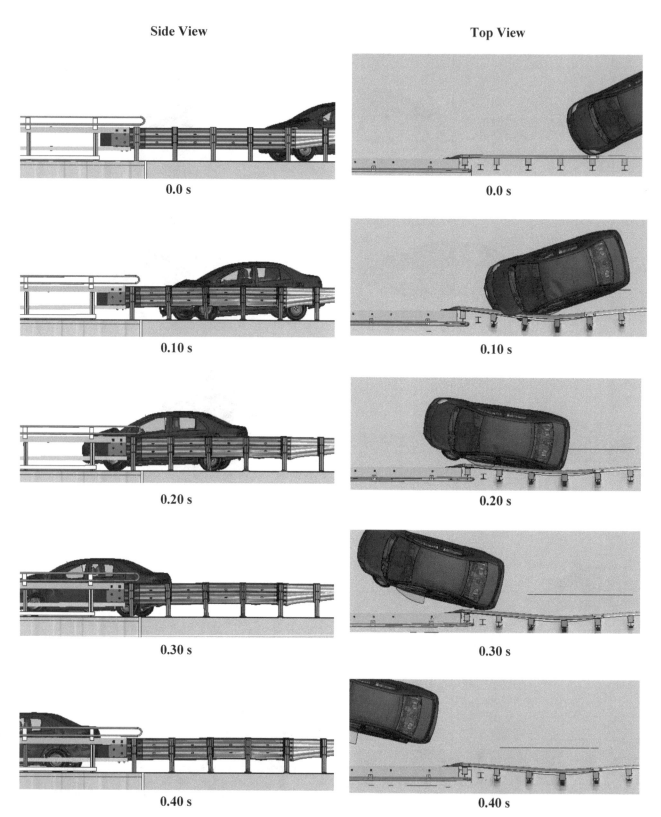

**Figure 117.** *Sequential images of passenger car (1100C) impact simulation for Thrie beam transition, Case 2.*

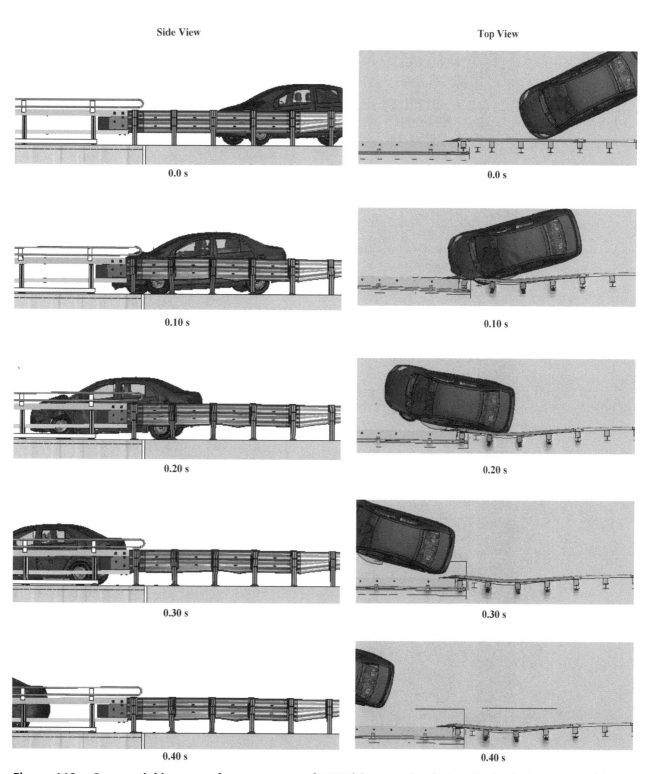

*Figure 118.  Sequential images of passenger car (1100C) impact simulation for Thrie beam transition, Case 3.*

**Table 80. Summary table of MASH Test 3-20 Thrie beam transition CIP analysis.**

| Variable | Measurement | Variable | Measurement | Variable | Measurement |
|---|---|---|---|---|---|
| **Case 1: 1100C—1 ft upstream of fourth transition post** | | **Case 2: 1100C—fifth transition post** | | **Case 3: 1100C—1 ft downstream of fourth transition post** | |
| Deflection (in.) | | Deflection (in.) | | Deflection (in.) | |
| Dynamic | 12.05 | Dynamic | 11.5 | Dynamic | 12.1 |
| Permanent | 10.1 | Permanent | 9.6 | Permanent | 9.9 |
| OIV (ft/s) | | OIV (ft/s) | | OIV (ft/s) | |
| $X$ | 21.0 | $X$ | 20.0 | $X$ | 20.7 |
| $Y$ | 27.2 | $Y$ | 30.5 | $Y$ | 29.9 |
| Stability (deg) | | Stability (deg) | | Stability (deg) | |
| Roll | 3.2 | Roll | 2.5 | Roll | 3.3 |
| Pitch | 2.4 | Pitch | 2.5 | Pitch | 2.6 |
| Yaw | 39.8 | Yaw | 39.7 | Yaw | 41.4 |
| Ridedown acceleration ($g$) | | Ridedown acceleration ($g$) | | Ridedown acceleration ($g$) | |
| $X$ | 9.2 | $X$ | 8.6 | $X$ | 7.7 |
| $Y$ | 16.2 | $Y$ | 8.4 | $Y$ | 9.4 |

The impact location for Case 2 allowed for more interaction with the end of the multifunctional LON barrier. However, the lateral ORA value for Case 1 was almost twice that recorded for Case 2. On the basis of the impact simulation results, Case 1 was determined to be the CIP for the passenger car crash tests.

### MASH Test 3-21 Simulations (2270C)

Since the passenger car (1100C) met MASH TL-3 evaluation criteria, impact simulations for the pickup truck (2270P) were conducted to assess the crashworthiness of the proposed system with regard to pickup truck impact conditions and to investigate the proposed CIP for testing. For the same reason reported in the previous section regarding the passenger car investigation method, only downstream impact simulations were conducted to account for pickup truck impacts. The following impact locations were considered in the investigation of the system's crashworthiness under 2270P impact (Figure 119):

- Case 1: Impact location = 2 ft downstream of fourth transition post.
- Case 2: Impact location = at fourth transition post.
- Case 3: Impact location = at fifth transition post.

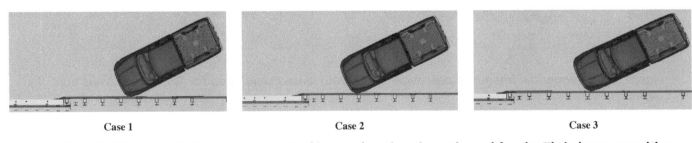

Case 1                 Case 2                 Case 3

*Figure 119. MASH Test 3-21: Downstream critical impact locations investigated for the Thrie beam transition.*

The selection of the impact locations was based on previous transition design and testing experience. Cases were selected with the objective of maximizing the potential for vehicle instability and pocketing on the end of the multifunctional barrier (near the transition connection).

During all the simulations conducted with consideration of different CIPs, the pickup truck was successfully contained and redirected and maintained its stability during the impact event. Figures 120 through 122 show the sequential images of the impact simulations of the pickup truck (2270P). Table 81 shows the summary of numerical and TRAP analysis results. The occupant risk factors for all cases met the MASH TL-3 evaluation criteria. On the basis of the results of the simulations and the predicted interaction between the pickup truck and the system during impact, Case 1 was determined to be the most critical for consideration for full-scale testing.

## Conclusion

The proposed Thrie beam transition system shows promise for meeting MASH requirements for both the pickup truck (MASH Test 3-21) and the passenger car (MASH Test 3-20) impacting at the downstream portion of the transition. On the basis of the simulation design, the CIP for the passenger car (1100C) and the pickup truck (2270P) is 1 ft upstream and 2 ft upstream of the fourth transition post, respectively.

As mentioned previously, the design and layout of the upstream configuration of this Thrie beam transition system are similar to the TxDOT Thrie beam transition. The upstream end of the TxDOT Thrie beam transition is considered MASH compliant on the basis of a professional opinion developed under the Roadside Safety Pooled Fund program (*34*). The research team recommends using the professional opinion developed for the TxDOT Thrie beam transition for the upstream end of the proposed transition. If testing of the upstream end of the proposed transition is desired, further funding will be needed to conduct the full-scale crash tests.

Side View                                   Top View

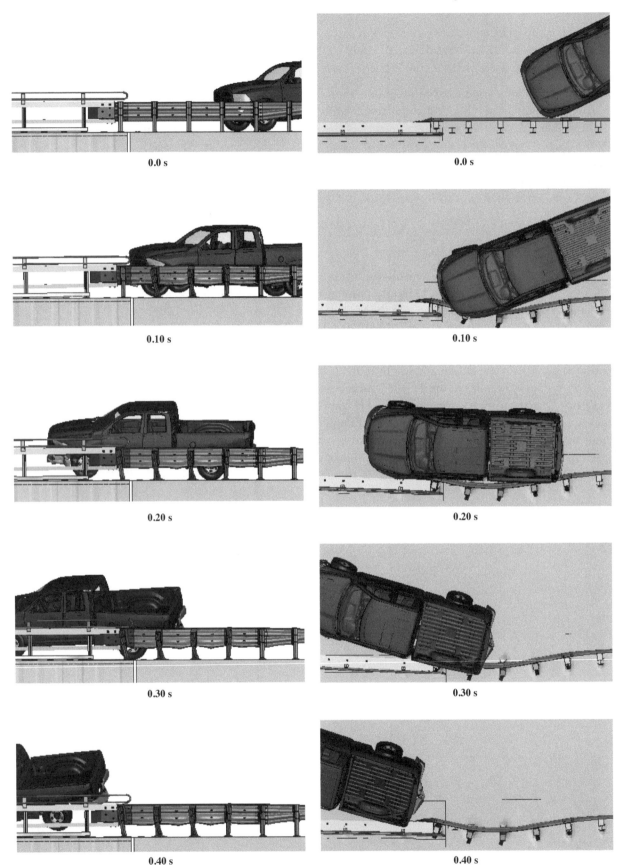

Figure 120. Sequential images of pickup truck (2270P) impact simulation for Thrie beam transition, Case 1.

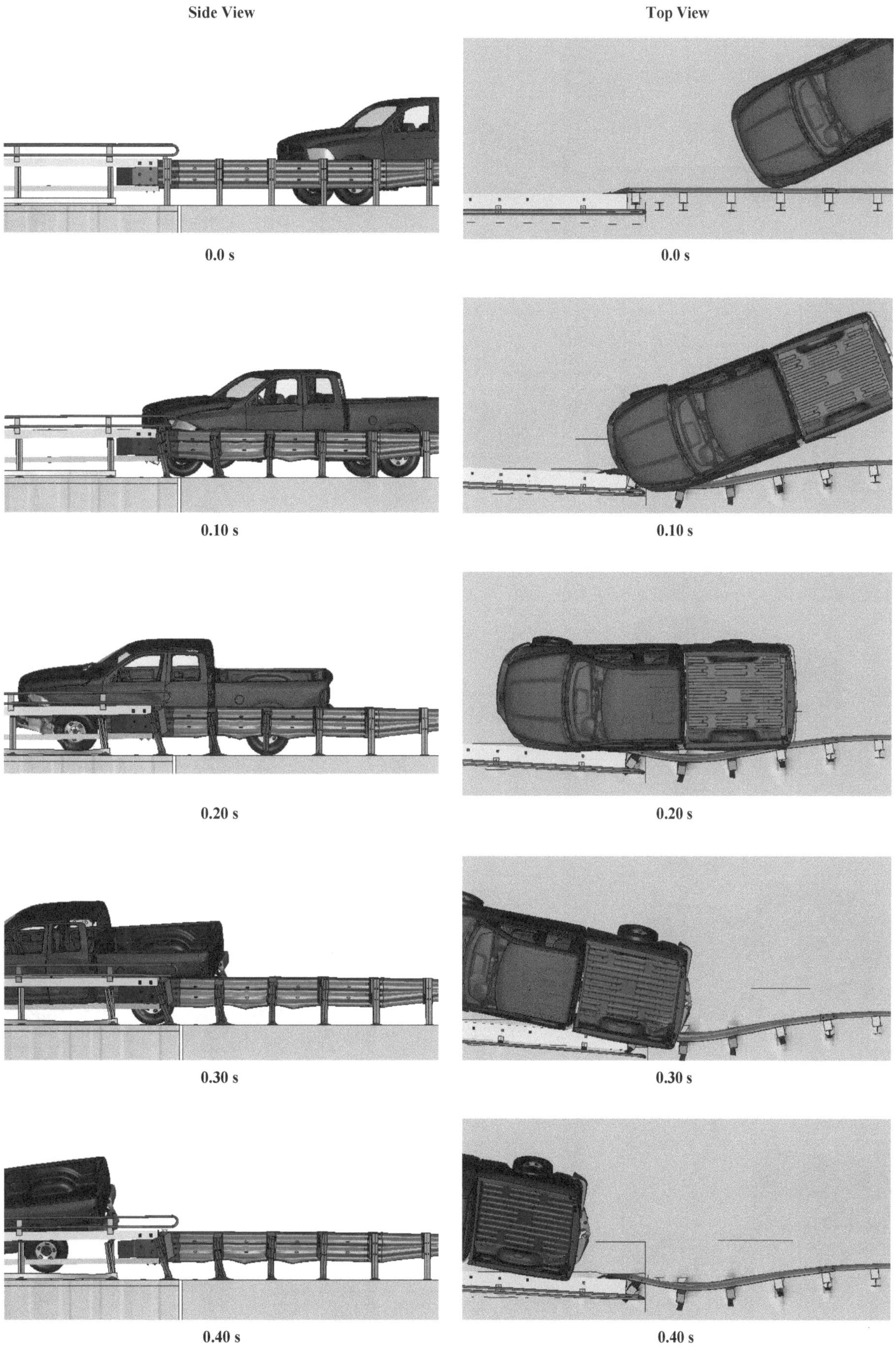

Side View       Top View

0.0 s       0.0 s

0.10 s       0.10 s

0.20 s       0.20 s

0.30 s       0.30 s

0.40 s       0.40 s

Figure 121.   Sequential images of pickup truck (2270P) impact simulation for Thrie beam transition, Case 2.

Side View                                          Top View

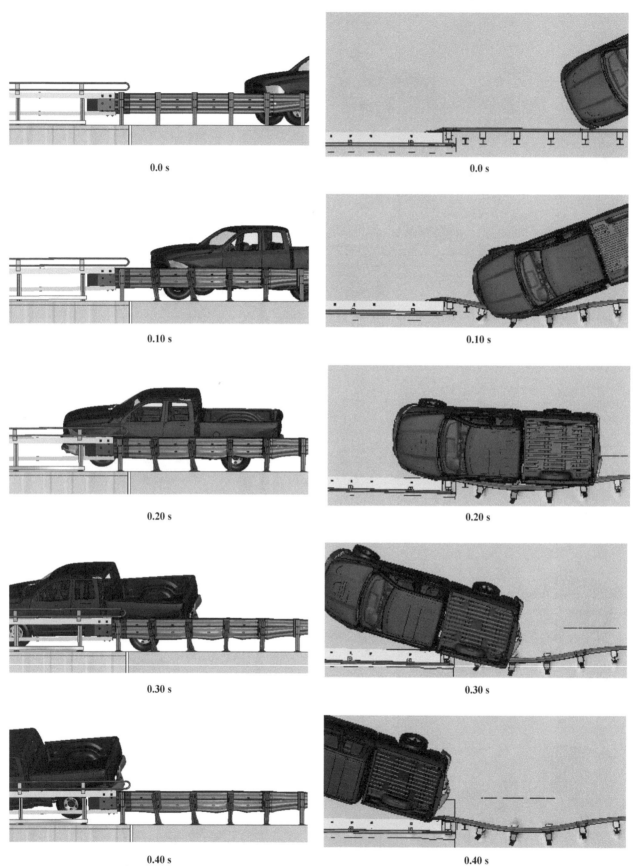

0.0 s                                              0.0 s

0.10 s                                             0.10 s

0.20 s                                             0.20 s

0.30 s                                             0.30 s

0.40 s                                             0.40 s

*Figure 122.    Sequential images of pickup truck (2270P) impact simulation for Thrie beam transition, Case 3.*

**Table 81.   Summary table of MASH Test 3-21 Thrie beam transition CIP analysis.**

| Variable | Measurement | Variable | Measurement | Variable | Measurement |
|---|---|---|---|---|---|
| **Case 1: 1100C—2 ft upstream of fourth transition post** | | **Case 2: 1100C—fourth transition post** | | **Case 3: 1100C—1 ft downstream of fourth transition post** | |
| Deflection (in.) | | Deflection (in.) | | Deflection (in.) | |
| Dynamic | 19.3 | Dynamic | 20.4 | Dynamic | 19.1 |
| Permanent | 16.6 | Permanent | 17.6 | Permanent | 16.6 |
| OIV (ft/s) | | OIV (ft/s) | | OIV (ft/s) | |
| X | 5.7 | X | 6.1 | X | 5.3 |
| Y | 7.0 | Y | 6.9 | Y | 7.1 |
| Stability (deg) | | Stability (deg) | | Stability (deg) | |
| Roll | 33.6 | Roll | 25.0 | Roll | 36.4 |
| Pitch | 6.9 | Pitch | 7.4 | Pitch | 5.8 |
| Yaw | 42.7 | Yaw | 35.4 | Yaw | 42.1 |
| Ridedown acceleration (g) | | Ridedown acceleration (g) | | Ridedown acceleration (g) | |
| X | 5.9 | X | 8.7 | X | 7.4 |
| Y | 11.0 | Y | 8.0 | Y | 11.6 |

# CHAPTER 14

# System Details for MASH Tests 3-20 and 3-21

## Test Article and Installation Details

The length of the test installation was 255 ft 8 in. The upstream end of the installation had a 79-ft section of guardrail and terminated at the upstream end with a steel post W-beam cable anchorage system. One section of Thrie beam guardrail was connected to the upstream end of the multifunctional rail, and a nonsymmetrical Thrie beam to W-beam connection was used to attach the upstream end of the Thrie beam to a W-beam guardrail. The downstream end of the installation was anchored with a steel post W-beam cable anchorage system that was approximately 9 ft 4 in. long. The multifunctional barrier was constructed of an HSS with dimensions of $12 \times 6 \times \frac{1}{4}$ in. with its top located 32 in. above grade. The rub rail was an HSS with dimensions of $4 \times 4 \times \frac{1}{4}$ in. with its top located 13 in. above grade. The rails were supported by $W6 \times 8.5$ posts spaced at 66 in. on center.

The field side handrails of the multifunctional barrier were fabricated of HSS 1.90-in.-diameter $\times$ 0.145-in.-thick tubing. Their centers were located 35 in. and 41 in. above grade, respectively. A cane rail, also on the field side, was fabricated from an 11-gauge 4-in.-wide plate with its bottom edge 1 in. above grade.

The posts of the multifunctional barrier were set in a 19-in.-wide, 4-in.-thick continuous band of grout, with 24-in.-wide, 4-in.-thick concrete slabs on both sides. The traffic side faces of the posts were 4 in. from the joint between the concrete and grout.

Due to an error during construction prior to MASH Test 3-21 (Crash Test 612541-01-3), Post 12 (the post placed in the middle of the Thrie beam to W-beam asymmetric transition rail) had a W-beam blockout with one 10-in. guardrail bolt as opposed to the transition blockout with two 10-in. guardrail bolts that the original drawings called for. This error was corrected for the MASH Test 3-20 (Crash Test 612541-01-4), and the drawings in Appendix F reflect what was tested. Because Post 12 was upstream of the impact location for Crash Tests 612541-01-3 and 612541-01-4, the error was determined not to be a factor in the outcome of the crash tests. (Note: This opinion/interpretation is outside the scope of the TTI Proving Ground's A2LA accreditation.)

Figure 123 presents the overall information on the multifunctional barrier transition for Crash Test 612541-01-3, and Figures 124 through 129 provide photographs of the installation. Appendix F provides further details on the multifunctional barrier transition for Crash Test 612541-01-3. Drawings were provided by the TTI Proving Ground, and construction was performed by TTI Proving Ground personnel.

For Crash Test 612541-01-4, the section of the multifunctional barrier that was the farthest upstream was removed, and the concrete and grout were cut out because of damage from the previous test, Crash Test 612541-01-3. This removal shortened the overall length of the installation by 16 ft 6 in., making the total length 239 ft 2 in. All other details of the installation remained the same.

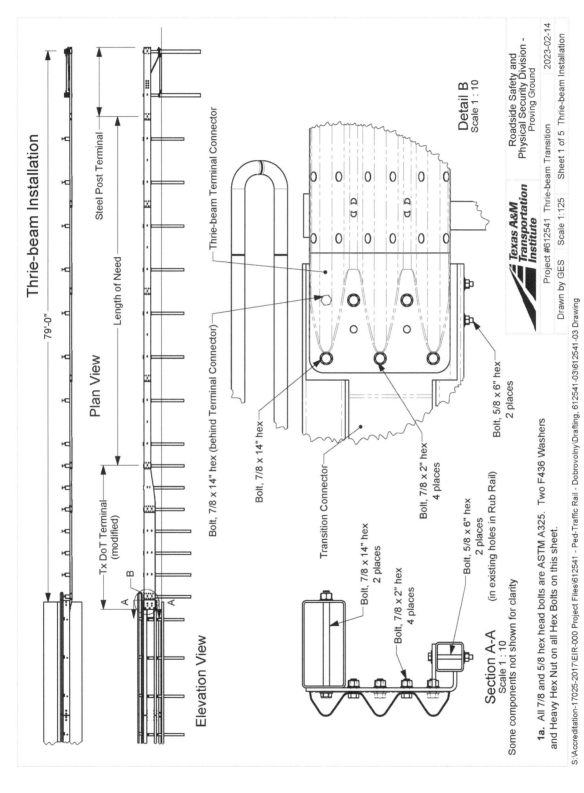

**Figure 123. Details on multifunctional barrier transition for Crash Test 612541-01-3.**

*Figure 124. Multifunctional barrier transition prior to Crash Test 612541-01-3.*

*Figure 125. Downstream view of the multifunctional barrier transition prior to Crash Test 612541-01-3.*

*Figure 126. Field side of the multifunctional barrier transition prior to Crash Test 612541-01-3.*

*Figure 127.   Field side of the multifunctional barrier transition at the transition prior to Crash Test 612541-01-3.*

*Figure 128.   Close-up view of a transition post on the multifunctional barrier transition prior to Crash Test 612541-01-3.*

*Figure 129.    In-line view of the multifunctional barrier transition prior to Crash Test 612541-01-3.*

Figure 130 presents the overall information on the multifunctional barrier transition for Crash Test 612541-01-4, and Figures 131 through 134 provide photographs of the installation. Appendix E provides further details on the multifunctional barrier transition for Crash Test 612541-01-4. Drawings were provided by the TTI Proving Ground, and construction was performed by TTI Proving Ground personnel.

## Design Modifications During Tests

No modifications were made during testing.

## Material Specifications

Appendix I provides material certification documents for the materials used to install/construct the multifunctional barrier transition. For information on the concrete, see Table 47.

## Soil Conditions

The test installation was installed in standard soil meeting Type 1 Grade D of AASHTO standard specification M147-17 "Materials for Aggregate and Soil Aggregate Subbase, Base, and Surface Courses." In accordance with Appendix B of MASH, the soil strength was measured the day of the crash test. During installation of the pedestrian traffic rail transition for full-scale crash testing, two 6-ft-long W6 × 16 posts were installed in the immediate vicinity of the pedestrian traffic rail transition with the same fill materials and installation procedures used in the test installation and the standard dynamic test. Table B.1 in MASH Appendix B (*1*) presents minimum soil strength properties established through the dynamic testing performed in accordance with MASH Appendix B.

The minimum post loads are shown in Table 82 and Table 83. Table 82 shows the loads on the post at the specified deflections on the day of MASH Test 3-21, February 15, 2023. The backfill material in which the multifunctional barrier transition was installed met the minimum MASH requirements for soil strength. Table 83 shows the loads on the post at the specified deflections on the day of MASH Test 3-20, March 1, 2023. The backfill material in which the multifunctional barrier transition was installed met the minimum MASH requirements for soil strength.

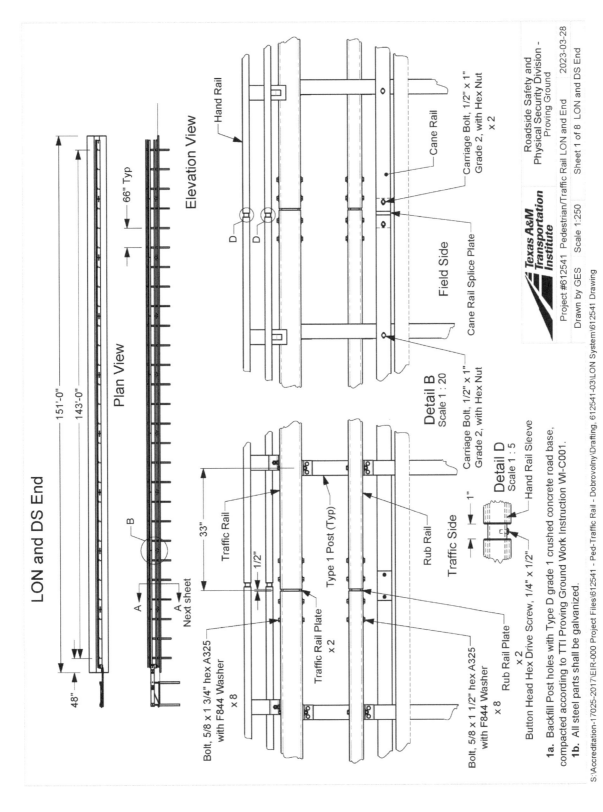

Figure 130. *Details on multifunctional barrier LON for Crash Test 612541-01-4.*

*Figure 131.  Multifunctional barrier transition prior to Crash Test 612541-01-4.*

*Figure 132.  Downstream view of the multifunctional barrier transition prior to Crash Test 612541-01-4.*

*Figure 133.  Field side of the multifunctional barrier transition prior to Crash Test 612541-01-4.*

*Figure 134.   Field side of the multifunctional barrier transition prior to Crash Test 612541-01-4.*

Table 82.   Soil strength for Crash Test 612541-01-3.

| Displacement (in.) | Minimum Load (lb) | Actual Load (lb) |
|:---:|:---:|:---:|
| 5 | 4,420 | 7,515 |
| 10 | 4,981 | 8,454 |
| 15 | 5,282 | 8,878 |

Table 83.   Soil strength for Crash Test 612541-01-4.

| Displacement (in.) | Minimum Load (lb) | Actual Load (lb) |
|:---:|:---:|:---:|
| 5 | 4,420 | 8,757 |
| 10 | 4,981 | 10,363 |
| 15 | 5,282 | 10,999 |

# Test Requirements and Evaluation Criteria for MASH Tests 3-20 and 3-21

## Performed Crash Test Matrix

Table 84 shows the test conditions and evaluation criteria for MASH TL-3 for transitions. The target CIPs for each test were determined on the basis of the FE simulations performed in Chapter 13 and using the information provided in MASH Section 2.2.1 and Section 2.3.2. Figure 135 shows the target CIP for MASH TL-3 tests on the multifunctional barrier transition. The crash tests and data analysis procedures were in accordance with guidelines presented in MASH. Chapter 4 presents brief descriptions of these procedures.

**Table 84. Test conditions and evaluation criteria specified for MASH TL-3 longitudinal barrier.**

| Test Designation | Test Vehicle | Impact Conditions | | Evaluation Criteria[a] |
| | | Speed (mi/h) | Angle (deg) | |
|---|---|---|---|---|
| 3-20 | 1100C | 62 | 25 | A, D, F, H, I |
| 3-21 | 2270P | 62 | 25 | A, D, F, H, I |

[a]Detailed information on the evaluation criteria is given in Table 51 in Chapter 8.

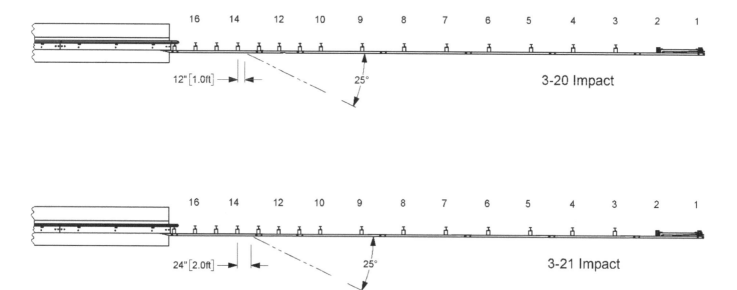

*Figure 135. Target CIP for MASH TL-3 tests on multifunctional barrier transition.*

## Evaluation Criteria

The appropriate safety evaluation criteria from Tables 2.2 and 5.1 of MASH were used to evaluate the transition crash tests reported herein. Table 84 lists the test conditions and evaluation criteria required for MASH TL-3. Detailed information on the evaluation criteria is given in Table 51 in Chapter 8.

# CHAPTER 16

# MASH Test 3-20 (Crash Test 612541-01-4)

## Test Designation and Actual Impact Conditions

The MASH impact conditions and exit parameters for Test 612541-01-4 are given in Table 85 and Table 86, respectively. Figure 136 and Figure 137 depict the setup of the target impact.

## Weather Conditions

Table 87 provides the weather conditions for Crash Test 612541-01-4.

**Table 85. Impact conditions for MASH Test 3-20 (Crash Test 612541-01-4).**

| Test Parameter | Specification | Tolerance | Measured |
|---|---|---|---|
| Impact speed (mi/h) | 62 | ±2.5 | 62.6 |
| Impact angle (deg) | 25 | ±1.5 | 25.5 |
| Impact severity (kip-ft) | 51 | ≥51 | 58.9 |
| Impact location [distance (in.) upstream of centerline of Post 14] | 12 | ±12 | 8 |

**Table 86. Exit parameters for MASH Test 3-20 (Crash Test 612541-01-4).**

| Exit Parameter | Measured |
|---|---|
| Speed (mi/h) | 48.3 |
| Trajectory (deg) | 11.6 |
| Heading (deg) | 11.6 |
| Brakes applied post impact (s) | 2.7 |
| Vehicle at rest position | 230 ft downstream of impact point<br>93 ft to the traffic side<br>30 deg left |
| Comments | Vehicle remained upright and stable.<br>Vehicle crossed the exit box[a] at 40 ft downstream from loss of contact and satisfied the exit box criteria described in MASH. |

[a]Not less than 32.8 ft downstream from loss of contact for cars and pickups is optimal.

*Figure 136.   Multifunctional barrier transition/test vehicle geometrics for Crash Test 612541-01-4.*

*Figure 137.   Multifunctional barrier transition/test vehicle impact location for Crash Test 612541-01-4.*

Table 87.   Weather conditions for Crash Test 612541-01-4 (2023-03-01, AM).

| Condition | Measurement |
|---|---|
| Wind speed (mi/h) | 17 |
| Wind direction (deg) | 188 |
| Temperature (°F) | 79 |
| Relative humidity (%) | 79 |
| Vehicle traveling (deg) | 195 |

## Test Vehicle

Figure 138 and Figure 139 show the 2018 Nissan Versa used for the crash test. Table 88 gives the vehicle measurements. Figure G.1 in Appendix G, Section G.1, gives additional dimensions and information about the vehicle.

*Figure 138.   Impact side of test vehicle before Crash Test 612541-01-4.*

*Figure 139.   Opposite of the impact side of the test vehicle before Crash Test 612541-01-4.*

**Table 88.   Vehicle measurements for Crash Test 612541-01-4.**

| Test Parameter | MASH | Allowed Tolerance | Measured |
|---|---|---|---|
| Dummy (if applicable)$^a$ (lb) | 165 | N/A | 165 |
| Inertial weight (lb) | 2,420 | ±55 | 2,427 |
| Gross static$^a$ (lb) | 2,585 | ±55 | 2,592 |
| Wheelbase (in.) | 98 | ±5 | 102.4 |
| Front overhang (in.) | 35 | ±4 | 32.5 |
| Overall length (in.) | 169 | ±8 | 175.4 |
| Overall width (in.) | 65 | ±3 | 66.7 |
| Hood height (in.) | 28 | ±4 | 30.5 |
| Track width$^b$ (in.) | 59 | ±2 | 58.4 |
| CG aft of front axle$^c$ (in.) | 39 | ±4 | 41.85 |
| CG above ground$^{c,d}$ (in.) | N/A | N/A | N/A |

$^a$ If a dummy is used, the gross static vehicle mass includes the mass of the dummy.
$^b$ Average of front and rear axles.
$^c$ For test inertial mass.
$^d$ 2270P vehicle must meet minimum CG height requirement.

## Test Description

Table 89 lists events that occurred during Crash Test 612541-01-4. Figures G.4, G.5, and G.6 in Appendix G, Section G.2, present sequential photographs from the test.

## Damage to Test Installation

The rail was scuffed at impact. Table 90 reports the post displacement and lean of the installation, and Table 91 describes the deflection and working width of the multifunctional barrier transition. Figure 140 and Figure 141 show the damage to the pedestrian traffic rail transition.

**Table 89.  Events during Crash Test 612541-01-4.**

| Time (s) | Event |
|---|---|
| 0.0000 | Vehicle impacted the installation. |
| 0.0150 | Posts 14 and 15 began to lean toward field side. |
| 0.0280 | Posts 13 and 16 began to lean toward field side. |
| 0.0300 | Vehicle began to redirect. |
| 0.0410 | Post 17 began to lean toward field side. |
| 0.1520 | Vehicle was parallel with installation. |
| 0.1590 | Passenger side of rear bumper contacted rail. |
| 0.2720 | Vehicle lost contact with the rail traveling 48.3 mi/h at a trajectory and heading of 11.6 deg. |

**Table 90.  Post displacement details for multifunctional barrier transition for Crash Test 612541-01-4.**

| Post | Soil Gap (in.) | | Lean from Vertical Toward Field Side (deg) |
| | Traffic Side | Field Side | |
|---|---|---|---|
| 13 | ¼ | — | 1.5 |
| 14 | 1 | ½ | 2 |
| 15 | — | 1 | 3 |
| 16 | — | ¾ | 1 |
| 17 | — | ¼ | 1 |

**Table 91.  Deflection and working width of the multifunctional barrier transition for Crash Test 612541-01-4.**

| Test Parameter | Measured |
|---|---|
| Permanent deflection/location (in.) | 2.75 toward field side, 2 ft downstream from Post 14 |
| Dynamic deflection (in.) | 6.8 toward field side at Post 15 |
| Working width[a] and height (in.) | 24.1 at a height of 31.8 at Post 15 |

[a] Per MASH, "The working width is the maximum dynamic lateral position of any major part of the system or vehicle. These measurements are all relative to the pre-impact traffic face of the test article." In other words, the working width is the total barrier width plus the maximum dynamic intrusion of any portion of the barrier or test vehicle past the field side edge of the barrier.

*Figure 140.   Multifunctional barrier transition after test at impact location for Crash Test 612541-01-4.*

*Figure 141.   Field side of the multifunctional barrier transition after Crash Test 612541-01-4.*

## Damage to Test Vehicle

Figure 142 and Figure 143 show the damage sustained by the vehicle. Figure 144 and Figure 145 show the interior of the test vehicle. Table 92 and Table 93 provide details on the occupant compartment deformation and exterior vehicle damage, respectively. Figures G.2 and G.3 in Appendix G, Section G.1, provide exterior crush and occupant compartment measurements.

## Occupant Risk Factors

Data from the accelerometers were digitized for evaluation of occupant risk, and the results are shown in Table 94. Figure G.7 in Appendix G, Section G.3, shows the vehicle angular displacements, and Figures G.8 through G.10 in Appendix G, Section G.4, show acceleration versus time traces.

## Test Summary

Figure 146 summarizes the results of MASH Crash Test 612541-01-4.

*Figure 142.   Impact side of test vehicle after Crash Test 612541-01-4.*

*Figure 143.   Rear impact side of test vehicle after Crash Test 612541-01-4.*

*Figure 144.   Overall interior of test vehicle after Crash Test 612541-01-4.*

*Figure 145.    Interior of test vehicle on impact side after Crash Test 612541-01-4.*

**Table 92.    Occupant compartment deformation for Crash Test 612541-01-4.**

| Test Parameter | Specification (in.) | Measured (in.) |
|---|---|---|
| Roof | ≤4.0 | 0.0 |
| Windshield | ≤3.0 | 0.0 |
| A and B pillars | ≤5.0 overall, ≤3.0 lateral | 0.0 |
| Foot well/toe pan | ≤9.0 | 0.0 |
| Floor pan/transmission tunnel | ≤12.0 | 0.0 |
| Side front panel | ≤12.0 | 0.5 |
| Front door (above seat) | ≤9.0 | 1.0 |
| Front door (below seat) | ≤12.0 | 0.0 |

**Table 93.    Exterior vehicle damage for Crash Test 612541-01-4.**

| Part of Vehicle | Damage |
|---|---|
| Side windows | Side windows remained intact |
| Maximum exterior deformation | 10 in. in the front plane at the passenger side front corner at bumper height |
| VDS | 01RFQ4 |
| CDC | 01FREW2 |
| Fuel tank damage | None |
| Description of damage to vehicle | The front bumper, radiator and support, right and left headlights, right front quarter fender, right front tire and rim, right front strut and tower, right front door, right rear door, right rear quarter fender, right rear tire and rim, and rear bumper were damaged. The right front door had a 2.75-in. gap at the top. |

**Table 94.  Occupant risk factors for Crash Test 612541-01-4.**

| Test Parameter | MASH[a] | Measured | Time (s) |
|---|---|---|---|
| OIV (ft/s) | | | |
| X | ≤40.0<br>*30.0* | 17.9 | 0.0847 on right side of interior |
| Y | ≤40.0<br>*30.0* | 30.4 | 0.0847 on right side of interior |
| Ridedown (*g*) | | | |
| X | ≤20.49<br>*15.0* | 5.6 | 0.0847–0.0947 |
| Y | ≤20.49<br>*15.0* | 9.4 | 0.0881–0.0981 |
| THIV (m/s) | N/A | 10.6 | 0.0829 on right side of interior |
| ASI | N/A | 2.0 | 0.0543–0.1043 |
| Max. 0.050-s average (*g*) | | | |
| X | N/A | −9.5 | 0.0379–0.0879 |
| Y | N/A | −16.3 | 0.0275–0.0775 |
| Vertical | N/A | 2.1 | 0.0842–0.1342 |
| Roll (deg) | ≤75 | 10.1 | 2.0000 |
| Pitch (deg) | ≤75 | 2.3 | 0.2266 |
| Yaw (deg) | N/A | 49.3 | 2.0000 |

[a] Values in italics are the preferred MASH values.

| Sequential Photographs | | Test Agency | Texas A&M Transportation Institute (TTI) |
|---|---|---|---|
| | | Test Standard/Test No. | MASH 2016, Test 3-20 |
| | | TTI Project No. | 612541-01-4 |
| | | Test Date | 2023-03-01 |
| **0.000 s** | | **TEST ARTICLE** | |
| | | Type | Longitudinal barrier |
| | | Name | Pedestrian Traffic Rail Transition |
| | | Length | approx. 239 ft 2 in. |
| | | Key Materials: LON | Traffic side: HSS 12- × 6- × ¼-in. traffic rail, HSS 4- × 4- × ¼-in. rub rail, W6 × 8.5 posts spaced at 66 in. Field side: HSS round 1.9-in.-diameter × 0.145-in.-thick (Sch 40) ASTM A500 Grade B tubing × 2, and 12-gauge, 4-in.-wide plate cane rail |
| | | Key Materials: Transition & Terminal | Thrie beam and W-beam guardrail, 72-in.- and 84-in.-long W6 × 8.5 wide flange guardrail posts; steel post end terminal |
| **0.200 s** | | Soil Type and Condition | AASHTO M147-17 Type 1 Grading D (crushed concrete) |
| | | **TEST VEHICLE** | |
| | | Type/Designation | 1100C |
| | | Year, Make and Model | 2018 Nissan Versa |
| | | Inertial Weight (lb) | 2,427 |
| | | Dummy (lb) | 165 |
| | | Gross Static (lb) | 2,592 |
| | | **IMPACT CONDITIONS** | |
| | | Impact Speed (mi/h) | 62.6 |
| | | Impact Angle (deg) | 25.5 |
| | | Impact Location | 8 in. upstream from the centerline of Post 14 |
| | | Impact Severity (kip-ft) | 58.9 |
| **0.400 s** | | **EXIT CONDITIONS** | |
| | | Exit Speed (mi/h) | 48.3 |
| | | Trajectory/Heading Angle (deg) | 11.6/11.6 |
| | | Exit Box Criteria | Crossed the exit box 40 ft downstream from loss of contact. |
| | | Stopping Distance | 230 ft downstream 93 ft to the traffic side |
| | | **TEST ARTICLE DEFLECTIONS** | |
| | | Dynamic (in.) | 6.8 |
| | | Permanent (in.) | 2.75 |
| | | Working Width/Height (in.) | 24.1/31.8 |
| | | **VEHICLE DAMAGE** | |
| | | VDS | 01RFQ4 |
| | | CDC | 01FREW2 |
| | | Max. Ext. Deformation (in.) | 10 |
| **0.600 s** | | Max. Occupant Compartment Deformation | 1 in. in the front passenger door |

| OCCUPANT RISK VALUES | | | | | | | |
|---|---|---|---|---|---|---|---|
| Long. OIV (ft/s) | 17.9 | Long. Ridedown (g) | 5.6 | Max. 50-ms Long. (g) | -9.5 | Max. Roll (deg) | 10.1 |
| Lat. OIV (ft/s) | 30.4 | Lat. Ridedown (g) | 9.4 | Max. 50-ms Lat. (g) | -16.3 | Max. Pitch (deg) | 2.3 |
| THIV (m/s) | 10.6 | ASI | 2.0 | Max. 50-ms Vert. (g) | 2.1 | Max. Yaw (deg) | 49.3 |

**Figure 146. Summary of results for MASH Test 3-20 (Crash Test 612541-01-4) on multifunctional barrier transition.**

# CHAPTER 17

# MASH Test 3-21
# (Crash Test 612541-01-3)

## Test Designation and Actual Impact Conditions

The MASH impact conditions and exit parameters for Crash Test 612541-01-3 are given in Table 95 and Table 96, respectively. Figure 147 and Figure 148 depict the setup of the target impact.

## Weather Conditions

Table 97 provides the weather conditions for Crash Test 612541-01-3.

Table 95.  Impact conditions for MASH Test 3-21
(Crash Test 612541-01-3).

| Test Parameter | Specification | Tolerance | Measured |
|---|---|---|---|
| Impact speed (mi/h) | 62 | ±2.5 | 62.2 |
| Impact angle (deg) | 25 | ±1.5 | 24.7 |
| Impact severity (kip-ft) | 106 | ≥106 | 113.8 |
| Impact location [distance (in.) upstream of centerline of Post 14] | 24 | ±12 | 20.9 |

Table 96.  Exit parameters for MASH Test 3-21
(Crash Test 612541-01-3).

| Exit Parameter | Measured |
|---|---|
| Speed (mi/h) | 46.7 |
| Trajectory (deg) | 8.6 |
| Heading (deg) | 13.4 |
| Brakes applied post impact (s) | 3.5 |
| Vehicle at rest position | 246 ft downstream of impact point<br>24 ft to the traffic side<br>5 deg right |
| Comments | Vehicle remained upright and stable.<br>Vehicle crossed the exit box[a] 48 ft downstream from loss of contact and satisfied the exit box criteria described in MASH. |

[a] Not less than 32.8 ft downstream from loss of contact for cars and pickups is optimal.

*Figure 147.   Multifunctional barrier transition/test vehicle geometrics for Crash Test 612541-01-3.*

*Figure 148.   Multifunctional barrier transition/test vehicle impact location for Crash Test 612541-01-3.*

**Table 97.   Weather conditions for Crash Test 612541-01-3 (2023-02-15, AM).**

| Condition | Measurement |
|---|---|
| Wind speed (mi/h) | 11 |
| Wind direction (deg) | 182 |
| Temperature (°F) | 72 |
| Relative humidity (%) | 91 |
| Vehicle traveling (deg) | 195 |

## Test Vehicle

Figure 149 and Figure 150 show the 2018 Ram 1500 used for the crash test. Table 98 shows the vehicle measurements. Figure H.1 in Appendix H, Section H.1, gives additional dimensions and information about the vehicle.

***Figure 149.   Impact side of test vehicle before Crash Test 612541-01-3.***

***Figure 150.   Opposite of impact side of the test vehicle before Crash Test 612541-01-3.***

**Table 98.   Vehicle measurements for Crash Test 612541-01-3.**

| Test Parameter | MASH | Allowed Tolerance | Measured |
|---|---|---|---|
| Dummy (if applicable)[a] (lb) | 165 | N/A | 165 |
| Inertial weight (lb) | 5,000 | ±110 | 5,037 |
| Gross static[a] (lb) | 5,165 | ±110 | 5,202 |
| Wheelbase (in.) | 148 | ±12 | 140.5 |
| Front overhang (in.) | 39 | ±3 | 40 |
| Overall length (in.) | 237 | ±13 | 227.5 |
| Overall width (in.) | 78 | ±2 | 78.5 |
| Hood height (in.) | 43 | ±4 | 46.0 |
| Track width[b] (in.) | 67 | ±1.5 | 68.25 |
| CG aft of front axle[c] (in.) | 63 | ±4 | 60.6 |
| CG above ground[c,d] (in.) | 28 | ≥28 | 28.4 |

[a] If a dummy is used, the gross static vehicle mass includes the mass of the dummy.
[b] Average of front and rear axles.
[c] For test inertial mass.
[d] 2270P vehicle must meet minimum CG height requirement.

## Test Description

Table 99 lists events that occurred during Crash Test 612541-01-3. Figures H.4, H.5, and H.6 in Appendix H, Section H.2, present sequential photographs from the test.

## Damage to Test Installation

The rail was scuffed and deformed at impact, and the grout separated from the traffic side of the concrete slab at Posts 18 and 19. The grout was also cracked and broken up around Post 18. Table 100 reports the post displacement and lean of the installation, and Table 101 describes the deflection and working width of the multifunctional barrier transition. Figure 151 and Figure 152 show the damage to the multifunctional barrier transition.

## Damage to Test Vehicle

Figure 153 and Figure 154 show the damage sustained by the vehicle. Figure 155 and Figure 156 show the interior of the test vehicle. Table 102 and Table 103 provide details on the occupant compartment deformation and exterior vehicle damage. Figures H.2 and H.3 in Appendix H.1 provide exterior crush and occupant compartment measurements.

**Table 99.   Events during Crash Test 612541-01-3.**

| Time (s) | Events |
|---|---|
| 0 | Vehicle impacted the installation. |
| 0.014 | Posts 13 and 14 began to lean toward field side. |
| 0.021 | Posts 12, 15, and 16 began to lean toward field side. |
| 0.033 | Vehicle began to redirect. |
| 0.036 | Post 17 began to lean toward field side. |
| 0.101 | Front driver's side tire began to leave pavement. |
| 0.115 | Front right fender contacted rail. |
| 0.186 | Vehicle was parallel with installation. |
| 0.675 | Vehicle lost contact with the rail traveling 46.7 mi/h, at a trajectory and heading of 8.6 and 13.4 deg, respectively. |

**Table 100.   Post displacement details for multifunctional barrier transition for Crash Test 612541-01-3.**

| Post | Soil Gap (in.) | | Lean from Vertical Toward Field Side (deg) |
|---|---|---|---|
| | **Traffic Side** | **Field Side** | |
| 9–11 | Soil disturbed | | — |
| 12 | 1 | — | 1.5 |
| 13 | 2½ | ½ | 7 |
| 14 | 4¾ | ¾ | 12 |
| 15 | Soil filled back in | | 15 |
| 16 | Soil filled back in | | 13 |
| 17 | Soil filled back in | | 6 |
| 18 | ¾ | ½ | 1.5 |
| 19 | ¼ | ⅛ | — |

### Table 101. Deflection and working width of the multifunctional barrier transition for Crash Test 612541-01-3.

| Test Parameter | Measured |
|---|---|
| Permanent deflection/location (in.) | 10.25 toward field side, at the centerline of Post 15 |
| Dynamic deflection (in.) | 16.3 toward field side, between Posts 15 and 16 |
| Working width[a] and height (in.) | 34.8 at a height of 31.0 at the top field side of Post 15 |

[a] Per MASH, "The working width is the maximum dynamic lateral position of any major part of the system or vehicle. These measurements are all relative to the pre-impact traffic face of the test article." In other words, the working width is the total barrier width plus the maximum dynamic intrusion of any portion of the barrier or test vehicle past the field side edge of the barrier.

*Figure 151.   Multifunctional barrier transition after test at impact location for Crash Test 612541-01-3.*

*Figure 152.   In-line view of the multifunctional barrier transition after Crash Test 612541-01-3.*

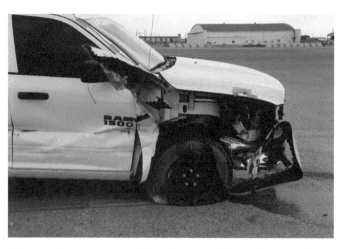

*Figure 153.  Impact side of test vehicle after Crash Test 612541-01-3.*

*Figure 154.  Rear impact side of test vehicle after Crash Test 612541-01-3.*

*Figure 155.  Overall interior of test vehicle after Crash Test 612541-01-3.*

*Figure 156.   Interior of test vehicle on impact side after Crash Test 612541-01-3.*

**Table 102.   Occupant compartment deformation for Crash Test 612541-01-3.**

| Test Parameter | Specification (in.) | Measured (in.) |
|---|---|---|
| Roof | ≤4.0 | 0.0 |
| Windshield | ≤3.0 | 0.0 |
| A and B pillars | ≤5.0 overall. ≤3.0 lateral | 0.0 |
| Foot well/toe pan | ≤9.0 | 0.0 |
| Floor pan/transmission tunnel | ≤12.0 | 0.0 |
| Side front panel | ≤12.0 | 0.5 |
| Front door (above seat) | ≤9.0 | 0.5 |
| Front door (below seat) | ≤12.0 | 0.0 |

**Table 103.   Exterior vehicle damage for Crash Test 612541-01-3.**

| Part of Vehicle | Damage |
|---|---|
| Side windows | Side windows remained intact |
| Maximum exterior deformation | 12 in. in the front plane at the right front corner at bumper height |
| VDS | 01FRQ3 |
| CDC | 01FREW2 |
| Fuel tank damage | None |
| Description of damage to vehicle | The front bumper, hood, grill, right front fender, right headlight, right front tire and rim, right frame rail, radiator, support, windshield (caused by torsion of body from impact), right front door, right rear door, right cab corner, right rear quarter fender, right taillight, and rear bumper were damaged. The windshield had small cracks on the lower right side, the right front door had a 2-in. gap at the top, and the right rear door had a 1.5-in. gap at the top. |

## Occupant Risk Factors

Data from the accelerometers were digitized for evaluation of occupant risk, and the results are shown in Table 104. Figure H.7 in Appendix H, Section H.3, shows the vehicle angular displacements, and Figures H.8 through H.10 in Appendix H, Section H.4, show acceleration versus time traces.

## Test Summary

Figure 157 summarizes the results of MASH Crash Test 612541-01-3.

**Table 104.   Occupant risk factors for Crash Test 612541-01-3.**

| Test Parameter | MASH[a] | Measured | Time (s) |
|---|---|---|---|
| OIV (ft/s) | | | |
| X | ≤40.0 *30.0* | 17.7 | 0.1153 on right side of interior |
| Y | ≤40.0 *30.0* | 21.4 | 0.1153 on right side of interior |
| Ridedown (g) | | | |
| X | ≤20.49 *15.0* | 7.4 | 0.1308–0.1408 |
| Y | ≤20.49 *15.0* | 14.5 | 0.2068–0.2168 |
| THIV (m/s) | N/A | 8.1 | 0.1115 on right side of interior |
| ASI | N/A | 1.1 | 0.0681–0.1181 |
| Max. 0.050-s average (g) | | | |
| X | N/A | −6.9 | 0.0638–0.1138 |
| Y | N/A | −8.6 | 0.0451–0.0951 |
| Vertical | N/A | 4.4 | 0.2550–0.3050 |
| Roll (deg) | ≤75 | 33.3 | 0.6062 |
| Pitch (deg) | ≤75 | 5.9 | 0.5627 |
| Yaw (deg) | N/A | 41.6 | 0.7953 |

[a] Values in italics are the preferred MASH values.

| Sequential Photographs | | | |
|---|---|---|---|
| **0.000 s** | Test Agency | Texas A&M Transportation Institute (TTI) | |
| | Test Standard/Test No. | MASH 2016, Test 3-21 | |
| | TTI Project No. | 612541-01-3 | |
| | Test Date | 2023-02-15 | |
| | **TEST ARTICLE** | | |
| | Type | Longitudinal Barrier | |
| | Name | Pedestrian Traffic Rail Transition | |
| | Length | 255 ft 8 in. | |
| | Key Materials: LON | Traffic side: HSS 12- × 6- × ¼-in. traffic rail, HSS 4- × 4- × ¼-in. rub rail, W6 × 8.5 posts spaced at 66 in. Field side: HSS Round 1.9-in.-diameter × 0.145-in.-thick (Sch 40) ASTM A500 Grade B tubing × 2, and 12 gauge, 4-in. wide plate cane rail. | |
| **0.200 s** | Key Materials: Transition & Terminal | Thrie beam and W-beam guardrail, 72-in. and 84-in. wide flange guardrail posts; steel post end terminal | |
| | Soil Type and Condition | AASHTO M147-17 Type 1 Grading D (crushed concrete) | |
| | **TEST VEHICLE** | | |
| | Type/Designation | 2270P | |
| | Year, Make and Model | 2018 Ram 1500 | |
| | Inertial Weight (lb) | 5,037 | |
| | Dummy (lb) | 165 | |
| | Gross Static (lb) | 5,202 | |
| | **IMPACT CONDITIONS** | | |
| | Impact Speed (mi/h) | 62.2 | |
| | Impact Angle (deg) | 24.7 | |
| **0.400 s** | Impact Location | 20.9 in. upstream from the centerline of Post 14. | |
| | Impact Severity (kip-ft) | 113.8 | |
| | **EXIT CONDITIONS** | | |
| | Exit Speed (mi/h) | 46.7 | |
| | Trajectory/Heading Angle (deg) | 8.6/13.4 | |
| | Exit Box Criteria | Vehicle crossed the exit box 48 ft downstream from loss of contact. | |
| | Stopping Distance | 246 ft downstream 24 ft to the traffic side | |
| | **TEST ARTICLE DEFLECTIONS** | | |
| | Dynamic (in.) | 16.3 | |
| | Permanent (in.) | 10.25 | |
| **0.600 s** | Working Width/Height (in.) | 34.8/31.0 | |
| | **VEHICLE DAMAGE** | | |
| | VDS | 01FRQ3 | |
| | CDC | 01FREW2 | |
| | Max. Ext. Deformation (in.) | 12 | |
| | Max. Occupant Compartment Deformation | 0.5 in. in the door and side panel | |

| OCCUPANT RISK VALUES | | | | | | | |
|---|---|---|---|---|---|---|---|
| Long. OIV (ft/s) | 17.7 | Long. Ridedown (g) | 7.4 | Max. 50-ms Long. (g) | −6.9 | Max. Roll (deg) | 33.3 |
| Lat. OIV (ft/s) | 21.4 | Lat. Ridedown (g) | 14.5 | Max. 50-ms Lat. (g) | −8.6 | Max. Pitch (deg) | 5.9 |
| THIV (m/s) | 8.1 | ASI | 1.1 | Max. 50-ms Vert. (g) | 4.4 | Max. Yaw (deg) | 41.6 |

**Figure 157.    Summary of results for MASH Test 3-21 (Crash Test 612541-01-3) on multifunctional barrier transition.**

CHAPTER 18

# Conclusions, Recommendations, and Suggested Research

## Summary and Conclusions

Under this project, research was performed to (*a*) develop a new multifunctional barrier system that complied with the specific requirements needed for the accommodation of pedestrians (including those with disabilities), bicyclists, and motor vehicles; and (*b*) conduct full-scale crash tests and provide standard drawings for the system. The research approach included collecting relevant literature and information on current practices pertaining to the separation of vulnerable users from traffic, conducting a survey to identify barrier systems commonly used to separate vulnerable users from traffic and the desired/needed improvements to those systems, and developing design options for a new multifunctional barrier system and transition.

Six different barrier design options were proposed. The design concept selected by the project panel was developed by using FE impact simulations. The final barrier system design was tested and evaluated according to the requirements of MASH Tests 3-10 and 3-11. Both tests successfully met MASH TL-3 evaluation criteria.

The new multifunctional barrier system met goals for both the traffic and vulnerable user sides of the barrier. The maximum dynamic deflection under MASH TL-3 impact conditions was only 16 in., which was significantly less than the target deflection limit of 24 in. established by the project panel at the onset of the project. No debris was generated by the barrier during the design impacts under MASH conditions. Some inevitable debris from the vehicle was present, but this was primarily composed of lightweight plastic pieces and should not pose a significant threat to vulnerable users outside the deflection limits of the multifunctional barrier.

Additionally, this research developed a transition system to connect the new multifunctional barrier to a conventional strong-post W-beam guardrail installation. The selected Thrie beam transition system was tested and evaluated in accordance with the specifications of MASH Tests 3-20 and 3-21, and the system met the MASH TL-3 evaluation criteria.

Table 105 shows that both the multifunctional barrier and the transition met the performance criteria for MASH TL-3 longitudinal barrier systems. Because the multifunctional barrier and transition met the MASH TL-3 performance criteria for barrier systems, a letter to request Federal Aid Reimbursement Eligibility of Highway Safety Hardware was drafted. The contents of that letter are presented in Appendix J.

## Recommendations

On the basis of the outcomes of this research, the new multifunctional barrier and associated transition system that were developed are recommended for use when site conditions require positive barrier protection to separate traffic and nonmotorized transportation facilities such

**Table 105. Assessment summary for MASH TL-3 tests of multifunctional barrier and transition.**

| Evaluation Criteria[a] | Description | MASH 3-10: Crash Test 612541-01-2 | MASH 3-11: Crash Test 612541-01-1 | MASH 3-20: Crash Test 612541-01-4 | MASH 3-21: Crash Test 612541-01-3 |
|---|---|---|---|---|---|
| A | Contain, redirect, or controlled stop | S | S | S | S |
| D | No penetration into occupant compartment | S | S | S | S |
| F | Roll and pitch limit | S | S | S | S |
| H | OIV threshold | S | S | S | S |
| I | Ridedown threshold | S | S | S | S |
| | Overall evaluation | Pass | Pass | Pass | Pass |

Note: S = satisfactory.
[a] See Table 51 in Chapter 8 for details.

as sidewalks, bicycle facilities, and shared-use paths. The barrier and transition systems satisfy MASH TL-3 criteria and are, therefore, considered acceptable for use on high-speed facilities. Detailed drawings of the multifunctional barrier system are provided in Appendix B. Detailed drawings of the transition from the multifunctional barrier system and conventional strong-post W-beam guardrail are provided in Appendices E and F. These detailed drawings can be used by interested transportation agencies to develop standards for the implementation of these systems. Their use at appropriate locations should enhance the safety of vulnerable users while maintaining MASH TL-3 performance for motorists.

Although the approach guardrail attached to the developed transition was terminated with a downstream anchor terminal, termination with a MASH-crashworthy terminal is an acceptable option when the end of the terminal will be within the clear zone of opposing traffic. A MASH-compliant TL-3 terminal can be connected anywhere beyond the asymmetric Thrie beam to W-beam transition section from an impact performance standpoint. The need and length of any associated approach rail between the MASH terminal and multifunctional barrier transition should be determined on the basis of a user agency's design manual.

Note that the transition and its approach guardrail will not provide the same level of protection for vulnerable users behind the barrier as the multifunctional barrier system. Any standard approach guardrail or terminal system beyond the multifunctional barrier and its transition will have considerably more deflection and potentially more debris. Such circumstances may arise when an intersecting roadway is encountered, and the multifunctional barrier needs to be terminated with a crashworthy MASH terminal. In this or similar scenarios, user agencies may consider transitioning the nonmotorized transportation facilities further from the barrier at these locations, as depicted in Figure 158.

## Suggested Research

This research has led to the development of a new multifunctional barrier. It was developed to have limited dynamic deflection under a design traffic impact for MASH TL-3 conditions to limit its penetration into the shared use space behind the barrier. The barrier system that was developed has a maximum dynamic deflection of 16 in. compared to conventional strong-post

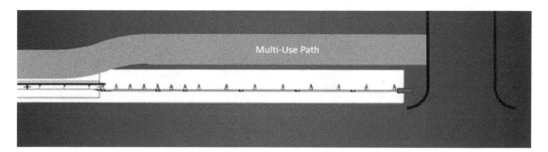

***Figure 158.  Offset of multiuse path from standard guardrail or guardrail terminal.***

W-beam guardrail that typically has dynamic deflections in the range of 42 in. or more. Additional research can be performed to develop other multifunctional barrier systems that have different ranges of deflection if desired. As deflection is permitted to increase, the cost of a barrier typically decreases.

A MASH TL-3 compliant transition system was also developed to transition the stiffness and geometry of the multifunctional barrier system to a conventional strong-post W-beam guardrail to permits its termination with a MASH compliant W-beam guardrail terminal. This transition incorporates nested Thrie beam rail and reduced post spacing. As described herein, the impact performance of an alternate W-beam transition with extended rub rail appears promising and could provide a more cost-effective transition system for the multifunctional barrier. Further research and testing are needed to verify if this design will comply with MASH criteria.

Additional research could also be conducted to assist user agencies with determination of site criteria that merits the implementation of the new multifunctional barrier system, including the proximity of the shared-use path from vehicular traffic. While implementation at many locations may be intuitive, a more comprehensive benefit-cost or risk analysis could assist the decision process at some locations. In-service performance evaluation of the new multifunctional barrier system and transition would also be useful in understanding its in-field impact performance for both traffic and vulnerable users, and determining if improvements could be incorporated into future versions of the system. This includes evaluation of potential debris from a vehicle impact onto the trail side of the barrier.

Future research could evaluate the comfort levels of vulnerable users on the trail side of the barrier and its utility and function for those users, including those with disabilities. Such research would assist with understanding how the barrier could be improved.

# References

1. AASHTO. *Manual for Assessing Safety Hardware*, 2nd ed. Washington, DC, 2016.
2. AASHTO. *Guide for the Development of Bicycle Facilities*, 4th ed. Washington, DC, 2012.
3. U.S. Access Board. Public Right-of-Way Accessibility Guidelines. https://www.access-board.gov/prowag/.
4. Mogawer, W. S., Austerman, A. J., and Gazzi, J. J. *Shared Use Path Fencing Usage*. Vermont Agency of Transportation, Montpelier, 2007.
5. Texas Department of Transportation. *Bridge Railing Manual*. Austin, 2018.
6. Ritter, M. A. Chapter 10: Rail Systems for Timber Decks, in *Timber Bridges: Design, Construction, Inspection, and Maintenance*. Forest Service, U.S. Department of Agriculture, Washington, DC, 1990.
7. Lechtenberg, K. A., Faller, R. K., Bielenberg, R. W., Schmidt, J. D., Guajardo, A. L., and Reid, J. D. *Development of a Crashworthy Pedestrian Rail*. Wisconsin Department of Transportation, Madison, 2016.
8. AASHTO. *LRFD Bridge Design Specifications*, 9th ed. Washington, DC, 2020.
9. AASHTO. *Guide for the Planning, Design, and Operation of Pedestrian Facilities*, 1st ed. Washington, DC, 2004.
10. AASHTO. *Guide for the Planning, Design, and Operation of Pedestrian Facilities*, 2nd ed. Washington, DC, 2021.
11. Sarkar, S. Evaluation of Different Types of Pedestrian-Vehicle Separations. *Transportation Research Record: Journal of the Transportation Research Board* 1502, 1995, pp. 83–95.
12. Sanders, R. L. We Can All Get Along: The Alignment of Driver and Bicyclist Roadway Design Preferences in the San Francisco Bay Area. *Transportation Research Part A: Policy and Practice* 91, 2016, pp. 120–133. https://doi.org/10.1016/j.tra.2016.06.002.
13. Sanders, R. L. *Examining the Cycle: How Perceived and Actual Bicycling Risk Influence Cycling Frequency, Roadway Design Preferences, and Support for Cycling Among Bay Area Residents*. PhD dissertation, University of California, Berkeley, 2013.
14. Li, Z., Wang, W., Liu, P., and Ragland, D. R. Physical Environments Influencing Bicyclists' Perception of Comfort on Separated and On-Street Bicycle Facilities. *Transportation Research Part D: Transport and Environment* 17(3), 2012, pp. 256–261.
15. DuBose, B. 2011. Physically Separated Bikeways: A Game Changer for Bicycle Mode Split? *ITE Journal* 81(4), 2011, p. 54.
16. Huybers, S., Van Houten, R., and Malenfant, J. E. L. Reducing Conflicts Between Motor Vehicles and Pedestrians: The Separate and Combined Effects of Pavement Markings and a Sign Prompt. *Journal of Applied Behavior Analysis* 37(4), 2004, pp. 445–456. https://doi.org/10.1901/jaba.2004.37-445.
17. McNeil, N., Monsere, C. M., and Dill, J. Influence of Bike Lane Buffer Types on Perceived Comfort and Safety of Bicyclists and Potential Bicyclists. *Transportation Research Record: Journal of the Transportation Research Board* 2520, 2015, pp. 132–142.
18. Caltrans. Roadside Management Toolbox. https://dot.ca.gov/programs/design/lap-roadside-management-toolbox.
19. Dunn, M. *Evaluation of DuroTrim Vegetation Control Mats*. Iowa Department of Transportation, Ames, 2002. http://publications.iowa.gov/19902/.
20. Yelverton, F., and Gannon, T. *Vegetation Management Under Guardrails for North Carolina Roadsides*. No. FHWA/NC/2004-02. U.S. Department of Transportation, Washington, DC, 2003. https://ntlrepository.blob.core.windows.net/lib/24000/24700/24799/Final_Report_2001-06.pdf.
21. Bligh, R. P., Skinger, N. R., Abu-Odeh, A. Y., Roschke, P. N., Menges, W. L., and Haug, R. R. *Dynamic Response of Guardrail Systems Encased in Pavement Mow Strips*. No. FHWA/TX-04/0-4162-2. Texas Department of Transportation, Austin, 2004. https://static.tti.tamu.edu/tti.tamu.edu/documents/0-4162-2.pdf.
22. Raine, W. Tire-Rubber Anti-Vegetation Tile Evaluation. Recycled Materials Resource Center, Quarterly and Final Report for RMRC Research Project No. 30. 2004. https://rmrc.wisc.edu/wp-content/uploads/2012/10/P30Final.pdf.

23. Arsenault, A., Teeter-Balin, J., Velinsky, S. A., and White, W. 2008. *Alternatives to Labor Intensive Tasks in Roadside Vegetation Maintenance* (No. UCD-ARR-08-06-30-01). AHMCT Research Center, University of California, Davis, 2008. https://dot.ca.gov/-/media/dot-media/programs/research-innovation-system -information/documents/f0016966-ucd-arr-08-06-30-04.pdf.

24. Arrington, D. R., Bligh, R. P., and Menges, W. L. *Alternative Design of Guardrail Posts in Asphalt or Concrete Mowing Pads.* Washington State Department of Transportation, Olympia, 2009. http://www.roadsidepooledfund .org/wp-content/uploads/2011/03/405160-14-1.pdf.

25. Willard, R. G., Morin, J. R., and Tang, O. K., *Assessment of Alternatives in Vegetation Management at the Pavement Edge.* No. WA-RD 736.1. Washington State Department of Transportation, Olympia, 2010. https:// www.wsdot.wa.gov/research/reports/fullreports/736.1.pdf.

26. Barton, S., and Budischak, V. *Guardrail Vegetation Management in Delaware.* Delaware Center for Transportation. Delaware Center for Transportation, Newark, 2013. https://cpb-us-w2.wpmucdn.com/sites.udel .edu/dist/1/1139/files/2013/10/Rpt-247-Guardrail-vegetation-Barton-PLSC-1bw8586.pdf.

27. Scott, D. W., Stewart, L. K., and White, D. W. *Crash Tests on Guardrail Systems Embedded in Asphalt Vegetation Barriers in Accordance with GDOT Design Specifications.* No. FHWA-GA-18-1626. Georgia Department of Transportation, Atlanta, 2018. https://rosap.ntl.bts.gov/view/dot/40283.

28. Sheikh, N. M., Menges, W. L., and Kuhn, D. L. *MASH TL-3 Evaluation of 31-Inch W-Beam Guardrail with Wood and Steel Posts in Concrete Mow Strip.* No. 608551-01-1-5. Washington State Department of Transportation, Olympia, 2019. https://www.roadsidepooledfund.org/wp-content/uploads/2017/06/TRNo608551 -1-45-Final.pdf.

29. Ross, H. E., Jr., Sicking, D. L., Zimmer, R. A., and Michie, J. D. 1993. *NCHRP Report 350: Recommended Procedures for the Safety Performance Evaluation of Highway Features.* Transportation Research Board, Washington, D.C., 1993.

30. Michie, J. D. *NCHRP Report 230: Recommended Procedures for the Safety Performance Evaluation of Highway Appurtenances.* Transportation Research Board, Washington, DC, 1981.

31. AASHTO. *Roadside Design Guide,* 4th ed. Washington, DC, 2011.

32. Letter to Aris Stathopoulos, New York Metropolitan Transportation Authority, Bridges and Tunnels, from Wanda L. Menges, TTI Proving Ground, Jan. 30, 2017. https://www.roadsidepooledfund.org/wp-content /uploads/2017/04/b274-1.pdf.

33. Bligh, R., Abu-Odeh, A., and Menges, W. L. *MASH Test 3-10 on 31-Inch W-Beam Guardrail with Standard Offset Blocks.* No. FHWA/TX-11/9-1002-4. Texas Department of Transportation, Austin, 2011. https://static .tti.tamu.edu/tti.tamu.edu/documents/9-1002-4.pdf.

34. Moran, S., and Bligh, R. *TxDOT Thrie-Beam Transition to Concrete Barrier MASH TL-3 Study Pooled Fund-Engineering Support. Letter Report.* Texas A&M Transportation Institute, College Station, 2020. https://www .roadsidepooledfund.org/wp-content/uploads/2020/05/TxDOT-Thrie-Beam-Transition-to-Concrete-Barrier -Professional-Opinion-Letter-Report.pdf.

# Acronyms and Abbreviations

| | |
|---|---|
| ADA | Americans with Disability Act |
| ARDVAC | Advanced Roadway Debris Vacuum |
| ASI | acceleration severity index |
| A2LA | American Association for Laboratory Accreditation |
| Caltrans | California Department of Transportation |
| CDC | collision deformation classification |
| CG | center of gravity |
| CIP | critical impact point |
| CNRB | Constrained Nodal Rigid Body |
| CSCM | Continuous Surface Cap Model |
| DAS | data acquisition system |
| deg | degree(s) |
| DOT | department of transportation |
| ext | exterior |
| FE | finite element |
| FRP | fiber-reinforced polymer |
| ft | foot, feet |
| $g$ | acceleration due to gravity |
| GDOT | Georgia Department of Transportation |
| HDPE | high-density polyethylene |
| HPBO | heavy-post blocked-out |
| HSS | hollow structural section |
| in. | inch(es) |
| IEC | International Electrotechnical Commission |
| ISO | International Organization for Standardization |
| kg/m$^3$ | kilograms per cubic meter |
| kPa | kilopascals |
| ksi | kips per square inch |
| lb | pound(s) |
| lb/ft$^3$ | pounds per cubic foot |
| lat. | latitude |
| LON | length of need |
| long. | longitude |
| MA | moving average acceleration |
| MASH | *Manual for Assessing Safety Hardware* |
| MGS | Midwest Guardrail System |
| m | meter |
| mi/h | mile(s) per hour |

| | |
|---|---|
| MPA | megapascals |
| MwRSF | Midwest Roadside Safety Facility |
| N/A | not applicable |
| NIST | National Institute of Standards and Technology |
| ODOT | Oregon Department of Transportation |
| OIV | occupant impact velocity |
| ORA | occupant ridedown acceleration |
| OSHA | Occupational Safety and Health Administration |
| PennDOT | Pennsylvania Department of Transportation |
| PHD | peak head deceleration |
| PROWAG | Public Right-of-Way Accessibility Guidelines |
| psi | pounds per square inch |
| PVC | polyvinyl chloride |
| ROW | right-of-way |
| RSVVP | Roadside Safety Verification and Validation Program |
| s | second(s) |
| sch | schedule |
| TBTA | Triborough Bridge and Tunnel Authority |
| THIV | theoretical head impact velocity |
| TL | test level |
| TRAP | Test Risk Assessment Program |
| TTI | Texas A&M Transportation Institute |
| TxDOT | Texas Department of Transportation |
| UV | ultraviolet |
| VDS | vehicle damage scale |
| vert. | vertical |

# Appendices

Appendices A through J can be found on the National Academies Press (NAP) website (nap .nationalacademies.org) by searching for *NCHRP Research Report 1116: Development of a MASH Barrier to Shield Pedestrians, Bicyclists, and Other Vulnerable Users from Motor Vehicles* and looking under "Resources." Appendices B, E, and F are also included here.

The appendices on the NAP website are grouped in two files: "Technical Drawings and Information for FHWA Eligibility Filing: Appendices B, E, F, and J" and "Survey, Crash Test Data, and Supporting Certification Documents: Appendices A, C, D, G, H, and I."

## Technical Drawings and Information for FHWA Eligibility Filing: Appendices B, E, F, and J

Appendix B:  Details of the Pedestrian Traffic Rail for MASH Tests 3-10 and 3-11
Appendix E:  Details of the Pedestrian Traffic Rail Transition for MASH Test 3-20
Appendix F:  Details of the Pedestrian Traffic Rail Transition for MASH Test 3-21
Appendix J:  FHWA Eligibility Request Form for the Pedestrian Traffic Rail and Transition

## Survey, Crash Test Data, and Supporting Certification Documents: Appendices A, C, D, G, H, and I

Appendix A:  Survey
Appendix C:  MASH Test 3-10 (Crash Test No. 612541-01-2)
Appendix D:  MASH Test 3-11 (Crash Test No. 612541-01-1)
Appendix G:  MASH Test 3-20 (Crash Test 612541-01-4)
Appendix H:  MASH Test 3-21 (Crash Test 612541-01-3)
Appendix I:  Supporting Certification Documents

# Details of the Pedestrian Traffic Rail for MASH Tests 3-10 and 3-11

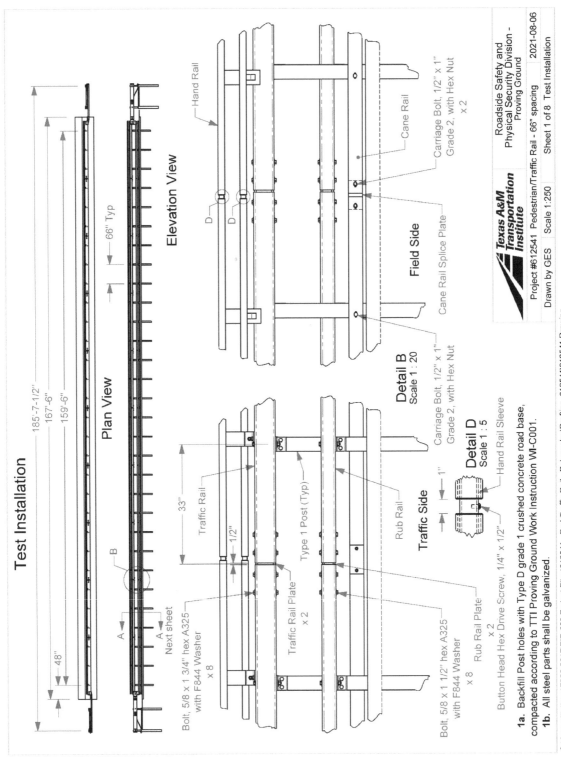

Test Installation

Plan View

Elevation View

185'-7-1/2"
167'-6"
159'-6"
48"
66" Typ

A
B
A
Next sheet

Bolt, 5/8 x 1 3/4" hex A325
with F844 Washer
x 8

Bolt, 5/8 x 1 1/2" hex A325
with F844 Washer
x 8

Traffic Rail Plate
x 2

Rub Rail Plate
x 2

Button Head Hex Drive Screw, 1/4" x 1/2"

Traffic Rail

33"

1/2"

Type 1 Post (Typ)

Rub Rail

Traffic Side

Hand Rail

Cane Rail

Carriage Bolt, 1/2" x 1"
Grade 2, with Hex Nut
x 2

Field Side

Cane Rail Splice Plate

Detail B
Scale 1 : 20

Carriage Bolt, 1/2" x 1"
Grade 2, with Hex Nut

Detail D
Scale 1 : 5

1"

Hand Rail Sleeve

**1a.** Backfill Post holes with Type D grade 1 crushed concrete road base,
compacted according to TTI Proving Ground Work Instruction WI-C001.
**1b.** All steel parts shall be galvanized.

Texas A&M
Transportation
Institute

Roadside Safety and
Physical Security Division -
Proving Ground

Project #612541 Pedestrian/Traffic Rail - 66" spacing          2021-08-06

Drawn by GES      Scale 1:250      Sheet 1 of 8   Test Installation

Q:\Accreditation-17025-2017\EIR-000 Project Files\612541 - Ped-Traffic Rail - Dobrovolny\Drafting, 612541\612541 Drawing

B-2

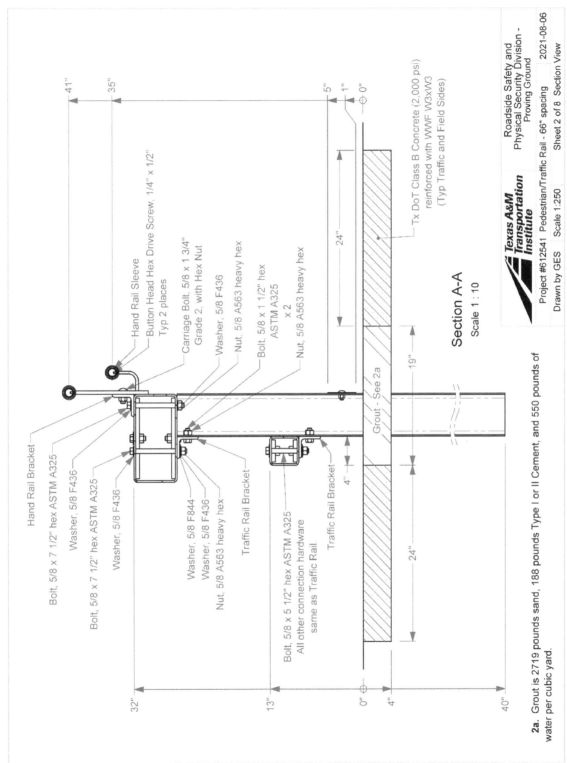

Hand Rail Bracket

Bolt, 5/8 x 7 1/2" hex ASTM A325

Washer, 5/8 F436

Bolt, 5/8 x 7 1/2" hex ASTM A325

Washer, 5/8 F436

Washer, 5/8 F844
Washer, 5/8 F436
Nut, 5/8 A563 heavy hex

Traffic Rail Bracket

Bolt, 5/8 x 5 1/2" hex ASTM A325
All other connection hardware
same as Traffic Rail

Traffic Rail Bracket

Hand Rail Sleeve

Button Head Hex Drive Screw, 1/4" x 1/2"
Typ 2 places

Carriage Bolt, 5/8 x 1 3/4"
Grade 2, with Hex Nut

Washer, 5/8 F436

Nut, 5/8 A563 heavy hex

Bolt, 5/8 x 1 1/2" hex
ASTM A325
x 2

Nut, 5/8 A563 heavy hex

Tx DoT Class B Concrete (2,000 psi)
reinforced with WWF W3xW3
(Typ Traffic and Field Sides)

Grout - See 2a

Section A-A
Scale 1 : 10

41"

35"

32"

13'

0"

4"

40"

5"

1"

0"

24"

19"

24"

4"

**2a.** Grout is 2719 pounds sand, 188 pounds Type I or II Cement, and 550 pounds of
water per cubic yard.

Texas A&M
Transportation
Institute

Roadside Safety and
Physical Security Division -
Proving Ground

2021-08-06

Project #612541 Pedestrian/Traffic Rail - 66" spacing

Drawn by GES    Scale 1:250    Sheet 2 of 8   Section View

Q:\Accreditation-17025-2017\EIR-000 Project Files\612541 - Ped-Traffic Rail - Dobrovolny\Drafting, 612541\612541 Drawing

B-3

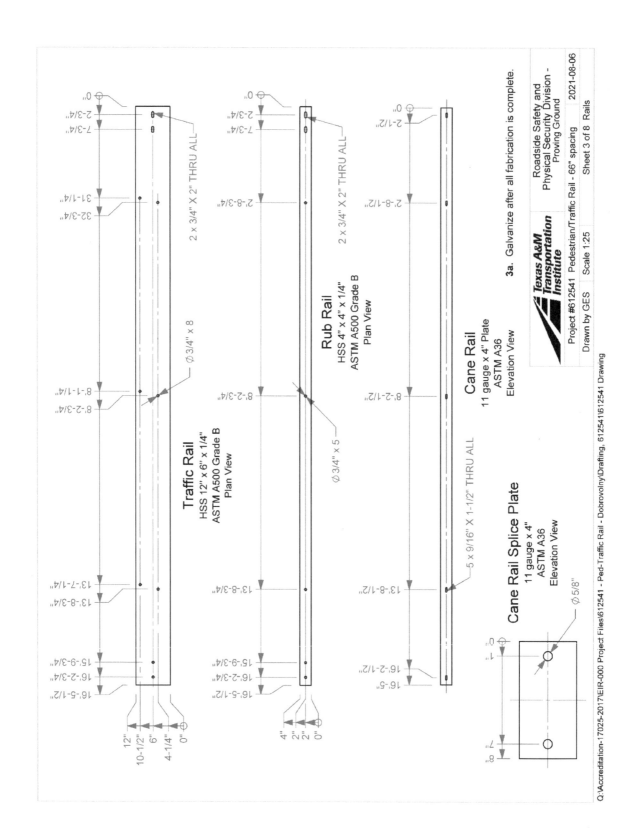

Traffic Rail
HSS 12" x 6" x 1/4"
ASTM A500 Grade B
Plan View

Ø 3/4" x 8

2 x 3/4" X 2" THRU ALL

Rub Rail
HSS 4" x 4" x 1/4"
ASTM A500 Grade B
Plan View

Ø 3/4" x 5

2 x 3/4" X 2" THRU ALL

Cane Rail
11 gauge x 4" Plate
ASTM A36
Elevation View

5 x 9/16" X 1-1/2" THRU ALL

Cane Rail Splice Plate
11 gauge x 4"
ASTM A36
Elevation View

Ø 5/8"

3a. Galvanize after all fabrication is complete.

Texas A&M Transportation Institute

Roadside Safety and Physical Security Division - Proving Ground

Project #612541 Pedestrian/Traffic Rail - 66" spacing   2021-08-06

Drawn by GES      Scale 1:25      Sheet 3 of 8  Rails

Q:\Accreditation-17025-2017\EIR-000 Project Files\612541 - Ped-Traffic Rail - Dobrovolny\Drafting, 612541\612541 Drawing

B-4

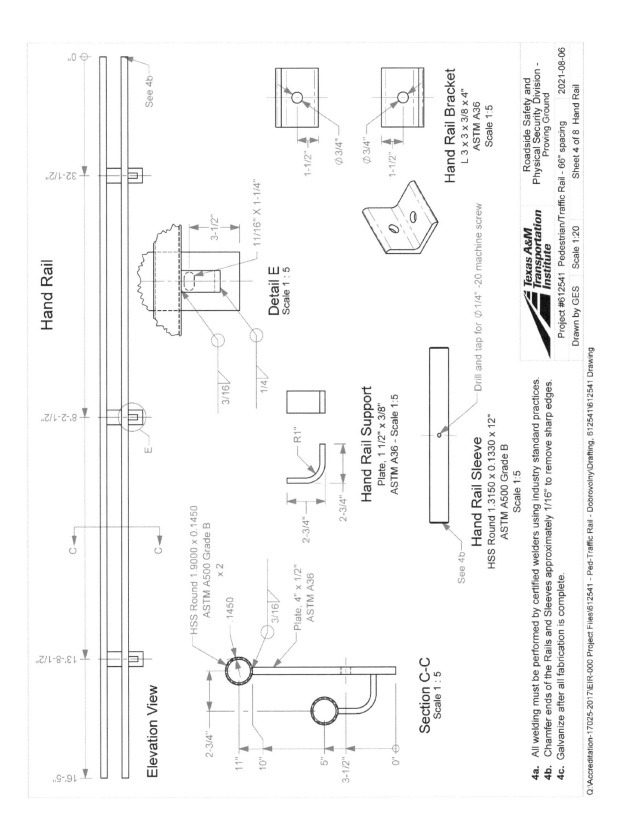

# Hand Rail

**Elevation View**

0"
32-1/2"
8'-2-1/2"
13'-8-1/2"
16'-5"

See 4b

C
C
E

HSS Round 1.9000 x 0.1450
ASTM A500 Grade B
x 2

.1450
3/16

Plate, 4" x 1/2"
ASTM A36

2-3/4"
11"
10"
5"
3-1/2"
0"

**Section C-C**
Scale 1 : 5

3-1/2"
11/16" X 1-1/4"

**Detail E**
Scale 1 : 5

3/16
1/4

R 1"
2-3/4"
2-3/4"

**Hand Rail Support**
Plate, 1 1/2" x 3/8"
ASTM A36 - Scale 1:5

See 4b

**Hand Rail Sleeve**
HSS Round 1.3150 x 0.1330 x 12"
ASTM A500 Grade B
Scale 1:5

Drill and tap for Ø 1/4" -20 machine screw

Ø 3/4"
1-1/2"
Ø 3/4"
1-1/2"

**Hand Rail Bracket**
L 3 x 3 x 3/8 x 4"
ASTM A36
Scale 1:5

4a.  All welding must be performed by certified welders using industry standard practices.
4b.  Chamfer ends of the Rails and Sleeves approximately 1/16" to remove sharp edges.
4c.  Galvanize after all fabrication is complete.

Texas A&M Transportation Institute

Roadside Safety and Physical Security Division - Proving Ground

Project #612541  Pedestrian/Traffic Rail - 66" spacing    2021-08-06

Drawn by GES      Scale 1:20      Sheet 4 of 8  Hand Rail

# Joint Plates

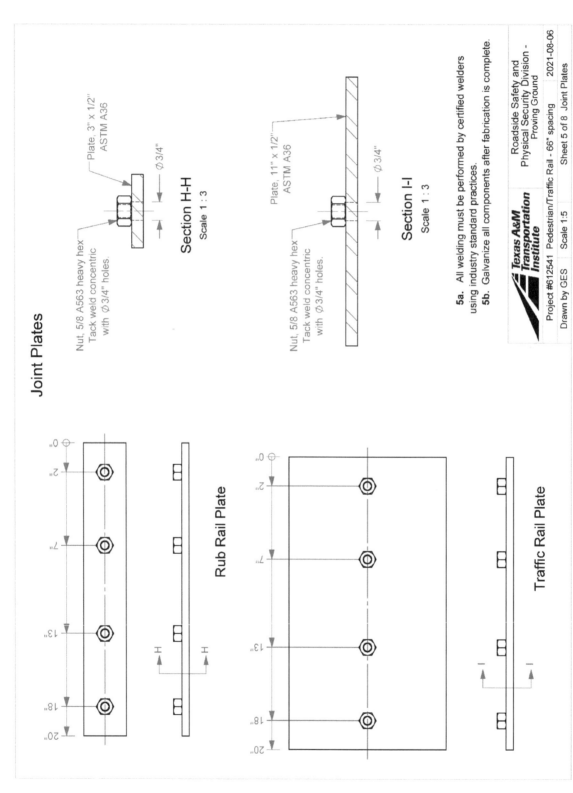

**Section H-H**
Scale 1 : 3

Plate, 3" x 1/2"
ASTM A36

Ø 3/4"

Nut, 5/8 A563 heavy hex
Tack weld concentric
with Ø 3/4" holes.

**Section I-I**
Scale 1 : 3

Plate, 11" x 1/2"
ASTM A36

Ø 3/4"

Nut, 5/8 A563 heavy hex
Tack weld concentric
with Ø 3/4" holes.

**Rub Rail Plate**

0"  2"  7"  13"  18"  20"

**Traffic Rail Plate**

0"  2"  7"  13"  18"  20"

5a. All welding must be performed by certified welders using industry standard practices.

5b. Galvanize all components after fabrication is complete.

**Texas A&M Transportation Institute**

Roadside Safety and Physical Security Division - Proving Ground

2021-08-06

Project #612541  Pedestrian/Traffic Rail - 66" spacing

Sheet 5 of 8  Joint Plates

Drawn by GES  Scale 1:5

Q:\Accreditation-17025-2017\EIR-000 Project Files\612541 - Ped-Traffic Rail - Dobrovolny\Drafting, 612541\612541 Drawing

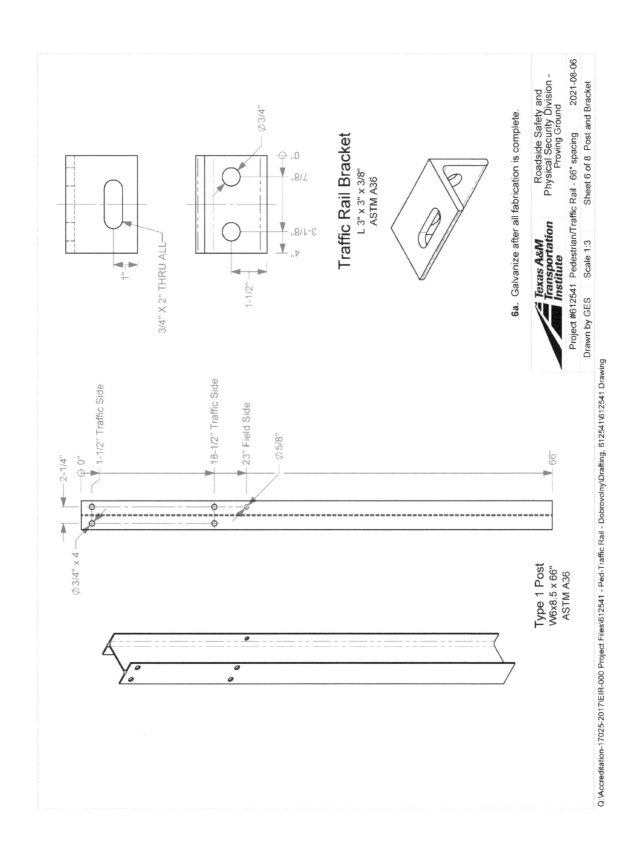

Traffic Rail Bracket
L 3" x 3" x 3/8"
ASTM A36

Ø 3/4"

3/4" X 2" THRU ALL

1"

0"

7/8"

3-1/8"

4"

1-1/2"

Type 1 Post
W6x8.5 x 66"
ASTM A36

2-1/4"

0"

1-1/2" Traffic Side

18-1/2" Traffic Side

23" Field Side

Ø 5/8"

66"

Ø 3/4" x 4

6a. Galvanize after all fabrication is complete.

Texas A&M
Transportation
Institute

Roadside Safety and
Physical Security Division -
Proving Ground

2021-08-06

Project #612541  Pedestrian/Traffic Rail - 66" spacing

Drawn by GES    Scale 1:3    Sheet 6 of 8  Post and Bracket

Q:\Accreditation-17025-2017\EIR-000 Project Files\612541 - Ped-Traffic Rail - Dobrovolny\Drafting, 612541\612541 Drawing

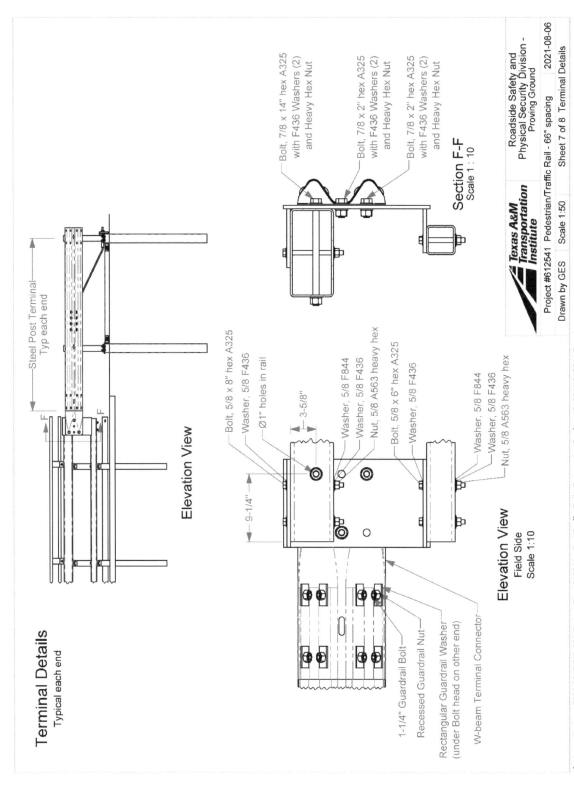

**Terminal Details**
Typical each end

Steel Post Terminal
Typ each end

**Elevation View**

Bolt, 7/8 x 14" hex A325
with F436 Washers (2)
and Heavy Hex Nut

Bolt, 7/8 x 2" hex A325
with F436 Washers (2)
and Heavy Hex Nut

Bolt, 7/8 x 2" hex A325
with F436 Washers (2)
and Heavy Hex Nut

**Section F-F**
Scale 1 : 10

Bolt, 5/8 x 8" hex A325
Washer, 5/8 F436
Ø1" holes in rail

3-5/8"

9-1/4"

Washer, 5/8 F844
Washer, 5/8 F436
Nut, 5/8 A563 heavy hex

Bolt, 5/8 x 6" hex A325
Washer, 5/8 F436

Washer, 5/8 F844
Washer, 5/8 F436
Nut, 5/8 A563 heavy hex

1-1/4" Guardrail Bolt

Recessed Guardrail Nut

Rectangular Guardrail Washer
(under Bolt head on other end)

W-beam Terminal Connector

**Elevation View**
Field Side
Scale 1:10

Texas A&M Transportation Institute

Roadside Safety and Physical Security Division - Proving Ground

2021-08-06

Project #612541 Pedestrian/Traffic Rail - 66" spacing

Scale 1:50

Sheet 7 of 8 Terminal Details

Drawn by GES

Q:\Accreditation-17025-2017\EIR-000 Project Files\612541 - Ped-Traffic Rail - Dobrovolny\Drafting, 612541\612541 Drawing

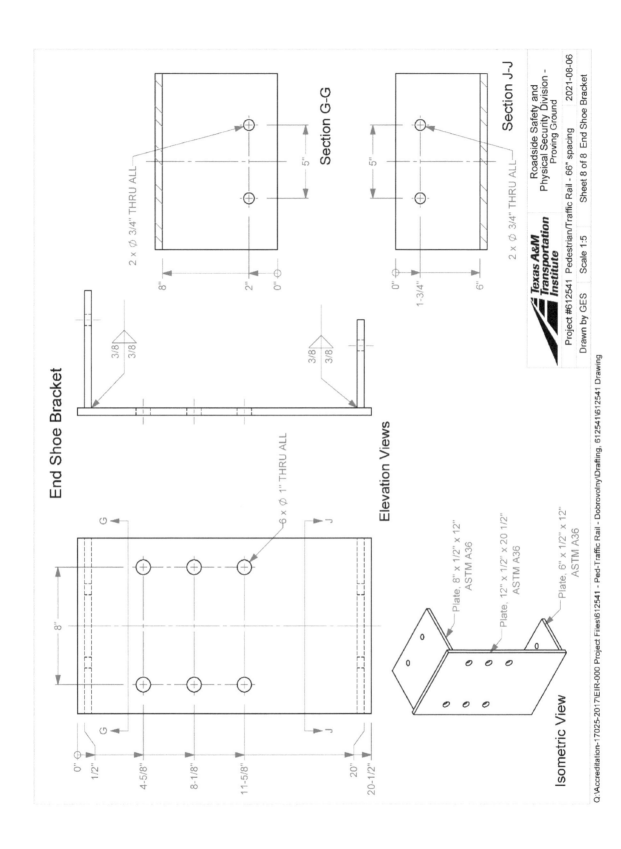

End Shoe Bracket

Section G-G

2 x ⌀ 3/4" THRU ALL

8"
2"
0"
5"

Section J-J

2 x ⌀ 3/4" THRU ALL

0"
1-3/4"
6"
5"

Elevation Views

3/8
3/8

3/8
3/8

6 x ⌀ 1" THRU ALL

G
J

8"

Isometric View

0"
1/2"
4-5/8"
8-1/8"
11-5/8"
20"
20-1/2"

G
J

Plate, 8" x 1/2" x 12"
ASTM A36

Plate, 12" x 1/2" x 20 1/2"
ASTM A36

Plate, 6" x 1/2" x 12"
ASTM A36

Texas A&M Transportation Institute

Roadside Safety and Physical Security Division - Proving Ground

Project #612541  Pedestrian/Traffic Rail - 66" spacing      2021-08-06

Drawn by GES      Scale 1:5      Sheet 8 of 8  End Shoe Bracket

Q:\Accreditation-17025-2017\EIR-000 Project Files\612541 - Ped-Traffic Rail - Dobrovolny\Drafting, 612541\612541 Drawing

B-9

# Terminal Details

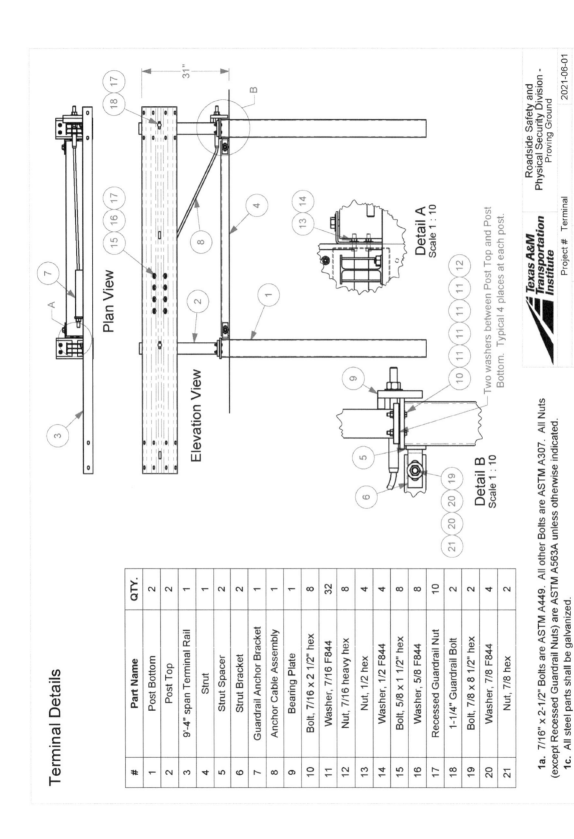

Plan View

Elevation View

31"

Detail A
Scale 1 : 10

Detail B
Scale 1 : 10

Two washers between Post Top and Post Bottom. Typical 4 places at each post.

| # | Part Name | QTY. |
|---|-----------|------|
| 1 | Post Bottom | 2 |
| 2 | Post Top | 2 |
| 3 | 9'-4" span Terminal Rail | 1 |
| 4 | Strut | 1 |
| 5 | Strut Spacer | 2 |
| 6 | Strut Bracket | 2 |
| 7 | Guardrail Anchor Bracket | 1 |
| 8 | Anchor Cable Assembly | 1 |
| 9 | Bearing Plate | 1 |
| 10 | Bolt, 7/16 x 2 1/2" hex | 8 |
| 11 | Washer, 7/16 F844 | 32 |
| 12 | Nut, 7/16 heavy hex | 8 |
| 13 | Nut, 1/2 hex | 4 |
| 14 | Washer, 1/2 F844 | 4 |
| 15 | Bolt, 5/8 x 1 1/2" hex | 8 |
| 16 | Washer, 5/8 F844 | 8 |
| 17 | Recessed Guardrail Nut | 10 |
| 18 | 1-1/4" Guardrail Bolt | 2 |
| 19 | Bolt, 7/8 x 8 1/2" hex | 2 |
| 20 | Washer, 7/8 F844 | 4 |
| 21 | Nut, 7/8 hex | 2 |

1a. 7/16" x 2-1/2" Bolts are ASTM A449. All other Bolts are ASTM A307. All Nuts (except Recessed Guardrail Nuts) are ASTM A563A unless otherwise indicated.
1c. All steel parts shall be galvanized.

Texas A&M Transportation Institute

Roadside Safety and Physical Security Division - Proving Ground

Project # Terminal

Scale 1:25

2021-06-01

Sheet 1 of 6  Terminal Details

Drawn by GES

T:\Drafting Department\Solidworks\Standard Parts\Guardrail Parts and Subs\Guardrail Drawings\Midwest Terminal

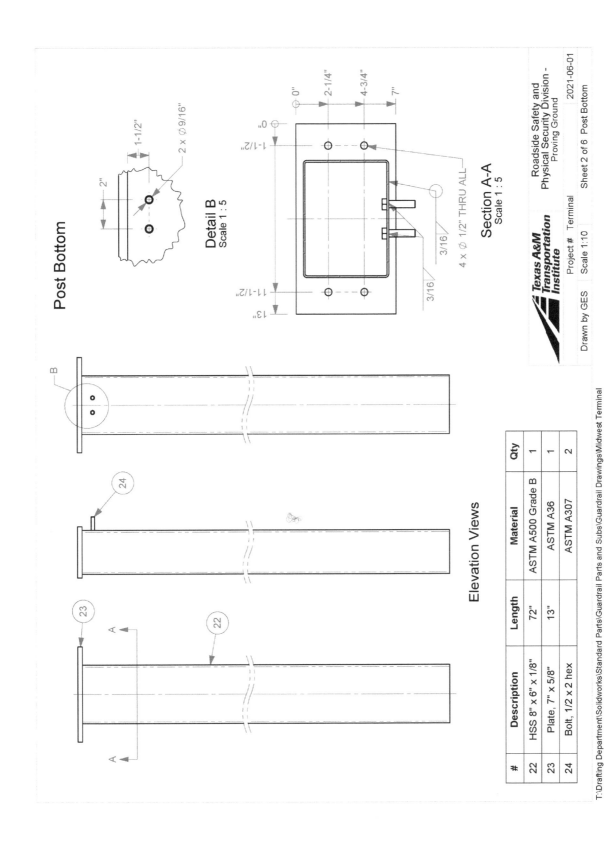

Post Bottom

Detail B
Scale 1 : 5

2"
1-1/2"
2 x Ø 9/16"

Section A-A
Scale 1 : 5

0"
2-1/4"
4-3/4"
7"

0"
1-1/2"
11-1/2"
13"

3/16
3/16

4 x Ø 1/2" THRU ALL

Elevation Views

| # | Description | Length | Material | Qty |
|---|-------------|--------|----------|-----|
| 22 | HSS 8" x 6" x 1/8" | 72" | ASTM A500 Grade B | 1 |
| 23 | Plate, 7" x 5/8" | 13" | ASTM A36 | 1 |
| 24 | Bolt, 1/2 x 2 hex | | ASTM A307 | 2 |

Texas A&M Transportation Institute

Roadside Safety and Physical Security Division -
Proving Ground

2021-06-01

Project # Terminal

Sheet 2 of 6  Post Bottom

Drawn by GES   Scale 1:10

T:\Drafting Department\Solidworks\Standard Parts\Guardrail Parts and Subs\Guardrail Drawings\Midwest Terminal

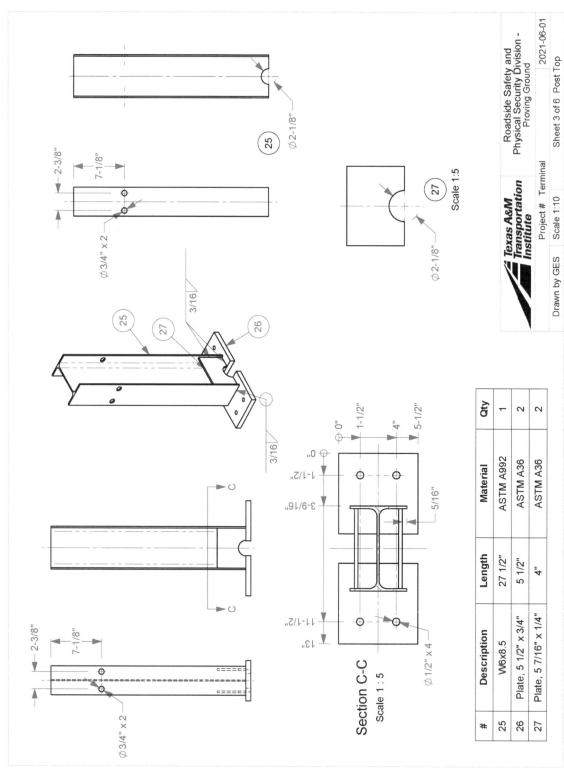

Section C-C
Scale 1 : 5

| # | Description | Length | Material | Qty |
|---|---|---|---|---|
| 25 | W6x8.5 | 27 1/2" | ASTM A992 | 1 |
| 26 | Plate, 5 1/2" x 3/4" | 5 1/2" | ASTM A36 | 2 |
| 27 | Plate, 5 7/16" x 1/4" | 4" | ASTM A36 | 2 |

T:\Drafting Department\Solidworks\Standard Parts\Guardrail Parts and Subs\Guardrail Drawings\Midwest Terminal

Texas A&M Transportation Institute

Roadside Safety and Physical Security Division - Proving Ground

2021-06-01

Sheet 3 of 6 Post Top

Project # Terminal

Drawn by GES    Scale 1:10

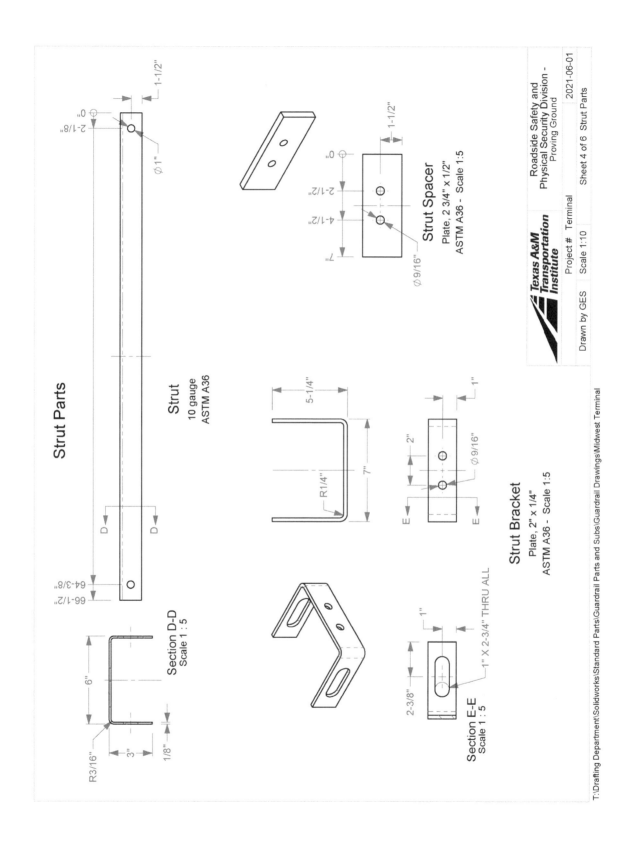

Strut Parts

Strut
10 gauge
ASTM A36

Section D-D
Scale 1 : 5

Strut Spacer
Plate, 2 3/4" x 1/2"
ASTM A36 - Scale 1:5

Strut Bracket
Plate, 2" x 1/4"
ASTM A36 - Scale 1:5

Section E-E
Scale 1 : 5

Roadside Safety and
Physical Security Division -
Proving Ground

Texas A&M
Transportation
Institute

Project # Terminal

Drawn by GES    Scale 1:10    Sheet 4 of 6   Strut Parts

2021-06-01

T:\Drafting Department\Solidworks\Standard Parts\Guardrail Parts and Subs\Guardrail Drawings\Midwest Terminal

B-13

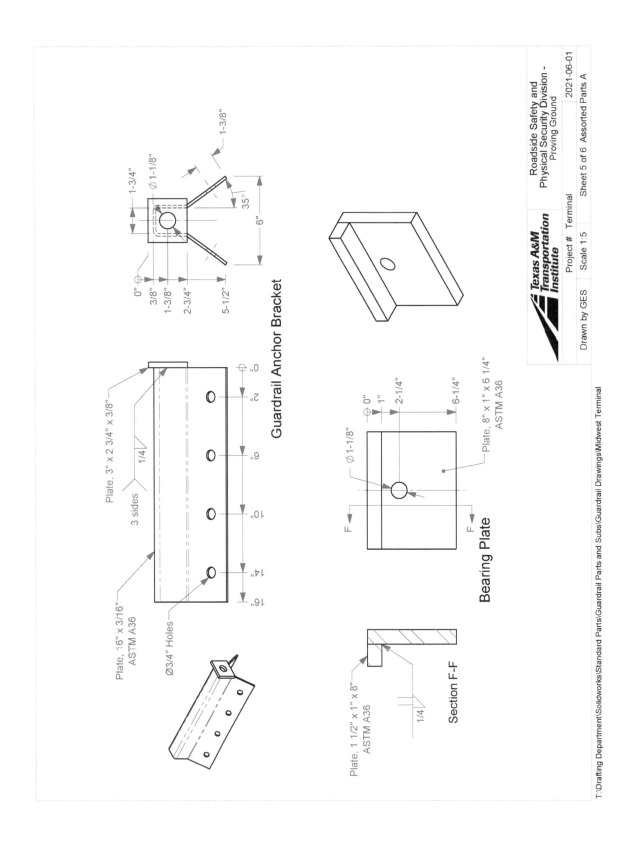

Guardrail Anchor Bracket

Ø 1-1/8"

1-3/4"

1-3/8"

35°

6"

0"
3/8"
1-3/8"
2-3/4"
5-1/2"

Plate, 3" x 2 3/4" x 3/8"

1/4"

3 sides

Plate, 16" x 3/16"
ASTM A36

Ø3/4" Holes

0"
2"
6"
10"
14"
16"

Bearing Plate

Ø 1-1/8"

0"
1"
2-1/4"
6-1/4"

Plate, 8" x 1" x 6 1/4"
ASTM A36

F

F

Section F-F

Plate, 1 1/2" x 1" x 8"
ASTM A36

1/4"

Texas A&M
Transportation
Institute

Roadside Safety and
Physical Security Division -
Proving Ground

2021-06-01

Project #   Terminal

Scale 1:5

Sheet 5 of 6   Assorted Parts A

Drawn by GES

T:\Drafting Department\Solidworks\Standard Parts\Guardrail Parts and Subs\Guardrail Drawings\Midwest Terminal

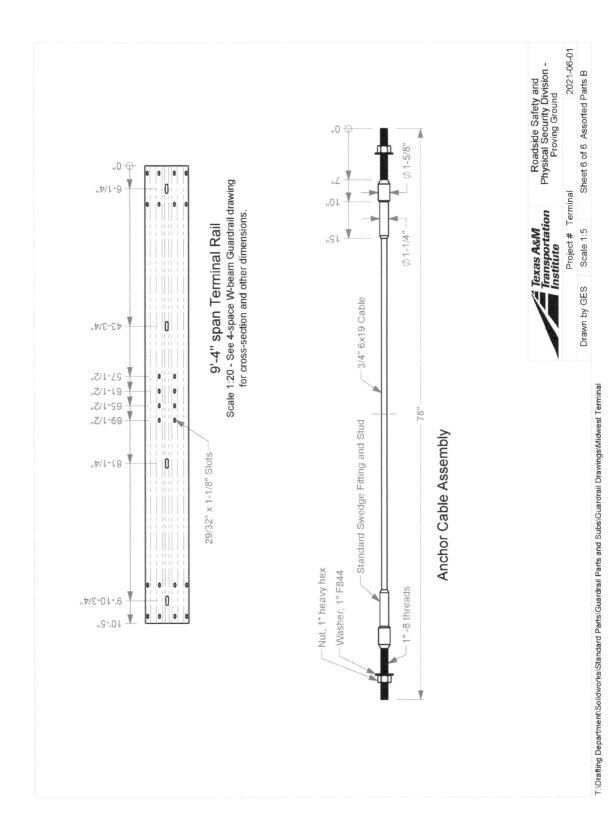

9'-4" span Terminal Rail

Scale 1:20 - See 4-space W-beam Guardrail drawing for cross-section and other dimensions.

29/32" x 1-1/8" Slots

Anchor Cable Assembly

Nut, 1" heavy hex

Washer, 1" F844

Standard Swedge Fitting and Stud

3/4" 6x19 Cable

1"-8 threads

Ø 1-5/8"

Ø 1-1/4"

Texas A&M Transportation Institute

Roadside Safety and Physical Security Division - Proving Ground

2021-06-01

Project # Terminal

Sheet 6 of 6 Assorted Parts B

Drawn by GES

Scale 1:5

T:\Drafting Department\Solidworks\Standard Parts\Guardrail Parts and Subs\Guardrail Drawings\Midwest Terminal

# W-beam Terminal Connector

See W-beam Guardrail drawing for all dimensions not shown here.

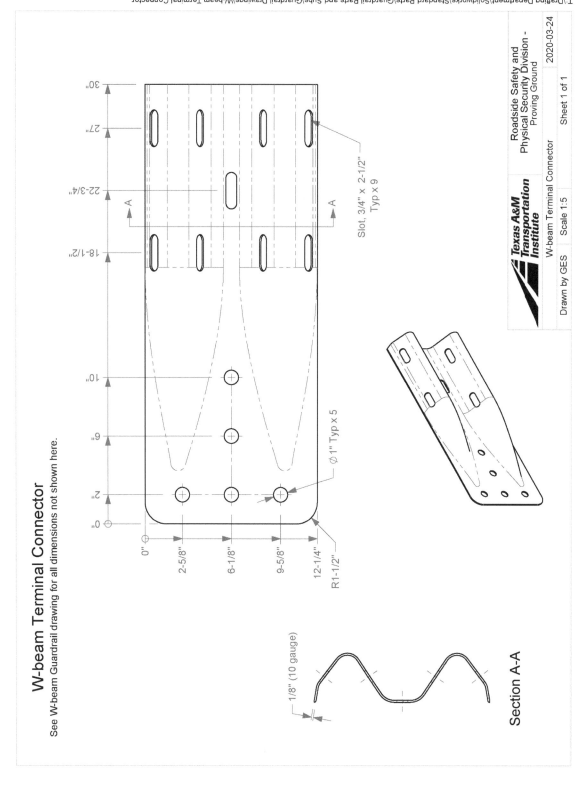

Slot, 3/4" x 2-1/2"
Typ x 9

Ø 1" Typ x 5

R1-1/2"

Section A-A

1/8" (10 gauge)

| | |
|---|---|
| Roadside Safety and Physical Security Division - Proving Ground | 2020-03-24 |
| Texas A&M Transportation Institute | Sheet 1 of 1 |
| W-beam Terminal Connector | Scale 1:5 |
| Drawn by GES | |

Rectangular Guardrail Washer

0.20" thick

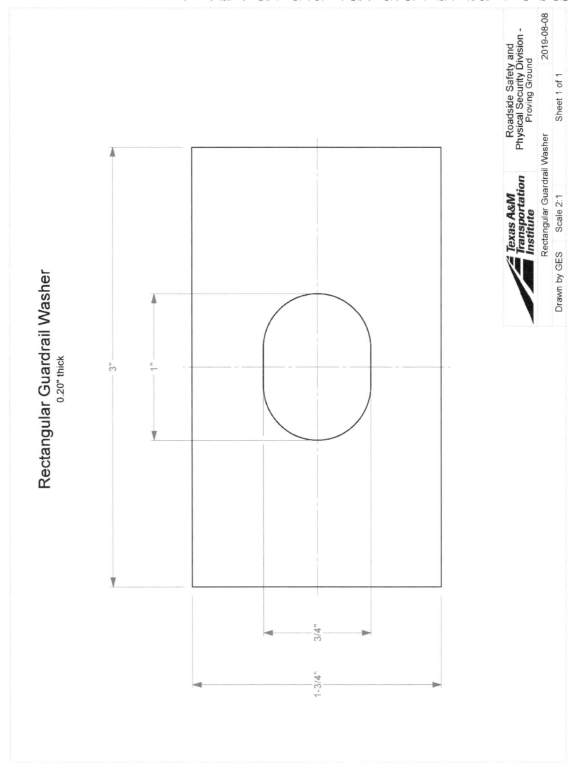

3"

1"

3/4"

1-3/4"

Texas A&M
Transportation
Institute

Roadside Safety and
Physical Security Division -
Proving Ground

2019-08-08

Rectangular Guardrail Washer

Drawn by GES          Scale 2:1          Sheet 1 of 1

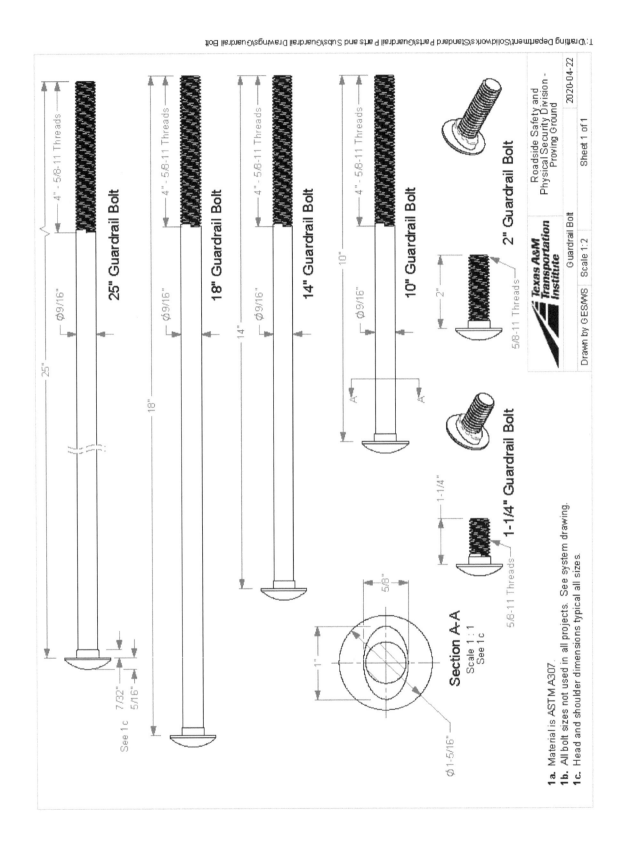

25" Guardrail Bolt

18" Guardrail Bolt

14" Guardrail Bolt

10" Guardrail Bolt

2" Guardrail Bolt

1-1/4" Guardrail Bolt

4" - 5/8-11 Threads

Ø9/16"

5/8-11 Threads

2"

1-1/4"

5/8-11 Threads

Section A-A
Scale 1 : 1
See 1c

5/8"

1"

Ø1-5/16"

7/32"

5/16"

See 1c

1a. Material is ASTM A307.
1b. All bolt sizes not used in all projects. See system drawing.
1c. Head and shoulder dimensions typical all sizes.

Texas A&M Transportation Institute

Roadside Safety and Physical Security Division - Proving Ground

2020-04-22

Guardrail Bolt

Drawn by GES/WS    Scale 1:2    Sheet 1 of 1

Recessed Guardrail Nut

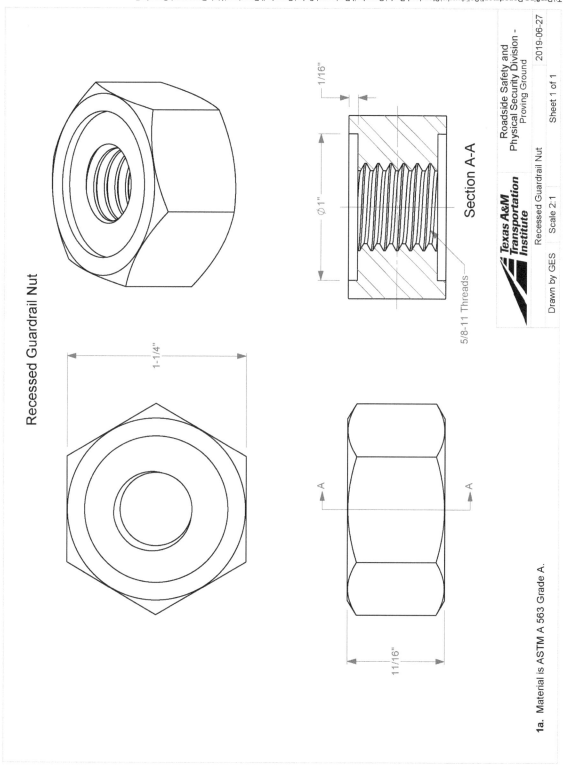

1-1/4"

11/16"

Section A-A

5/8-11 Threads

Ø 1"

1/16"

A

A

| Roadside Safety and Physical Security Division - Proving Ground | 2019-06-27 |
|---|---|

Texas A&M Transportation Institute

| | Recessed Guardrail Nut | Sheet 1 of 1 |
|---|---|---|
| Drawn by GES | Scale 2:1 | |

1a.  Material is ASTM A 563 Grade A.

# Details of the Pedestrian Traffic Rail Transition for MASH Test 3-20

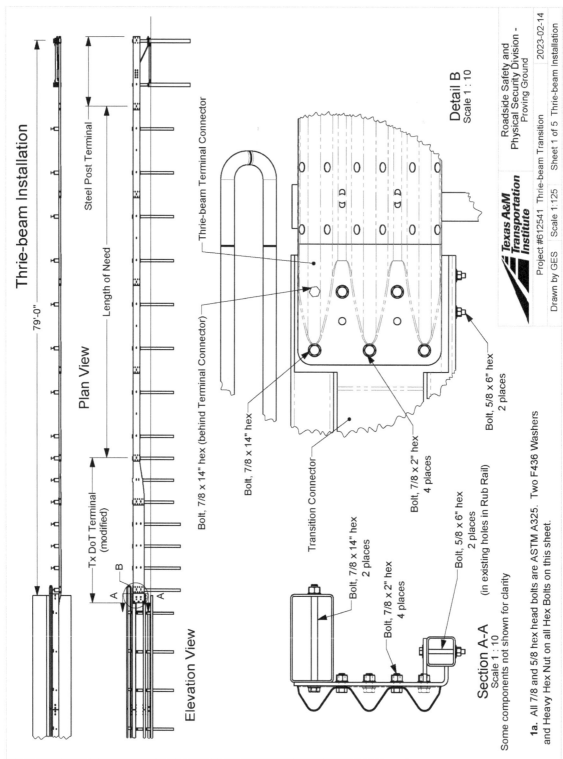

# Thrie-beam Installation

## Plan View

79'-0"

Steel Post Terminal

Length of Need

Tx DoT Terminal (modified)

A
B
A

## Elevation View

Thrie-beam Terminal Connector

Bolt, 7/8 x 14" hex (behind Terminal Connector)

Bolt, 7/8 x 14" hex

Transition Connector

Bolt, 7/8 x 14" hex
2 places

Bolt, 7/8 x 2" hex
4 places

Bolt, 5/8 x 6" hex
2 places

## Section A-A
Scale 1 : 10
(in existing holes in Rub Rail)
Some components not shown for clarity

Bolt, 7/8 x 2" hex
4 places

Bolt, 5/8 x 6" hex
2 places

## Detail B
Scale 1 : 10

**1a.** All 7/8 and 5/8 hex head bolts are ASTM A325. Two F436 Washers and Heavy Hex Nut on all Hex Bolts on this sheet.

Roadside Safety and Physical Security Division - Proving Ground

2023-02-14

Texas A&M Transportation Institute

Project #612541   Thrie-beam Transition

Drawn by GES   Scale 1:125   Sheet 1 of 5   Thrie-beam Installation

S:\Accreditation-17025-2017\EIR-000 Project Files\612541 - Ped-Traffic Rail - Dobrovolny\Drafting, 612541-03\612541-03 Drawing

Field Side

Drill holes through Traffic Rail for these bolts. See inset below.

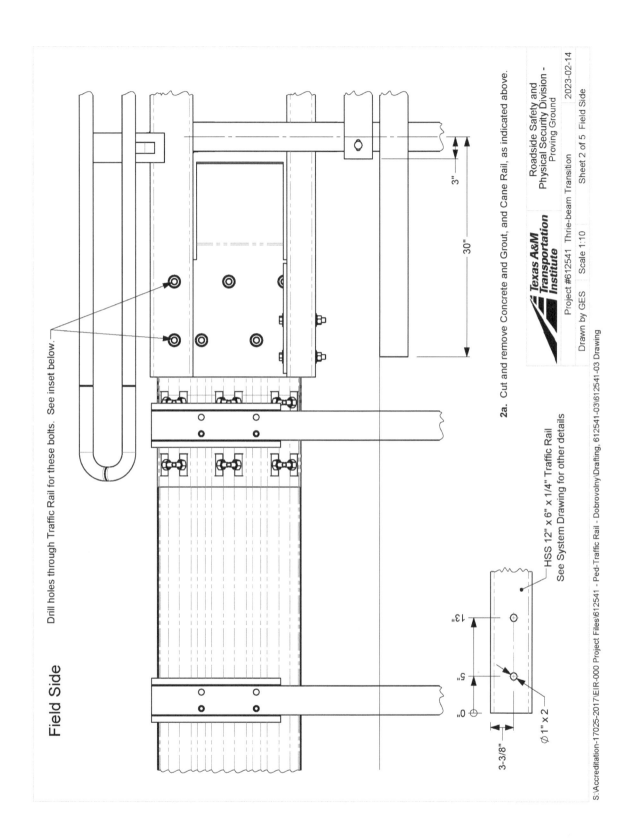

2a. Cut and remove Concrete and Grout, and Cane Rail, as indicated above.

3"

30"

13"

5"

0"

3-3/8"

⌀ 1" x 2

HSS 12" x 6" x 1/4" Traffic Rail
See System Drawing for other details

Roadside Safety and
Physical Security Division -
Proving Ground

Texas A&M
Transportation
Institute

2023-02-14

Project #612541  Thrie-beam Transition

Drawn by GES   Scale 1:10    Sheet 2 of 5   Field Side

S:\Accreditation-17025-2017\EIR-000 Project Files\612541 - Ped-Traffic Rail - Dobrovolny\Drafting, 612541-03\612541-03 Drawing

E-3

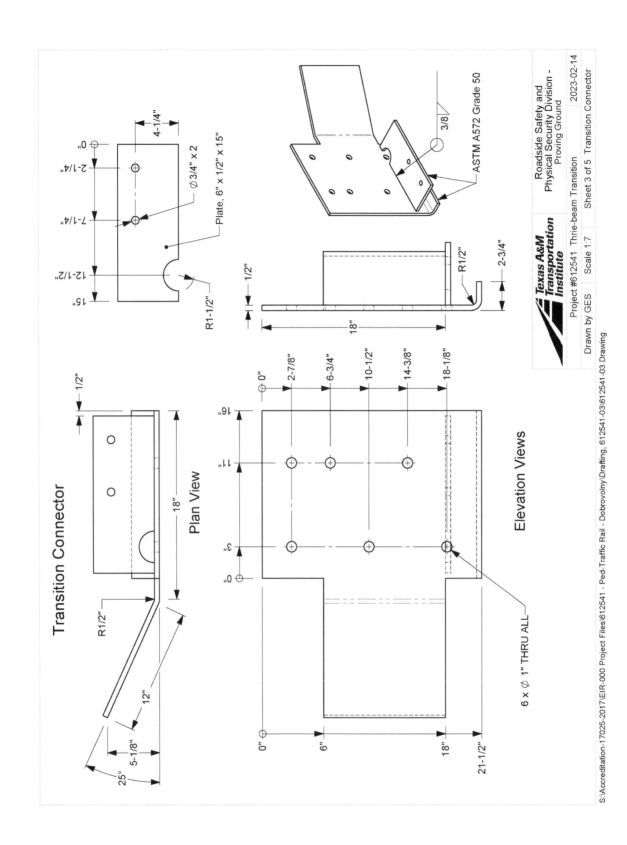

Transition Connector

Plan View

Elevation Views

Plate, 6" x 1/2" x 15"

⌀ 3/4" x 2

R1-1/2"

ASTM A572 Grade 50

6 x ⌀ 1" THRU ALL

R1/2"

25°

Texas A&M Transportation Institute

Roadside Safety and Physical Security Division - Proving Ground

Project #612541   Thrie-beam Transition            2023-02-14

Scale 1:7          Sheet 3 of 5   Transition Connector

Drawn by GES

S:\Accreditation-17025-2017\EIR-000 Project Files\612541 - Ped-Traffic Rail - Dobrovolny\Drafting, 612541-03\612541-03 Drawing

E-4

# Terminal Hand Rail

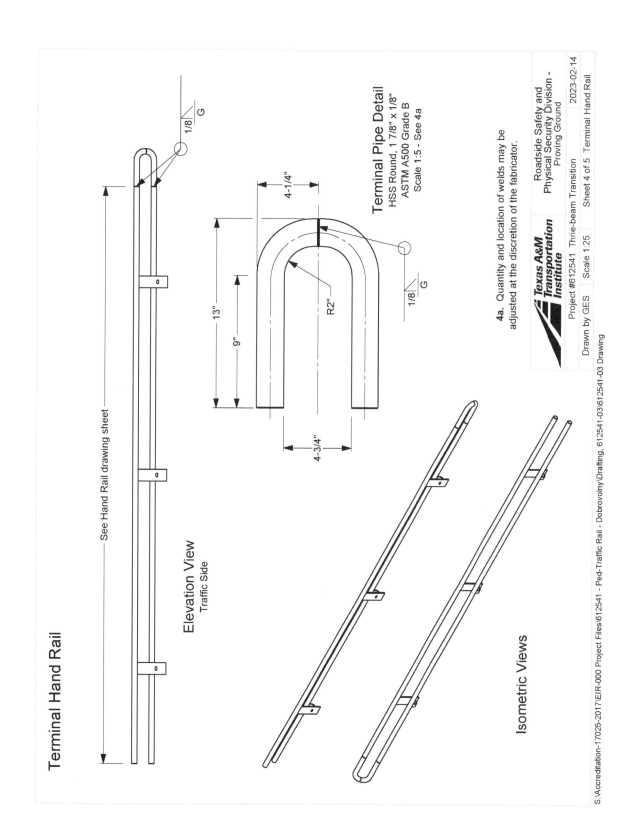

See Hand Rail drawing sheet

**Elevation View**
Traffic Side

1/8 / G

## Terminal Pipe Detail

HSS Round, 1 7/8" x 1/8"
ASTM A500 Grade B
Scale 1:5 - See 4a

4-1/4"

13"

9"

R2"

4-3/4"

1/8 / G

**4a.** Quantity and location of welds may be adjusted at the discretion of the fabricator.

**Isometric Views**

Texas A&M Transportation Institute

Roadside Safety and Physical Security Division - Proving Ground

2023-02-14

Project #612541   Thrie-beam Transition

Sheet 4 of 5   Terminal Hand Rail

Drawn by GES | Scale 1:25

S:\Accreditation-17025-2017\EIR-000 Project Files\612541 - Ped-Traffic Rail - Dobrovolny\Drafting, 612541-03\612541-03 Drawing

E-5

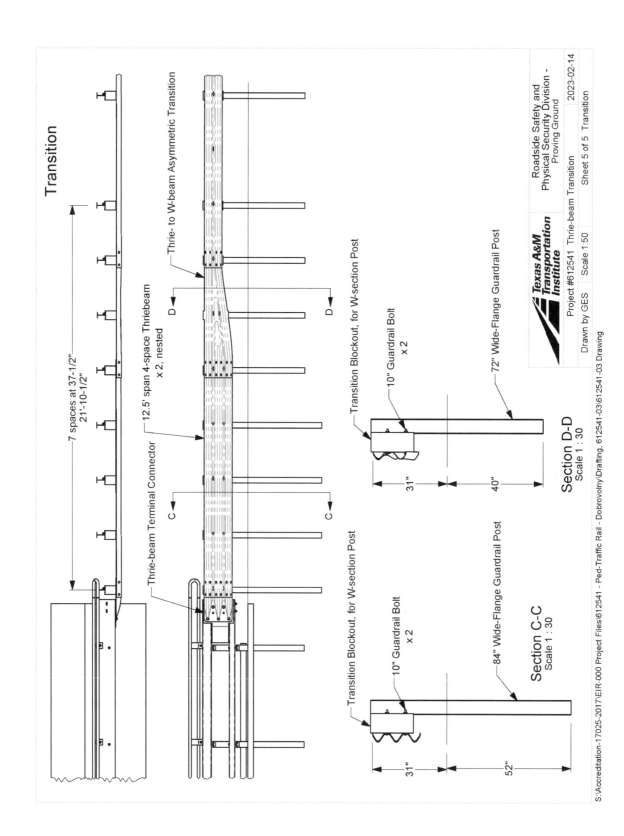

Transition

7 spaces at 37-1/2"
21'-10-1/2"

Thrie- to W-beam Asymmetric Transition

12.5' span 4-space Thriebeam x 2, nested

Thrie-beam Terminal Connector

D

D

C

C

Transition Blockout, for W-section Post

10" Guardrail Bolt x 2

72" Wide-Flange Guardrail Post

31"

40"

Section D-D
Scale 1 : 30

Transition Blockout, for W-section Post

10" Guardrail Bolt x 2

84" Wide-Flange Guardrail Post

31"

52"

Section C-C
Scale 1 : 30

Texas A&M Transportation Institute

Roadside Safety and Physical Security Division - Proving Ground

2023-02-14

Project #612541  Thrie-beam Transition

Scale 1:50

Sheet 5 of 5   Transition

Drawn by GES

S:\Accreditation-17025-2017\EIR-000 Project Files\612541 - Ped-Traffic Rail - Dobrovolny\Drafting, 612541-03\612541-03 Drawing

E-6

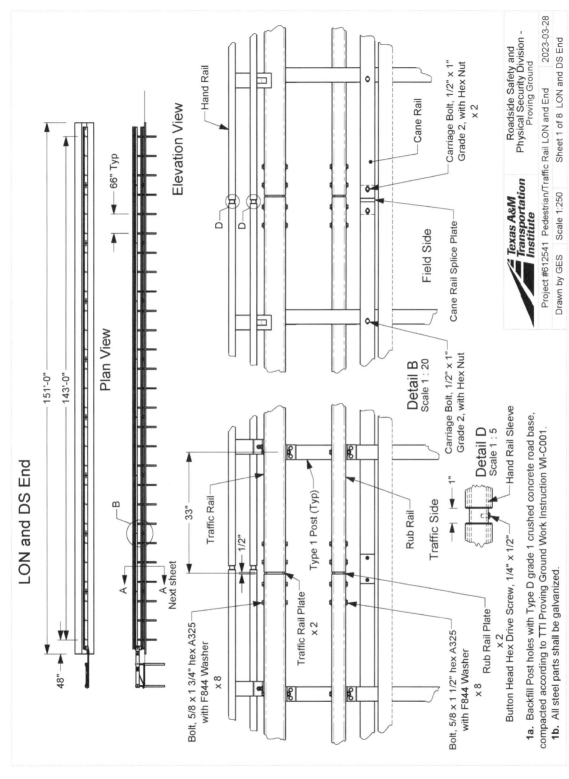

# LON and DS End

## Plan View

151'-0"

143'-0"

48"

66" Typ

A

A
Next sheet

B

## Elevation View

Hand Rail

D

D

Field Side

Carriage Bolt, 1/2" x 1" Grade 2, with Hex Nut x 2

Cane Rail

Cane Rail Splice Plate

### Detail B
Scale 1 : 20

Carriage Bolt, 1/2" x 1" Grade 2, with Hex Nut

### Detail D
Scale 1 : 5

Hand Rail Sleeve

1"

Traffic Rail

1/2"

Type 1 Post (Typ)

Rub Rail

Traffic Side

Bolt, 5/8 x 1 3/4" hex A325 with F844 Washer x 8

33"

Traffic Rail Plate x 2

Bolt, 5/8 x 1 1/2" hex A325 with F844 Washer x 8

Rub Rail Plate x 2

Button Head Hex Drive Screw, 1/4" x 1/2"

**1a.** Backfill Post holes with Type D grade 1 crushed concrete road base, compacted according to TTI Proving Ground Work Instruction WI-C001.

**1b.** All steel parts shall be galvanized.

Texas A&M Transportation Institute

Roadside Safety and Physical Security Division - Proving Ground

Project #612541  Pedestrian/Traffic Rail LON and End  2023-03-28

Drawn by GES  Scale 1:250  Sheet 1 of 8  LON and DS End

Scale 1:250

S:\Accreditation-17025-2017\EIR-000 Project Files\612541 - Ped-Traffic Rail - Dobrovolny\Drafting, 612541-03\LON System\612541 Drawing

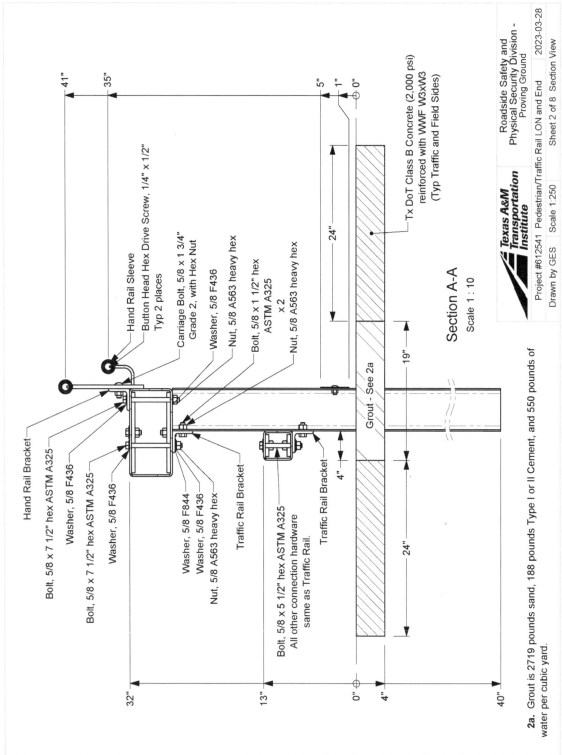

Hand Rail Bracket

Bolt, 5/8 x 7 1/2" hex ASTM A325

Washer, 5/8 F436

Bolt, 5/8 x 7 1/2" hex ASTM A325

Washer, 5/8 F436

Washer, 5/8 F844
Washer, 5/8 F436
Nut, 5/8 A563 heavy hex

Traffic Rail Bracket

Bolt, 5/8 x 5 1/2" hex ASTM A325
All other connection hardware
same as Traffic Rail.

Traffic Rail Bracket

Hand Rail Sleeve

Button Head Hex Drive Screw, 1/4" x 1/2"
Typ 2 places

Carriage Bolt, 5/8 x 1 3/4"
Grade 2, with Hex Nut

Washer, 5/8 F436

Nut, 5/8 A563 heavy hex

Bolt, 5/8 x 1 1/2" hex
ASTM A325
x 2

Nut, 5/8 A563 heavy hex

Grout - See 2a

Tx DoT Class B Concrete (2,000 psi)
reinforced with WWF W3xW3
(Typ Traffic and Field Sides)

Section A-A
Scale 1 : 10

41"
35"
5"
1"
0"
24"
19"
4"
32"
13"
0"
4"
24"
40"

**2a.** Grout is 2719 pounds sand, 188 pounds Type I or II Cement, and 550 pounds of water per cubic yard.

Texas A&M
Transportation
Institute

Roadside Safety and
Physical Security Division -
Proving Ground

2023-03-28

Project #612541  Pedestrian/Traffic Rail LON and End

Drawn by GES  Scale 1:250  Sheet 2 of 8  Section View

S:\Accreditation-17025-2017\EIR-000 Project Files\612541 - Ped-Traffic Rail - Dobrovolny\Drafting, 612541-03\LON System\612541 Drawing

E-8

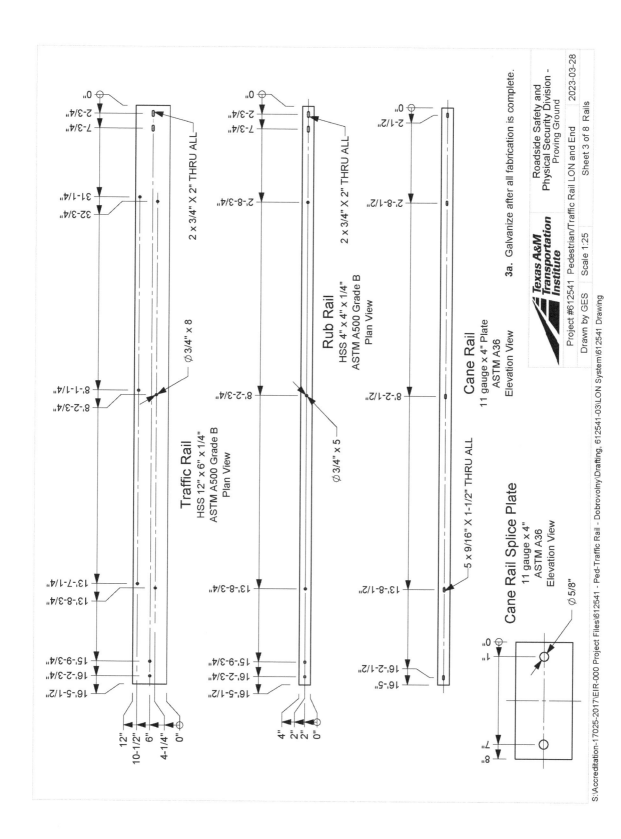

**Traffic Rail**
HSS 12" x 6" x 1/4"
ASTM A500 Grade B
Plan View

ø 3/4" x 8

2 x 3/4" X 2" THRU ALL

0"
2-3/4"
7-3/4"
31-1/4"
32-3/4"
8'-1-1/4"
8'-2-3/4"
13'-7-1/4"
13'-8-3/4"
15'-9-3/4"
16'-2-3/4"
16'-5-1/2"

12"
10-1/2"
6"
4-1/4"
0"

**Rub Rail**
HSS 4" x 4" x 1/4"
ASTM A500 Grade B
Plan View

ø 3/4" x 5

2 x 3/4" X 2" THRU ALL

0"
2-3/4"
7-3/4"
2'-8-3/4"
8'-2-3/4"
13'-8-3/4"
15'-9-3/4"
16'-2-3/4"
16'-5-1/2"

4"
2"
2"
0"

**Cane Rail**
11 gauge x 4" Plate
ASTM A36
Elevation View

5 x 9/16" X 1-1/2" THRU ALL

0"
2-1/2"
2'-8-1/2"
8'-2-1/2"
13'-8-1/2"
16'-2-1/2"
16'-5"

**Cane Rail Splice Plate**
11 gauge x 4"
ASTM A36
Elevation View

ø 5/8"

0"
1"
7"
8"

3a. Galvanize after all fabrication is complete.

Texas A&M Transportation Institute

Roadside Safety and Physical Security Division - Proving Ground

Project #612541  Pedestrian/Traffic Rail LON and End

2023-03-28

Drawn by GES

Scale 1:25

Sheet 3 of 8  Rails

S:\Accreditation-17025-2017\EIR-000 Project Files\612541 - Ped-Traffic Rail - Dobrovolny\Drafting, 612541-03\LON System\612541 Drawing

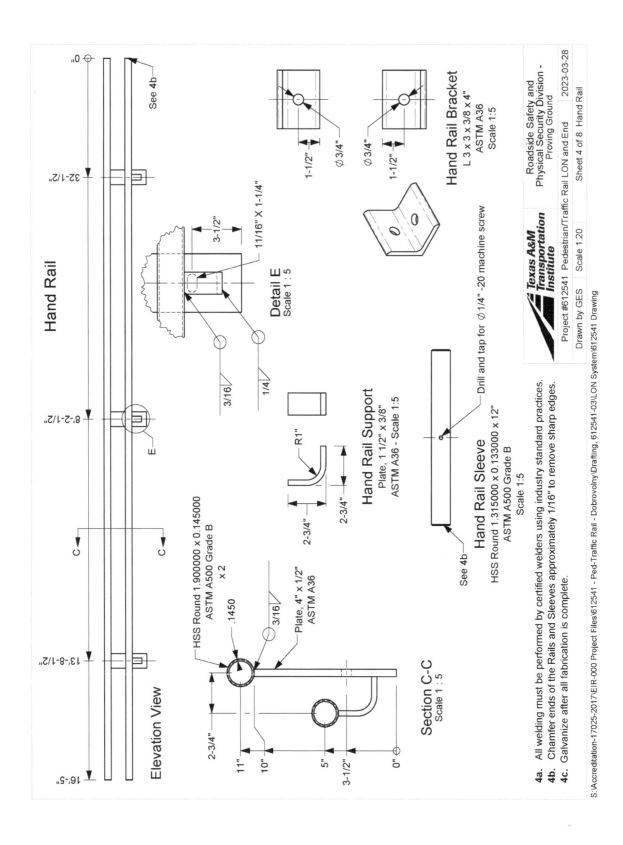

# Hand Rail

## Elevation View

0"

32-1/2"

8'-2-1/2"

13'-8-1/2"

16'-5"

See 4b

C

C

E

## Detail E
Scale 1 : 5

3-1/2"

11/16" X 1-1/4"

3/16

1/4

## Hand Rail Support
Plate, 1 1/2" x 3/8"
ASTM A36 - Scale 1:5

R1"

2-3/4"

2-3/4"

## Hand Rail Sleeve
HSS Round 1.315000 x 0.133000 x 12"
ASTM A500 Grade B
Scale 1:5

Drill and tap for ⌀ 1/4"-20 machine screw

See 4b

## Section C-C
Scale 1 : 5

HSS Round 1.900000 x 0.145000
ASTM A500 Grade B
x 2

.1450

3/16

Plate, 4" x 1/2"
ASTM A36

2-3/4"

11"

10"

5"

3-1/2"

0"

## Hand Rail Bracket
L 3 x 3 x 3/8 x 4"
ASTM A36
Scale 1:5

⌀ 3/4"

1-1/2"

⌀ 3/4"

1-1/2"

**4a.** All welding must be performed by certified welders using industry standard practices.
**4b.** Chamfer ends of the Rails and Sleeves approximately 1/16" to remove sharp edges.
**4c.** Galvanize after all fabrication is complete.

Texas A&M Transportation Institute

Roadside Safety and Physical Security Division - Proving Ground

Project #612541   Pedestrian/Traffic Rail LON and End   2023-03-28

Drawn by GES   Scale 1:20   Sheet 4 of 8   Hand Rail

S:\Accreditation-17025-2017\EIR-000 Project Files\612541 - Ped-Traffic Rail - Dobrovolny\Drafting, 612541-03\LON System\612541 Drawing

E-10

# Joint Plates

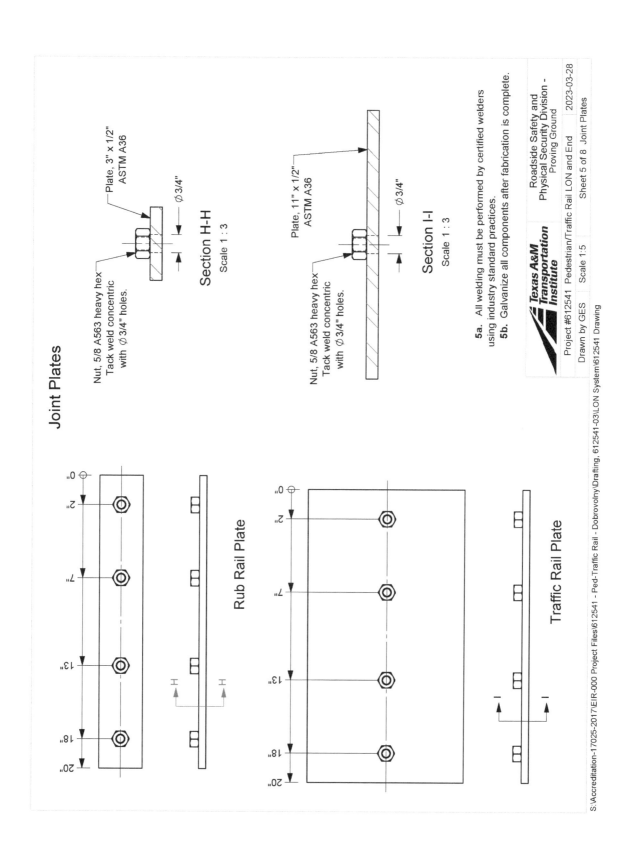

Plate, 3" x 1/2"
ASTM A36

Nut, 5/8 A563 heavy hex
Tack weld concentric
with ∅ 3/4" holes.

∅ 3/4"

## Section H-H
Scale 1 : 3

Plate, 11" x 1/2"
ASTM A36

Nut, 5/8 A563 heavy hex
Tack weld concentric
with ∅ 3/4" holes.

∅ 3/4"

## Section I-I
Scale 1 : 3

**Rub Rail Plate**

0"
2"
7"
13"
18"
20"

**Traffic Rail Plate**

0"
2"
7"
13"
18"
20"

**5a.** All welding must be performed by certified welders using industry standard practices.
**5b.** Galvanize all components after fabrication is complete.

**Texas A&M Transportation Institute**

Roadside Safety and Physical Security Division - Proving Ground

Project #612541  Pedestrian/Traffic Rail LON and End  2023-03-28

Drawn by GES    Scale 1:5    Sheet 5 of 8  Joint Plates

S:\Accreditation-17025-2017\EIR-000 Project Files\612541 - Ped-Traffic Rail - Dobrovolny\Drafting, 612541-03\LON System\612541 Drawing

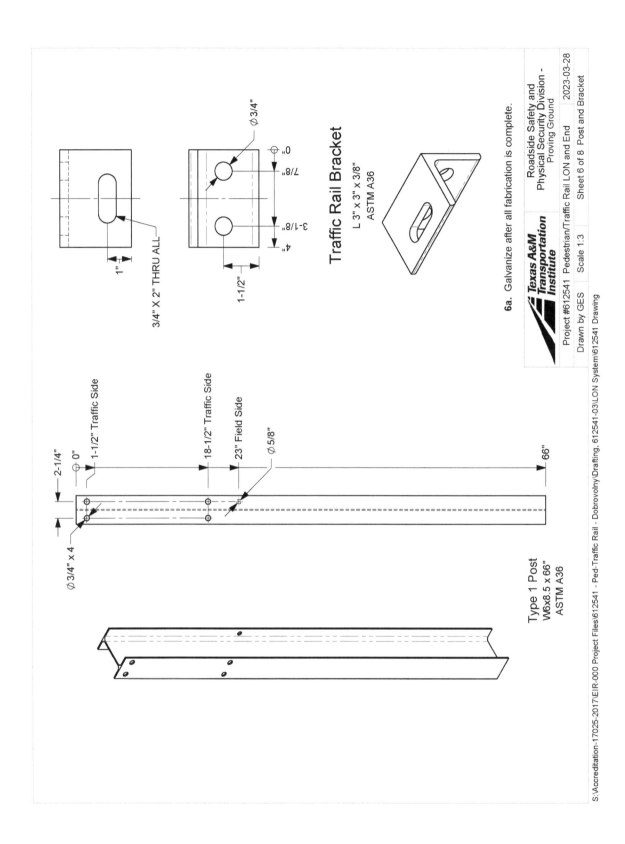

**Traffic Rail Bracket**

L 3" x 3" x 3/8"
ASTM A36

3/4" X 2" THRU ALL

1"

Ø 3/4"

0"
7/8"
3-1/8"
4"

1-1/2"

**Type 1 Post**

W6x8.5 x 66"
ASTM A36

Ø 3/4" x 4

2-1/4"
0"
1-1/2" Traffic Side
18-1/2" Traffic Side
23" Field Side

Ø 5/8"

66"

6a. Galvanize after all fabrication is complete.

Texas A&M
Transportation
Institute

Roadside Safety and
Physical Security Division -
Proving Ground

2023-03-28

Project #612541   Pedestrian/Traffic Rail LON and End

Drawn by GES   Scale 1:3   Sheet 6 of 8   Post and Bracket

S:\Accreditation-17025-2017\EIR-000 Project Files\612541 - Ped-Traffic Rail - Dobrovolny\Drafting, 612541-03\LON System\612541 Drawing

E-12

# Downstream Terminal Details

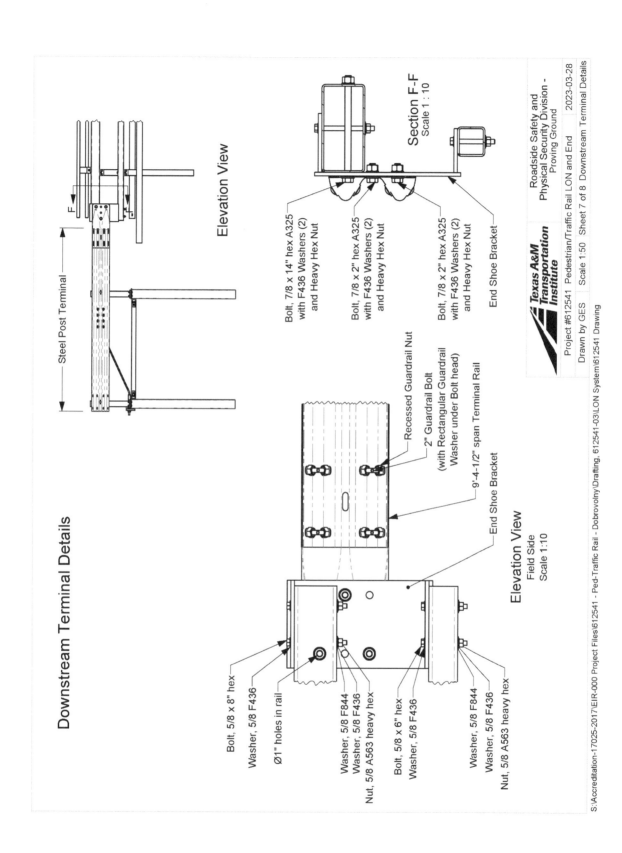

Steel Post Terminal

**Elevation View**

Bolt, 7/8 x 14" hex A325 with F436 Washers (2) and Heavy Hex Nut

Bolt, 7/8 x 2" hex A325 with F436 Washers (2) and Heavy Hex Nut

Bolt, 7/8 x 2" hex A325 with F436 Washers (2) and Heavy Hex Nut

End Shoe Bracket

**Section F-F**
Scale 1 : 10

Recessed Guardrail Nut

2" Guardrail Bolt (with Rectangular Guardrail Washer under Bolt head)

9'-4-1/2" span Terminal Rail

End Shoe Bracket

**Elevation View**
Field Side
Scale 1:10

Bolt, 5/8 x 8" hex

Washer, 5/8 F436

Ø1" holes in rail

Washer, 5/8 F844

Washer, 5/8 F436

Nut, 5/8 A563 heavy hex

Bolt, 5/8 x 6" hex

Washer, 5/8 F436

Washer, 5/8 F844

Washer, 5/8 F436

Nut, 5/8 A563 heavy hex

**Texas A&M Transportation Institute**

Roadside Safety and Physical Security Division - Proving Ground

2023-03-28

Project #612541  Pedestrian/Traffic Rail LON and End

Drawn by GES

Scale 1:50  Sheet 7 of 8  Downstream Terminal Details

S:\Accreditation-17025-2017\EIR-000 Project Files\612541 - Ped-Traffic Rail - Dobrovolny\Drafting, 612541-03\LON System\612541 Drawing

E-13

# End Shoe Bracket

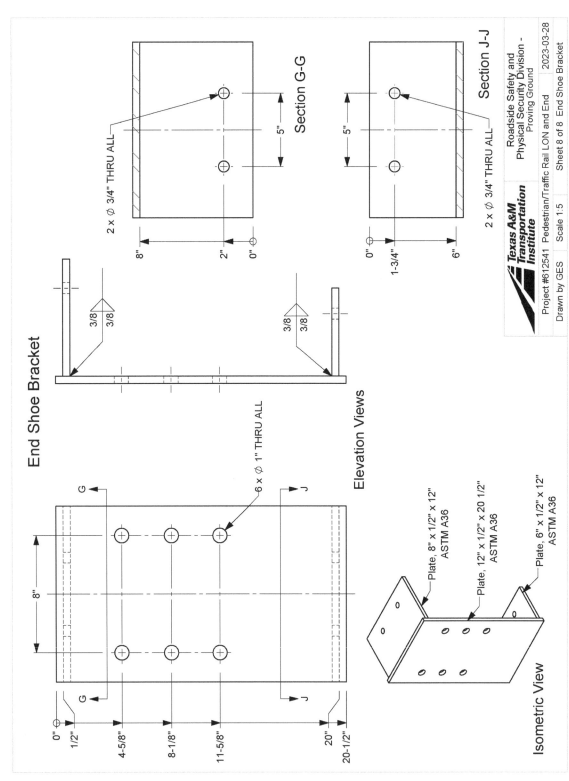

## Section G-G

2 x ⌀ 3/4" THRU ALL

8"
2"
0"
5"

## Section J-J

2 x ⌀ 3/4" THRU ALL

0"
1-3/4"
6"
5"

## Elevation Views

3/8
3/8

3/8
3/8

6 x ⌀ 1" THRU ALL

G
G
J
J

8"

0"
1/2"
4-5/8"
8-1/8"
11-5/8"
20"
20-1/2"

## Isometric View

Plate, 8" x 1/2" x 12"
ASTM A36

Plate, 12" x 1/2" x 20 1/2"
ASTM A36

Plate, 6" x 1/2" x 12"
ASTM A36

Texas A&M Transportation Institute

Project #612541   Pedestrian/Traffic Rail LON and End

Roadside Safety and Physical Security Division - Proving Ground

2023-03-28

Drawn by GES   Scale 1:5   Sheet 8 of 8   End Shoe Bracket

S:\Accreditation-17025-2017\EIR-000 Project Files\612541 - Ped-Traffic Rail - Dobrovolny\Drafting, 612541-03\LON System\612541 Drawing

E-14

# Steel Post Terminal Details

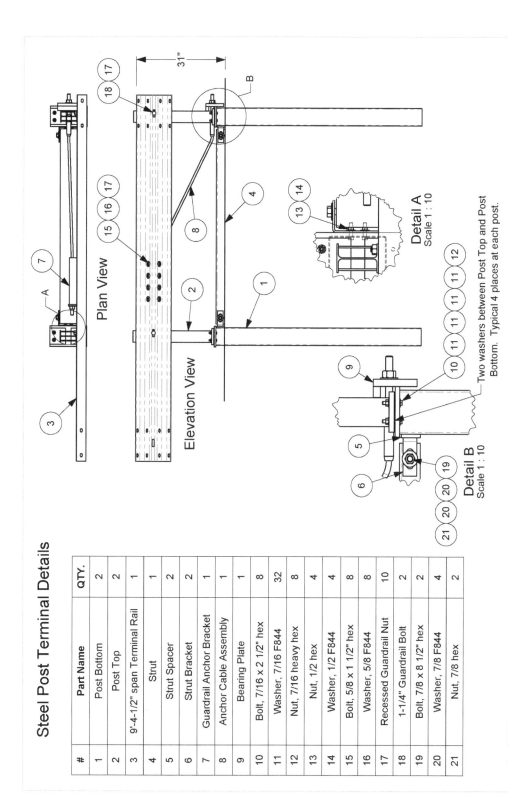

Plan View

Elevation View

Detail A
Scale 1 : 10

Detail B
Scale 1 : 10

31"

Two washers between Post Top and Post Bottom. Typical 4 places at each post.

| # | Part Name | QTY. |
|---|-----------|------|
| 1 | Post Bottom | 2 |
| 2 | Post Top | 2 |
| 3 | 9'-4-1/2" span Terminal Rail | 1 |
| 4 | Strut | 1 |
| 5 | Strut Spacer | 2 |
| 6 | Strut Bracket | 2 |
| 7 | Guardrail Anchor Bracket | 1 |
| 8 | Anchor Cable Assembly | 1 |
| 9 | Bearing Plate | 1 |
| 10 | Bolt, 7/16 x 2 1/2" hex | 8 |
| 11 | Washer, 7/16 F844 | 32 |
| 12 | Nut, 7/16 heavy hex | 8 |
| 13 | Nut, 1/2 hex | 4 |
| 14 | Washer, 1/2 F844 | 4 |
| 15 | Bolt, 5/8 x 1 1/2" hex | 8 |
| 16 | Washer, 5/8 F844 | 8 |
| 17 | Recessed Guardrail Nut | 10 |
| 18 | 1-1/4" Guardrail Bolt | 2 |
| 19 | Bolt, 7/8 x 8 1/2" hex | 2 |
| 20 | Washer, 7/8 F844 | 4 |
| 21 | Nut, 7/8 hex | 2 |

**1a.** 7/16" x 2-1/2" Bolts are ASTM A449. All other Bolts are ASTM A307. All Nuts (except Recessed Guardrail Nuts) are ASTM A563A unless otherwise indicated.
**1b.** All steel parts shall be galvanized.
**1c.** This specific terminal configuration has not been tested. It is used as a barrier anchorage device for crash testing purposes.

Texas A&M Transportation Institute

Roadside Safety and Physical Security Division - Proving Ground

| Drawn by GES | Project # | Terminal | 2023-02-08 |
|---|---|---|---|
| | Scale 1:25 | | Sheet 1 of 6  Terminal Details |

S:\engrfact\Drafting Department\Solidworks\Standard Parts\Guardrail Parts and Subs\Guardrail Drawings\Steel Post Terminal

E-15

Post Bottom

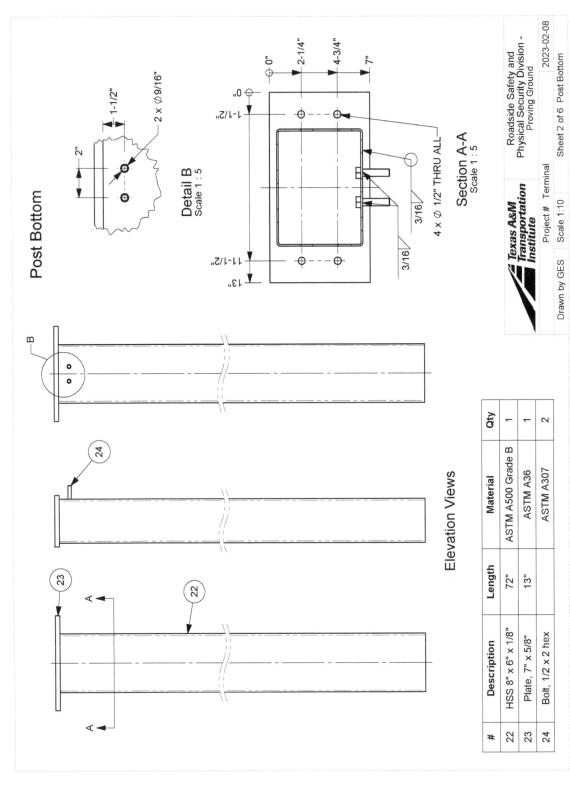

Detail B
Scale 1 : 5

2 x Ø 9/16"

2"
1-1/2"

Section A-A
Scale 1 : 5

4 x Ø 1/2" THRU ALL

3/16

3/16

0"
2-1/4"
4-3/4"
7"

0"
11-1/2"
11-1/2"
13"

Elevation Views

| # | Description | Length | Material | Qty |
|---|---|---|---|---|
| 22 | HSS 8" x 6" x 1/8" | 72" | ASTM A500 Grade B | 1 |
| 23 | Plate, 7" x 5/8" | 13" | ASTM A36 | 1 |
| 24 | Bolt, 1/2 x 2 hex | | ASTM A307 | 2 |

Texas A&M
Transportation
Institute

Roadside Safety and
Physical Security Division -
Proving Ground

Project # Terminal        2023-02-08

Drawn by GES    Scale 1:10    Sheet 2 of 6  Post Bottom

S:\engrfact\Drafting Department\Solidworks\Standard Parts\Guardrail Parts and Subs\Standard Parts\Guardrail Drawings\Steel Post Terminal

E-16

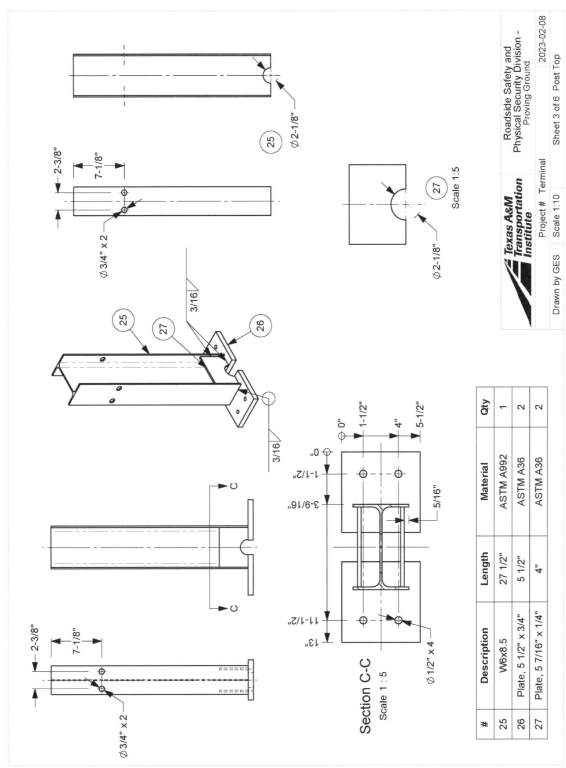

Ø2-1/8"

25

2-3/8"
7-1/8"

Ø3/4" x 2

27

Scale 1:5

Ø2-1/8"

3/16

25

27

26

3/16

C

C

2-3/8"
7-1/8"

Ø3/4" x 2

Section C-C
Scale 1 : 5

0"
1-1/2"
4"
5-1/2"

0"

1-1/2"

3-9/16"

5/16"

11-1/2"

13"

Ø1/2" x 4

| # | Description | Length | Material | Qty |
|---|---|---|---|---|
| 25 | W6x8.5 | 27 1/2" | ASTM A992 | 1 |
| 26 | Plate, 5 1/2" x 3/4" | 5 1/2" | ASTM A36 | 2 |
| 27 | Plate, 5 7/16" x 1/4" | 4" | ASTM A36 | 2 |

Roadside Safety and
Physical Security Division -
Proving Ground

2023-02-08

Sheet 3 of 6   Post Top

Texas A&M
Transportation
Institute

Project #  Terminal

Scale 1:10

Drawn by GES

S:\engrfact\Drafting Department\Solidworks\Standard Parts\Guardrail Parts and Subs\Guardrail Drawings\Steel Post Terminal

E-17

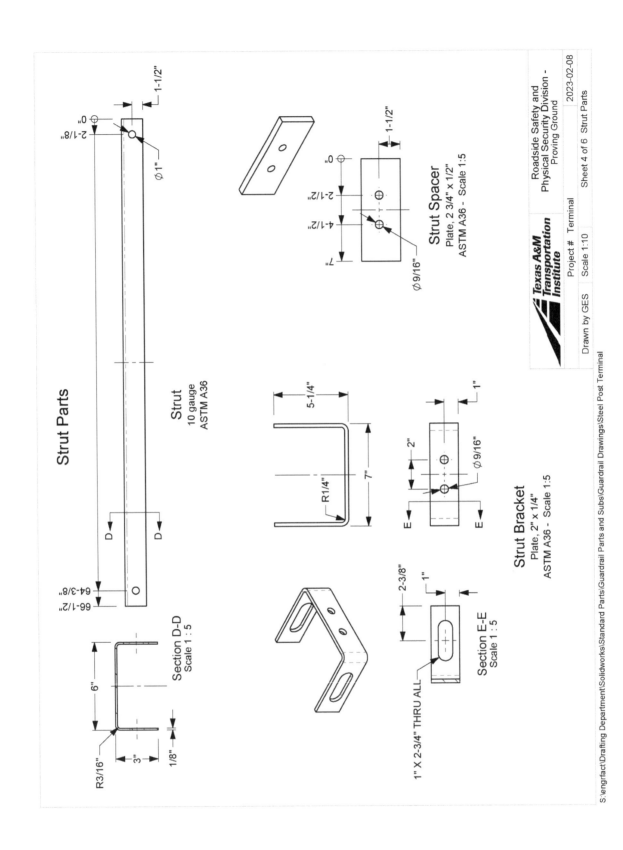

## Strut Parts

**Strut**
10 gauge
ASTM A36

Section D-D
Scale 1:5

Section E-E
Scale 1:5

1" X 2-3/4" THRU ALL

**Strut Bracket**
Plate, 2" x 1/4"
ASTM A36 -  Scale 1:5

**Strut Spacer**
Plate, 2 3/4" x 1/2"
ASTM A36 -  Scale 1:5

Texas A&M
Transportation
Institute

Roadside Safety and
Physical Security Division -
Proving Ground

2023-02-08

Drawn by GES

Project #  Terminal

Scale 1:10

Sheet 4 of 6  Strut Parts

S:\engrfact\Drafting Department\Solidworks\Standard Parts\Guardrail Parts and Subs\Guardrail Drawings\Steel Post Terminal

E-18

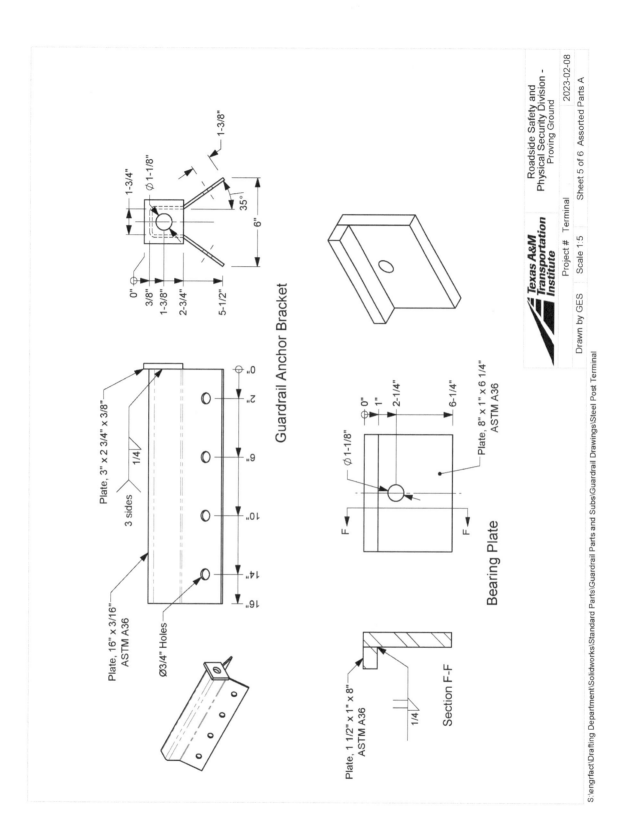

Guardrail Anchor Bracket

Plate, 3" x 2 3/4" x 3/8"

1/4

3 sides

Plate, 16" x 3/16"
ASTM A36

Ø3/4" Holes

0"
2"
6"
10"
14"
16"

1-3/4"
Ø1-1/8"
1-3/8"
35°
6"

0"
3/8"
1-3/8"
2-3/4"
5-1/2"

Bearing Plate

Ø1-1/8"

0"
1"
2-1/4"
6-1/4"

Plate, 8" x 1" x 6 1/4"
ASTM A36

F
F

Section F-F

Plate, 1 1/2" x 1" x 8"
ASTM A36

1/4

Texas A&M Transportation Institute

Roadside Safety and Physical Security Division - Proving Ground

Project # Terminal

Drawn by GES

Scale 1:5

2023-02-08

Sheet 5 of 6   Assorted Parts A

S:\engrfact\Drafting Department\Solidworks\Standard Parts\Guardrail Parts and Subs\Guardrail Drawings\Steel Post Terminal

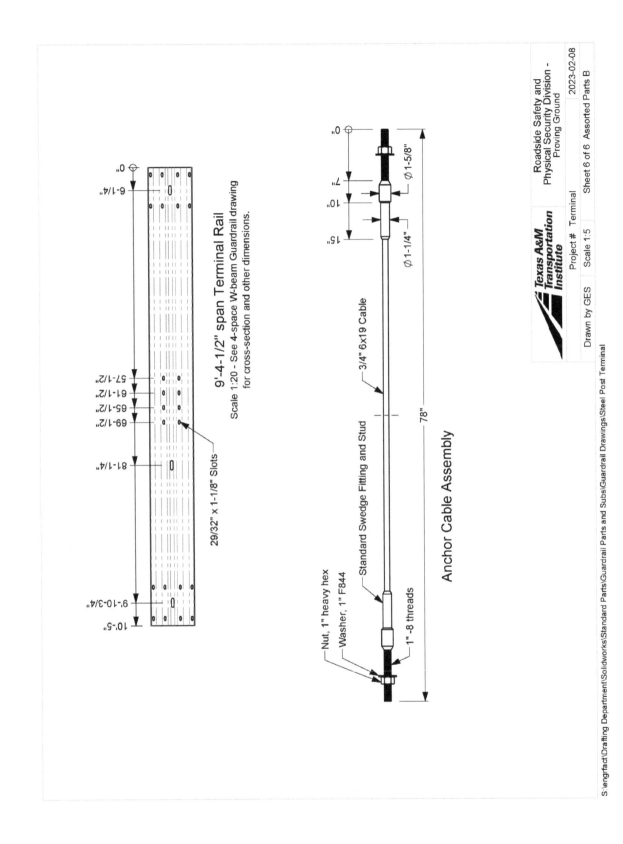

9'-4-1/2" span Terminal Rail

Scale 1:20 - See 4-space W-beam Guardrail drawing for cross-section and other dimensions.

29/32" x 1-1/8" Slots

Anchor Cable Assembly

3/4" 6x19 Cable

Standard Swedge Fitting and Stud

Nut, 1" heavy hex

Washer, 1" F844

1"-8 threads

Roadside Safety and Physical Security Division - Proving Ground

2023-02-08

Texas A&M Transportation Institute

Project # Terminal

Drawn by GES     Scale 1:5     Sheet 6 of 6     Assorted Parts B

S:\engrfact\Drafting Department\Solidworks\Standard Parts\Guardrail Parts and Subs\Guardrail Drawings\Steel Post Terminal

72" Wide Flange Guardrail Post

Section A-A
Scale 1 : 3

5.830
.194
3.940
.170

Elevation View

0"
7"
14-5/8"
72"
1-1/8"

A
A

Ø 13/16" x 2, both flanges

Isometric View

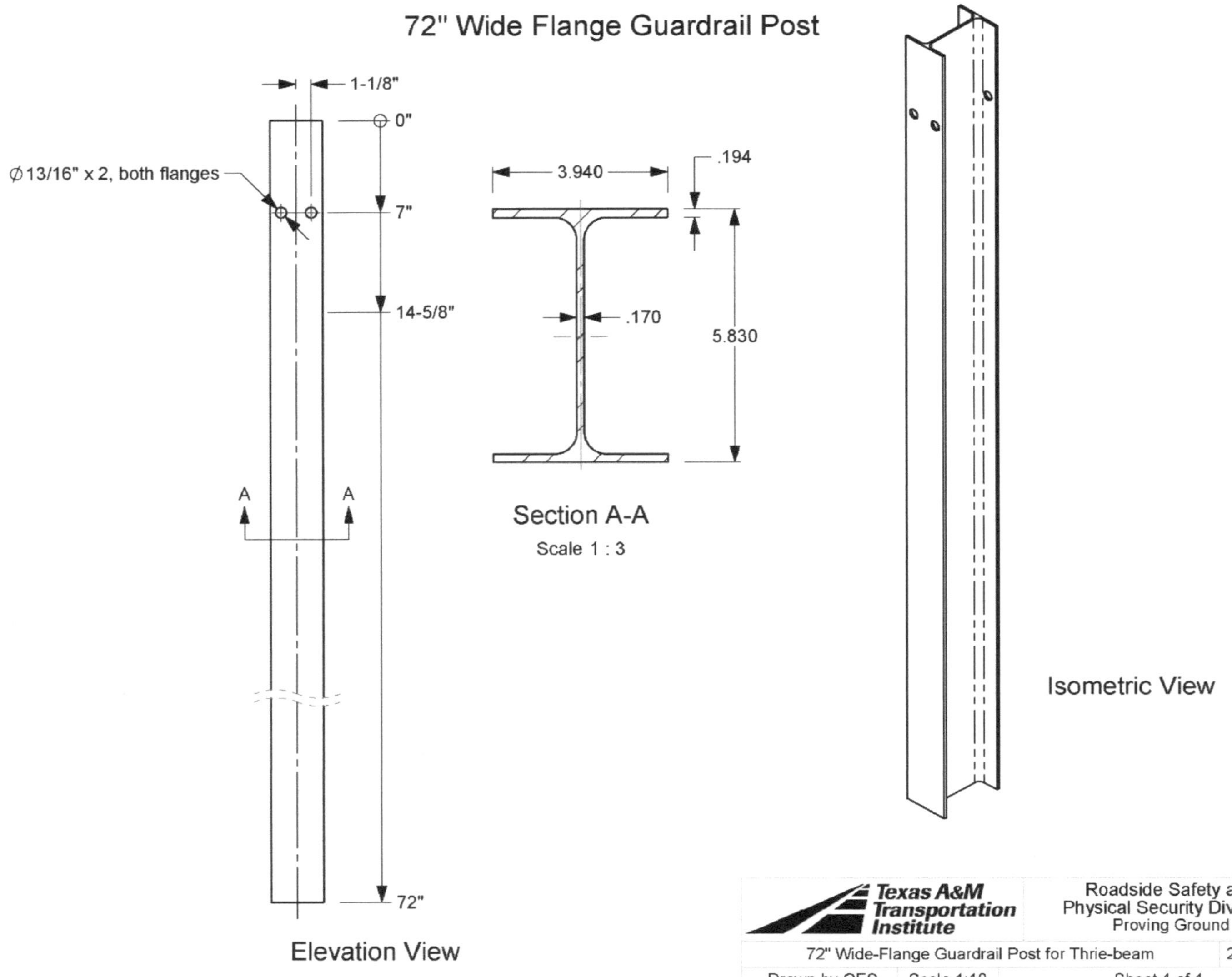

Texas A&M Transportation Institute

Roadside Safety and Physical Security Division - Proving Ground

72" Wide-Flange Guardrail Post for Thrie-beam

Drawn by GES | Scale 1:10 | 2022-07-08 | Sheet 1 of 1

T:\Drafting Department\Solidworks\Standard Parts\Guardrail Parts and Subs\Guardrail Drawings\Post, 72" Wide Flange for W-beam

E-21

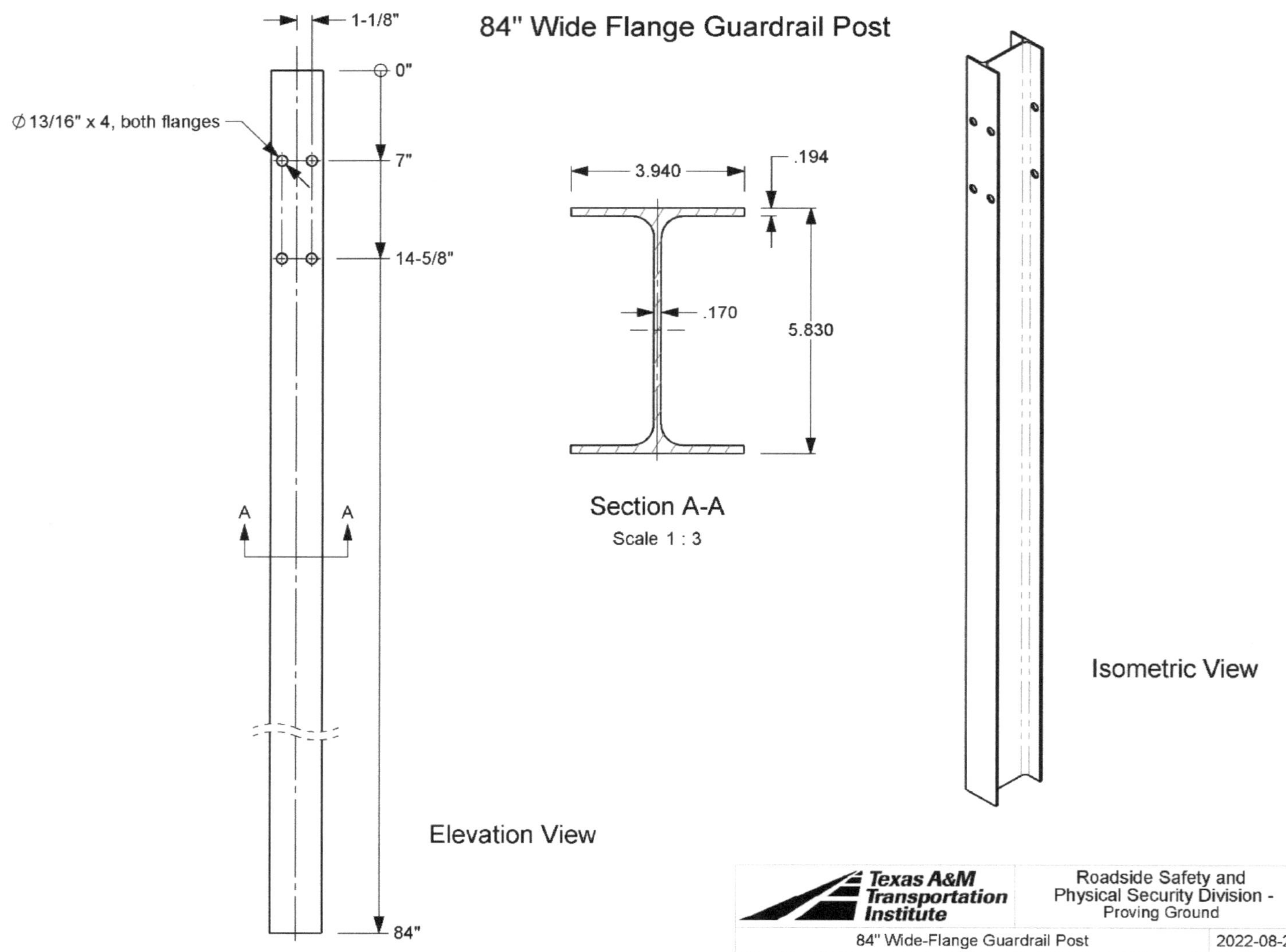
1-1/8"
84" Wide Flange Guardrail Post
0"
∅ 13/16" x 4, both flanges
7"
14-5/8"
84"
A
A
Elevation View
3.940
.194
.170
5.830
Section A-A
Scale 1 : 3
Isometric View

| Texas A&M Transportation Institute | | Roadside Safety and Physical Security Division - Proving Ground |
|---|---|---|
| 84" Wide-Flange Guardrail Post | | 2022-08-23 |
| Drawn by GES | Scale 1:10 | Sheet 1 of 1 |

T:\Drafting Department\Solidworks\Standard Parts\Guardrail Parts and Subs\Guardrail Drawings\Post, 84" Wide Flange Guardrail Post

Rectangular Guardrail Washer
0.20" thick

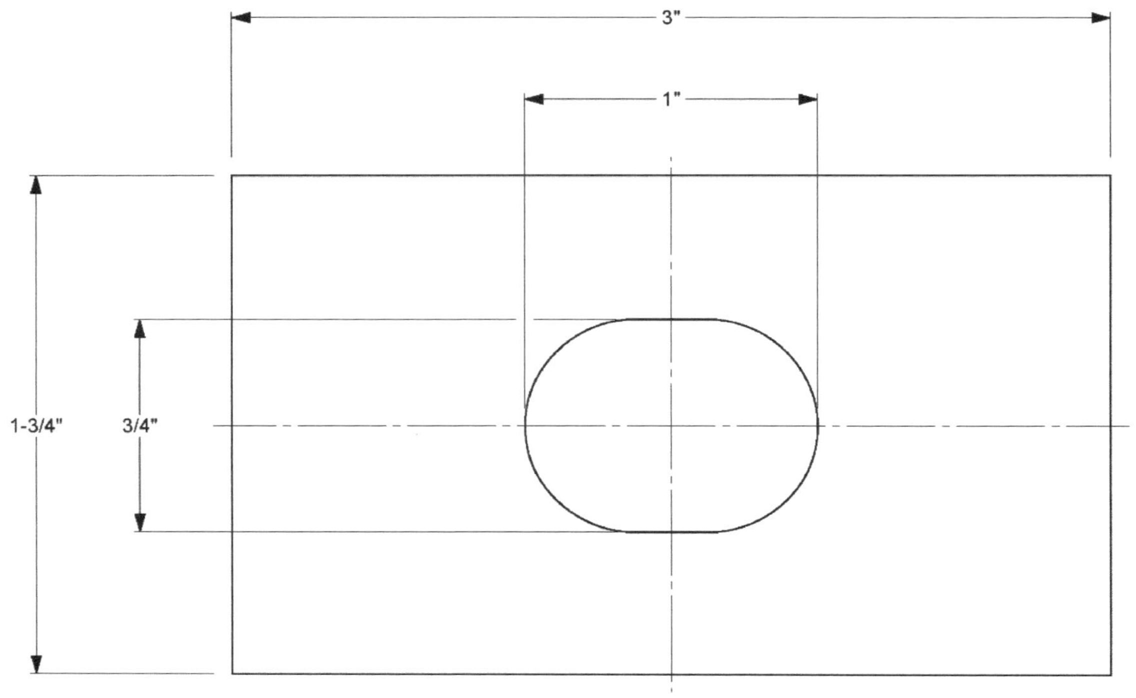

3"

1"

3/4"

1-3/4"

Texas A&M
Transportation
Institute

Roadside Safety and
Physical Security Division -
Proving Ground

2022-07-08

Rectangular Guardrail Washer

Sheet 1 of 1

Drawn by GES

Scale 2:1

E-23

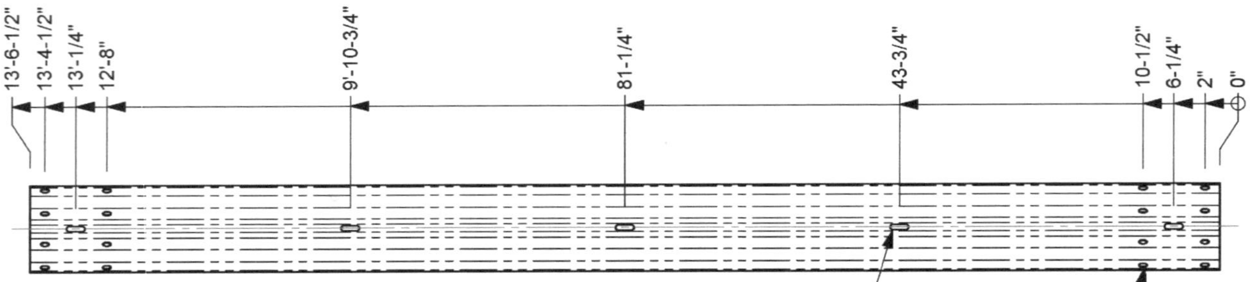

## Elevation View

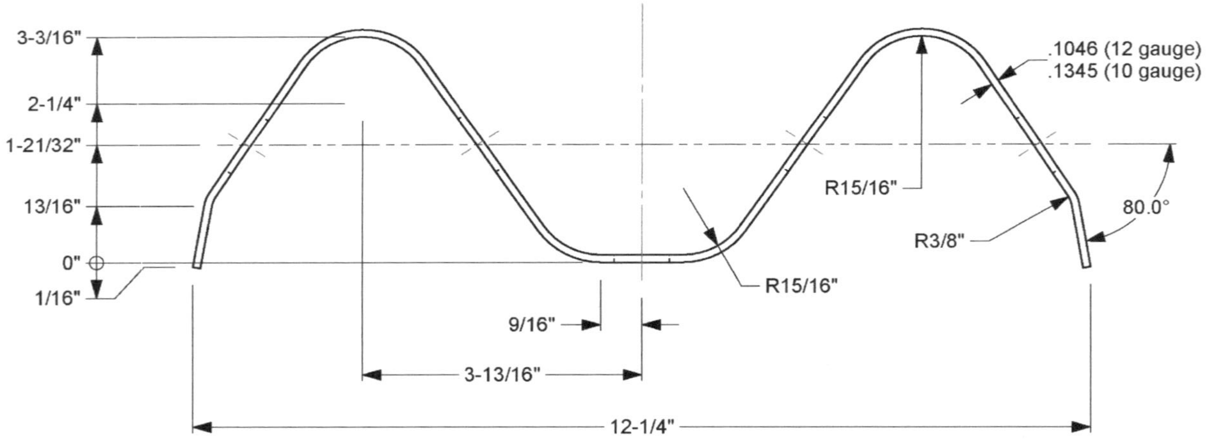

0"
2"
6-1/4"
10-1/2"

29/32" x 1-1/8" Slot
Typ x 8 each end

43-3/4"

3/4" x 2-1/2" Slot
Typ x 5
See 1b

81-1/4"

9'-10-3/4"

12'-8"
13'-1/4"
13'-4-1/2"
13'-6-1/2"

## Section View

.1046 (12 gauge)
.1345 (10 gauge)

80.0°

R3/8"

R15/16"

R15/16"

12-1/4"

9/16"

3-13/16"

3-3/16"
2-1/4"
1-21/32"
13/16"
0"
1/16"

**1a.** Manufacture per AASHTO M180 specifications.
**1b.** 4-space Guardrail is shown. Slots typical x 3 for 2-space W-beam spaced at 75", and typical x 9 for 8-space W-beam spaced at 18-3/4". Slots are typical x 4 at 37-1/2" for 9'-4-1/2" span W-beam.

| | |
|---|---|
| Texas A&M Transportation Institute | Roadside Safety and Physical Security Division - Proving Ground |
| | W-beam Guardrail |
| Drawn by GES | Scale 1:20 | Sheet 1 of 1 |
| | 2022-07-13 |

E-24

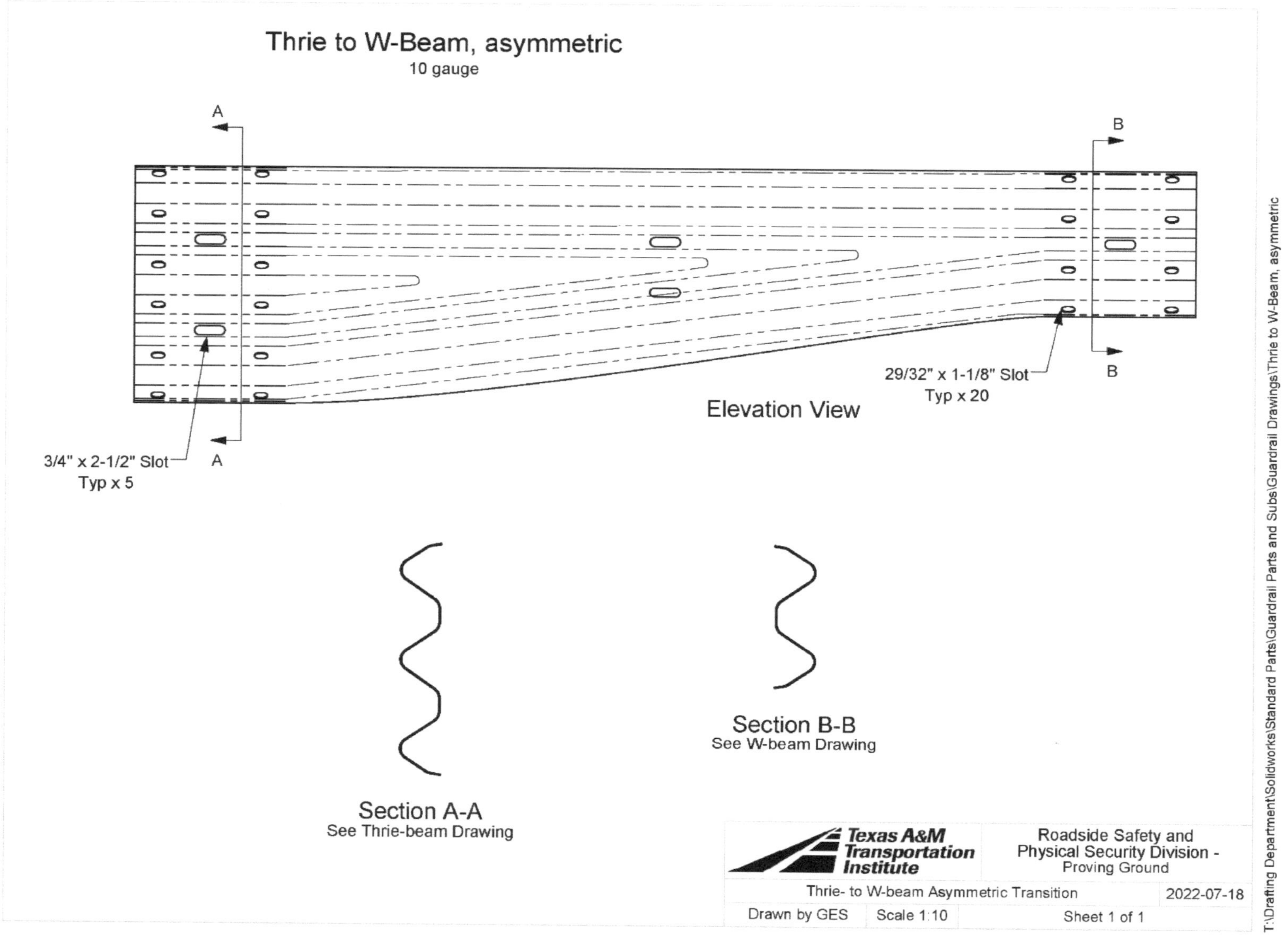

# Thrie to W-Beam, asymmetric
## 10 gauge

**Elevation View**

29/32" x 1-1/8" Slot
Typ x 20

3/4" x 2-1/2" Slot
Typ x 5

A

B

**Section A-A**
See Thrie-beam Drawing

**Section B-B**
See W-beam Drawing

Texas A&M
Transportation
Institute

Roadside Safety and
Physical Security Division -
Proving Ground

2022-07-18

Thrie- to W-beam Asymmetric Transition

Sheet 1 of 1

Drawn by GES

Scale 1:10

T:\Drafting Department\Solidworks\Standard Parts\Guardrail Parts and Subs\Guardrail Drawings\Thrie to W-Beam, asymmetric

# Transition Blockout for W-section Post

All dimensions except hole diameter are nominal

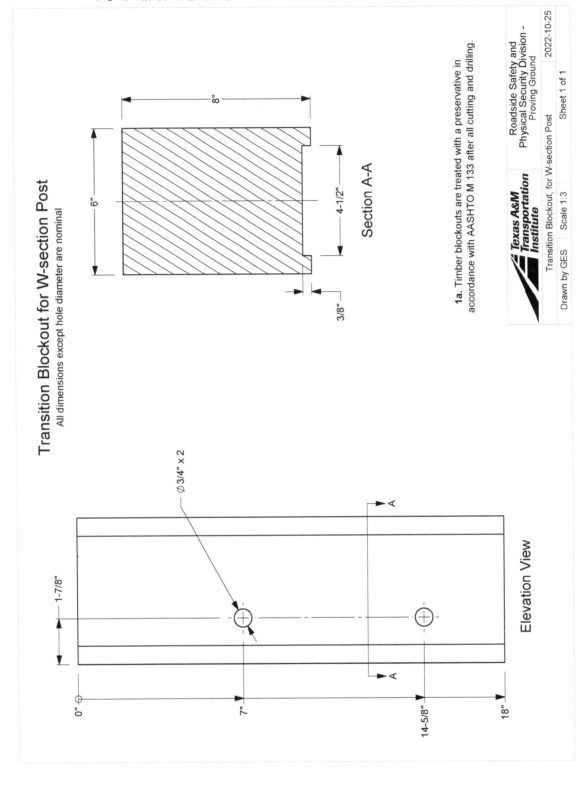

Section A-A

Elevation View

**1a.** Timber blockouts are treated with a preservative in accordance with AASHTO M 133 after all cutting and drilling.

| Texas A&M Transportation Institute | Roadside Safety and Physical Security Division - Proving Ground | 2022-10-25 |
|---|---|---|
| | Transition Blockout, for W-section Post | Sheet 1 of 1 |
| Drawn by GES | Scale 1:3 | |

# Timber Blockout for W-section Post

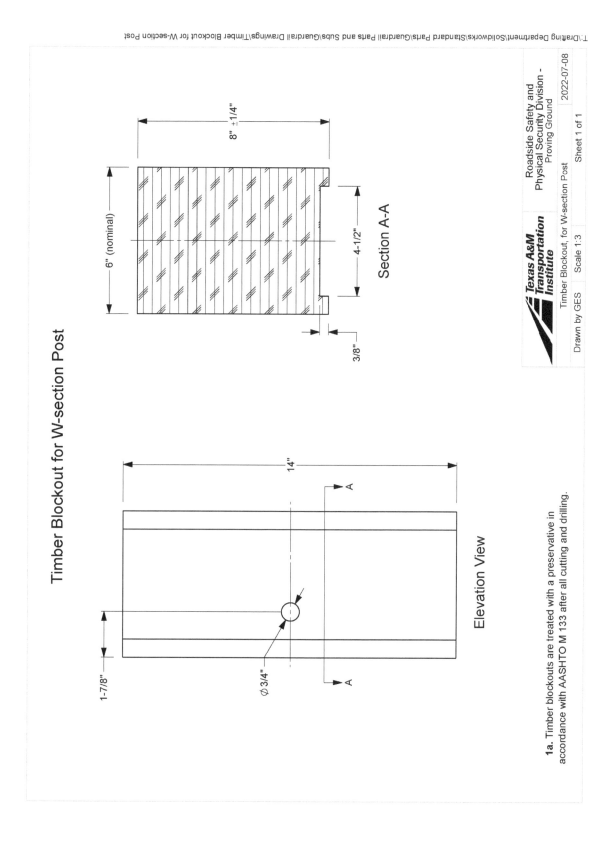

Section A-A

8" ±1/4"

6" (nominal)

4-1/2"

3/8"

Elevation View

14"

1-7/8"

∅ 3/4"

A

A

**1a.** Timber blockouts are treated with a preservative in accordance with AASHTO M 133 after all cutting and drilling.

| | |
|---|---|
| Roadside Safety and Physical Security Division - Proving Ground | 2022-07-08 |
| Texas A&M Transportation Institute | |
| Timber Blockout, for W-section Post | Sheet 1 of 1 |
| Drawn by GES | Scale 1:3 |

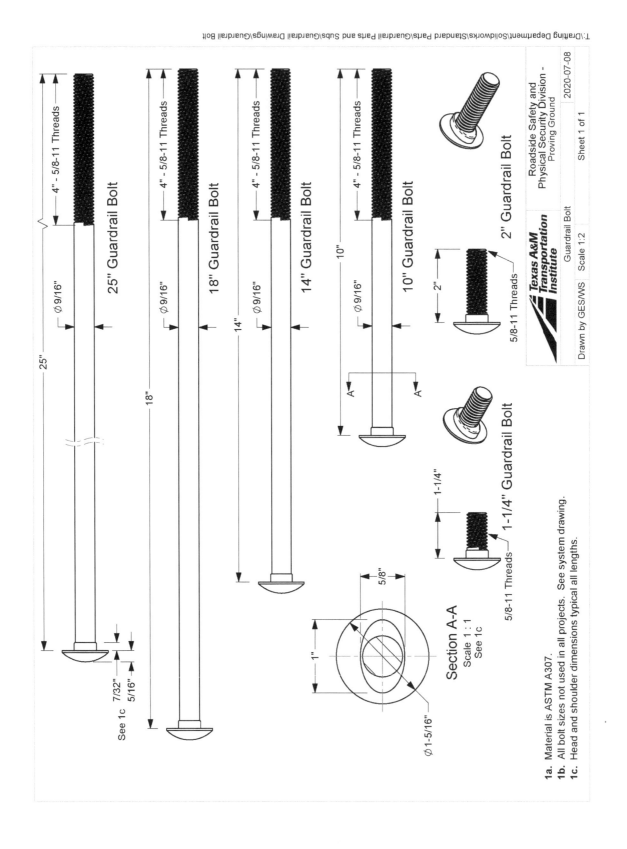

25" Guardrail Bolt

4" - 5/8-11 Threads

⌀ 9/16"

25"

See 1c   7/32"   5/16"

18" Guardrail Bolt

4" - 5/8-11 Threads

⌀ 9/16"

18"

14" Guardrail Bolt

4" - 5/8-11 Threads

⌀ 9/16"

14"

10" Guardrail Bolt

4" - 5/8-11 Threads

⌀ 9/16"

10"

A
A

2" Guardrail Bolt

2"

5/8-11 Threads

1-1/4" Guardrail Bolt

1-1/4"

5/8-11 Threads

Section A-A
Scale 1 : 1
See 1c

5/8"

1"

⌀ 1-5/16"

Roadside Safety and
Physical Security Division -
Proving Ground

Texas A&M
Transportation
Institute

Guardrail Bolt

2020-07-08

Sheet 1 of 1

Scale 1:2

Drawn by GES/WS

**1a.** Material is ASTM A307.
**1b.** All bolt sizes not used in all projects.  See system drawing.
**1c.** Head and shoulder dimensions typical all lengths.

E-28

Recessed Guardrail Nut

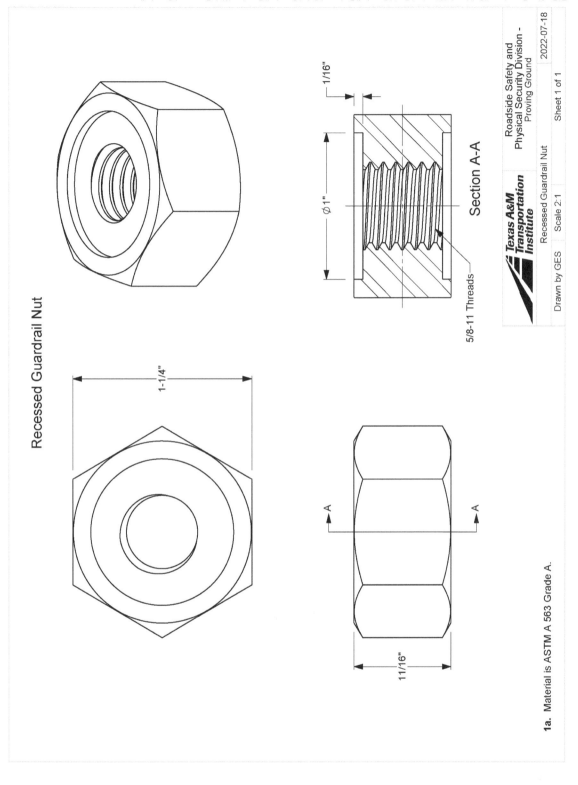

Section A-A

5/8-11 Threads

1/16"

Ø1"

1-1/4"

11/16"

A

A

| Texas A&M Transportation Institute | Roadside Safety and Physical Security Division - Proving Ground | 2022-07-18 |
| --- | --- | --- |
| | Recessed Guardrail Nut | Sheet 1 of 1 |
| Drawn by GES | Scale 2:1 | |

**1a.** Material is ASTM A 563 Grade A.

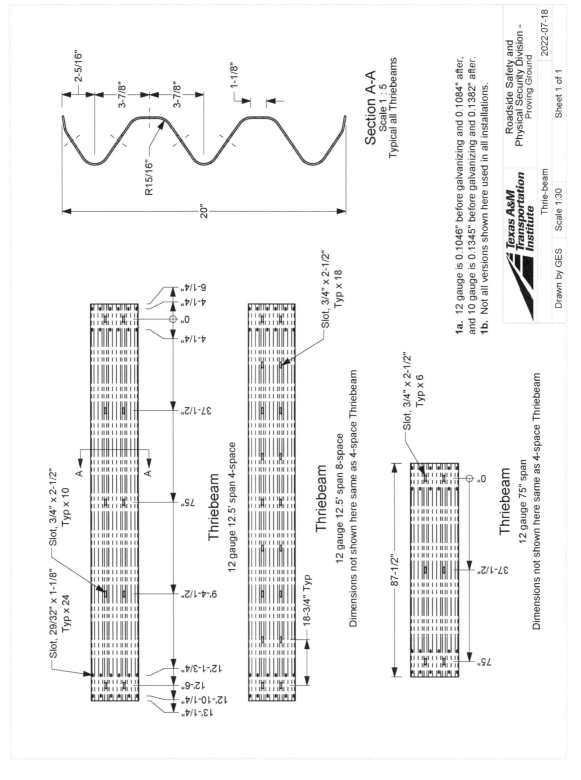

**Section A-A**
Scale 1 : 5
Typical all Thriebeams

2-5/16"
3-7/8"
3-7/8"
1-1/8"
R15/16"
20"

Slot, 29/32" x 1-1/8"
Typ x 24

Slot, 3/4" x 2-1/2"
Typ x 10

A   A

6-1/4"
4-1/4"
0"
4-1/4"

37-1/2"

75"

9'-4-1/2"

12'-1-3/4"
12'-6"
12'-10-1/4"
13'-1/4"

**Thriebeam**
12 gauge 12.5' span 4-space

Slot, 3/4" x 2-1/2"
Typ x 18

18-3/4" Typ

**Thriebeam**
12 gauge 12.5' span 8-space

Dimensions not shown here same as 4-space Thriebeam

Slot, 3/4" x 2-1/2"
Typ x 6

87-1/2"

0"
37-1/2"
75"

**Thriebeam**
12 gauge 75" span

Dimensions not shown here same as 4-space Thriebeam

**1a.** 12 gauge is 0.1046" before galvanizing and 0.1084" after,
and 10 gauge is 0.1345" before galvanizing and 0.1382" after.
**1b.** Not all versions shown here used in all installations.

Roadside Safety and
Physical Security Division -
Proving Ground

2022-07-18

Thrie-beam

Drawn by GES    Scale 1:30    Sheet 1 of 1

Texas A&M
Transportation
Institute

E-30

# W-beam Terminal Connector

See W-beam Guardrail drawing for all dimensions not shown here.

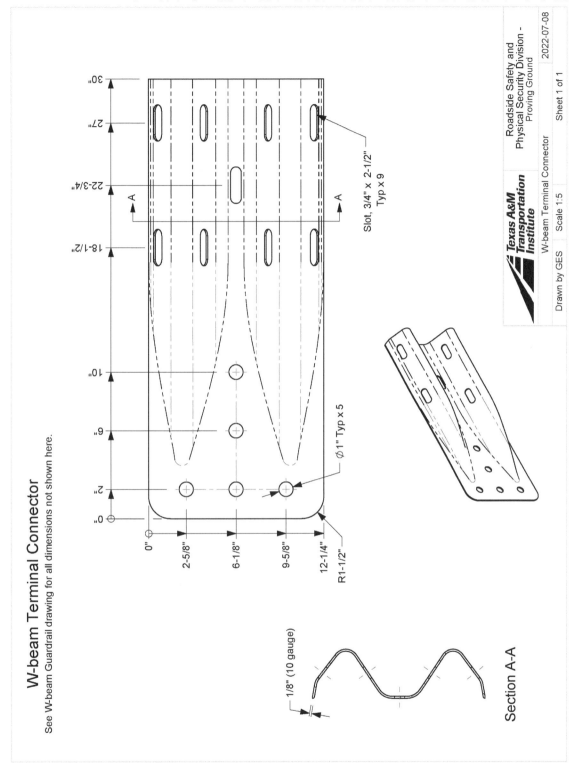

Slot, 3/4" x 2-1/2" Typ x 9

∅1" Typ x 5

R1-1/2"

0"
2-5/8"
6-1/8"
9-5/8"
12-1/4"

30"
27"
22-3/4"
18-1/2"
10"
9"
2"
0"

1/8" (10 gauge)

Section A-A

| | | |
|---|---|---|
| Roadside Safety and Physical Security Division - Proving Ground | | 2022-07-08 |
| Texas A&M Transportation Institute | | |
| W-beam Terminal Connector | | Sheet 1 of 1 |
| Drawn by GES | Scale 1:5 | |

# Thrie-beam End Shoe

10 gauge (0.1345" before galvanizing)

R2"
7 x Ø1"
3/4" x 2-1/2" Slots
Slot, 15/16" x 3"
Typ x 12
See Thrie-beam drawing
for cross-section.
0"
2-3/8"
6-3/16"
10"
13-13/16"
17-5/8"
20"
30"
28"
24"
20"
11-1/2"
7-1/4"
3"
0"


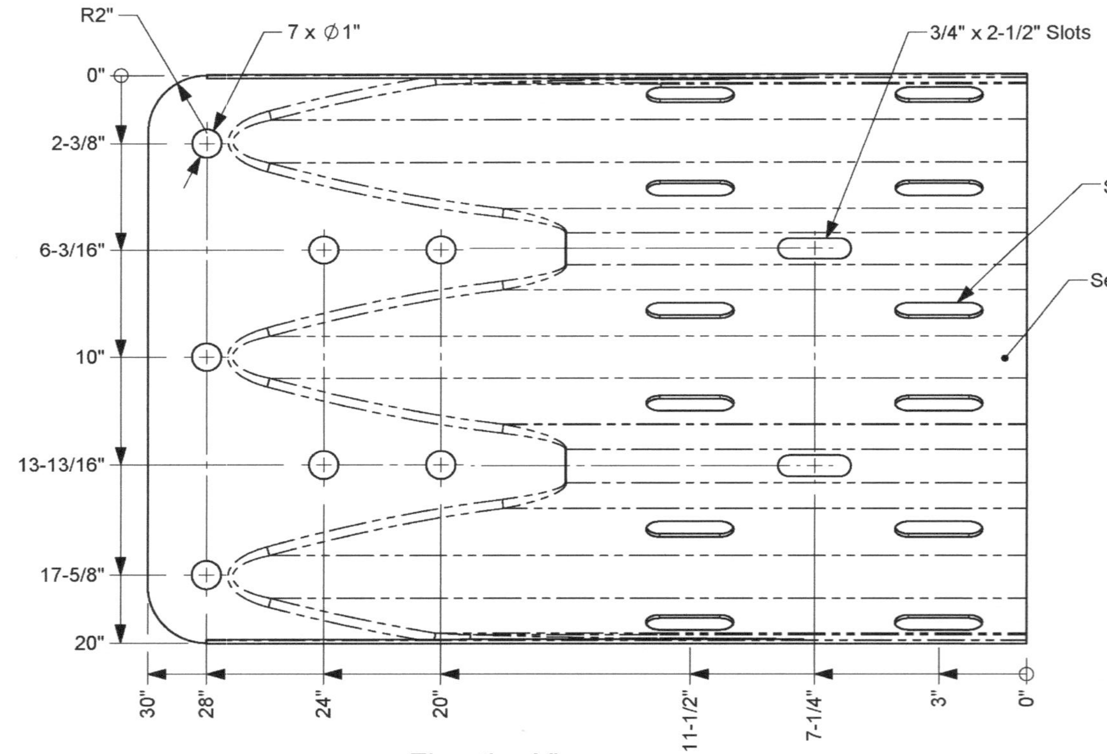

Elevation View

Isometric View

| Texas A&M Transportation Institute | Roadside Safety and Physical Security Division - Proving Ground | |
|---|---|---|
| Thrie-beam Terminal Connector | | 202-07-18 |
| Drawn by GES | Scale 1:5 | Sheet 1 of 1 |

T:\Drafting Department\Solidworks\Standard Parts\Guardrail Parts and Subs\Guardrail Drawings\Thrie-beam End Shoe

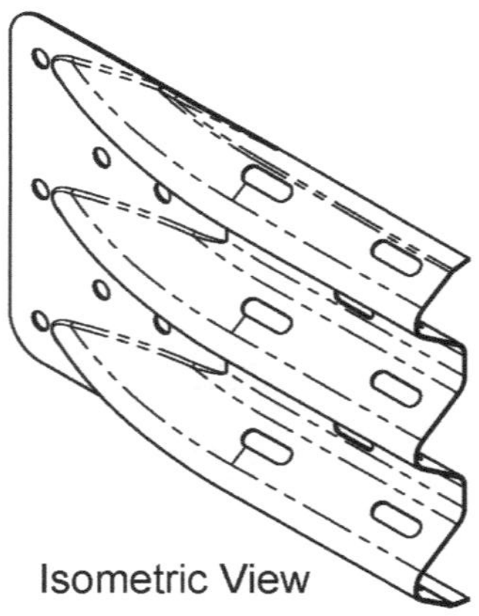

# Details of the Pedestrian Traffic Rail Transition for MASH Test 3-21

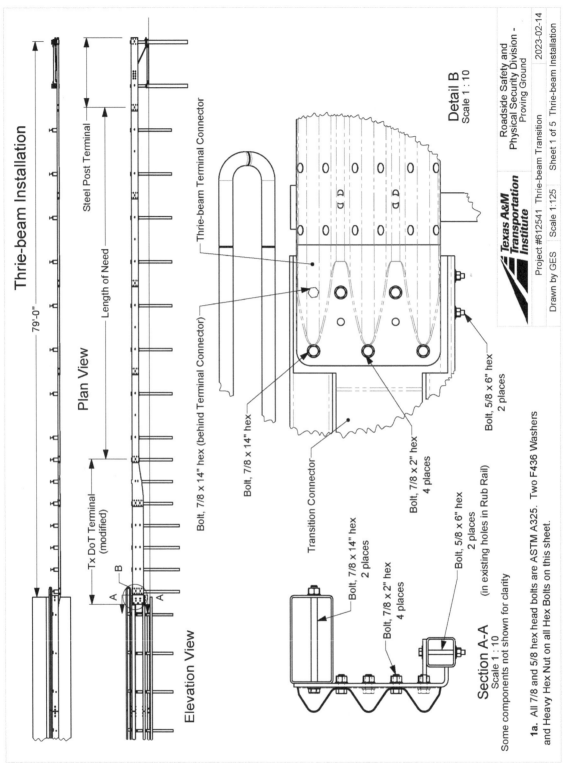

# Thrie-beam Installation

79'-0"

## Plan View

Steel Post Terminal

Length of Need

Thrie-beam Terminal Connector

Bolt, 7/8 x 14" hex (behind Terminal Connector)

TxDoT Terminal (modified)

A
B

A
A

## Elevation View

Bolt, 7/8 x 14" hex

Transition Connector

Bolt, 7/8 x 2" hex
4 places

Bolt, 5/8 x 6" hex
2 places

Bolt, 7/8 x 14" hex
2 places

Bolt, 7/8 x 2" hex
4 places

Bolt, 5/8 x 6" hex
2 places

## Section A-A
Scale 1 : 10    (in existing holes in Rub Rail)
Some components not shown for clarity

**1a.** All 7/8 and 5/8 hex head bolts are ASTM A325. Two F436 Washers and Heavy Hex Nut on all Hex Bolts on this sheet.

## Detail B
Scale 1 : 10

Texas A&M
Transportation
Institute

Roadside Safety and
Physical Security Division -
Proving Ground

2023-02-14

Project #612541  Thrie-beam Transition

Drawn by GES     Scale 1:125     Sheet 1 of 5   Thrie-beam Installation

S:\Accreditation-17025-2017\EIR-000 Project Files\612541 - Ped-Traffic Rail - Dobrovolny\Drafting, 612541-03\612541-03 Drawing

F-2

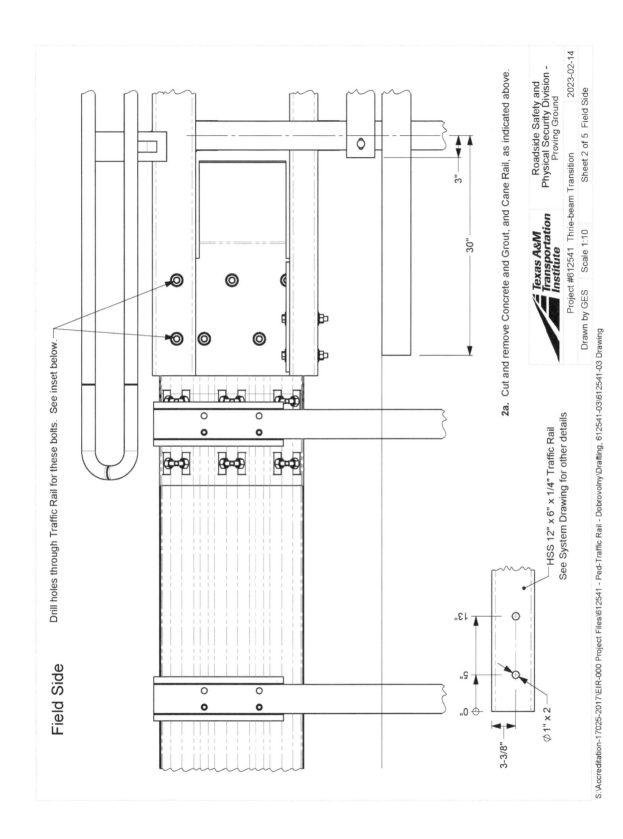

Field Side

Drill holes through Traffic Rail for these bolts. See inset below.

3"

30"

2a. Cut and remove Concrete and Grout, and Cane Rail, as indicated above.

HSS 12" x 6" x 1/4" Traffic Rail
See System Drawing for other details

13"

5"

0"

3-3/8"

Ø 1" x 2

Texas A&M
Transportation
Institute

Roadside Safety and
Physical Security Division -
Proving Ground

Project #612541 Thrie-beam Transition    2023-02-14

Drawn by GES    Scale 1:10    Sheet 2 of 5   Field Side

S:\Accreditation-17025-2017\IEIR-000 Project Files\612541 - Ped-Traffic Rail - Dobrovolny\Drafting, 612541-03\612541-03 Drawing

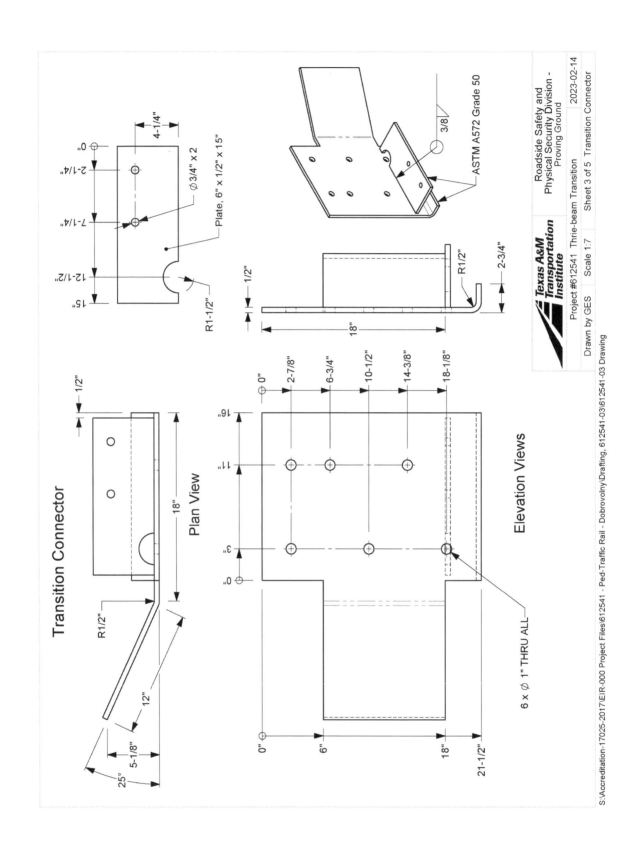

Transition Connector

Plan View

Elevation Views

Plate, 6" x 1/2" x 15"

∅ 3/4" x 2

R1-1/2"

4-1/4"
0"
2-1/4"
7-1/4"
12-1/2"
15"

1/2"

18"

R1/2"

R1/2"

1/2"

2-3/4"

ASTM A572 Grade 50

3/8

16"
11"
3"
0"

0"
2-7/8"
6-3/4"
10-1/2"
14-3/8"
18-1/8"

0"
6"
18"
21-1/2"

6 x ∅ 1" THRU ALL

R1/2"

12"

5-1/8"

25°

Roadside Safety and
Physical Security Division -
Proving Ground

Texas A&M
Transportation
Institute

Project #612541  Thrie-beam Transition          2023-02-14

Drawn by GES     Scale 1:7     Sheet 3 of 5  Transition Connector

S:\Accreditation-17025-2017\EIR-000 Project Files\612541 - Ped-Traffic Rail - Dobrovolny\Drafting, 612541-03\612541-03 Drawing

F-4

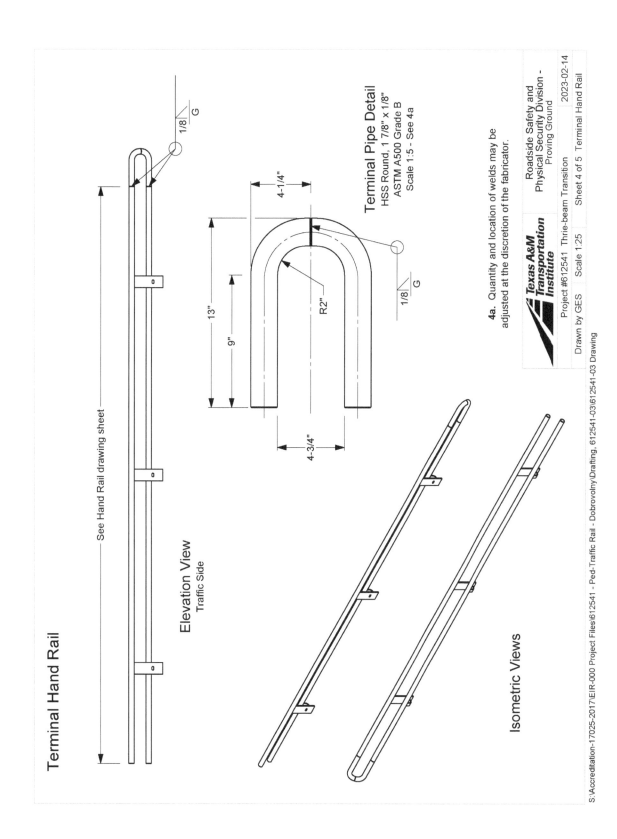

# Terminal Hand Rail

See Hand Rail drawing sheet

## Elevation View
Traffic Side

1/8 ⟍ G

## Terminal Pipe Detail
HSS Round, 1 7/8" x 1/8"
ASTM A500 Grade B
Scale 1:5 - See 4a

4-1/4"

R2"

13"

9"

4-3/4"

1/8 ⟍ G

**4a.** Quantity and location of welds may be adjusted at the discretion of the fabricator.

## Isometric Views

<table>
<tr><td colspan="3">Texas A&M<br>Transportation<br>Institute</td><td>Roadside Safety and<br>Physical Security Division -<br>Proving Ground</td></tr>
<tr><td colspan="3">Project #612541  Thrie-beam Transition</td><td>2023-02-14</td></tr>
<tr><td>Drawn by GES</td><td>Scale 1:25</td><td colspan="2">Sheet 4 of 5   Terminal Hand Rail</td></tr>
</table>

S:\Accreditation-17025-2017\EIR-000 Project Files\612541 - Ped-Traffic Rail - Dobrovolny\Drafting, 612541-03\612541-03 Drawing

F-5

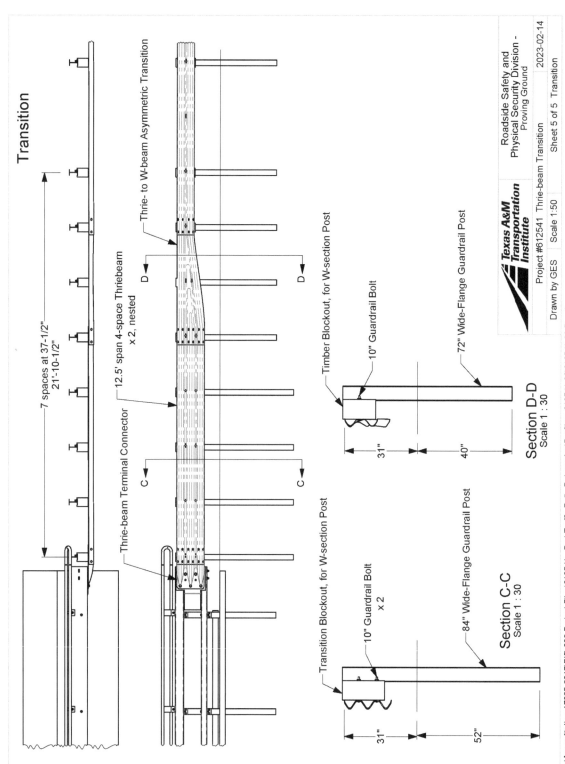

Transition

7 spaces at 37-1/2"
21'-10-1/2"

Thrie- to W-beam Asymmetric Transition

12.5' span 4-space Thriebeam x 2, nested

Thrie-beam Terminal Connector

Transition Blockout, for W-section Post

Timber Blockout, for W-section Post

10" Guardrail Bolt

72" Wide-Flange Guardrail Post

31"

40"

**Section D-D**
Scale 1 : 30

10" Guardrail Bolt x 2

84" Wide-Flange Guardrail Post

31"

52"

**Section C-C**
Scale 1 : 30

Texas A&M Transportation Institute

Roadside Safety and Physical Security Division - Proving Ground

Project #612541 Thrie-beam Transition

2023-02-14

Drawn by GES    Scale 1:50    Sheet 5 of 5  Transition

S:\Accreditation-17025-2017\EIR-000 Project Files\612541 - Ped-Traffic Rail - Dobrovolny\Drafting, 612541-03\612541-03 Drawing

F-6

# LON and DS End

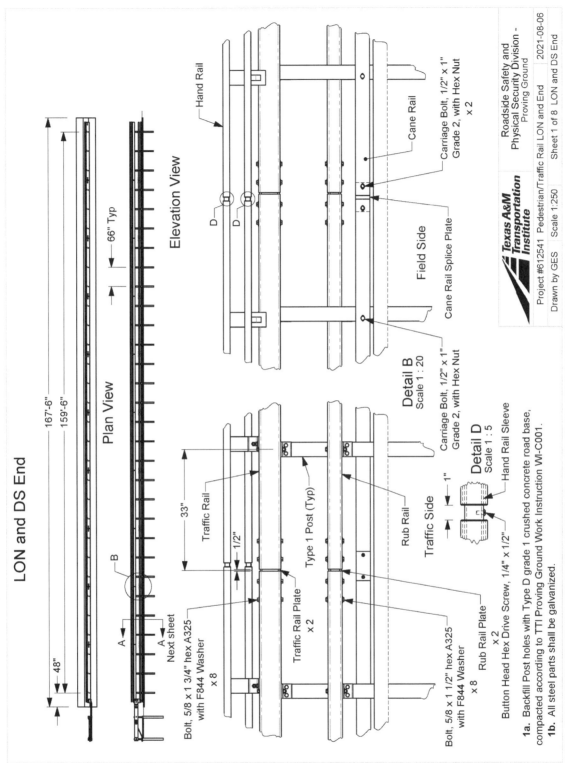

**Plan View**

**Elevation View**

167'-6"
159'-6"
48"
66" Typ

33"
1/2"
1"

A
A
Next sheet
B
B

Hand Rail

D
D

Cane Rail

Carriage Bolt, 1/2" x 1"
Grade 2, with Hex Nut
x 2

Field Side

Cane Rail Splice Plate

**Detail B**
Scale 1 : 20

Carriage Bolt, 1/2" x 1"
Grade 2, with Hex Nut

**Detail D**
Scale 1 : 5

Hand Rail Sleeve

Traffic Rail

Type 1 Post (Typ)

Rub Rail

Traffic Side

Traffic Rail Plate
x 2

Rub Rail Plate
x 2

Bolt, 5/8 x 1 3/4" hex A325
with F844 Washer
x 8

Bolt, 5/8 x 1 1/2" hex A325
with F844 Washer
x 8

Button Head Hex Drive Screw, 1/4" x 1/2"

**1a.** Backfill Post holes with Type D grade 1 crushed concrete road base,
compacted according to TTI Proving Ground Work Instruction WI-C001.
**1b.** All steel parts shall be galvanized.

Texas A&M
Transportation
Institute

Roadside Safety and
Physical Security Division -
Proving Ground

Project #612541  Pedestrian/Traffic Rail LON and End     2021-08-06

Drawn by GES | Scale 1:250 | Sheet 1 of 8  LON and DS End

S:\Accreditation-17025-2017\EIR-000 Project Files\612541 - Ped-Traffic Rail - Dobrovolny\Drafting, 612541-03\LON System\612541 Drawing

F-7

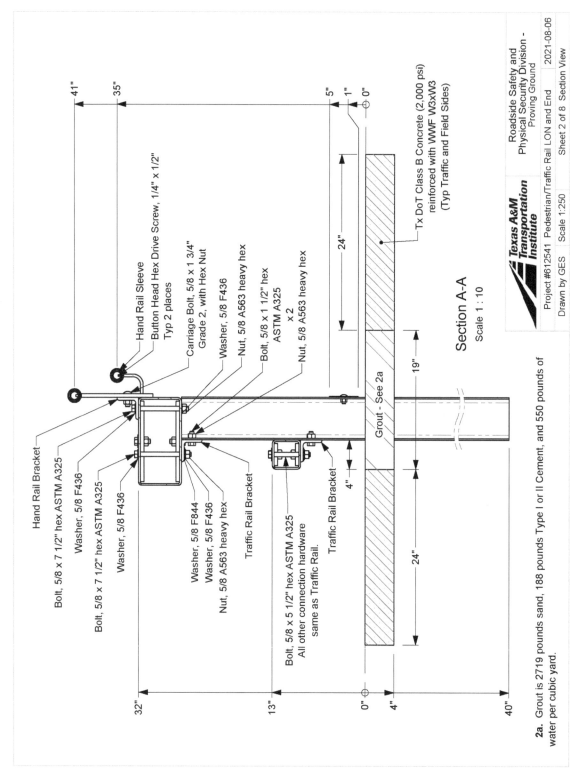

Hand Rail Bracket

Bolt, 5/8 x 7 1/2" hex ASTM A325

Washer, 5/8 F436

Bolt, 5/8 x 7 1/2" hex ASTM A325

Washer, 5/8 F436

Washer, 5/8 F844

Washer, 5/8 F436

Nut, 5/8 A563 heavy hex

Traffic Rail Bracket

Bolt, 5/8 x 5 1/2" hex ASTM A325
All other connection hardware
same as Traffic Rail.

Traffic Rail Bracket

Hand Rail Sleeve

Button Head Hex Drive Screw, 1/4" x 1/2"
Typ 2 places

Carriage Bolt, 5/8 x 1 3/4"
Grade 2, with Hex Nut

Washer, 5/8 F436

Nut, 5/8 A563 heavy hex

Bolt, 5/8 x 1 1/2" hex
ASTM A325
x 2

Nut, 5/8 A563 heavy hex

Tx DoT Class B Concrete (2,000 psi)
reinforced with WWF W3xW3
(Typ Traffic and Field Sides)

Grout - See 2a

41"

35"

32"

13"

0"

4"

40"

5"

1"

0"

24"

19"

4"

24"

Section A-A

Scale 1 : 10

**2a.** Grout is 2719 pounds sand, 188 pounds Type I or II Cement, and 550 pounds of water per cubic yard.

Texas A&M
Transportation
Institute

Roadside Safety and
Physical Security Division -
Proving Ground

Project #612541  Pedestrian/Traffic Rail LON and End      2021-08-06

Drawn by GES    Scale 1:250    Sheet 2 of 8  Section View

S:\Accreditation-17025-2017\EIR-000 Project Files\612541 - Ped-Traffic Rail - Dobrovolny\Drafting, 612541-03\LON System\612541 Drawing

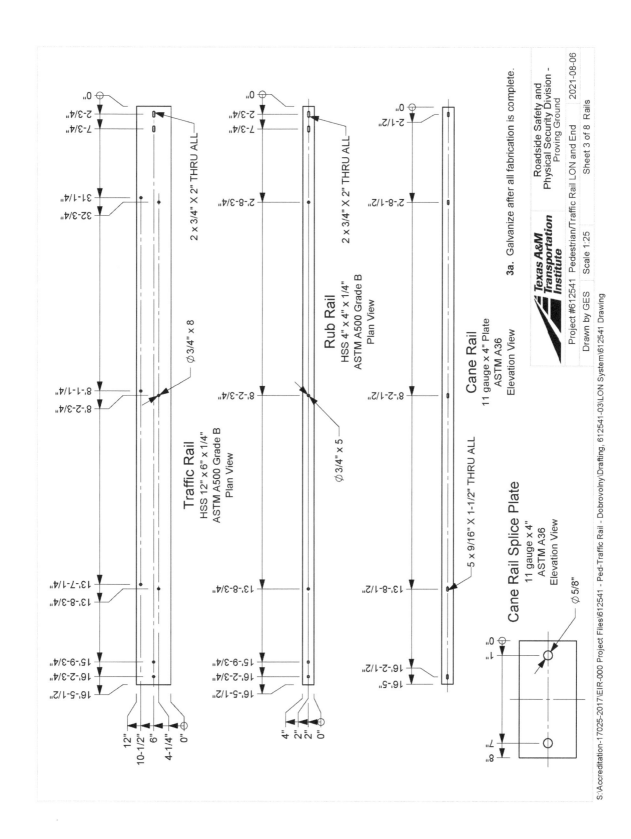

**Traffic Rail**
HSS 12" x 6" x 1/4"
ASTM A500 Grade B
Plan View

Ø 3/4" x 8

2 x 3/4" X 2" THRU ALL

**Rub Rail**
HSS 4" x 4" x 1/4"
ASTM A500 Grade B
Plan View

Ø 3/4" x 5

2 x 3/4" X 2" THRU ALL

**Cane Rail**
11 gauge x 4" Plate
ASTM A36
Elevation View

5 x 9/16" X 1-1/2" THRU ALL

**Cane Rail Splice Plate**
11 gauge x 4"
ASTM A36
Elevation View

Ø 5/8"

3a. Galvanize after all fabrication is complete.

Texas A&M Transportation Institute

Roadside Safety and Physical Security Division - Proving Ground

2021-08-06

Project #612541  Pedestrian/Traffic Rail LON and End

Drawn by GES  Scale 1:25  Sheet 3 of 8  Rails

S:\Accreditation-17025-2017\EIR-000 Project Files\612541 - Ped-Traffic Rail - Dobrovolny\Drafting, 612541-03\LON System\612541 Drawing

F-9

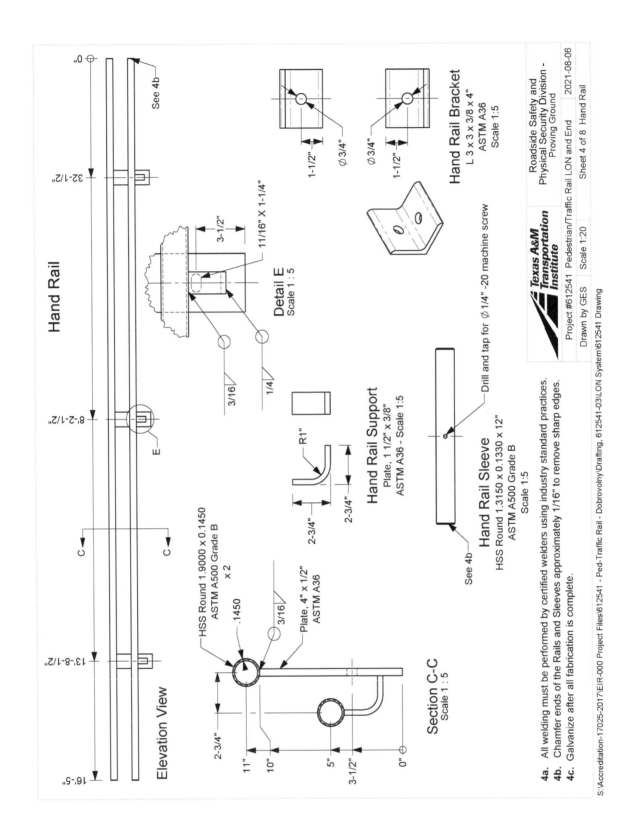

# Hand Rail

## Elevation View

0"

32-1/2"

See 4b

8'-2-1/2"

13'-8-1/2"

16'-5"

E

C

C

## Detail E
Scale 1 : 5

3-1/2"

11/16" X 1-1/4"

3/16

1/4

## Hand Rail Support
Plate, 1 1/2" x 3/8"
ASTM A36 - Scale 1:5

R1"

2-3/4"

2-3/4"

## Hand Rail Sleeve
HSS Round 1.3150 x 0.1330 x 12"
ASTM A500 Grade B
Scale 1:5

See 4b

Drill and tap for ⌀ 1/4"-20 machine screw

## Section C-C
Scale 1 : 5

HSS Round 1.9000 x 0.1450
ASTM A500 Grade B
x 2

.1450

3/16

Plate, 4" x 1/2"
ASTM A36

2-3/4"

11"

10"

5"

3-1/2"

0"

## Hand Rail Bracket
L 3 x 3 x 3/8 x 4"
ASTM A36
Scale 1:5

⌀ 3/4"

1-1/2"

⌀ 3/4"

1-1/2"

**4a.** All welding must be performed by certified welders using industry standard practices.
**4b.** Chamfer ends of the Rails and Sleeves approximately 1/16" to remove sharp edges.
**4c.** Galvanize after all fabrication is complete.

Texas A&M
Transportation
Institute

Roadside Safety and
Physical Security Division -
Proving Ground

2021-08-06

Project #612541  Pedestrian/Traffic Rail LON and End

Drawn by GES

Scale 1:20

Sheet 4 of 8  Hand Rail

S:\Accreditation-17025-2017\EIR-000 Project Files\612541 - Ped-Traffic Rail - Dobrovolny\Drafting, 612541-03\LON System\612541 Drawing

F-10

# Joint Plates

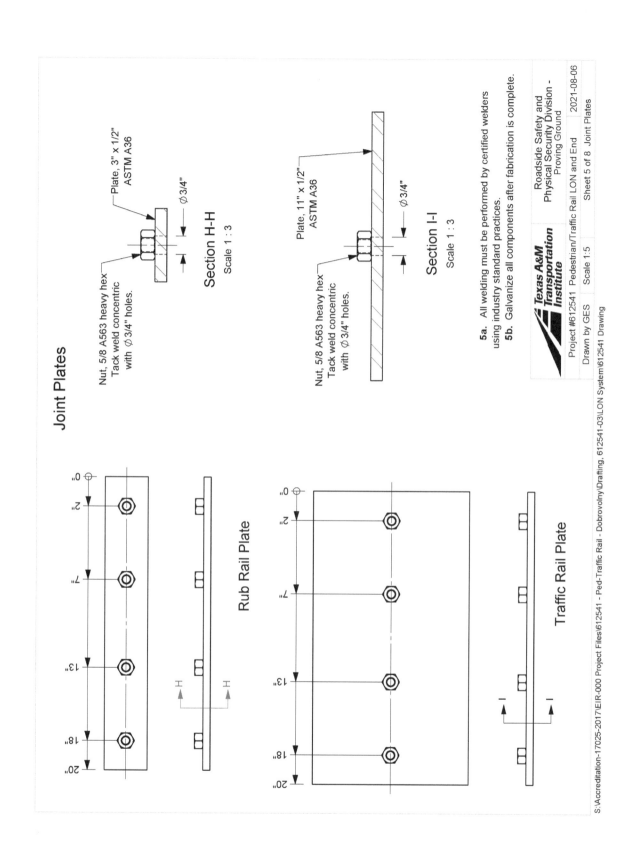

Plate, 3" x 1/2" ASTM A36

Nut, 5/8 A563 heavy hex
Tack weld concentric with ⌀ 3/4" holes.

⌀ 3/4"

## Section H-H
Scale 1 : 3

Plate, 11" x 1/2" ASTM A36

Nut, 5/8 A563 heavy hex
Tack weld concentric with ⌀ 3/4" holes.

⌀ 3/4"

## Section I-I
Scale 1 : 5

**5a.** All welding must be performed by certified welders using industry standard practices.

**5b.** Galvanize all components after fabrication is complete.

Rub Rail Plate

Traffic Rail Plate

0"  2"  7"  13"  18"  20"

H   H

I   I

**Texas A&M Transportation Institute**

Roadside Safety and Physical Security Division - Proving Ground    2021-08-06

Project #612541  Pedestrian/Traffic Rail LON and End

Drawn by GES    Scale 1:5    Sheet 5 of 8   Joint Plates

S:\Accreditation-17025-2017\EIR-000 Project Files\612541 - Ped-Traffic Rail - Dobrovolny\Drafting, 612541-03\ILON System\612541 Drawing

F-11

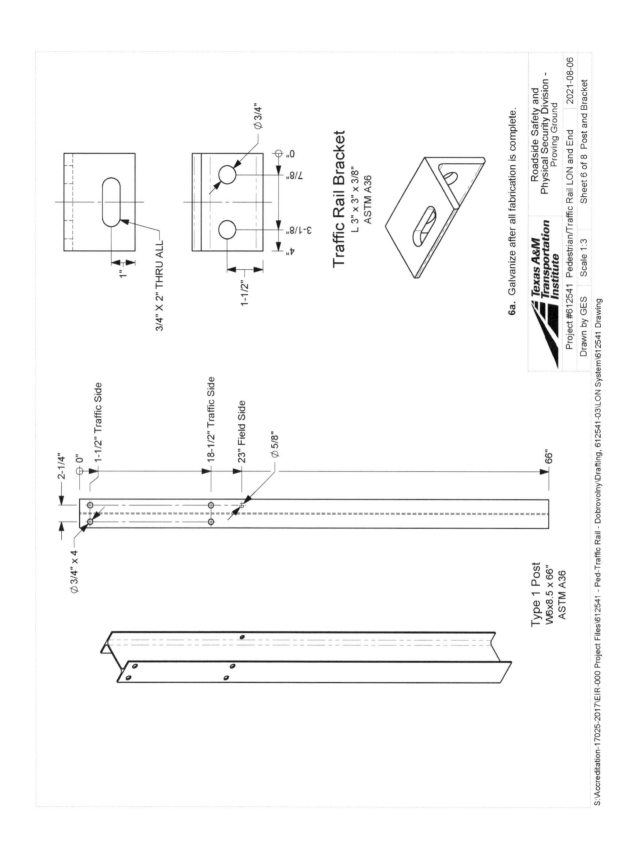

**Traffic Rail Bracket**
L 3" x 3" x 3/8"
ASTM A36

∅ 3/4"

0"

7/8"

3-1/8"

4"

1-1/2"

3/4" X 2" THRU ALL

1"

6a. Galvanize after all fabrication is complete.

2-1/4"

0"

1-1/2" Traffic Side

18-1/2" Traffic Side

23" Field Side

∅ 5/8"

66"

∅ 3/4" x 4

**Type 1 Post**
W6x8.5 x 66"
ASTM A36

Texas A&M
Transportation
Institute

Roadside Safety and
Physical Security Division -
Proving Ground

2021-08-06

Project #612541 Pedestrian/Traffic Rail LON and End

Drawn by GES

Scale 1:3

Sheet 6 of 8 Post and Bracket

S:\Accreditation-17025-2017\EIR-000 Project Files\612541 - Ped-Traffic Rail - Dobrovolny\Drafting, 612541-03\LON System\612541 Drawing

# Downstream Terminal Details

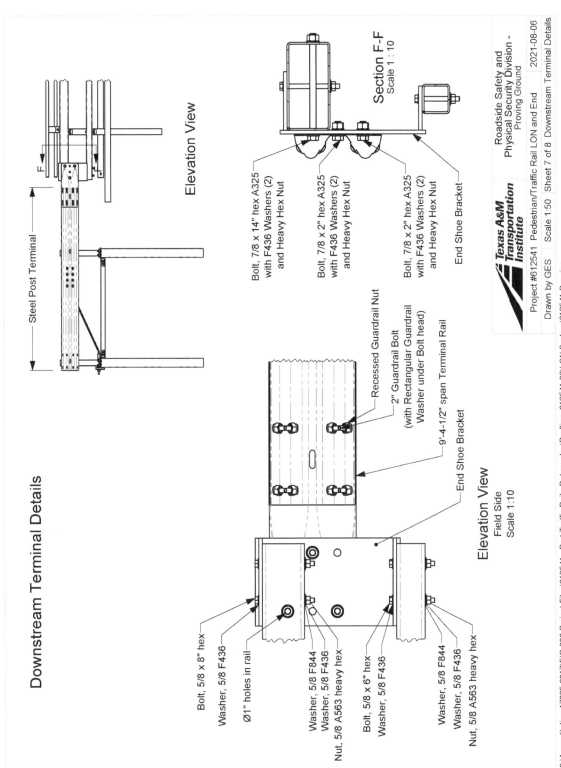

Elevation View

Steel Post Terminal

F

## Section F-F
Scale 1 : 10

Bolt, 7/8 x 14" hex A325 with F436 Washers (2) and Heavy Hex Nut

Bolt, 7/8 x 2" hex A325 with F436 Washers (2) and Heavy Hex Nut

Bolt, 7/8 x 2" hex A325 with F436 Washers (2) and Heavy Hex Nut

End Shoe Bracket

Recessed Guardrail Nut

2" Guardrail Bolt (with Rectangular Guardrail Washer under Bolt head)

9'-4-1/2" span Terminal Rail

End Shoe Bracket

## Elevation View
Field Side
Scale 1:10

Bolt, 5/8 x 8" hex

Washer, 5/8 F436

Ø1" holes in rail

Washer, 5/8 F844
Washer, 5/8 F436
Nut, 5/8 A563 heavy hex

Bolt, 5/8 x 6" hex

Washer, 5/8 F436

Washer, 5/8 F844
Washer, 5/8 F436
Nut, 5/8 A563 heavy hex

Texas A&M Transportation Institute

Roadside Safety and Physical Security Division - Proving Ground

2021-08-06

Project #612541 Pedestrian/Traffic Rail LON and End

Drawn by GES    Scale 1:50    Sheet 7 of 8 Downstream Terminal Details

S:\Accreditation-17025-2017\EIR-000 Project Files\612541 - Ped-Traffic Rail - Dobrovolny\Drafting, 612541-03\LON System\612541 Drawing

F-13

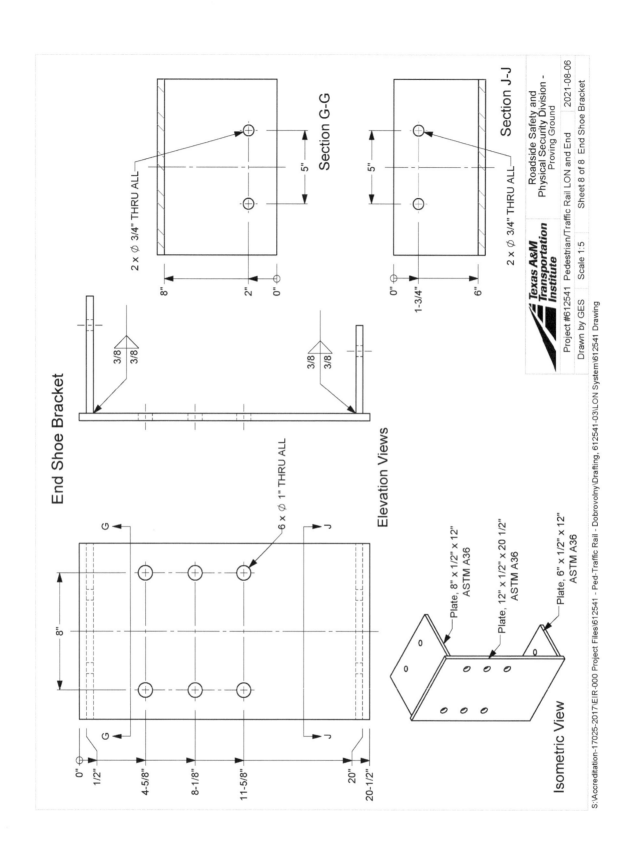

# End Shoe Bracket

Section G-G

2 × ⌀ 3/4" THRU ALL

8"
2"
0"
5"

Section J-J

2 × ⌀ 3/4" THRU ALL

0"
1-3/4"
6"
5"

3/8
3/8

3/8
3/8

Elevation Views

G
G

J
J

6 × ⌀ 1" THRU ALL

8"

0"
1/2"
4-5/8"
8-1/8"
11-5/8"
20"
20-1/2"

Isometric View

Plate, 8" × 1/2" × 12"
ASTM A36

Plate, 12" × 1/2" × 20 1/2"
ASTM A36

Plate, 6" × 1/2" × 12"
ASTM A36

Texas A&M
Transportation
Institute

Project #612541  Pedestrian/Traffic Rail LON and End

Roadside Safety and
Physical Security Division -
Proving Ground

2021-08-06

Drawn by GES    Scale 1:5    Sheet 8 of 8  End Shoe Bracket

S:\Accreditation-17025-2017\EIR-000 Project Files\612541 - Ped-Traffic Rail - Dobrovolny\Drafting, 612541-03\LON System\612541 Drawing

F-14

# Steel Post Terminal Details

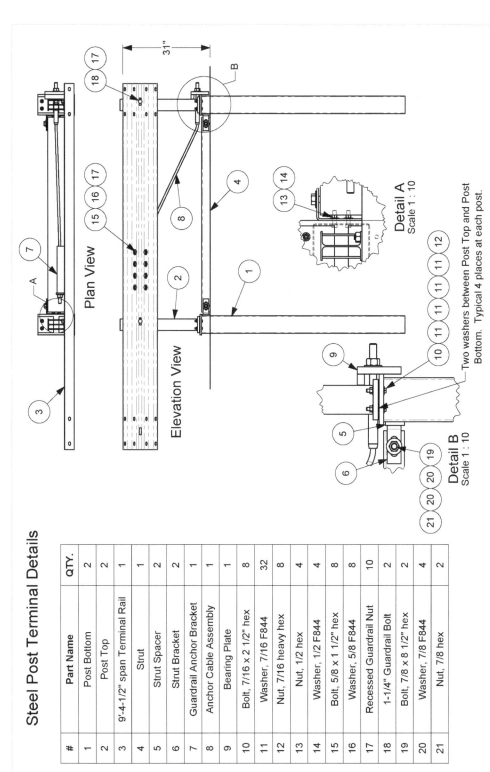

**Plan View**

**Elevation View**

31"

**Detail A**
Scale 1 : 10

**Detail B**
Scale 1 : 10

Two washers between Post Top and Post Bottom. Typical 4 places at each post.

| # | Part Name | QTY. |
|---|-----------|------|
| 1 | Post Bottom | 2 |
| 2 | Post Top | 2 |
| 3 | 9'-4-1/2" span Terminal Rail | 1 |
| 4 | Strut | 1 |
| 5 | Strut Spacer | 2 |
| 6 | Strut Bracket | 2 |
| 7 | Guardrail Anchor Bracket | 1 |
| 8 | Anchor Cable Assembly | 1 |
| 9 | Bearing Plate | 1 |
| 10 | Bolt, 7/16 x 2 1/2" hex | 8 |
| 11 | Washer, 7/16 F844 | 32 |
| 12 | Nut, 7/16 heavy hex | 8 |
| 13 | Nut, 1/2 hex | 4 |
| 14 | Washer, 1/2 F844 | 4 |
| 15 | Bolt, 5/8 x 1 1/2" hex | 8 |
| 16 | Washer, 5/8 F844 | 8 |
| 17 | Recessed Guardrail Nut | 10 |
| 18 | 1-1/4" Guardrail Bolt | 2 |
| 19 | Bolt, 7/8 x 8 1/2" hex | 2 |
| 20 | Washer, 7/8 F844 | 4 |
| 21 | Nut, 7/8 hex | 2 |

**1a.** 7/16" x 2-1/2" Bolts are ASTM A449. All other Bolts are ASTM A307. All Nuts (except Recessed Guardrail Nuts) are ASTM A563A unless otherwise indicated.

**1b.** All steel parts shall be galvanized.

**1c.** This specific terminal configuration has not been tested. It is used as a barrier anchorage device for crash testing purposes.

Texas A&M Transportation Institute

Roadside Safety and Physical Security Division - Proving Ground

2023-02-08

Project # Terminal

Scale 1:25

Sheet 1 of 6 Terminal Details

Drawn by GES

S:\engrfact\Drafting Department\Solidworks\Standard Parts\Guardrail Parts and Subs\Guardrail Drawings\Steel Post Terminal

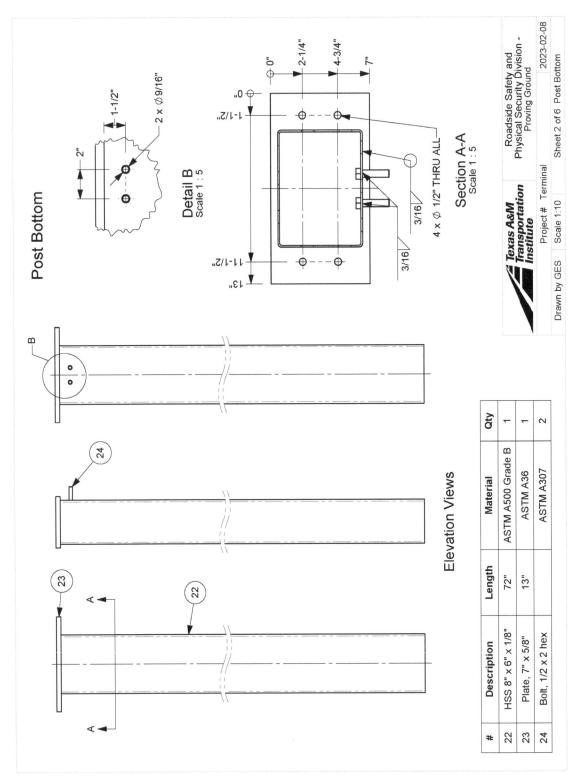

Post Bottom

Detail B
Scale 1 : 5

2 x Ø 9/16"
1-1/2"
2"

Section A-A
Scale 1 : 5

4 x Ø 1/2" THRU ALL
3/16
3/16

0"
2-1/4"
4-3/4"
7"

0"
11-1/2"
11-1/2"
13"

Elevation Views

B

24

23
A
A
22

| # | Description | Length | Material | Qty |
|---|---|---|---|---|
| 22 | HSS 8" x 6" x 1/8" | 72" | ASTM A500 Grade B | 1 |
| 23 | Plate, 7" x 5/8" | 13" | ASTM A36 | 1 |
| 24 | Bolt, 1/2 x 2 hex | | ASTM A307 | 2 |

Texas A&M
Transportation
Institute

Roadside Safety and
Physical Security Division -
Proving Ground

Project # Terminal

Drawn by GES | Scale 1:10 | Sheet 2 of 6  Post Bottom

2023-02-08

S:\engrfact\Drafting Department\Solidworks\Standard Parts and Subs\Guardrail Parts and Subs\Guardrail Drawings\Steel Post Terminal

F-16

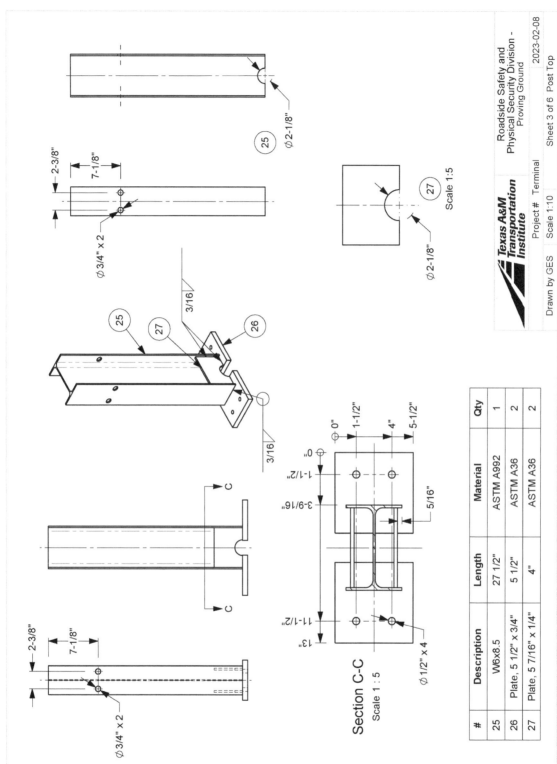

⌀ 2-1/8"

25

2-3/8"
7-1/8"

⌀ 3/4" x 2

27

⌀ 2-1/8"

Scale 1:5

3/16

25

27

26

3/16

C

C

2-3/8"
7-1/8"

⌀ 3/4" x 2

Section C-C
Scale 1 : 5

0"
1-1/2"
4"
5-1/2"

0"

1-1/2"

3-9/16"

5/16"

11-1/2"

13"

⌀ 1/2" x 4

| # | Description | Length | Material | Qty |
|---|---|---|---|---|
| 25 | W6x8.5 | 27 1/2" | ASTM A992 | 1 |
| 26 | Plate, 5 1/2" x 3/4" | 5 1/2" | ASTM A36 | 2 |
| 27 | Plate, 5 7/16" x 1/4" | 4" | ASTM A36 | 2 |

Texas A&M
Transportation
Institute

Roadside Safety and
Physical Security Division -
Proving Ground

2023-02-08

Project #   Terminal

Sheet 3 of 6   Post Top

Drawn by GES     Scale 1:10

S:\engrfact\Drafting Department\Solidworks\Standard Parts and Subs\Guardrail Parts and Subs\Guardrail Drawings\Steel Post Terminal

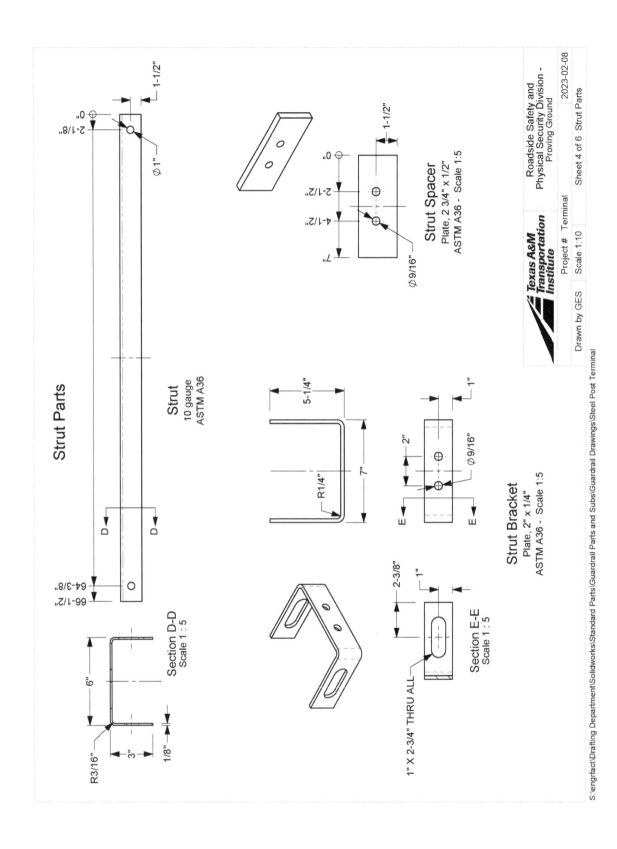

# Strut Parts

**Strut**
10 gauge
ASTM A36

Ø 1"

2-1/8"

0"

1-1/2"

64-3/8"

66-1/2"

D — D

**Section D-D**
Scale 1 : 5

6"

3"

R3/16"

1/8"

**Strut Spacer**
Plate, 2 3/4" x 1/2" - Scale 1:5
ASTM A36 -

Ø 9/16"

0"

2-1/2"

4-1/2"

7"

1-1/2"

**Strut Bracket**
Plate, 2" x 1/4" - Scale 1:5
ASTM A36 -

5-1/4"

7"

R1/4"

Ø 9/16"

2"

1"

E — E

**Section E-E**
Scale 1 : 5

2-3/8"

1"

1" X 2-3/4" THRU ALL

Texas A&M Transportation Institute

Roadside Safety and
Physical Security Division -
Proving Ground

2023-02-08

Project #  Terminal

Scale 1:10

Sheet 4 of 6   Strut Parts

Drawn by GES

S:\engrfact\Drafting Department\Solidworks\Standard Parts\Guardrail Parts and Subs\Guardrail Drawings\Steel Post Terminal

F-18

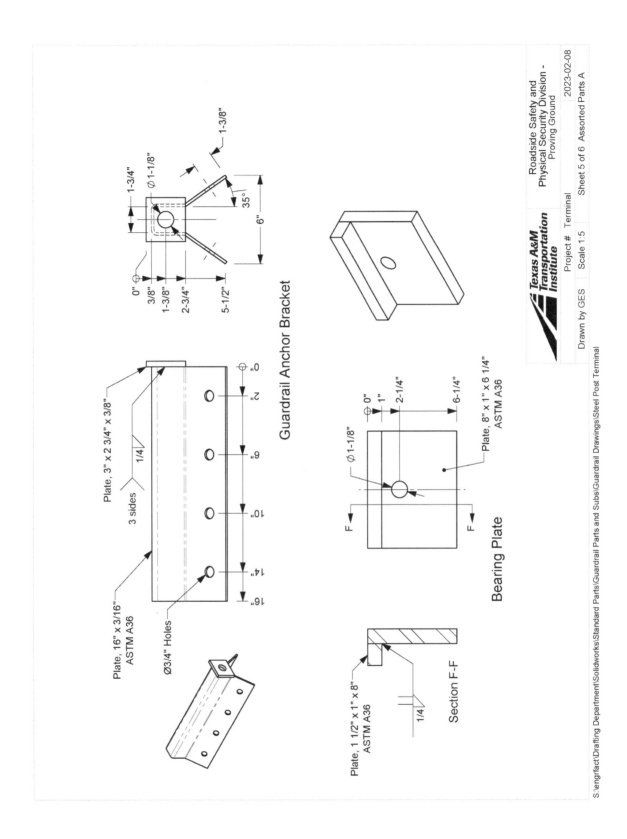

Guardrail Anchor Bracket

Plate, 3" x 2 3/4" x 3/8"
3 sides
Plate, 16" x 3/16"
ASTM A36
Ø3/4" Holes

Ø1-1/8"
1-3/4"
1-3/8"
35°
6"
0"
3/8"
1-3/8"
2-3/4"
5-1/2"

Bearing Plate

Ø1-1/8"
0"
1"
2-1/4"
6-1/4"
Plate, 8" x 1" x 6 1/4"
ASTM A36
F
F

Section F-F

Plate, 1 1/2" x 1" x 8"
ASTM A36
1/4

Roadside Safety and
Physical Security Division -
Proving Ground

Texas A&M
Transportation
Institute

Project #   Terminal
Scale 1:5
Sheet 5 of 6   Assorted Parts A
Drawn by GES
2023-02-08

S:\engrfact\Drafting Department\Solidworks\Standard Parts\Guardrail Parts and Subs\Guardrail Drawings\Steel Post Terminal

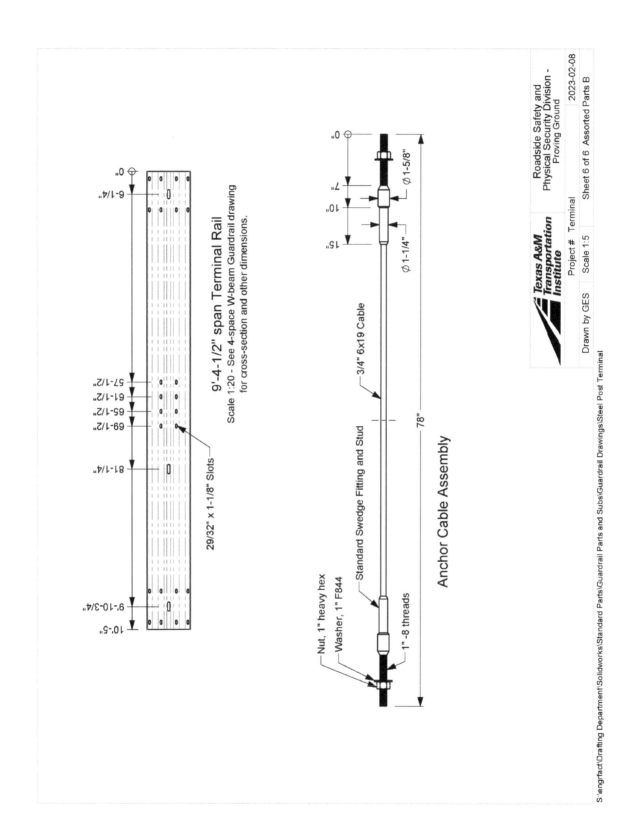

**9'-4-1/2" span Terminal Rail**

Scale 1:20 - See 4-space W-beam Guardrail drawing
for cross-section and other dimensions.

0"
6-1/4"
57-1/2"
61-1/2"
65-1/2"
69-1/2"
81-1/4"
9'-10-3/4"
10'-5"

29/32" x 1-1/8" Slots

**Anchor Cable Assembly**

0"
7"
10"
15"
Ø 1-5/8"
Ø 1-1/4"
78"

3/4" 6x19 Cable

Standard Swedge Fitting and Stud

Nut, 1" heavy hex
Washer, 1" F844
1"-8 threads

Roadside Safety and
Physical Security Division -
Proving Ground

2023-02-08

Texas A&M
Transportation
Institute

Project # Terminal    Sheet 6 of 6  Assorted Parts B

Drawn by GES    Scale 1:5

S:\engrfact\Drafting Department\Solidworks\Standard Parts\Guardrail Parts and Subs\Guardrail Drawings\Steel Post Terminal

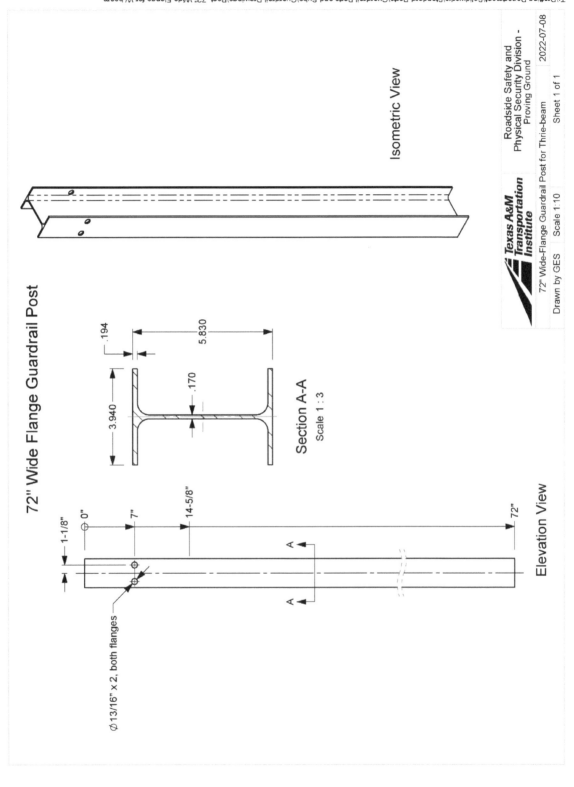

Isometric View

72" Wide Flange Guardrail Post

.194

5.830

3.940

.170

Section A-A

Scale 1 : 3

1-1/8"

0"

7"

14-5/8"

72"

A

A

Ø 13/16" x 2, both flanges

Elevation View

| Texas A&M Transportation Institute | Roadside Safety and Physical Security Division - Proving Ground | 2022-07-08 |
|---|---|---|
| | 72" Wide-Flange Guardrail Post for Thrie-beam | Sheet 1 of 1 |
| Drawn by GES | Scale 1:10 | |

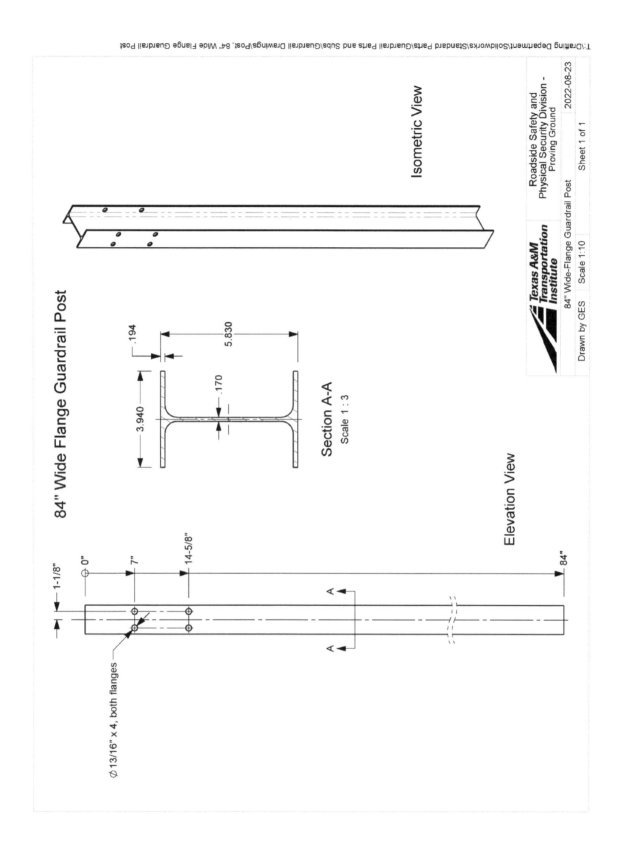

Isometric View

84" Wide Flange Guardrail Post

5.830

.194

3.940

.170

Section A-A
Scale 1 : 3

Elevation View

1-1/8"

0"

7"

14-5/8"

84"

A

A

Ø 13/16" x 4, both flanges

**Texas A&M Transportation Institute**

Roadside Safety and Physical Security Division - Proving Ground

2022-08-23

84" Wide-Flange Guardrail Post

Sheet 1 of 1

Drawn by GES | Scale 1:10

## Rectangular Guardrail Washer
0.20" thick

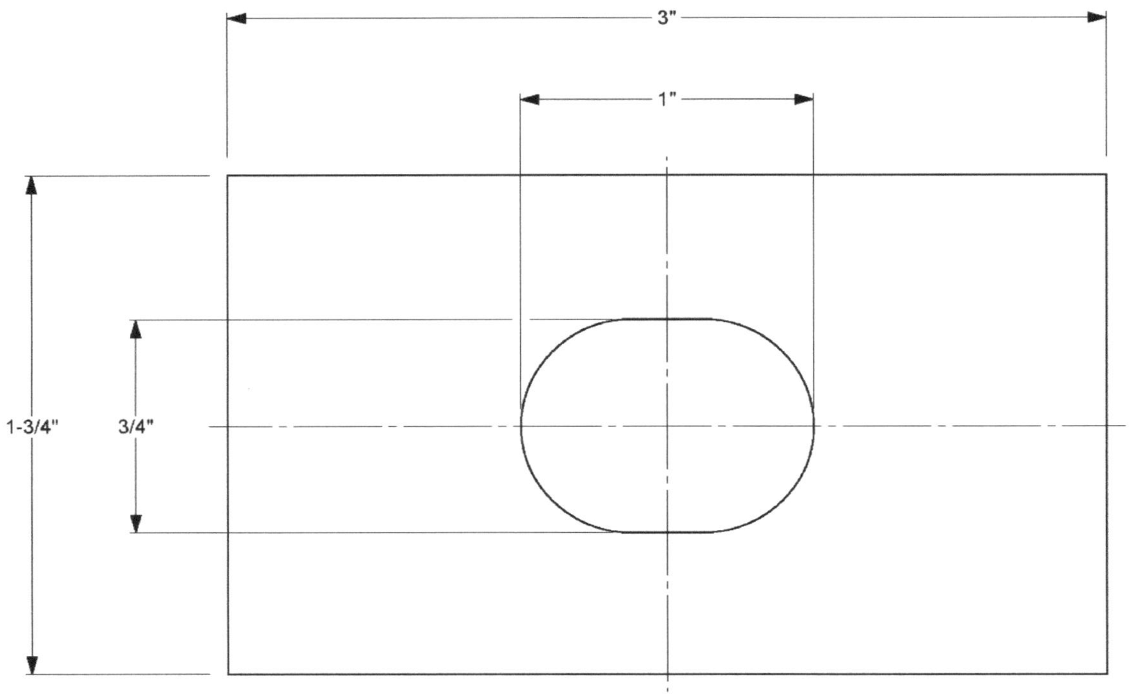

3"

1"

3/4"

1-3/4"

| Texas A&M Transportation Institute | Roadside Safety and Physical Security Division - Proving Ground | 2022-07-08 |
| --- | --- | --- |
| | Rectangular Guardrail Washer | Sheet 1 of 1 |
| Drawn by GES | Scale 2:1 | |

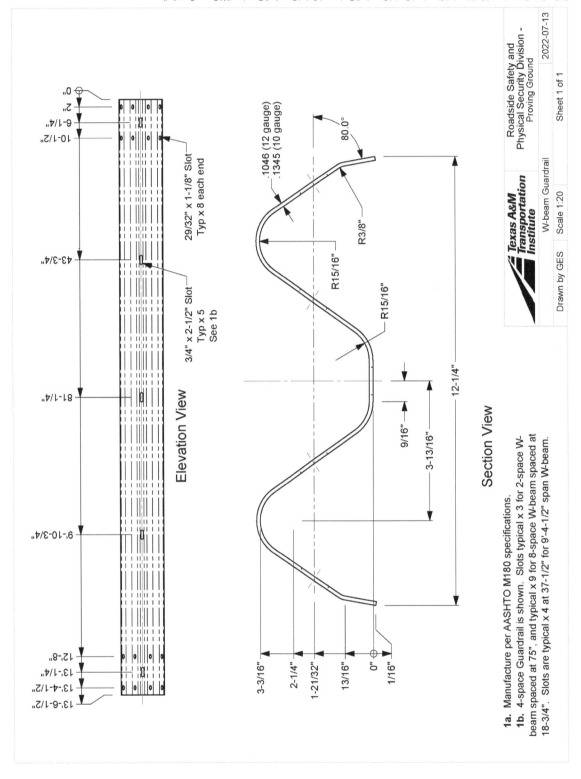

**Elevation View**

0"
2"
6-1/4"
10-1/2"

43-3/4"

81-1/4"

9'-10-3/4"

12'-8"
13'-1/4"
13'-4-1/2"
13'-6-1/2"

29/32" x 1-1/8" Slot
Typ x 8 each end

3/4" x 2-1/2" Slot
Typ x 5
See 1b

**Section View**

.1046 (12 gauge)
.1345 (10 gauge)

80.0°

R3/8"

R15/16"

R15/16"

12-1/4"

9/16"

3-13/16"

3-3/16"
2-1/4"
1-21/32"
13/16"
0"
1/16"

**1a.** Manufacture per AASHTO M180 specifications.
**1b.** 4-space Guardrail is shown. Slots typical x 3 for 2-space W-beam spaced at 75", and typical x 9 for 8-space W-beam spaced at 18-3/4". Slots are typical x 4 at 37-1/2" for 9'-4-1/2" span W-beam.

Texas A&M Transportation Institute

Roadside Safety and Physical Security Division - Proving Ground

2022-07-13

Sheet 1 of 1

W-beam Guardrail

Scale 1:20

Drawn by GES

F-24

Thrie to W-Beam, asymmetric
10 gauge

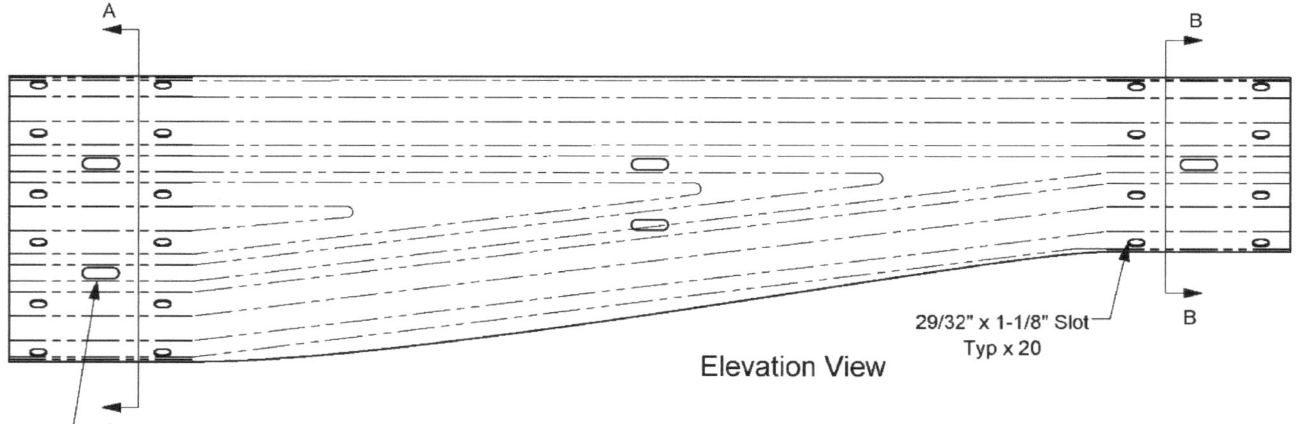

Elevation View

29/32" x 1-1/8" Slot
Typ x 20

3/4" x 2-1/2" Slot
Typ x 5

Section B-B
See W-beam Drawing

Section A-A
See Thrie-beam Drawing

Texas A&M Transportation Institute

Roadside Safety and Physical Security Division -
Proving Ground

Thrie- to W-beam Asymmetric Transition

Drawn by GES | Scale 1:10

2022-07-18

Sheet 1 of 1

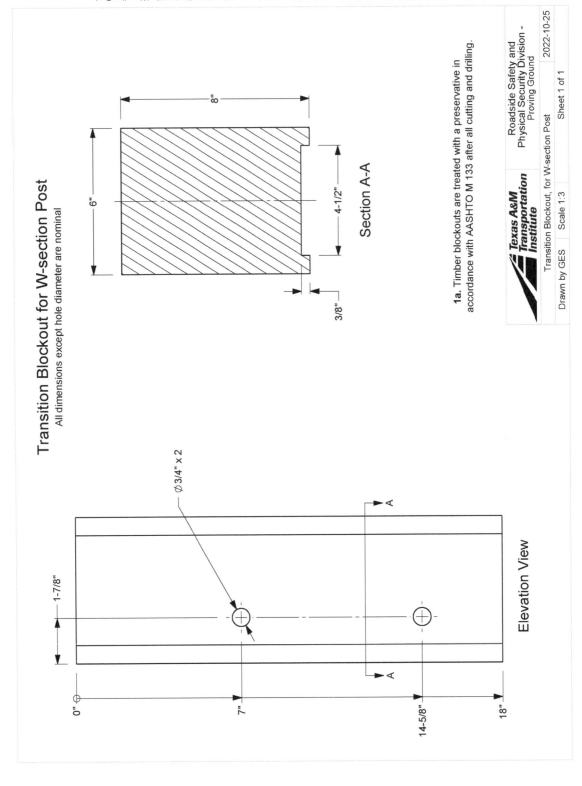

## Transition Blockout for W-section Post

All dimensions except hole diameter are nominal

8"

6"

4-1/2"

3/8"

Section A-A

Ø3/4" x 2

1-7/8"

0"

7"

14-5/8"

18"

A

A

Elevation View

1a. Timber blockouts are treated with a preservative in accordance with AASHTO M 133 after all cutting and drilling.

Texas A&M Transportation Institute

Roadside Safety and Physical Security Division - Proving Ground

2022-10-25

Transition Blockout, for W-section Post

Sheet 1 of 1

Drawn by GES

Scale 1:3

# Timber Blockout for W-section Post

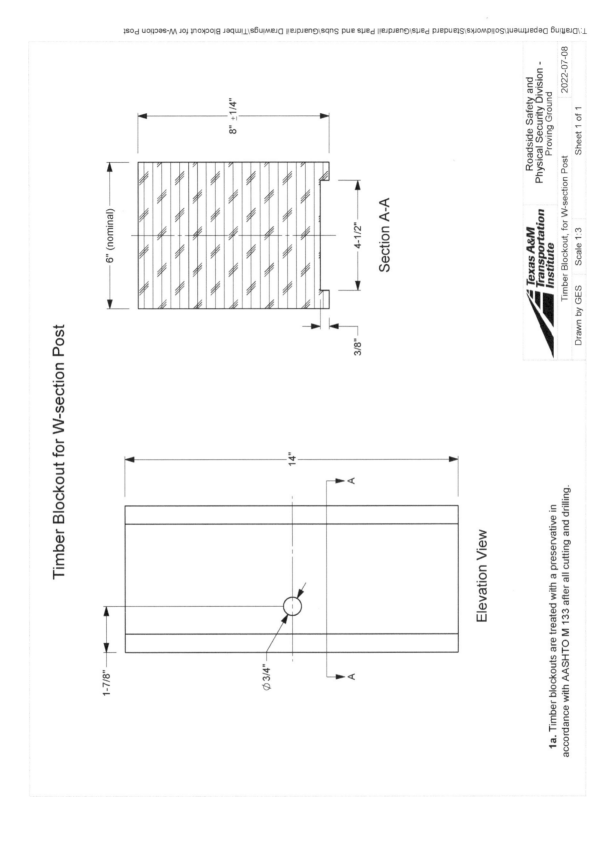

Section A-A

Elevation View

8" ±1/4"

6" (nominal)

4-1/2"

3/8"

14"

1-7/8"

Ø 3/4"

**1a.** Timber blockouts are treated with a preservative in accordance with AASHTO M 133 after all cutting and drilling.

Roadside Safety and
Physical Security Division -
Proving Ground

2022-07-08

Texas A&M
Transportation
Institute

Timber Blockout, for W-section Post

Sheet 1 of 1

Drawn by GES | Scale 1:3

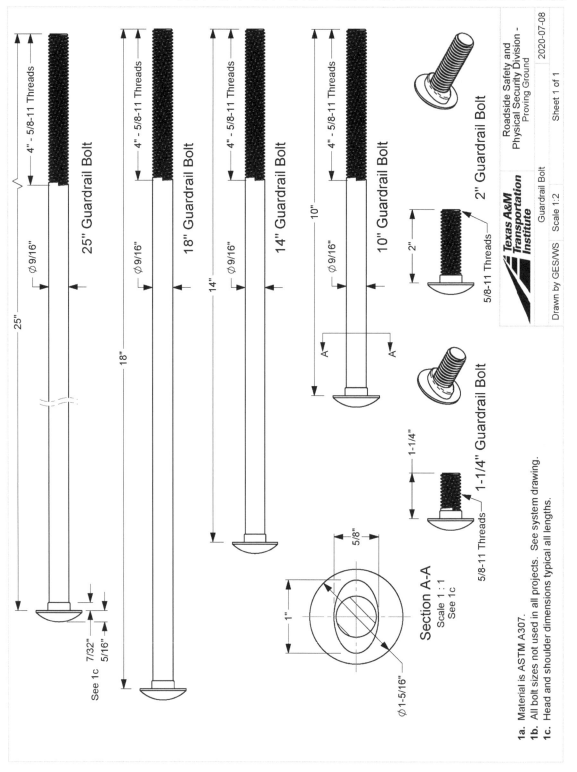

Section A-A
Scale 1 : 1
See 1c

Ø 1-5/16"

5/8"

1"

25" Guardrail Bolt
4" - 5/8-11 Threads
Ø 9/16"
25"
See 1c
7/32"
5/16"

18" Guardrail Bolt
4" - 5/8-11 Threads
Ø 9/16"
18"

14" Guardrail Bolt
4" - 5/8-11 Threads
Ø 9/16"
14"

10" Guardrail Bolt
4" - 5/8-11 Threads
Ø 9/16"
10"
A
A

2" Guardrail Bolt
5/8-11 Threads
2"

1-1/4" Guardrail Bolt
5/8-11 Threads
1-1/4"

**Texas A&M Transportation Institute**

Roadside Safety and Physical Security Division - Proving Ground

2020-07-08

Guardrail Bolt

Sheet 1 of 1

Drawn by GES/WS | Scale 1:2

1a. Material is ASTM A307.
1b. All bolt sizes not used in all projects. See system drawing.
1c. Head and shoulder dimensions typical all lengths.

F-28

Recessed Guardrail Nut

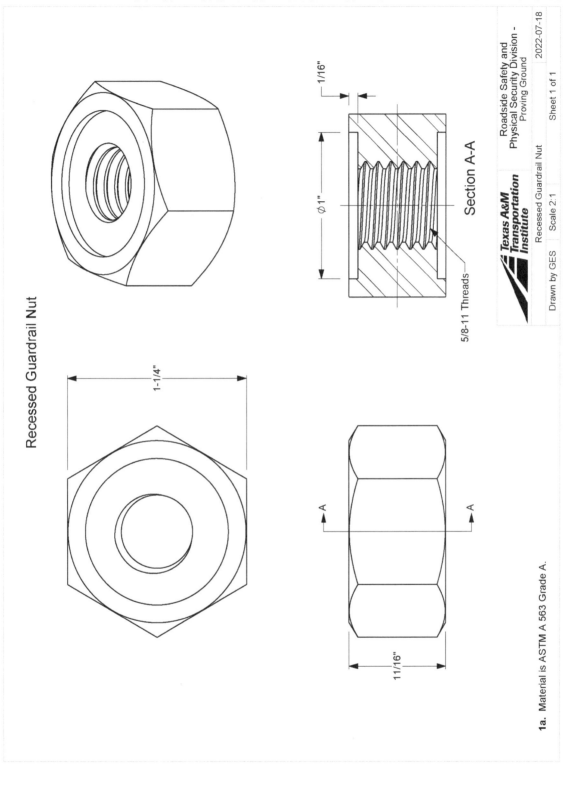

Section A-A

Ø 1"

1/16"

5/8-11 Threads

1-1/4"

11/16"

A

A

**Texas A&M Transportation Institute**

Roadside Safety and Physical Security Division - Proving Ground

2022-07-18

Recessed Guardrail Nut

Sheet 1 of 1

Drawn by GES

Scale 2:1

**1a.** Material is ASTM A 563 Grade A.

Section A-A
Scale 1 : 5
Typical all Thriebeams

Thriebeam
12 gauge 12.5' span 4-space

Thriebeam
12 gauge 12.5' span 8-space
Dimensions not shown here same as 4-space Thriebeam

Thriebeam
12 gauge 75" span
Dimensions not shown here same as 4-space Thriebeam

Slot, 3/4" x 2-1/2"
Typ x 18

Slot, 3/4" x 2-1/2"
Typ x 6

Slot, 3/4" x 2-1/2"
Typ x 10

Slot, 29/32" x 1-1/8"
Typ x 24

1a. 12 gauge is 0.1046" before galvanizing and 0.1084" after,
and 10 gauge is 0.1345" before galvanizing and 0.1382" after.
1b. Not all versions shown here used in all installations.

Texas A&M
Transportation
Institute

Roadside Safety and
Physical Security Division -
Proving Ground

Thrie-beam

Drawn by GES | Scale 1:30 | Scale 1:30

2022-07-18

Sheet 1 of 1

T:\Drafting Department\Solidworks\Standard Parts\Guardrail Parts and Subs\Guardrail Standard Drawings\Thrie-Beam

F-30

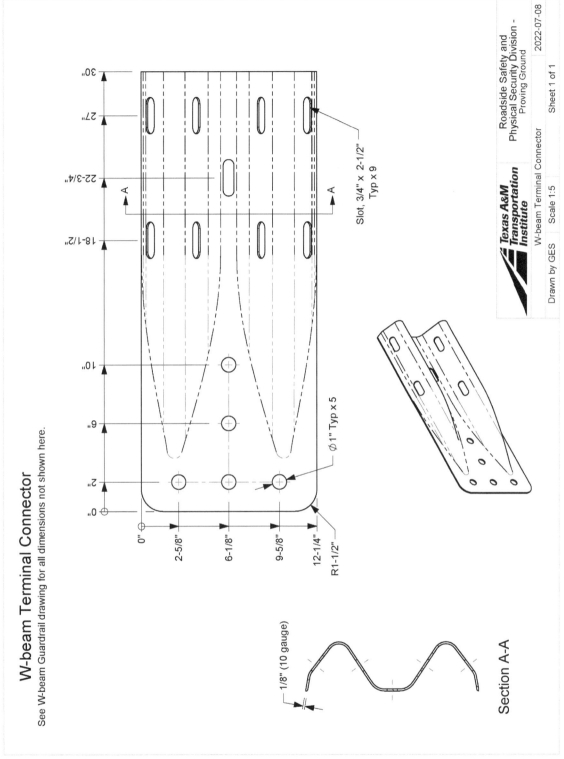

# W-beam Terminal Connector

See W-beam Guardrail drawing for all dimensions not shown here.

Slot, 3/4" x 2-1/2"
Typ x 9

Ø 1" Typ x 5

R1-1/2"

30"
27"
22-3/4"
18-1/2"
10"
6"
2"
0"

0"
2-5/8"
6-1/8"
9-5/8"
12-1/4"

A
A

1/8" (10 gauge)

Section A-A

| Texas A&M Transportation Institute | Roadside Safety and Physical Security Division - Proving Ground | |
|---|---|---|
| | W-beam Terminal Connector | 2022-07-08 |
| Drawn by GES | Scale 1:5 | Sheet 1 of 1 |

T:\Drafting Department\Solidworks\Standard Parts\Guardrail Parts and Subs\Guardrail Drawings\W-beam Terminal Connector

F-31

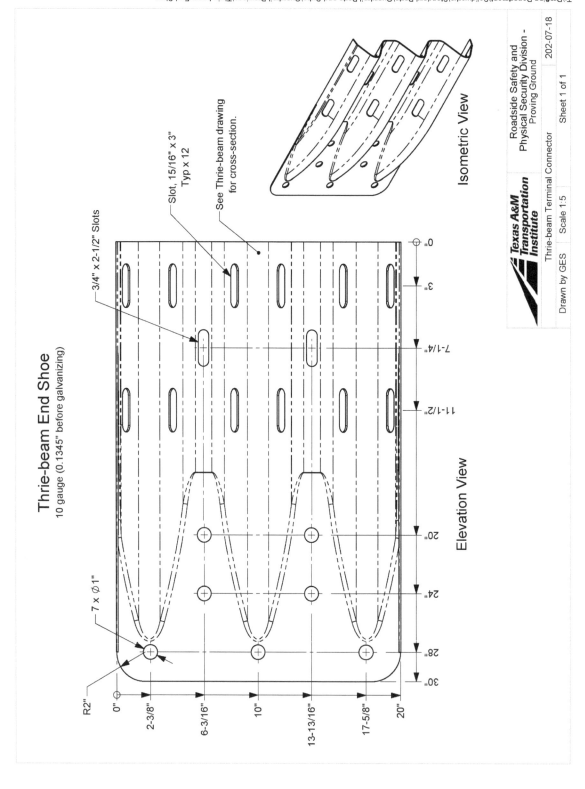

Thrie-beam End Shoe
10 gauge (0.1345" before galvanizing)

Slot, 15/16" x 3"
Typ x 12

See Thrie-beam drawing
for cross-section.

3/4" x 2-1/2" Slots

7 x ∅1"

R2"

Elevation View

Isometric View

| Roadside Safety and Physical Security Division - Proving Ground | 202-07-18 |
| Thrie-beam Terminal Connector | Sheet 1 of 1 |
| Texas A&M Transportation Institute | |
| Drawn by GES | Scale 1:5 |

F-32